IN THE NAME OF CHARITY

THE ROSSMINSTER AFFAIR

MICHAEL GILLARD

Chatto & Windus

LONDON

Published in 1987 by
Chatto & Windus Ltd
40–42 William IV St.
London WC2N 4DF

British Library Cataloguing in Publication Data

Gillard, Michael
In the name of charity: the Rossminster affair.
1. Tax evasion – Great Britain
I. Title
364.1'33   HJ2348.5
ISBN 0-7011-2859-3

Photoset by Rowland Phototypesetting Ltd
Bury St Edmunds, Suffolk
Printed by
Redwood Burn Ltd
Trowbridge, Wiltshire

CONTENTS

ILLUSTRATIONS

INTRODUCTION

Nobody loves the taxman. So it is not surprising that for a lengthy period, stretching through most of the 1970s, Roy Tucker was seen by many, accountants and non-accountants alike, as a reincarnated Robin Hood, even if he was robbing the government and the vast majority of taxpayers to give to the rich. The concept of someone clever enough to run rings round the Inland Revenue through loopholes in the taxes acts was appealing, especially in a socialist-run Britain beset by rising inflation and high taxation.

Once Tucker and Rossminster, the company which he formed with his fellow accountant, Ronald Plummer, broke out of the obscurity of specialist accountancy publications into the spotlight of Fleet Street newspapers, there was little criticism, except on the Left, of the phenomenon of tax avoidance on demand. Rossminster had made this available to anyone who could pay their fees, and Tucker's ingenuity was seen as something to wonder at and even applaud rather than as a cause for concern. Conservatives in particular rallied behind the position – long established in law – that avoidance, unlike evasion, was legal and therefore respectable.

But only Tucker and his close circle knew just how much his fill-in-the-numbers style of tax avoidance was costing Britain in lost revenue – revenue required to finance services and facilities, such as hospitals and roads, which those avoiding tax still enjoyed if others, less fortunate or less well advised, provided. Even when the multimillions involved were disclosed and the Inland Revenue went on the offensive, raiding Tucker's and Plummer's homes and offices, public opinion was still favourable, newspapers and courts ringing with denunciations of the taxman's excesses, not those of Tucker and Rossminster. But, at first imperceptibly and then with a suddenness which stunned Tucker and his supporters, a change in attitude occurred. This was brought about by the realisation in at least some legal and Conservative circles that what Tucker represented was both financially and socially unacceptable. The basis of the taxation system was being undermined. As Lord Templeman pointed out with telling irony, the totally artificial tax schemes marketed by Tucker and his imitators 'would render the payment of tax a voluntary exercise by the ignorant, the conscientious, the idle and the generality of taxpayers'.

That generality, the over 20 million Pay-As-You-Earn taxpayers, had no choice. They received their incomes with tax deducted at source. But many of them were also part of the 'black' economy – the casual workers and those with second jobs, done strictly for cash, around other people's homes, gardens and cars. By the end of the seventies the black economy was costing Britain more than £2000 million a year in tax evasion. The millions of offenders were unlikely to be discouraged from seeking to earn extra, untaxed income when they saw the rich avoiding tax with impunity. And 'any intelligent layman', observed Lord Bridge, would quickly realise that the wholly artificial Tucker tax schemes were not 'designed to achieve any substantial effect in the real world'. And Lord Wilberforce, then the premier tax judge among the Law Lords, stressed that tax was 'created to operate in the real world, not that of make believe'.

Such legal strictures came late in the day, when Tucker and Rossminster had effectively been put out of business. It had taken several years before the judges could bring themselves to face such simple realities. Until then they held the view that it was all very regrettable but a more important principle was at stake than a fair apportionment of the taxation burden among fellow citizens. 'It would be far more disagreeable to substitute the rule of caprice for that of law,' declared Lord Simon, holding the line that the judges were bound by decisions made thirty years or more before. But eventually Roy Tucker by the abusive nature of his tax schemes prised the blinkers from the judges' eyes and forced them to reconcile justice and the national interest. I would like to think that, along with a handful of other journalists, in particular Lorana Sullivan (then writing for the *Sunday Times*), I helped to change the public perception of Roy Tucker and Rossminster through the articles I wrote for *Private Eye* and the TV documentary produced with my Granada Television colleague Brian Blake for *World in Action*.

I had always struggled with mathematics and, despite a degree in economics, I found it impossible to complete my tax return unaided. The challenge presented by Roy Tucker and the taxes acts was for a long time all too easy to leave to others. Two events changed my attitude and started me down the road that led to this book. The first was a meeting in the summer of 1978 with a former Rossminster adviser. Over a bottle of wine in Soho he tried to explain to me the essentials of a crucial method used by Tucker to ensure that even if a tax scheme for companies did not succeed in the courts there would be no money left in the company to pay the tax. While grasping the 'heads I win, tails the taxman loses' message, I could not say that I fully understood the mechanics.

A year later, while the *Sunday Times* was closed by a lengthy dispute between management and the print unions, the homes of Tucker and his associates, including the new Conservative MP Tom Benyon, were raided by the Inland Revenue. Although the raids received wide publicity, it was clear that few journalists – given the enforced silence of Lorana Sullivan – understood Tucker's schemes, Rossminster's role or its close ties to senior figures in the two-month-old Conservative government.

It was the political dimension which all at once made Roy Tucker and Rossminster newsworthy to me and to *Private Eye*. Until then I had written only one item for *Private Eye* about Rossminster, in December 1978, recording the resignations earlier that year of some key insiders from certain Rossminster companies and suggesting, as proved correct, that this indicated problems ahead for Tucker and his associates. I now contacted my initial informant, who provided the links to the politicians together with further insights into the Rossminster operation. After the Revenue raids, a series of regular items about Rossminster appeared in *Private Eye* over the next three years.

However, the breakthrough in my understanding of Rossminster came when I met Arthur Lewis-Grey, its former managing director in Guernsey and the keeper of its offshore secrets. Amused that he lived at a house called Thatchers, I made a quizzical *Private Eye* reference to his role. A few days later he contacted the magazine. So began a series of very lengthy meetings over several months. With a photographic memory Lewis-Grey recalled names, dates and details. He provided notebooks full of information and leads for further inquiry, which I developed into further articles for *Private Eye*, two TV documentaries and now this book. Lewis-Grey provided this assistance initially on one condition – that he should not be identified as a source. His reason was a draconian severance agreement signed when he left Rossminster. But even that was outweighed by his belief that the public had to know what lay behind Rossminster. For that courageous decision I and many others owe him a considerable debt.

As a result of Lewis-Grey's cooperation I amassed hundreds of pages of company documents collected from the company registries in London and Douglas, Isle of Man, St Peter Port, Guernsey, St Helier, Jersey, and Panama, concerning Rossminster companies and those of its clients. Through these I was able to confirm the identities of clients and also trace details of the tax schemes they had carried out – once I knew the telltale clues to detect in the balance sheets. I was also able to unravel the convoluted chain of offshore ownership behind which Tucker and his associates had hidden their control of Rossminster.

It would have been impossible to discover much of what happened without the assistance of former employees of Tucker and Rossminster, a smattering of their clients, and several accountants who had a profound distaste for Tucker's and Plummer's activities. There was even a time, before their investigations faltered, when certain Inland Revenue officials were prepared to assist me on some of the more complex ramifications of Tucker's schemes and tell me how the Revenue viewed Rossminster. The incentive for this limited cooperation was the access I had to sources which they could not reach officially.

But the Inland Revenue remain their own worst enemies in dealing with journalists on tax matters. The belief of Rossminster insiders and their camp followers that there was a conspiracy between the Revenue and Rossminster's critics is a joke only those who have endeavoured to extract information from Somerset House can appreciate.

Perhaps the only thing Rossminster and the Inland Revenue share is the lack of co-operation consistently displayed towards my enquiries. No request I have made to Tucker and Plummer for an interview has been granted. In the course of writing this book I twice asked them for an opportunity to put to them the points I wished to raise and give them the chance to respond to the criticisms I make. Their reply was that they were unable to discuss Rossminster with me until all litigation with the Inland Revenue was resolved. This was unacceptable as it could take years. Their colleagues Desmond Miller and John Trotman also declined to be interviewed. While preparing their action against the Inland Revenue, however, neither Tucker nor Plummer felt constrained from assisting the author of *The Tax Raiders*, a book which took an unremitting pro-

Rossminster/anti-Revenue line. I have therefore taken the somewhat unusual course, where necessary, of relying on quotations from that book as reflecting the 'authorised' Tucker/Plummer view.

The story of Roy Tucker and Rossminster is important because tax avoidance was a significant facet of Britain in the seventies in the same way that Jim Slater, Slater, Walker and asset stripping characterised the sixties. It proved, as did Prohibition in another era, that a policy which lacks wide public support and acceptance will be honoured only in the breach by those who can find a way round or through its provisions. Furthermore, that search for loopholes leads to abuse and damage to society far beyond the policy's supposed benefits. The only ones to gain are those who can provide what the government seeks to deny.

That Rossminster lesson is becoming relevant again today because once more there is talk by some Labour politicians of a return to its 1974 policy of 'soak the rich', a group which it seems in Labour thinking now includes anyone earning more than £27,000 a year. This suggests that, not having learned from their mistake, they are intent on a repetition.

Michael Gillard
October 1986

LORD CLYDE'S SHOVEL

'Tax gatherers have been unpopular everywhere throughout the whole course of history. The payment of taxes is accompanied by a degree of reluctance greater in some persons than in others.'

These were the opening words of Lord Keith of Kinkel's 1983 report on the enforcement powers of the Inland Revenue and the Customs and Excise.[1]

Today legal tax avoidance and illegal tax evasion are financial facts of life in Britain. The boom that began in the sixties and accelerated throughout the seventies is still going strong in the second half of the eighties.

Legal tax avoidance has attracted not only the very rich but nearly all those who can afford it. Much further down the social scale, those whose goal is not so much wealth creation as meeting the costs of day-to-day life break the law and evade tax simply by not declaring their earnings from casual or second jobs. Both avoidance and evasion cost Britain dear. Certainly hundreds and possibly thousands of millions of pounds in tax have disappeared annually through cleverly exploited loopholes in the tax laws. This has involved such everyday matters as mortgages, insurance and pensions, loans, leasing and covenants to sophisticated and highly complex tax schemes.

Nobody did more to aid that great escape than Roy Tucker and Ronald Plummer, two accountants who were completely unknown at the start of the seventies but within ten years were celebrities and, to some, even heroes.

Although it only developed as specialised skill with the introduction of supertax in the early years of this century, tax avoidance is as old as taxes themselves. The concept of the trust, designed to preserve family wealth, has its origins in the Middle Ages; the window tax, introduced in 1796, resulted in windows being bricked up as a form of tax avoidance; with the introduction of income tax in 1799, the rich began thinking about ways of not paying when the rate was just a few pennies in the pound. The trebling of income tax to the equivalent of 15p in the pound with the outbreak of the First World War – which also prompted rises in profits tax from 9 per cent, and the end of tax exemption on profits earned abroad – spawned a growing community of tax advisers to whom the rich could turn for succour.

Those with large incomes quickly learned the first lesson of tax avoidance – turning highly taxed income into low- or untaxed capital. Until the introduction of a tax on short-term capital gains by the Conservatives in 1962 and the advent of the Wilson government two years later, taxes on capital were largely restricted to estate duty, payable on death: these were easily avoidable, or involved rates well below those payable on income. As a result, it was highly beneficial to forgo immediate income by investing in land, property or shares, which would appreciate in value and could be sold in future years taxfree. Still better was to place such appreciating assets in an overseas trust. So widespread had this abuse become that in 1936 the first steps were introduced to prevent the transfer abroad by British residents of UK assets, which became the basis of one of the key anti-avoidance measures, Section 478 of the Income and Corporation Taxes Act of 1970.

For the rich the years after the First World War became a battle to avoid on the one hand taxes on income or profits during one's lifetime and, on the other, taxes on capital after one's death. The introduction of excess profits tax during the Second World War opened a new front for the tax-avoidance adviser – namely, removing company profits from the taxman's grasp. As Britain climbed out of its postwar recession into the 'never had it so good' Conservative years of the fifties, the owners of private companies sought increasingly to avoid paying the Inland Revenue its share of escalating profits. A favourite device was the purchase of tax losses from other companies to offset against profits, which was achieved by simply acquiring defunct companies with a history of trading losses. Another familiar tactic was 'dividend stripping', the corporate version of the income-into-capital trick – the owners of a company would declare an abnormally large dividend on which the recipient could recover tax because he was either exempt from tax or had losses to offset against the payment. Another ploy was to generate 'paper' losses on shares in a company by declaring an abnormal dividend, thus reducing its assets. A fall in the share value could also be produced by sales of assets. This 'loss' could then be offset against income for tax purposes. Each new tax or increase in the rates of income tax, supertax, or surtax, or profits tax brought more custom for the tax advisers. But theirs was still very much a craft industry, dealing in bespoke products. Harold Wilson and his Chancellor of the Exchequer, James Callaghan, changed all that in 1964.

Two men made the resulting boom in legal tax avoidance possible. These unlikely patron saints of the tax avoider were David Ritchie, a Scottish mine manager who decided to invest in a passenger bus, and Frank Allman, a gardener employed on the Duke of Westminster's estate in Cheshire. For half a century the courts' decisions in their cases set the rules by which the Inland Revenue and the tax avoiders played their game, until the blatant excesses of Tucker and Plummer forced the Law Lords of the House of Lords to remove what Lord Diplock called 'the blinkers that the court . . . is enjoined to wear in Revenue cases'.

In 1926 David Ritchie set up the Ayrshire Pullman Motor Services company with one bus. His initial aim was to provide a business for his son-in-law, but when he left after a few months Ritchie continued the business with the help of his son. In 1927 Ritchie entered into a contract of copartnership with his five children backdated to the previous year. He had put up the company's £1600 capital as a loan, as well as making other advances, but was to receive only a 5 per cent interest payment. His children ran the business and shared the profits, but could take no dividends until his £1600 had been repaid. Ritchie was the part-time manager, but alone operated the bank account and signed all documents.

Despite these arrangements, the Inland Revenue adjudged Ritchie to be the sole partner and assessed him for income tax on the £9654 profits made from 1926 to 1929. Ritchie contested this claim, saying that because of the loan he was only a creditor, not a partner, and so did not participate in the profits. In December 1929 Ritchie appealed to the Court of Sessions in Edinburgh against the decision of the General Commissioners of Tax in favour of the Inland Revenue. As an indication of how the number of tax cases has grown since then, the appeal took only a year to reach the court: today it would take up to three years.

The Court of Sessions upheld Ritchie's appeal. Lord Clyde, the Lord President, was in no doubt why the canny Scot had so arranged the partnership with his children. It was to 'render the position of the family, as entitled to its profits, favourable in relation to the Inland Revenue both with regard to income tax to some extent, certainly with regard to super tax, and still more clearly with regard to death duties'.[2] If he was not a partner, then Ritchie could claim that the company's profits were not part of his personal income and so would avoid paying tax on those profits. The bus company would also not form part of his estate for death-duty purposes.

Lord Clyde saw nothing at all wrong with this, and went on to make a declaration that was to become the bill of rights for subsequent generations of tax avoiders with ambitions far beyond those of David Ritchie: 'No man in this country is under the smallest obligation, moral or other, so to arrange his legal relations to his business or to his property as to enable the Inland Revenue to put the largest possible shovel into his stores.'[3]

The door had been unlocked for those who now wanted to pay as little as possible of their wealth to the taxman. Almost six years later it swung wide open, courtesy of the House of Lords and some highly unusual arrangements for the payment of wages entered into between the Duke of Westminster, then as now Britain's richest landowner, and certain of his employees.

In 1930 the Duke executed deeds of covenant with Frank Allman, his gardener for twenty seven years, and others, ranging from a laundryman to an architect. Under the terms of the covenant Allman was to be paid £1.90 a week for seven years or his and the Duke's joint lives. This was achieved by the Duke making a cash payment in each year sufficient to produce an annual income, or annuity, for his gardener of £98.60 in each of the seven years. The advantage to the Duke was that such covenanted annuity payments could be deducted from his income and so reduce his personal tax bill. Allman was already employed at a fixed wage of £3 per week, but now he became entitled to £1.90 plus further payments for any services he rendered, making up the difference between the annuity and his former wage. The Duke then claimed that the annuities he had provided through the yearly cash payments were deductible against his income, so reducing his not inconsiderable surtax liability for the years 1929 to 1932.

The Inland Revenue did not agree. It said the payments were for services to be rendered to the Duke by those who remained in his employment, and so were not tax deductible. When this view was rejected by the Court of Appeal the Inland Revenue came before the House of Lords with an appeal in May 1935.

The key judgment in favour of the Duke came from Lord Tomlin. Reinforcing the philosophy of Lord Clyde, he declared, 'Every man is entitled if he can to order his affairs so that the tax attaching under the appropriate Acts is less than it otherwise would be.'[4] He went even further in encouraging the tax avoider, firmly squashing the idea, put forward by the Revenue, that the Law Lords were supposed to look at the substance of such artificial arrangements as that between the Duke and his gardener, and not just at their legal form: 'This so called doctrine of "the substance" seems to me to be nothing more than an attempt to make a man pay notwithstanding that he has so ordered his affairs that the amount of tax sought from him is not legally claimable.' All that mattered, pronounced the noble lord, was the legal effect of the transaction. So long as it *was* legal and the documents did not reveal a sham, in the purely legalistic sense of purporting to show other than what happened, then the form was all that counted.

With these words Lord Tomlin equipped his successors in Britain's highest court with the semantic blinkers they were to wear until Roy Tucker forced them to see the light. For the next forty-six years the Law Lords steadfastly refused to take them off – as was amply demonstrated when the Inland Revenue took on another of Britain's richest families, the Vesteys.

From early on William Vestey made clear his views about tax. He told the Royal Commission on Income Tax in 1919, 'The present position of affairs suits me admirably. I am abroad; I pay nothing.' Two years later, when Lloyd George – from whom he had bought his peerage – refused to give the Vesteys tax-exempt status, a family trust was set up in Paris with French resident trustees as a means of keeping the family fortune taxfree.

Trusts were, perhaps, the world's first tax-avoidance device, pioneered in Britain to help families avoid death duties. Assets such as land, property or shares are put in a trust or settlement by the owner or settlor who appoints as trustees two or more reliable individuals, usually lawyers or accountants, to administer the trust for the beneficiaries, normally family members. The settlor can disclaim any ownership or interest in the trust's assets – as can the trustees, who are merely nominees – so that it becomes very difficult for the Inland Revenue to determine who has an interest in the trust's assets or income, and so whom to tax. This way the value of the trust can grow for years without tax being paid. Even if tax is paid it is only on the income received, and at well below the rate at which that same

5

income would have been taxed in the settlor's hands. And the trust's assets may be distributed tax free to family members so long as it can be shown that they were not legally entitled to receive it, but only at the discretion of the trustees. Through the trust, highly taxed income is converted into lightly or zero-taxed capital – the goal of every tax avoider.

These already considerable advantages can be even further improved upon by establishing the trust and the trustees outside the United Kingdom, and so beyond the Inland Revenue's jurisdiction.

The French trust established by the Vesteys received £960,000 annually as rent on family-owned properties outside Britain which had been transferred into the trust's ownership. These were leased to the private Vestey master company in London, Union International. The trust's invested income was to accumulate for the benefit of the family in twenty one years' time, but in the meantime the two Vestey brothers, William and Edmund, continued to enjoy the use of these funds by way of interestfree loans.

Lord Vestey died in 1940; two years later, the Inland Revenue, armed with the provisions of the 1936 and 1938 Finance Acts, designed to prevent UK residents transferring assets abroad so that income would be received by foreign trustees on their behalf, sought to tax the Vestey estate and Edmund Vestey on the grounds that both had had the 'power to enjoy' the trust's income.

By this time the original Paris trust had been replaced by another twenty-one-year creation, transferring control of the assets to trustees in Uruguay, where the trust's records were kept, and to Argentina. Despite inflation, the accommodating trustees still leased the assets to Union International for the identical £960,000 a year.

The Inland Revenue won its case all the way – until the Vesteys reached the House of Lords in 1949 with an appeal against a tax bill of at least £6 million. Once again, though not doubting that the Vesteys had been avoiding tax, the Law Lords were far more concerned with whether they had been caught by the exact wording of the Acts. They decided they had not. Justifying this further victory for major-league tax avoidance, Lord Normand declared:

Parliament, in its attempts to keep pace with the ingenuity devoted to tax avoidance, may fall short of its purpose. That is a misfortune for the taxpayers who do not try to avoid their share of the burden, and it is disappointing to the Inland Revenue, but the Court will not stretch the terms of the taxing Acts in order to improve on the efforts of

Parliament and stop gaps which are left open by the statute. Tax avoidance is an evil but it would be the beginning of much greater evils if the courts were to overstretch the language of the statute to subject to taxation people of whom they disapproved.[5]

The Law Lords' consistent view of this 'evil' was that it was a matter for Parliament to legislate against. The courts were to be concerned only with the meaning of words, not with justice or fairness or even with what Parliament intended – particularly not with what Parliament intended. As the Master of the Rolls, Sir Wilfred Greene, had said in 1941, it was 'quite impossible to leave the contractual or other arrangements out of account'.[6]

The tax avoider needed no greater encouragement. What was good enough for the richest in the land would be good for anyone with the wit to spot the loopholes in the annual Finance Acts or the omnibus Income and Corporation Tax and Taxes Management Acts. Thirty years later, in November 1979, the House of Lords judges were still thinking along the same lines when they overruled the Inland Revenue's second assault on the Vesteys – an attempt to tax members of the family on the £2,600,000 they had received from the family trust between 1962 and 1966.

In finding for the Vesteys on that occasion, Lord Wilberforce recalled the words of Viscount Simon in a 1942 tax case:

Of recent years much ingenuity has been expended in certain quarters in attempting to devise methods of disposition of income by which those who were prepared to adopt them might enjoy the benefits of residence in this country while receiving the equivalent of such income without sharing in the appropriate burden of British taxation ... There is, of course, no doubt that they are within their legal rights, but that is no reason why their efforts, or those of the professional gentlemen who assist them in the matter, should be regarded as a commendable exercise of ingenuity or as a discharge of the duties of good citizenship. On the contrary, one result of such methods, if they succeed, is of course to increase the load of tax on the shoulders of the great body of good citizens who do not desire, or do not know how, to adopt these manoeuvres.[7]

But he still found in favour of the Vesteys not paying any tax. 'Let's face it, nobody pays more tax than they have to. We're all tax dodgers, aren't we?' was the relaxed response of the Old Etonian Edmund Vestey, who had received £920,000 from the trust taxfree, when questioned about his family's successful sixty-year-long campaign to keep the Inland Revenue from the door of its £1000 million fortune.[8]

Moreover, by the late seventies, far from being reviled, the 'professional gentlemen' were feted in the press for their brilliance and acclaimed by lawyers, accountants and Conservative politicians as examples to be followed, cleverly robbing the avaricious taxman. The cause of this social transformation from villain to hero had been the arrival of the Labour government in 1964.

Labour's return to power after thirteen years of Conservative rule immediately brought with it higher rates of both income and surtax, payable by those who earned over £50,000 a year, and the top combined tax rate for the highest paid became 91.25 per cent. Even the average wage-earner on PAYE now faced income tax at a standard rate of 41.25 per cent.

Labour also introduced new taxes, such as corporation tax on company profits at 40 per cent, as well as capital gains tax at 30 per cent on all capital profits and not just on the short-term gains taxed by the Conservatives. Announcing this new tax in November 1964, James Callaghan said, 'This measure will bring to an end the state of affairs in which hard work and great energy are fully taxed while the fruits of speculation and passive ownership escape untaxed.' Add to all these exchange control restrictions on transferring capital out of the country and the fall in the value of the pound, which was devalued in 1967, and the incentives for avoiding if not evading tax had received their greatest ever boost.

But perhaps the strongest incentive to both legal avoidance and illegal evasion was the application of tight government controls on wages and dividends during a sustained period of high inflation, which continued unchecked into the seventies. This applied in particular to capital gains tax, since the gains which were being taxed were not so much real as inflationary. 'Four fifths of the yield of capital gains tax was on inflationary gains, not real gains,' Sir William Pile, a former chairman of the Board of Inland Revenue explained: 'This led a number of people to feel, well, that's unjust, I may as well administer my own justice and I'm entitled to be my own Chancellor of the Exchequer. The only way you could add to your capital assets in real terms was to avoid the tax.' The reluctance of high income earners and the owners of profitable businesses to pay tax was further increased when the 1974 Labour government imposed a punitive 98 per cent top tax rate on incomes: this came on top of capital gains tax, the raising of corporation tax to 52 per cent, and the introduction of capital transfer tax to replace estate duty, which had become a largely voluntary tax. Those who until then would never have thought of breaking the law became more than prepared to go up to if not over the legal edge in order to preserve a bigger slice of their income and wealth. The impact was corrosive. For, as the Keith Committee report correctly observed, 'If some people are perceived to be escaping their obligations, great dissatisfaction is likely to be aroused among the majority of conscientious taxpayers.'

Among the 20 million paying tax under the PAYE system and the one-million-plus ranks of the self-employed, this dissatisfaction took the form of increasing tax evasion, the only escape route they could afford. This gave birth to the 'cash, no cheques' black economy of moonlighting garage mechanics, decorators, electricians and plumbers – not to mention the casual workers in industries like catering, whose very existence was unknown to the Inland Revenue. By 1979 Sir William Pile estimated that workers in the black economy cost £2000–£2500 million a year in lost tax revenue. He also admitted that even he participated in its growth by paying cash for work done around his home because it was the only way to get things done. Today the estimated loss from the black economy is put at £5000 million a year.

But while the poor broke the law and evaded, the rich stayed within the law and avoided – so much so that legal avoidance accounted for some £400–£500 million a year by the end of the seventies.

The coexistence of illegal tax evasion and legal tax avoidance on such a scale indicated the erosion in public honesty and moral values which had taken place in a country previously thought of as more honest than most when it came to paying tax. Britain is now no better than such pioneers of the black economy as Italy and France. Though spurred by the high tax policies of successive Labour governments as a means of financing increased public expenditure and, supposedly, redistributing wealth, this erosion was also encouraged by the way in which the courts consistently supported the right of the rich to run rings round the taxman. Not surprisingly, those unable to afford clever accountants and eminent lawyers saw nothing wrong in taking their own – illegal – steps to improve or protect their more modest incomes.

All this coincided with the emergence of a class of new money makers, earning fast fortunes in property development, stock-market operations, films and pop music. Like the old money class, the Vesteys and the Grosvenors, they did not wish to donate most of their more ephemeral wealth to Harold Wilson's socialist Britain, but unlike the Vesteys and the Grosvenors they did not count among their faithful retainers a family tax adviser. So was born the demand for a new breed of those 'professional gentlemen' of whom Viscount Simon had spoken so disparagingly –

advisers who could, like an illusionist, make tax liabilities disappear through increasingly artificial and intricate but ready-made tax schemes.

Such fiscal magicians became the focus of a countrywide network of accountants and lawyers. They in turn were plugged into an even more influential grid – that of the life insurance and pension-plan salesmen. From the fifties onwards insurance and pension schemes with their built-in tax concessions – premiums could be deducted from income before tax – boomed with the rise in the stock market and inflation. By the midsixties both were very big business. The use of insurance and pension policies to avoid tax suggested a second imperative for the eager tax adviser – that of finding an allowance against tax, such as insurance or pension premiums, and developing it into a loophole by astute use of the wording of the relevant statute, so as to create a situation never envisaged by the law makers or the Inland Revenue.

The amount of tax which could be saved by paying life insurance and pension premiums was limited and the benefits long-term. However, those who sold such policies knew clients who would be in the market for a proposal that could save them even more – and with benefits now, rather than in ten or twenty years' time. One of the first to see the potential was Colin Emson, who set up as a tax consultant in 1967. 'I went into advising clients on tax avoidance because I saw, in one particular case involving estate duty, just how unfair the tax system had become,' he explained; and he established Emson & Dudley – after Richard Empson and Edmund Dudley, Henry VIII's hated tax collectors – to advise clients on which ready-made tax scheme was suitable, or to suggest a 'bespoke' alternative.

Tax-avoidance schemes had long made use of annuities and other devices associated with the insurance industry, so there was already considerable cross-fertilisation between the insurance world and those who produced tax schemes. Labour taxation policies welded that loose arrangement into the alliance which eventually brought forth Rossminster and its imitators.

Although the tax-avoidance business was changing its form and recruiting new members, until 1974 the game was still largely played in the same fashion as before. The adviser produced a scheme for a limited number of clients which was usually designed either to change highly taxed income into lower-taxed capital or to defer tax into the indefinite future. The results and the method used to obtain them were then put before the local Inspector of Taxes who challenged it in the courts. If the taxpayer won, he paid no tax, and vice versa. It was all very gentlemanly, with no aces up the sleeve.

The tax-scheme promoter did not need an unsporting advantage, thanks to Lord Tomlin's doctrine and Lord Clyde's shovel, he already had an edge on the Inland Revenue. Given the power of precedent, the English courts were unlikely to examine the substance or reality of a tax scheme, or even its end result, but concentrated instead on the form and legality of each component part. However, this did not mean that the tax avoider was certain to win – indeed the House of Lords turned down a number of income-into-capital schemes based on the concept of 'dividend stripping'. But increasingly sophisticated schemes continued to get through.

In the battle to outwit the Inland Revenue by finding new loopholes, tax avoidance became increasingly dependent on ever more artificial schemes. The transactions underlying the schemes were not undertaken for any real commercial purpose, and bore little relation to the ways in which loans, leases or commercial deals were enacted in the real world, but were undertaken purely for tax-avoidance purposes. Such arrangements lacked any element of commercial reality and existed purely in the unreal world of artificial tax avoidance, in which the client began by owing the Inland Revenue money and ended with his debts erased. His only real contribution was paying a fee for the privilege of taking part in an elaborate vanishing trick.

Just how artificial such schemes had become was shown by the efforts of Julie Christie and David Frost to avoid paying tax on their superstar incomes. Show business quickly proved a fruitful field for the tax-avoidance promoters. Attempts to protect Hayley Mills's earnings as a child star for Walt Disney went all the way to the House of Lords – the Inland Revenue finally won in 1974. Companies like Constellation Investments and Management Agency and Music were floated on the stock market as a means of sheltering the earnings of sixties stars like the singers Tom Jones and Engelbert Humperdinck, swapping the ownership of the companies which owned the rights to their services for shares in the public company – yet another variant of the income-into-capital trick.

Following her international success in the films *Darling* and *Doctor Zhivago*, Julie Christie expected to earn £475,000 over the seven years from 1965 and was advised to carry out a highly complex tax scheme – so complex that, according to its co-creator, an attempted precis of the plan ran to some 15,000 words.[9] Other clients included Albert Finney,

Tommy Steele, Christopher Plummer and composer Malcolm Arnold.

Called the Open Commercial Trust, the stars' scheme featured many of the ingredients which were to be put to ample use by Roy Tucker and Rossminster. The 'pass the parcel' switching of matching 'paper' loans between several allied parties in a preordained sequence of transactions; the temporary provision of the money for these loans from a friendly outside bank, which reclaimed the money plus a fee and interest at the end of the sequence a few days later; and the tightly scripted completion meeting, at the beginning of which the tax payer had a tax liability and at the end of which he did not. Central to it all was the tax avoider's favourite instrument – the discretionary trust. This is a trust in which the beneficiaries are notionally at the discretion of the trustees. This will normally be exercised in keeping with the wishes of the settlor, and usually means his family; but until a distribution of the trust's income or capital is made, no tax will be paid.[10]

The scheme used by Julie Christie was firmly knocked on the head by Mr Justice, now Lord, Templeman in 1975 in the first of a series of anti-avoidance rulings made by him which would eventually change the views of the House of Lords. Terming the scheme a 'circle of payments' and a 'trick', the judge declared in the High Court, 'Circular payments disguised the fact that nothing was being accomplished save provision for the distribution of the profits ... complications are not trading and tax avoidance, whether successful or unsuccessful, is not by itself trading.'[11] Julie Christie decided not to appeal but to pay the tax.

Just how differently most judges saw the matter was shown that same year, when Lord Justice Russell pronounced, 'There can be a bona fide commercial transaction with the obtaining of a tax advantage as a main object.'[12]

The case the Inland Revenue fought and lost against David Frost illustrated another ever popular weapon in the tax avoider's armoury – the use of tax havens through which to channel income which would be highly taxed if received in the UK. These offshore tax havens were mostly islands, either around the coast of Britain, such as Jersey, Guernsey and the Isle of Man, or in the Caribbean, such as the Bahamas, Cayman, Turks and Caicos or British Virgin Islands: others include Gibraltar. Their attraction is low or no tax, political stability, the use of English as the language of commerce, and a British or partly British system of law. All are past or present British colonies, or are part of the British Isles for all but tax purposes, though a non-British favourite is the Netherlands Antilles off the Caribbean coast of South America.

From 1967 David Frost's substantial American earnings were paid through companies in the Bahamas and the Netherlands Antilles into a partnership set up in the Bahamas in which he had a 97 per cent interest in the profits and 99 per cent of the capital. The Inland Revenue assessed Frost for tax of £175,000 on his US earnings for the three years from 1969. It claimed that the partnership was not real, as the co-partner was merely a trust company and so produced no income. This argument lost all the way to the House of Lords, in January 1980. After the verdict, the *Financial Times*'s tax correspondent commented, 'The rules by which [the Revenue] and taxpayers play these games, under the genial umpiring of the courts, might seem to some people to be rationality taken to the point not only of absurdity but insanity.'[13]

The Christie and Frost schemes were the work of individual promoters with one or two bright ideas; but by the late sixties a new name had appeared on the tax-avoidance scene who revolutionised this approach by producing a whole series of schemes. These were far more sophisticated – in other words, far more artificial – than their predecessors, and could be sold on demand to companies and individuals, particularly in the property world, anxious to avoid not only corporation and income tax but taxes on development profits as well.

Godfrey Bradman had qualified as an accountant in the early sixties, taking a correspondence course while working as a £1.25-a-week clerk. He soon set up his own practice in the West End with his partner Bernard Faber, specialising in intricate tax-avoidance schemes for a select but growing band of private clients. Although he preferred the shadows to the spotlight, Bradman's fame spread along the accountancy and legal grapevines. (The outside world did not hear of Bradman and his activities until February 1974, when he suggested that a group of private individuals should pay the striking miners £80,000 a week to end the coal dispute which threatened to bring down the Conservative government. By then he was out of tax avoidance.)

In the late sixties and early seventies Godfrey Bradman was the man to see if you had a large tax problem. Soon the Inland Revenue were engaged in a number of long-running legal challenges to ever varying versions of Bradman schemes. The schemes were cleverly constructed out of a bewildering sequence of as many as twenty-five or more moves between a bevy of Bradman-linked companies. In one winning scheme the key company was named, with a touch of humour rarely present in tax matters, Excalibur.

Bradman's forte involved transactions which notionally stretched away into the future, with payment for a property deal being made in small annual sums spread over 200 years or by leases, the rents of which were payable over 250 or even 997 years, thereby avoiding any large taxable payment until the final year. His clients, however, would not have to wait anything like 997 years to enjoy their taxfree profit: that would be forthcoming within days after another Bradman company had acquired for cash the rights to the future payments.

Bradman's services did not come cheap: his commissions, charged on the amount of tax saved, could easily amount to between £50,000 and £100,000, or even more. But where profits of £500,000 or more were involved, the tax rate demanded by Chancellor Bradman represented a considerable saving on what the real Chancellor would have wanted.

At thirty-four the bespectacled Bradman, the quintessential accountant, was the undisputed king of tax avoidance, dominating it as no one had done before. But he was eager to use the profits he had earned to move into the more respectable and permanent realms of banking and property development – for, unlike many of those who engaged in promoting tax schemes, including Rossminster's founders Tucker and Plummer, Bradman was gifted with a good business sense.

In 1971 he launched his London Mercantile group, followed the next year by a bank, the London Mercantile Corporation. Bradman was by then at the height of his power and influence as the best and brightest 'inventor and purveyor' – to quote Templeman – of tax-avoidance schemes. With typical astuteness, Bradman chose that moment to retire.

As Bradman explains his decision, it was 'no longer worth straining my mind on advising others. I got bored with reading legislation in an attempt to outwit the draftsmen. It was an unnecessary use of skills.'[14] But in accountancy circles it was rumoured that Bradman, shrewd as ever, had negotiated a deal with the Inland Revenue, trading their vital recognition of London Mercantile Corporation as a bank for his agreement to stop marketing tax schemes. Those already sold would continue to be fought through the courts – the Excalibur scheme finally triumphed in the House of Lords in 1981 – but there would be no more. The gentlemanly, unpublicised contest between Godfrey Bradman and the Inland Revenue was to end in a truce.[15]

If this was so, it was a good deal for both sides. Ever the long-term thinker – as his tax schemes showed – Bradman realised that the game could not go on for ever. As one Finance Act closed a loophole he had exploited, so another would open, which the Revenue would then close once it had discovered the scheme, and so on; but the taxman could not always be relied upon merely to react to events. It would be simple to emulate the United States, Australia and other countries by passing legislation which would effectively make artificial avoidance schemes illegal. And with a Conservative government now in power, far more money could be made from property deals and from a bank than from being a cut-price Chancellor.

For the Inland Revenue Bradman's retirement and the disappearance of his 'off-the-peg' schemes meant the removal of one of their major headaches; but it also left a large and growing vacuum as the fast fortunes of the new money games multiplied and the property and stock-market booms spiralled towards the dizzy peaks they were to reach before the great crash in 1973–74. Bradman had shown the way, whetted appetites and created the market. The time was right for two other accountants to fill that vacuum. In the process they would turn tax avoidance from a craft designed for the few into a mass-production industry aimed at the many.

THE ROAD TO ROSSMINSTER

Accountancy is not a profession associated with society's movers and shakers; it tends to be identified with well-paid pinstriped orthodoxy rather than with controversy, still less with confronting the government.

There was nothing grey about Roy Tucker, except his suits. A diminutive, boyish figure with long hair, often to be seen cycling through Mayfair, Tucker, even in his thirties, still looked rather like the schoolboy genius who just might blow up the chemistry lab. One first-time visitor to Rossminster in the early days remarked to a director about the rather unkempt individual with whom they had just shared the lift, 'You must do something about your messenger boy. He gives the wrong impression for a respectable banking business.' He was informed he had just met Roy Tucker.

Ronald Plummer, on the other hand, prematurely grey and clinically precise, would have slipped easily into the stereotype of the accountant. Plummer's failure to impress hid considerable organisational and perceptive skills. Almost four years older than his colleague, Plummer was a perfect foil for Tucker's intellectual and conceptual brilliance.

Ronald Anthony Plummer was born in Maida Vale in September 1936. His birth certificate records that he was the son of a builder's labourer. In later years those who met him at Rossminster always found him very reticent and even embarrassed about his family background; by then his father, who had worked for London Transport, had died, and his mother was living in a semidetached house in Pinner, just outside London.

Plummer began his accountancy career on leaving school in 1952. Four years later, having obtained some O levels via a correspondence course, he joined the small Regent Street firm of Shacklady, Hudson, Crookes &

Co., who had advertised for articled clerks. The former senior partner Mervyn Hudson recalls him as 'a very bright clerk' who did well in his final examinations – 'he finished very high up the list.' On qualifying in 1961 Plummer joined one of the largest of the 'Big Eight' major international accountancy firms, Price Waterhouse. He worked in both the audit and management consultancy departments there before deciding on a career in merchant banking. He joined the prominent City bank Samuel Montagu's corporate finance department, handling takeover bids and deals.

As Plummer himself later described it in Rossminster's promotional literature, he became involved in tax matters 'by accident'. Tax considerations, such as the UK residence or nonresidence for tax purposes of companies and shareholders, and potential liabilities for capital gains tax (charged on the difference between the purchase and sale price of assets) or stamp duty (paid on the transfer of shares from one owner to another), are substantial factors in structuring takeover bids. So, as Plummer described it, he decided that 'if dealings with complex tax questions were to be undertaken, it would be advisable to return to the profession.'[1]

He joined the fastest-growing and most aggressive member of the 'Big Eight', the American firm Arthur Andersen, becoming a manager in its tax department. It was here, in 1968, that he first met Roy Tucker.

Roy Clifford Tucker not only came from a far less humble background than his future partner but had followed his father into accountancy. Also a Londoner, Tucker was born in July 1940 in Kingston. Somewhat inappropriately for someone who was to spend so much time helping the rich, his parents lived in Robin Hood Way. In 1953 Tucker was sent to St Paul's School in west London, where he made little mark on his contemporaries. 'He was very modest and retiring,' according to one former classmate. Another Old Pauline was less charitable – 'Roy Tucker was a nonenity at St Paul's.' Even so, he became the treasurer of the Gramophone and Physical societies, and joined the honour roll of Foundation Scholars, the brightest boys in the school.

Tucker specialised in mathematics, which he planned to read at Oxford. However, the boy who later took on the Inland Revenue, with up to £1000 million in tax at stake, failed the scholarship examination. Tucker used to tell people at Rossminster that he had not wanted to go to university,[2] but one of his St Paul's contemporaries says it was assumed that all the members of Tucker's mathematics group would go on to university as a matter of course.

Instead, Tucker joined the City firm of Sydenham, Snowden, Nicholson & Co. in 1960. With his A level pass in mathematics he qualified as an articled clerk in four years rather than the five years required of most of his peers, including Plummer. According to one of the firm's partners, he immediately demonstrated an interest in tax quite unusual among newly qualified accountants.

As a result, he was sent to a new office the firm had opened in Hereford to be the tax manager, dealing with a wide variety of personal tax and estate duty cases. Tucker stayed at Hereford for four years and seemed to relish his dealings with the Inland Revenue. 'He enjoyed doing battle with the Revenue, he liked to argue every point and prove them wrong and himself right,' according to one of his colleagues. 'He was very arrogant but you have to be arrogant to be a tax manager.' But although he did well with the firm, he seems not to have made the sort of impression that would have marked him out as a man to watch. 'When he left I did not feel a great sense of loss,' says a partner who knew him well.

Tucker left to join Arthur Andersen – then very much the firm to be with for up-and-coming young accountants – where he knew the tax partner, Robert Pereira. Andersen had only opened an office in Britain during the fifties, but was already beginning to rival the older, more established British accountancy firms and was eager to expand its UK business, especially among private clients. Ambitious young accountants, eager to gain experience of company audits instead of private clients' tax affairs and so enhance their career prospects, were attracted by the possibilities Andersen offered. The US accountancy firms were also ahead of those in Britain in new techniques and ideas. Arthur Andersen already had a large number of major companies as clients, creating different challenges on taxation matters both in Britain and abroad, and Ronald Plummer travelled extensively in the US while at Arthur Andersen, studying American tax techniques, some of which were utilised much later at Rossminster.

The tax department at Arthur Andersen included six or so tax managers and two or three tax partners. Each manager had a wide range of responsibilities and handled a client's entire tax affairs. It was an ideal school in which Tucker and Plummer could develop their approach to tax avoidance. They also met several like-minded accountants at Arthur

Andersen who were later to be involved with Rossminster or introduce business to them.

One of their contemporaries recalls how they appeared in those pre-Rossminster days. Plummer was 'pleasant but remote, not a revealing character'. He was seen as 'hard-nosed' and 'very commercial'. Tucker on the other hand was 'the funny little man with his collar turned up, babbling ideas, very imaginative, fast-thinking, with a fairly flexible approach which saw a lot of angles'. Most of these ideas and angles were, however, seen by his colleagues as 'off the wall'. Ironically, most of the 'Big Eight' accountancy firms were to be unimpressed by artificial tax avoidance and advised against Tucker's tax schemes. They were not confident that such highly artificial schemes would succeed in the courts.

Like most of their colleagues in the tax department, neither Plummer nor Tucker saw their future at Arthur Andersen. They saw it as a stepping stone to a more exciting and rewarding career in the City with a bank or with one of the stock-market whiz kids who dominated the financial columns at the start of the seventies. Arthur Andersen on a c.v. was an 'open sesame' to many such sought-after jobs.

Roy Tucker was already fascinated by the possibilities in tax avoidance, and had started devising his own tax schemes. His principle was very simple: 'After working out the avoidance objective the Revenue was trying to ban, you start thinking of other ways of reaching the same result.'[3]

Ronald Plummer left Arthur Andersen in May 1970 for a job that was the envy of all his colleagues in the tax department – that of tax adviser to Jim Slater's Slater, Walker Securities. Slater, Walker was then at the peak of its reputation as *the* financial phenomenon of the time. The most potent force in the stock market, it had created the concept of 'asset stripping' – buying control, for shares, of sleepy old companies that were heavy with assets but light on profits and selling off the component parts for cash, so realising capital profits which further elevated its own share price. By 1970 Slater, Walker's empire spanned the globe and had spawned a series of satellite companies run by Slater protégés and imitators. With a bank and an insurance company in-house, it seemed poised to join the City elite. As Plummer told it to his envious fellow tax managers, Jim Slater had interviewed him personally and had been so impressed by the fact that he asked for a higher salary than any of the other applicants that he gave him the job.

Plummer stayed almost three years with Slater, Walker. 'He appeared to have an onerous life, sitting at a desk with four telephones which rang singly, doubly or all at once,' says a former Slater, Walker colleague. 'To answer, instantly, tax queries from Jim Slater alone was a feat.' At the same time Plummer was developing ideas which were to be crucial in the formation and development of Rossminster. Like Arthur Andersen, Slater, Walker was to be a fertile source of future business associates and clients.

Of equal importance for the future was the fact that Slater, Walker's banking and insurance interests had already extended to Britain's home-grown tax havens, the Channel Islands and the Isle of Man, and Plummer made good contacts among the Slater representatives there. Although they are no different from the mainland where citizenship, defence and foreign relations are concerned, these offshore islands are not part of the UK for tax purposes. They are self-governing, and the Inland Revenue has no jurisdiction in them. Like the tax havens further afield, Jersey, Guernsey and the Isle of Man offer low tax to resident individuals and no tax on profits or assets to those who register companies but do no business locally, such companies pay a nominal annual duty or corporation tax, as well as offering bank accounts into which money can be deposited taxfree and in total secrecy by nonresidents. Once assets or income have been hidden by UK residents behind such companies or bank accounts, they will remain taxfree unless discovered by the Inland Revenue.

At Slater, Walker Plummer also learned how an in-house bank could enable a financial-services group to finance activities which an outside, orthodox bank would be wary of backing.

Finally, Slater himself illustrated how a particular loophole in the tax laws – the tax-exempt status of charities – could be utilised commercially for tax avoidance, so benefiting those whose interests were somewhat less altruistic. Any organisation registered as a recognised charity by the Charity Commissioners because of its supposed nonprofit motive is exempt from all tax on any income or assets received or on any capital gains it makes, so long as it uses its funds for purely charitable purposes and within the terms of the deed under which it is established. In February 1970 Jim Slater formed two charities – the Slater Foundation and the Helen Slater Charitable Trust. The trust was largely funded by the donation of a block of Slater, Walker shares, plus covenants from associated companies. All its income from share dealing, rents and covenants was donated to the foundation in order to keep its charitable status.[4]

Plummer was not only the group tax manager but advised Jim Slater on his personal tax affairs, so he would have been involved with the operations of the two charities even though they had been set up before he joined Slater, Walker. Plummer and Tucker were later to imitate the Slater concept, transforming charities into instruments of massive tax avoidance.

Plummer's departure to Slater, Walker cemented rather than broke his association with an equally restless Tucker. The following year Tucker decided to form his own practice, Roy Tucker & Co., for the purpose of marketing Bradman-style tax schemes. This was difficult to do while he was still at Arthur Andersen who, while not opposed to artificial tax schemes in principle, were increasingly uneasy at their tax manager's ambitions. 'I was frustrated under the Arthur Andersen umbrella because it was impossible to set up the necessary banking and financial structures,' Tucker recalled later.[5] He left in November 1971.

At Slater, Walker his friend Ron Plummer saw the possibilities, and quickly provided the answer. Plummer realised there was a riskfree profit to be made out of financing the circular transactions in tax schemes. For the Slater, Walker bank, financing tax avoidance was just one more type of unorthodox banking business which other banks did not touch.

Tucker initially operated out of City offices in Lombard Street, together with an ex-Andersen articled clerk, Tim Nicholas, and a secretary. He began by offering tax advice and selling schemes in a small way, but he stepped up gear in August 1972 with a move to offices in North Audley Street, Mayfair. Through his own connections and through Plummer, he began to put together a network of friends and associates who would later play important roles in forming, running and promoting Rossminster. Like Tim Nicholas, Nicholas Pilbrow was another ex-Andersen alumnus, while fellow accountant Richard Gardner and Barry Pilkington were former inspectors of taxes, and so knew the Revenue from the inside.

Gardner had already begun promoting his own tax schemes. After joining the Inland Revenue near his home in Chelmsford he had decided before completing his training that it was not for him. 'I met an Inspector who had been in fourteen posts in twenty-two years and I decided not to go on.' A bluff, burly, cheerful character, Gardner had qualified as a certified accountant and joined a number of insurance brokers, concentrating on estate duty planning: 'At least you had no aggravated clients, only a few aggrieved beneficiaries.' Then, in 1972, he decided to move again and considered applying for the advertised post of tax planner at a merchant bank. Before he could do so, however, his superior suggested he should speak to a 'very clever' man at Slater, Walker – who turned out to be Ron Plummer. Gardner soon realised that Slater, Walker was the bank in the advertisement, but he was not attracted by the idea. 'I decided I would rather be a big cog in a small wheel.'

Plummer then suggested he might like to join his friend Roy Tucker, who had recently opened his own practice. Gardner was not convinced. But a month later Plummer invited him to meet Tucker at a City pub. As a result of that meeting Gardner joined Roy Tucker & Co. in May 1972. The deal was that Tucker would take 25 per cent of his estate duty business and he would have 25 per cent of Tucker's tax business. But that was soon forgotten, says Gardner.

Tucker also made use of his connections with insurance salesmen and tax consultants like Simon Cardale and Colin Emson who had the clients and wanted the tax schemes. Finally there were the vital top-flight legal experts such as the leading tax QC Desmond Miller and the West End solicitor Jerrold Moser.

Freed from the constraints at Arthur Andersen, with Slater, Walker's financial backing and equipped with a network of salesmen with links to accountants and lawyers throughout the country, Roy Tucker was ready to assume the mantle of Godfrey Bradman, to redesign it and make it his own.

CHARITY BEGINS AT HOME

After his initial forays into the world of tax avoidance, Roy Tucker combined with his friend Ron Plummer to make the first substantial move towards their impending partnership with a tax scheme which was both simple and ingenious, and which was to flourish over the next five years. Once again it was designed to turn income into capital and so reduce the costly burden of surtax for higher income earners; and it met a growing demand for such schemes from their professional advisers.

Among these was Simon Cardale, then running his own insurance and investment advisory business in Belgravia. With Slater, Walker's backing Tucker, Plummer and Cardale combined to produce and market the first of the Capital Income Plans which later were to become a regular Rossminster feature. Initiated by Tucker as technical adviser, the Capital Income Plan introduced what became known as the Reverse Annuity Scheme. The concept was then taken to Plummer to refine and execute. To perfect it, Plummer required the services of two Slater, Walker group companies, together with the bank. The key was a little-known charity, Home and Overseas Voluntary Aid Services.

HOVAS had been formed on 30 December 1970 to 'relieve suffering amongst the aged, impotent or poor; to advance education and to further such other charitable objects as the company may see fit'. In reality this meant expediting the Capital Income Plan Mark 1.

A registered charity set up to benefit some cause, institution or group of individuals, or a company incorporated with similar charitable purposes, is tax-exempt. It can make profits through the purchase and sale of investments or receive as dividends the profits made by noncharitable companies, all tax free. Once it has been recognised as a charity by the Charity

Commissioners and thus by the Inland Revenue – which has a rarely used right of challenge – it need only ensure that its activities appear compatible with the objects for which the charity was formed. And if these are defined widely enough then virtually all things are possible. Jim Slater had spotted the nonaltruistic opportunities this loophole presented, as had the equally profit-conscious Godfrey Bradman, but Tucker and Plummer exploited the charity loophole to its utmost.

HOVAS was the first of a succession of charities to figure in their tax schemes – so much so that abuse of the tax-exempt status of charities was to become a Rossminster trademark.

Among the first two HOVAS directors was Brian Mepham, a chartered accountant friend of Plummer's who had been a junior partner in the firm at which he had done his articles. The firm, now called Fraser Threlford Crookes, had moved to the City and was later to be used a good deal by Rossminster. The other director was a Lloyd's underwriter, Robin Kershaw, whom Cardale introduced. They were joined in March 1971 by the Honourable Mary Berry, a daughter of Baron Fermoy and the former wife of the Conservative MP, Sir Anthony Berry. HOVAS was both a registered charity and a company formed for charitable purposes, and the shares in the company were held by the three directors.

Mary Berry had become involved with HOVAS as a result of meeting Roy Tucker. She was then involved in the Blackfriars Settlement charity project which Tucker knew. According to Mrs Berry, Tucker invited her to become a director, on the grounds that 'he would get rich clients to donate to the Blackfriars Settlement'. Her job was to research projects which would then receive donations from HOVAS once the money began to flow in – 'I was receiving applications or pricing projects so that if HOVAS received any money they knew what to do.' As far as Mrs Berry was concerned, HOVAS was a straightforward charity aiming to relieve suffering among the poor, not the rich. After all, its surplus funds were to be used 'exclusively for charitable purposes'.

Mrs Berry was appointed to the HOVAS board just as the tax avoidance season was moving into top gear ahead of the 5 April deadline. Capital Income Plan Mark 1 was now in action, and in an impressive vote of confidence Plummer, facing a £3500 surtax bill, became one of the first of its charity-conscious clients.

On 10 March HOVAS borrowed £1,430,000 from Baldrene, a Slater, Walker company of which Plummer was a director. The loan – costing almost double the Bank Rate, then 6½ per cent – was to purchase the right to a series of yearly annuity payments from high surtax payers. The scheme was described as 'simplicity itself' some six years later by the High Court judge Mr Justice Walton. As a charity HOVAS expected to recover the tax payable on the income from which the surtax payer paid the annuity, while the surtax payer hoped to deduct the gross pre-tax amount of the annuity from his total income, since it was paid to a charity, and so reduce his tax liability. HOVAS then paid the surtax payer a capital sum roughly equal to the amount of the annuity. This way the taxpayer saved the surtax he would otherwise have had to pay on the income equal to the amount of the annuity but received back almost all that he paid to the charity. Just how the scheme worked was set out, in Lord Wilberforce's words, with 'almost military precision' in a 'Most Confidential' letter circulated by Simon Cardale, who took a 5 per cent commission on each scheme sold.

Cardale took as his example a taxpayer earning £30,000 and facing 50 per cent surtax on almost half his income, costing him £7347. HOVAS would purchase the right to an annuity from the taxpayer for a cash payment of £44,800. In turn the taxpayer agreed to pay the charity five net annual payments of £9000, equivalent to the gross sum on which surtax was payable before deduction of income tax at the then standard 38 per cent rate. To guarantee that the five annuity payments were made, the taxpayer then purchased, with the money from the charity, promissory notes costing £45,000 from a finance company, as well as providing the £200 difference. Each note was for £9000 and repayable over five years. The taxpayer also had to provide some shares as extra security.

On the day on which the taxpayer signed the annuity agreement with HOVAS he was to open a deposit account with a merchant bank, into which he paid the sum of £15. Into this account would go the payment from HOVAS. He then paid the 5 per cent commission based on the amount received from HOVAS, and on receiving the money from the charity he purchased the promissory notes. Twenty-eight days after this the taxpayer made his first annuity payment of £9000 to HOVAS which, a day later, released to him a similar amount from the promissory notes. That process was then repeated on four more yearly occasions, at the end of which all his securities would be returned, together with his £45,000. At the end of his letter, Cardale summarised the outcome of these circular transactions:

'Result: the gross equivalent of the £9000 a year is £14,694. Mr X deducts this latter sum each year in computing his total income for surtax. With surtax at 50 per cent his annual saving is £7347.'

Cardale estimated the total cost to the taxpayer at £2513, for which he would receive a benefit over the five years of £37,418 – and 'his profit on the transaction is thus £34,905 FREE OF TAX.'

All this overlooked the fact that HOVAS had no funds with which to buy annuities without the Baldrene loan. And it could only obtain that loan if the purchasers of the annuities provided security which could be pledged to Baldrene. That was the reason for the promissory notes, which had to be purchased from another Slater, Walker company, Old Change Court (Investments). It was also the reason for requiring the further securities to be pledged.

Plummer was sold the scheme by Cardale at a special cut-rate commission. Instead of the normal 5 per cent fee, or £125, Plummer paid just £15. But it was partly his scheme and he, through Slater, Walker, was providing the means whereby Cardale had something to sell.

Plummer entered into the scheme at a completion meeting on 15 March 1971 involving all the parties – Plummer, Cardale, Baldrene, HOVAS, Old Change Court and Slater, Walker. Of those present, only Cardale was not in the Slater, Walker camp. Plummer agreed to pay HOVAS an amount equal to £500 a year net of income tax at the standard rate – £851 gross. In return HOVAS paid Plummer £2480 into an account at Slater, Walker, which he had just opened with a deposit of £40. Slater, Walker immediately paid £15 to Cardale as his fee and £2500 to Old Change in return for five promissory notes of £500 each. These were immediately lodged with HOVAS as security for the annuity payments and HOVAS in turn immediately lodged the same notes with Baldrene as security for the £2480 loan used to pay Plummer. Plummer also provided HOVAS with £300 with which to buy Midland Bank shares as further security, and HOVAS took out insurance on his life. All this was completed at the meeting by the signing of a number of standard, pre-prepared forms.

The scheme went into effect on 29 March when the first £500 payment was made by Slater, Walker to HOVAS on Plummer's behalf. This was done by means of bookkeeping entries in the two bank accounts inside Slater, Walker. No actual money changed hands. HOVAS then repaid Baldrene £500 and received in return a promissory note for the same amount which was released to Slater, Walker, who presented it to Old

Change for payment into Plummer's account. This procedure was to be repeated on one day in each of the next four years.

The only real money in the whole transaction was the £340 put up by Plummer to pay Cardale's fee, the premium on his life insurance, a small amount of one day's interest at Slater, Walker for the overdraft pending arrival of the promissory note repayment, and to buy the Midland Bank shares. The rest of the money was provided by Baldrene. Plummer got back from HOVAS each £500 he had paid them via Baldrene and Old Change: the money involved never went outside Slater, Walker. In return he expected to cut his income assessable for surtax by £2500 and so keep the benefit of the tax relief claimed by HOVAS. It was, as even a critic like Viscount Dilhorne had to admit, 'an ingenious, complicated and well thought-out scheme . . . to raid the Treasury using the technicalities of revenue law as the necessary weapons'.[1]

The cost to HOVAS was the 12 per cent interest it had to pay Baldrene for the loan. But if it could reclaim the tax payable by Plummer on that part of his income represented by the annuity, at the standard rate of income tax £351 on every £500, it would stand to receive £4255, £2500 from Plummer and the balance from the Inland Revenue.

All this assumed that the Inland Revenue would accept HOVAS's claim to be a charity and so be eligible for the tax refund. Without it there would be no 'surplus funds' with which to perform acts of charity other than that rendered to Plummer. The sufferings of the rich might have been relieved, but those of the aged, impotent and poor would have to continue.

For their first stab at marketing an off-the-peg tax-avoidance scheme CIP Mark 1 was a significant success. Including Plummer, forty taxpayers bought the scheme. HOVAS paid £1,466,000 for annuities, representing tax liabilities of £368,000 or an average of £9000 a year. A similar amount stood to be refunded to the charity. HOVAS received in the period to April 1972 an income of £919,461 before the expected tax refund. But expenses were high. Amortising the annuities and paying £184,000 interest to Slater, Walker on the Baldrene loan, plus insurance premiums, cost £786,000. Pending the arrival of the expected £368,000 tax rebate a mere £19.55 went to charity although £551,000 was held on deposit at Ralli Brothers – a Slater, Walker bank – earning £35,000 in interest. Roy Tucker did better as the auditor. His fees were £450.

A year later the tax situation was still unresolved, with £530,000 now being claimed. Still, despite interest on its bank deposit of £67,000, it seems that HOVAS would have been unable to donate £6000 to charity had it not received a similar donation from a non-annuity source, presumably to assist in maintaining the charitable fiction. In the year to April 1973, annuities costing a further £532,000 were bought. The annuity payments received had more than halved to £416,000 but the cost of financing them was £434,000 including £158,000 paid to Slater, Walker.

By the following year, to April 1974, all charitable work had ceased, although during that period another £817,000 had been paid for annuities. HOVAS was now claiming £637,000 from the Inland Revenue. Though no payments were made to charity, HOVAS was not without income, receiving £357,000 in annuity payments and £97,000 in bank interest. But there were no 'surplus funds', it seems, especially after paying Slater, Walker.

Well before HOVAS's role as a 'charity' came to an end, Mary Berry had become disenchanted. Little or no money had either come in or gone out for the promised purposes. She decided that she no longer could afford the time to be involved and resigned in June 1973.

The explanation for the lack of funds was that the Inland Revenue had refused to accept that HOVAS was entitled to reclaim the tax due on the annuity payments, on the grounds that the company had not used its income only for charitable purposes. This was still the Revenue's position in April 1975, shortly after Plummer made the last of his five annuity payments. By then the tax rebate claimed by HOVAS had reached £755,000.[2]

Since its establishment in December 1970, HOVAS had expended just £6219.55 on the charitable work it had proposed to carry out among the aged, impotent and poor. On the other hand, Slater, Walker had earned £651,000 in interest, and Simon Cardale up to £141,000, while the surtax-paying clients were hoping to avoid up to £2,815,000.

The Capital Income Plan Mark 2 featured Plummer and Tucker's next exploitation of charity – the Deprived Children's Aid Fund. The DCAF was formed almost a year after HOVAS, on 8 December 1971. Unlike its predecessor it was not a registered charity, but its articles of association said that it would apply all surplus funds from its main activity of investing in annuities to charitable purposes. The company was run from Tucker's offices at Audley House with Tim Nicholas as its secretary. Nicholas became the expert on the Capital Income Plan schemes, handling all their administration even after Rossminster had been formed. He was considered one of the few insiders to understand their labyrinthine ramifications. The DCAF auditors were Plummer's old firm Fraser Threlford & Crookes. The shares in the company were held by two Irish residents, Joseph Mullen and Neil Deane – Tucker, whose wife Annabel's family are Irish, has a home in Ireland.

The first two directors of DCAF were a City public relations man, David Pollock, and someone who was to feature regularly with Tucker and Plummer in the years ahead – Glyn Evans, the managing director of the City commodity dealers, E. Bailey. Pollock had come in as a result of his friendship with an associate of Simon Cardale, and he had assumed that the idea originated with Cardale rather than with Tucker and Plummer. He realised the charity's real purpose, admitting that he 'knew it was linked to a tax scheme and that there was a tax wheeze going through the courts'. Evans had met Tucker and Plummer as a result of their fascination with commodity investment both as a means of making money and as a vehicle for tax avoidance.

CIP Mark 2 was launched with Cardale's assistance in early 1972. Like all the various versions of the Capital Income Plan it had slight differences from the original Reverse Annuity concept, but the aim of switching income into capital was the same. It was as successful as the original. About fifty individuals bought the scheme saving – according to Tucker – about £150,000 in tax.[3] Unfortunately one client died soon after buying the scheme and this cost DCAF £81,000 in lost annuities.

In the period up to April 1973, DCAF bought annuities costing £834,000, almost half those of HOVAS; in return it received payments totalling £627,000. This was made possible by a £2 million loan from Securities Dublin, a small bank Rossminster was later to acquire. The company had deposited £1,230,000 with Alpane, a Slater, Walker company, which was later replaced by Pemberley, a company controlled by John Glauser, Plummer's Slater, Walker colleague in Guernsey. Alpane dropped out because Slater, Walker became disillusioned about the profits from the exercise and concerned about both the costs and the possible tax consequences of its involvement. Alpane was a Bermuda company, and the particular area of concern was Section 482 of the Taxes Act, which prevents the transfer of business by a UK resident company to a non-resident company without Treasury permission. 'The joke was that it was all pain and no profit,' recalls a former Slater, Walker executive. 'The scheme was fiendishly complicated, the sums involved were small because the number of clients was too few, there was a lot of work, not much profit and we were skating on thin ice with the Revenue.' Slater, Walker also decided to sell Alpane's HOVAS predecessor, Baldrene.

As with HOVAS, only more so, investing in annuities was far too costly a business to leave much over for deprived children. In its first year DCAF donated precisely £30 to 'charitable work' from a total income of £717,000, and the following year £5000 from £262,000. But then, as one of the scheme's buyers, self proclaimed 'pessimistic solicitor' Richard Sotnick admitted, the furtherance of charity was not part of his purpose. Roy Tucker later estimated his profit from the scheme at £10,000 – 'It wasn't much, but it provided us with working capital.'[4]

'We selected charities from the mail,' recalls David Pollock. Money went to a Cheshire Home but mainly to several children's charities. 'It just went on a few kids' outings' was how one Rossminster insider put it. But by 1975 the Revenue's resistance to accepting HOVAS as a charity had begun to spill over onto DCAF. No more annuities were purchased and so the flow of annuity payments slowed. That year, however, the company did pay £250 to charity, and over £1500 the year after.

David Pollock resigned in April 1977. 'I was told the charity was folding. There was no point in staying. I was just a cipher. There were just two or three meetings a year.'[5] But well before Pollock left it was clear that the company and its supposed charitable work had no future. Like that of HOVAS, its charitable status and thereby its right to reclaim the vital tax rebate had been disputed by the Inland Revenue. Instead of being owed up to £542,000 by the Revenue, the company faced a possible bill of £53,000 in income tax and corporation tax on the capital gains from its annuities.[6]

Tucker and Plummer deny that they misused the spirit or intention of charities for tax-avoidance purposes. But the figures speak for themselves. Even in those charities which did make substantial donations to charitable causes – and HOVAS and DCAF were certainly not among them – the benefit to the charity paled into virtual invisibility in comparison with the benefits to Tucker, Cardale and their clients.

As David Forrest, secretary of the Charity Commissioners, makes clear, the test of a charity is its 'poise'. Is the fund-raising activity or trade in which it is engaged tangential to its major purpose, as the Oxfam shops are, or is it predominant? In the case of both HOVAS and DCAF there is little doubt that they were engaged primarily in a trade, the purchase of annuities, which far outweighed any charitable activity.

But if the tax troubles of HOVAS and DCAF meant less relief of suffering among the aged and among deprived children than had been intended, the suffering of the high income earners who had bought the Capital Income Plan knew no bounds. For if HOVAS and DCAF did not have charitable status, then the claim for tax relief on the donations paid to them would be ineffective, and it was estimated that tax of at least £4 million was at stake.

The Inland Revenue duly rejected claims for deductions on the HOVAS and DCAF donations. But Cardale's clients found an unexpected – if necessary for client consumption – champion, Ronald Plummer. As supervisor of as well as participant in the scheme, and facing personal surtax assessments for £11,126 covering the three years 1970 to 1973, he decided to contest the Revenue's decision. This legal battle was to continue until 1979.[7] By then the Reverse Annuity concept had been nullified by the Finance Act 1977.

Chapter 4

IN MARX WE TRUST

In addition to the Reverse Annuity schemes, during the 1972 and 1973 avoidance seasons Tucker and Plummer – together with Nicholas Pilbrow and a new partner, the solicitor Jerrold Moser – came up with a new offering, devised to avoid capital gains tax. The Exempt Debt Scheme entrenched their standing as the budding Bradmans.

With his bouffant hairstyle, fashionable suits and telephone in his Rolls-Royce, Jerrold Moser was an unlawyerlike lawyer who might well have seemed more at home in Manhattan than Mayfair. He was already well known for his expertise in tax matters, had done a lot of business with Bradman in the sixties, and had a clientele liberally sprinkled with names well known in the City and the worlds of property and 'fringe' banking.

Moser provided the legal drafting for the Exempt Debt Scheme, which was ready to be marketed towards the end of 1971. The concept came from Tucker, while Plummer involved Slater, Walker once more as the bankers. The marketing was to be handled by Pilbrow through his Mayfair tax consultancy, Dovercliffe Consultants. The fee, to be shared among the four partners, was to be 8 per cent of the tax saved, 2 per cent more than that for the Capital Income Plan Mark 2. It was a seller's market.

The partners' arrangements for benefiting from the sale of the Exempt Debt Scheme were secret and highly complex. They marked the beginning of Tucker's and Plummer's long and continuing love affair with the hazy concepts contained in the offshore discretionary trust.

The discretionary trust has been a leading instrument of tax avoidance since the introduction of estate duty after World War One. The added refinement of locating such a trust outside the jurisdiction of the Inland Revenue was increasingly practised in the twenties and thirties by the

Vesteys and others. But it is not necessary to go abroad to achieve the desired effect when a short trip to the Channel Islands or the Isle of Man will do quite as well. The discretionary trust may not have done very much for the Treasury, but it has generated a multimillion-pound business for the lawyers of these nearby havens.

The basic concept of the offshore discretionary trust is to transfer legal ownership of assets from the present UK resident and taxable owner to the trust's nonresident, untaxable trustees. Under a deed of trust the beneficiaries of the trust, decided at the trustees' discretion, have no legal right or power to enjoy its income or capital but merely the right to be considered when the trustees distribute either. Until they actually receive any of the trust's assets the beneficiaries can in this way resist almost any Revenue attempt to make them account for or pay tax on the trust's assets and income. Similarly, the settlor – the individual who sets up the trust – can deny any further interest in it, even if he is a UK resident. Only capital transfer tax is a problem, but one that can be easily solved. The trustees, being in a tax haven, are beyond the Revenue's jurisdiction.

An offshore discretionary trust is usually created with funds from a settlor who is preferably not a UK resident: the settlor can be either an individual or a company, and need not be identified. It is important that the settlor is not a beneficiary, otherwise the Revenue may take this as evidence of a taxable 'power to enjoy'. A trust can be established with as little as £10; once it is established, UK assets can be acquired by the trust or it can receive the right to income which, if received in the UK, would be taxable.

The settlor appoints trustees – usually lawyers in a tax haven, who have the added advantage of being able to hide behind client confidentiality. The trustees administer the affairs of the trust, the assets of which are held by a company often set up in a separate tax haven for added obfuscation. The trustees will usually be equipped with either a schedule of intended beneficiaries in its deed of trust or, more probably, this will be left to the discretion of the trustees acting on the instruction of the settlor or his representative. But the trustees are certain to know for whom the trust was set up or acquired. It is possible to buy ready-made trusts, and all offshore trust companies carry a stock on the shelf ready for instant use. The beneficiaries of the trust are often identified by a letter of wishes indicating to whom the trustees should look for instructions about the use or disbursement of the trust's funds. This may say who the real beneficiaries are to be. The trustees can then by deed appoint the trust funds to the stated or intended beneficiary. To make sure that these instructions are carried out, the settlor usually appoints a protector who can override the trustees if necessary. All such trusts must have an ultimate beneficiary stated in the deed of trust, such as the blind, deaf or spastic of Guernsey or Jersey. These act as the beneficiary of last resort, who should never be needed. Such worthy causes appeared often in the trusts associated with Tucker and Plummer, and they were to benefit even less than Home and Overseas Voluntary Aid Services or the Deprived Children's Aid Fund.

All the trust consists of is a file of documents kept in conditions of complete secrecy in a lawyer's office in the Channel Islands, the Isle of Man, Gibraltar, Bermuda or Liechtenstein. Because it is a discretionary trust – the discretion being notionally with the trustees – the real or intended beneficiaries can deny any interest: only the trustees can disprove that and they are unlikely to do so. To prove that they have no interest in the trust, the beneficiaries can make futile requests for information from the trustees in absolute confidence that if they are not the stated beneficiaries such requests will be ignored. The Inland Revenue finds it impossible to penetrate this façade.

Once assets have been placed in such a trust or accumulated there by a UK resident they will be free of all tax. The Inland Revenue seeks to prevent the transfer of assets offshore by UK residents through Section 482 of the Income and Corporation Taxes Act. Under Section 482 it can tax a settlor or a beneficiary if it can prove that they have the 'power to enjoy' the offshore trust's assets or income – the tactic tried without success with the Vesteys. Despite such restrictions and the sensitivity of the Inland Revenue's antennae to their creation or existence, the number of such discretionary trusts has mushroomed in keeping with the burden of taxation and with it the resistance on behalf of the haves to giving up any more of their wealth than can be wrested from them.

Lawyers in the Channel Islands, the Isle of Man and Gibraltar show little or no compunction about creating trusts for the benefit of UK residents who are clearly seeking to escape tax. Ironically, neither Jersey nor Guernsey, the favoured offshore locations for discretionary trusts, have any trust law on the statute books: trusts are based on British law, which does not apply in the Channel Islands. The attitude of the tax-haven lawyers can best be compared with the three wise monkeys, except that it is very expensive to have them keep their eyes, ears and mouths shut. Even before the dismantling of exchange control in 1979, with that facility available on the doorstep, Section 482 was less than watertight. It was difficult but not impossible to transfer assets outside the UK: all that was required was to sell assets at below their real value to the offshore trust, which then sold them on at the real value and pocketed the profit taxfree. Even simpler was to arrange for the right to future income or assets to be acquired by the offshore trust instead of being received in the UK. The Inland Revenue would not necessarily even know that these assets or income existed.

The route to Jersey and Guernsey was already well trodden by the time that Tucker, Plummer, Pilbrow and Moser began to consider how to shelter from tax the anticipated profits from marketing the Exempt Debt Scheme. It was decided that trusts should be set up to receive each partner's share of the expected profits – Trumpet for Tucker, Pandora for Plummer, Piano for Pilbrow and Marx for Moser. The complex arrangements were made in Jersey by Brian Hamilton, an associate of Tucker and Plummer who was closely involved in trust company business.

Hamilton formed a Bahamas company which was responsible for organising the Exempt Debt Scheme and paying legal fees and other expenses, and which signed a marketing agreement with Pilbrow's company Dovercliffe. A second Bahamas company received all sums paid by Dovercliffe for the rights to the scheme. But when, in 1972, the Bahamas were excluded from a shrunken Sterling Area, to facilitate the payments due from the UK companies the assets of the two Bahamas companies were transferred to Paget Investments (Jersey) and a Manx company, Ridge, whose shares were settled on the Ridge Trust, a discretionary trust which gave the trustees the power to add beneficiaries, including the trustees of other trusts. Later in 1973 Ridge was put into liquidation, and in December 1973 the Ridge trustees distributed £35,000 each to the trustees of the Trumpet, Pandora, Piano and Marx trusts which had been settled by the Jersey advocate Michael Voisin. Ridge retained £50,000 to finance the legal costs of a test case on the Exempt Debt Scheme. The four trusts who shared the £140,000 were accumulation settlements, which meant there could be no distribution of income or capital until the trust was terminated. The trustees were the Rocquaine Trust company in Guernsey, run by the accountant John Glauser, who worked for the local Slater, Walker company, and the advocate de Vic Carey, a prominent member of the Guernsey States or parliament.

As a result of these arrangements the four inventors of the Exempt Debt Scheme could now claim that they were neither the settlors nor transferors in relation to the Ridge Trust or the four other trusts; that their rights to any profits from the scheme were only an unenforceable expectation of an unprotectable idea dependent on Hamilton's and Voisin's generosity, and so not a legally recognised asset; and that they could not receive any distribution from the trust. All this added up to not having to make any disclosure to the Inland Revenue – and if anything *was* disclosed, no tax was payable.

The reality behind the trust structure was, however, somewhat different. The Trumpet Trust's funds were later appointed by the trustees to Roy Tucker's brother Keith, a chartered surveyor, once he had emigrated to Belgium and as a result could play an increasing role in sheltering his brother's wealth from tax. Instructions about the investment of these funds usually reached Rocquaine not from Keith Tucker in Belgium but from Roy Tucker in London, as those concerning the Pandora Trust came from Plummer. A letter of wishes to the trustees of the Piano Trust indicated that they were to look to Pilbrow for instructions. A similar arrangement probably existed between Moser and the Marx Trust.[1] Moser was also paid onshore £24,000 in consultancy fees by Pilbrow companies for legal work on the Exempt Debt Scheme.

Once these offshore structures were in place, the quartet began selling the latest tax-avoidance scheme in December 1971, including a new sales gimmick – legal opinions from senior members of the Revenue Bar attesting to its likely success. This was to become a hallmark of the Tucker sales pitch, which when coupled with the promise to fight a test case against the Inland Revenue to prove counsel's opinion correct amounted to an irresistible combination.

To put a legal seal of approval on the Exempt Debt Scheme, the services were recruited of George Graham QC and a then leading junior barrister, Andrew Park – who was to become a familiar name in the legal opinions that accompanied Tucker sales packages – along with an opinion from a prominent company-law expert, Michael Wheeler QC. Such opinions were traditionally given privately to clients and their solicitors: their use by the clients as marketing tools to sell tax schemes was a novel approach. It seems that there were few objections from the Revenue Bar.

A letter from Pilbrow to potential clients made clear another aspect of the marketing approach which was to become Tucker standard, namely secrecy: 'It is essential both from our point of view in order to protect the scheme and from your point of view to maximise the chances of success of the scheme, that it suffers the minimum of exposure.' This may have been designed in the first place to keep the idea from potential rivals – the Reverse Annuity Scheme had very soon been imitated by other tax-scheme promoters – but equally if not more important was to prevent its details from being exposed to the Inland Revenue for as long as possible. It was no longer a matter of putting the scheme to the local tax inspector and challenging him to prove it did not legally work. The Tucker approach was to make it as hard as possible for him to realise that a scheme existed at all; and the lack of centralisation within the Inland Revenue could mean that the wide marketing of a particular scheme might not be detected until very late in the game. This greatly increased the number of clients to whom the scheme could be sold as well as the chances of success in avoiding disallowance of the relief claimed, let alone a test-case challenge or legislation to close the loophole. From the start Tucker and Plummer considered secrecy and minimal or no disclosure to the Revenue, until legally required, to be essential.

The Exempt Debt Scheme set out to create a strictly notional capital loss, which could be used to offset a very real capital gains tax liability. This involved fifteen steps taken over a period of approximately two weeks. It relied on cash provided by Slater, Walker and companies controlled by Pilbrow – through Masterdene Finance, established in March 1972, of which he and Tucker were directors – and Tim Nicholas, the master of the Capital Income Plan.

The client began by acquiring a new company, which immediately made a 'rights' issue of new shares for cash. The client's company then agreed to make two loans to the new company repayable on demand after thirty years and thirty-one years. Each loan paid interest at 11 per cent. After receiving one interest payment on each loan the client's company then exercised an option to reduce the interest on the first loan to zero and raise that on the second to 22 per cent. It then paid up the share capital required by the 'rights' issue made by the new company, after which the client's company sold the second 22 per cent loan to Masterdene Finance for its market value less a small discount, creating a 'paper' profit. The finance company then sold the loan to a subsidiary of the new company which promptly went into voluntary liquidation and distributed its only asset, the 22 per cent loan, to the new company. It was now the new company's turn to go into liquidation, whereupon the first, now zero-interest, loan was repaid to the client's company – as was the second 22 per cent loan, but at a premium and not at par as in the case of the first loan. The client's company now agreed to sell these shares to T. J. Nicholas Holdings in return for loan stock issued by that company. This resulted in the client's company making a 'paper' capital loss on the value of its shares in the new company equal to the real gain on which it was seeking to avoid tax. The client's company then sold that loan stock for cash to Guardclose, the parent of T. J. Nicholas. At the end of the chain the 'paper' profit on selling the second 22 per cent loan cancelled out the 'paper' loss on the sale of the shares in the new company; but the capital loss could be offset against the real capital gains tax liability which had brought the client into the scheme in the first place.

In a bid to gild these circular transactions with a veneer of reality, the Pilbrow letter to clients stated, 'There is no binding arrangement or undertaking to the effect that once the first step has been taken, then every other step must be taken in its appointed order . . . as a matter of law (the client) is free to withdraw at any time and so are all the other contemplated parties.' But that was merely for the record, and the courts. The truth was very different, as Lord Templeman was to make clear in his witty demolition of the charade when it eventually came before the Court of Appeal. It was, he said,

Yet another circular game in which the taxpayer and a few hired performers act out a play; nothing happens save that the Houdini taxpayer appears to escape from the manacles of tax. The game is recognisable by four rules. First, the play is devised and scripted prior to performance. Secondly, real money and real documents are circulated and exchanged. Thirdly, the money is returned by the end of the performance. Fourthly, the financial position of the actors is the same at the end as it was in the beginning save that the taxpayer in the course of the performance pays the hired actors for their services. The object of the performance is to create the illusion that something has happened, that Hamlet has been killed and that Bottom did don an ass's head so that tax advantages can be claimed as if something had happened. The audience are informed that the actors reserve the right to walk out in the middle of the performance but in fact they are the creatures of the consultant who has sold and the taxpayer who has bought the play; the actors are never in a position to make a profit and there is no chance that they will go on strike. The critics are mistakenly informed that the play is based on a classic masterpiece called *The Duke of Westminster* but in that piece the old retainer entered the theatre with his salary and left with a genuine entitlement to his salary and to an additional annuity.[2]

Or, as a Pilbrow letter to clients baldly declared, 'The scheme is a pure tax avoidance scheme and has no commercial justification insofar as there is no prospect of [the client] making a profit; indeed he is certain to make a loss representing the cost of undertaking the scheme.'

The Exempt Debt Scheme was bought by between twenty and thirty Tucker clients in 1972 and 1973 seeking to avoid capital gains tax on gains totalling about £15 million – a potential tax liability of up to £4,500,000. Among them were the Ramsays, a family of farmers from Scotton in Lincolnshire.

To provide the necessary funds to finance the different ambitions of his three sons, William Ramsay sold the freehold of Westgate Farm and leased it back from the purchasers in November 1972, as a result of which the family company, W. T. Ramsay, made a capital profit of £193,000. Two brothers then left, one to farm and the other to go into a garage business, leaving the elder brother, Robert Ramsay, to run the farm. The sale, however, had produced a substantial tax liability for W. T. Ramsay. As Robert Ramsey explained, 'We wanted to be able to roll over the cash from the farm for the future rather than pay so much of it in tax.' As a result of an introduction by the estate agent who had handled the sale, he met Pilbrow and Moser in February 1973.

Robert Ramsay agreed to buy the scheme at a cost of £14,000, but not before there had been some opposition within the Ramsay family:

My father was not particularly in favour. He said we would have a lot of trouble later and our affairs would be put under the microscope by the Inland Revenue. My mother was also against it as she thought it was wrong to engage in such a scheme which was unfair on other taxpayers. But I was fighting for my own, it had nothing to do with morality, it was simply a matter of pounds, shillings and pence.

Between 23 February and 9 March Robert Ramsay took part in a series of meetings regarding Caithmead, a new investment company which W. T. Ramsay had acquired for the purpose of making and selling the loans – made with Slater, Walker money – by which it hoped to create a 'paper' capital loss which would wipe out the tax liability on the profit from the sale of the farm.

On 23 February W. T. Ramsay acquired two preferred ordinary shares in the recently formed Caithmead, which then made a 34 for 1 'rights' issue of new shares. Slater, Walker provided a loan facility to W. T. Ramsay so that it could make two loans of £218,750 each to Caithmead. On 2 March, Ramsay exercised its option to drop the interest rate on one loan to zero and double the other to 22 per cent; Caithmead called upon Ramsay to pay up the £184,654 due on the 68 new shares it had issued; and Ramsay agreed to sell the 22 per cent loan to Masterdene Finance, a subsidiary of Dovercliffe, for £373,763. Masterdene also bought options to buy the other zero coupon loan and Ramsay's shares in Caithmead. The total payment was £391,481, giving a capital profit of £172,731. Seven days later Masterdene sold the 22 per cent loan to Caithrole, a subsidiary of Caithmead, for £394,673. Caithrole then went into liquidation; the 22 per cent loan due by Caithmead was then extinguished in settlement for the exactly similar amount due to be repaid by Caithrole as a return of its share capital. Caithmead now went into liquidation, making the first zero coupon loan repayable to Ramsay, who received £218,750. Ramsay agreed to sell its seventy shares in Caithmead – which had cost £185,034, but were now of little value – to T. J. Nicholas Holdings, a company run out of Tucker's offices, in exchange for £9387 in loan stock, which was promptly sold on at the same price to Guardclose. Ramsay had thereby made a 'loss' of £175,647 on its investment in Caithmead. Although all but £2916 of this was covered by its 'profit' on the sale of the loan to Masterdene, Ramsay now hoped that this paper 'loss' would offset the liability for tax on the profit from selling Westgate Farm.

Dovercliffe received a fee of £12,000, and Masterdene £2000. Most of these proceeds, however, were destined for the offshore Ridge Trust and the beneficiaries of the Trumpet, Pandora, Piano and Marx Trusts. Slater, Walker had earned the interest on the £622,500 it had provided over the fourteen days it took for the money to move in a circle via W. T. Ramsay, Caithmead, Caithrole, Masterdene Finance, T. J. Nicholas Holdings and Guardclose back to Slater, Walker; Tucker later estimated that Slater, Walker took 'the lion's share' of the profits.[3] But the Exempt Debt Scheme had also been Tucker and Plummer's most profitable venture yet. At least £210,000 was ultimately paid to the four offshore trusts out of commissions totalling between £300,000 and £400,000. But whereas for the promoters these profits were nonrefundable, there was no such guarantee about the tax the clients were paying to avoid. As Pilbrow made clear in his letter, 'There is no guarantee that the anticipated tax relief will result from the implementation of the scheme and we can accept no responsibility or liability whatsoever for any expense or loss incurred as a result of the scheme being embarked upon.'

Such statements were *pro forma* for tax schemes in order to protect the promoters from any future legal liability, but clients felt no lack of confidence in the effectiveness of the scheme. Like the other Exempt Debt Scheme purchasers, Robert Ramsay went away confident that he had outwitted the taxman.

With the capital provided by the Reverse Annuity and Exempt Debt schemes and Tucker's growing reputation in the tax world behind them, by the spring of 1973 Tucker and Plummer were preparing to move into tax avoidance full-time. From now on they planned to have their own marketing and banking vehicles, so enabling them to keep all the profits. This new venture was to be in association with Richard Gardner and three new names – the accountant John Trotman, the aspiring Conservative M P Tom Benyon and the leading tax Q C Desmond Miller.

THE BIRTH OF ROSSMINSTER

Although the Rossminster Group did not come into existence until July 1973, following Plummer's departure from Slater, Walker four months earlier, planning for its formation had been in progress since early in the year. Although riskfree profits could be made in a matter of days from financing tax schemes, they were still petty cash in comparison with what could be made by Slater, Walker in the stock market or through property deals. But, as Plummer explained later,

Jim Slater was making so much money on other things then that he didn't really want to make it through financing tax schemes, which he didn't completely understand. But I could see that the demand for schemes was there. I had seen the need for financial advice to be provided for companies who wanted to engage in sophisticated arrangements which sometimes scare banks and bank managers.[1]

This difference of outlook is not hard to understand. Slater and Plummer were very different animals, as Tom Benyon – who, despite having worked for Slater, Walker did not meet Jim Slater until he visited the Rossminster offices – is quick to point out: 'Jim was cavalier and would take gambles. Ron had a building-society mind. He would never do a deal unless there was no downside.'

The Rossminster concept was brilliantly simple. Instead of relying on the individual efforts of Cardale, Pilbrow or Nicholas to market, and Slater, Walker to finance, schemes which Tucker and Plummer devised, both functions would be handled in-house. In addition to being more profitable it would give both men greater control over their creations. Future schemes could be marketed more aggressively by an organisation solely dedicated to the promotion of tax avoidance. Their own company could also advertise for clients, which Tucker, as a professional accountant, could not do. It could handle a number of tax schemes at one time, whereas most of the individual salesmen only had the organisation to handle one. This would enable tax avoidance schemes which met the differing needs and deadlines of income tax, corporation tax and capital gains tax to be sold throughout the year, instead of incurring a mad rush to meet individual requirements before the tax year ended on 5 April.

The formation of Rossminster created for the first time an organisation whose sole business was the mass marketing and financing of 'off-the-peg' rather than 'bespoke' tax schemes, in which all the client had to do was fill in the numbers for the tax to be avoided and pay his fee. Tax avoidance was fast replacing its discreet, Harrods image of the past with that of the supermarket. An assembly line was being constructed in which Tucker, the scheme maker, joined with Plummer, the organiser and financier, to supply schemes for avoiding tax to anyone who preferred to pay a little to Rossminster rather than a lot to the Revenue. Within months there would be long queues outside Tucker's offices. But it would be much longer before the Inland Revenue woke up to the revolution that had changed the tax game in a fundamental and, for the Treasury, highly damaging fashion.

Having decided to form a company to market and finance Tucker's tax schemes, their next queston was what to call it. Tom Benyon claims the credit for the name Rossminster. 'They were looking for something very solid, very English,' says one former insider. They found it, according to Benyon, in a combination drawn from the Scottish county of Ross and Cromarty – 'anything to do with Scotland, like the Scottish Widows insurance company, has that image of little old ladies and their money' – and the equally reassuring National Westminster Bank, where the new company was to open its first account. The allusions were ideal. The name Rossminster was replete with useful images with which to cloak such an esoteric, controversial and far from patriotic activity as tax avoidance.

The respectable image was further enhanced by appointing Desmond Miller as chairman. Miller's involvement was of inestimable prestige value. The youngest son of the Bishop of Cashel and Waterford, Miller had emerged from Oxford and wartime service in the army, where he reached the rank of Lieutenant Colonel, to become one of the most prominent members of the Revenue Bar. He had twice been a member of the Bar's General Council, Master of the Bench of the Inner Temple and chairman of the influential Taxation and Retirement Benefit committees.

At the age of fifty-eight he was considering retirement within a few years, and so the offer from Tucker and Plummer – in the course of a legal conference at which he was being consulted on a tax scheme – was very attractive. Like most tax barristers Desmond Miller took a 'robust' line on avoidance. He saw nothing either socially or morally wrong in exploiting legal loopholes or legislative grey areas to enable the rich to avoid contributing their share of the costs of the society in which they lived. All that mattered was whether what was proposed was illegal. Questions about the ethics of tax avoidance were dismissed as 'Boy Scout morality'. Those who disagreed with his analysis thought his attitude was 'amoral'.

Miller was no stranger to Tucker and Plummer, and not just through providing legal advice. He had met Plummer when he was at Slater, Walker and in 1972 had joined him in a relatively short-lived venture, VAT Planning & Publications, which organised conferences on value added tax. Another director was Patrick Roney, who became Rossminster's main lawyer. The managing director was the architect of VAT, barrister Humphrey Mainprice.

It was also through Plummer that Tom Benyon, another Slater, Walker alumnus, was recruited. After Wellington and Sandhurst, Benyon had spent four years in Kenya and Aden with the Scots Guards and in Muscat on secondment to the Sultan of Oman's forces. He left the army on health grounds and joined the Slater, Walker insurance broking arm. While there, he met and liked Plummer. Then, in 1972, he told his superior, Arthur Piercy – later also to join Rossminster – that he wanted to leave and make money. Piercy told him that Plummer had an idea for a bank. 'The idea then was to concentrate on bonds not tax, but this changed.' says Benyon. Although no tax expert, Benyon, then thirty-two, was a very good salesman. Intellectually lightweight, he had the knack of explaining the benefits and the workings of schemes in simple and convincing language. His amiable appearance and pleasant manner made him both encouraging and reassuring to clients.

Benyon had already decided to deploy his salesman's talents in the political arena, and was actively looking for a constituency to contest for the Conservatives at the next election. But first he needed to make himself financially independent. Tucker and Plummer were not slow to appreciate the possibilities he presented. Benyon agreed to join Rossminster for £12,000 a year and the promise of a shareholding.

Richard Gardner, then thirty-five, was by now almost entirely occupied with the administration of Tucker's tax schemes through Richard Gardner

& Partners, which had been formed in 1972. His own tax scheme activities had suffered a serious setback. A much more outspoken and less cerebral character than either Tucker or Plummer, Gardner had developed the Special Gift Scheme for avoiding estate duty. 'I had five counsels' opinions but they were all wrong,' he cheerfully recalls. 'We had all missed one crucial point.' Prone to falling asleep at legal conferences, Gardner tells of how, after the Inland Revenue had challenged the scheme, he went to a vital meeting with counsel, dozed off and awoke to hear the senior QC present intoning, 'I'm afraid there is no hope.' This left him with little to do but assist Tucker despite their original partnership arrangement. 'I became Roy Tucker's creature.'

John Trotman had gone into accountancy with Coopers & Lybrand direct from school and had been qualified almost ten years. He had met Plummer at Samuel Montagu. The youngest of the six, he was self-effacing despite a liking for monogrammed shirts. 'John should never have left Coopers,' says one former colleague. 'He was not able to cope with the outside world.' Trotman became group finance director, which with Tucker, Plummer and Gardner involved was something of a non-job. Trotman made little impression on those who met him, and as such was the perfect accountant.

A former adviser to Rossminster who met all the individuals involved in the early days had this to say of them:

They had an obsessive interest in tax. They were all fairly right-wing people. They took the view that it was a bit of a moral crusade – especially after the Labour Party raised the tax rates to 83 per cent and 98 per cent. They saw themselves as using the law to defeat the law. They were very, very clear that what they were doing was absolutely legal and they got rather indignant if one suggested that it might even be immoral. They viewed people who criticised them with a varying degree of emotions from concern to contempt because a number of the criticisms were highly emotional as they saw it. But some I think they felt were likely to attract legislation and they viewed those with concern.

Miller and Tucker he characterised as 'intellectual bullies'. Of Tucker he says:

He was the dynamo, he was the ship's engine. He was the chap who produced the schemes in consultation with other people but there was no doubt that his was the brain that actually produced the ways round the legislation. Roy is a person who intellectual-ises about almost everything. He lived a pretty spartan life. He had none of the furnishings which many people have in their offices. Some people are obsessed by horse racing form, some people are obsessed by crosswords and chess, Roy was obsessed by tax.

The diminutive Tucker – 'a walking compendium of the taxes acts' – was often to be seen trotting alongside the much taller, commanding figure of Miller deep in discussion on some fine point of legal interpretation.

Plummer was a very different personality: 'He wasn't such an interesting person as Roy. But it was his idea. He told me once that he started it because he could not get Jim Slater to understand the schemes and therefore Slater would not finance them. So he started his own bank, which was a brilliant piece of lateral thinking.'

From the beginning neither Tucker nor Gardner were publicly linked with Rossminster. Neither appeared as directors although both were shareholders. Tucker, like Plummer, held a 45 per cent interest and Gardner was to have a 5 per cent interest. Although within a year or so it was an open secret at least inside Rossminster, in the early days it was not admitted that Tucker, together with Plummer, was the controlling shareholder. The exact nature of the relationship between Rossminster and Roy Tucker & Co. was also kept secret and was still being concealed late in 1974, as a letter written by Plummer on 14 October reveals:

As far as correspondence or discussions are concerned between a member of either organisation and a third party we continue to stress that Rossminster's role in tax schemes devised by Roy Tucker & Co. is limited to providing banking facilities and that Roy Tucker & Co. and Rossminster are entirely separate organisations.

Within the two organisations it is known by all senior staff that family interests of the principals of Roy Tucker & Co. have, directly or indirectly, shareholding interests in Rossminster.

We have considered it right not to withhold such information although exact percentages are not disclosed. As far as secretaries and receptionists are concerned the position is limited to informing them of the close business relationships which exist between the two separate organisations.

If an outside party asks us for details of the shareholding position of the Rossminster Group our standard reply is: it is privately owned and the directors and their families have the controlling interest.[2]

Such an answer of course omitted any reference to the fact that Tucker had a similar share stake to that of Plummer, but was not a director.

This pretence was still being preserved a year later when Miller approached Guernsey advocate Roger Perrot about the possibility of his becoming a local director of the Rossminster company there. Tucker, who was to meet Perrot had the advocate wanted the directorship, which he

ROY TUCKER & CO.

INTERNAL MEMORANDUM

Date...... 15 October 19⁻

1 Hanover Square
London W1R 9RD
Telephone:
01-493 3671
Telex 269097

From...... ROY C. TUCKER

To...... R.M. Gardner, ~~T.J~~ Nicholas,
D.B. Pilkington, W.S. Cairns

Subject...... RELATIONSHIP BETWEEN ROSSMINSTER & ROY TUCKER & CO.

Recent events have shown the importance that must be
attached to not blurring the distinctions between the
Rossminster Group and Roy Tucker & Co. through expediency.

In this connection I enclose a letter from Ron Plummer
of Rossminster to John Glauser outlining the relationship
between Rossminster & Roy Tucker & Co. which please read.
I shall be having a private word with each one of you about
this during the next few days.

Dealing with the relationship between Rossminster and Roy Tucker
and Co., there has been no change in our policy of maintaining the
separate nature of the two organisations. To restate :-

> As far as correspondence or discussions are concerned
> between a member of either organisation and a third
> party we continue to stress that Rossminster's role in
> tax schemes devised by Roy Tucker & Co. is limited to
> providing banking facilities and that Roy Tucker & Co.
> and Rossminster are entirely separate organisations.
> If you are aware of any departure from this policy,
> please let me know at once.

> Within the two organisations it is known by all senior
> staff that family interests of the principals of Roy
> Tucker & Co. have directly or indirectly, shareholding
> interests in Rossminster and that therefore there should be
> no conflict of interests.

> We have considered it right not to withhold such inform-
> ation although exact percentages are not disclosed.
> As far as secretaries and receptionists are concerned
> the position is limited to informing them of the close
> business relationships which exists between the two

separate organisations and periodically a memorandum is
sent out by me to Rossminster staff on this basis.

Shareholdings   ../2

If an outside party asks us for details of the shareholding position
of The Rossminster Group our standard reply is :-

> It is privately owned and the directors and their families
> have the controlling interest. There are no institutional
> shareholders.

We have recently thought it worthwhile to review the form of working
relationship between Rossminster and Roy Tucker & Co. and in
particular the involvement of Rossminster staff in what might loosely
be described as promotion of tax schemes designed by Roy Tucker
and Co. The outcome is that we consider that no change should be
made in our present policy at least until April, 1975. Whilst there
are obvious long term advantages to be gained by the Rossminster
Group from being less active in the promotion of tax schemes and
from having a less close business relationship with Roy Tucker & Co.
we think that the probable loss of substantial profits (both to
Rossminster and to Roy Tucker & Co.) does not justify such action
for the current tax year.

A short speech of welcome will be made by Desmond Miller at the declined, was described by Miller as 'a friend and business associate advising generally'.[3] For almost Rossminster's entire existence, the outside world was told that Rossminster was merely the independent financier and promoter of an otherwise unconnected Tucker's scheme.

Although equal partners with Plummer, Tucker was seen by insiders throughout Rossminster's existence as the dominant figure. 'Ron would always defer to Roy,' recalls a Tucker associate. 'Whenever RAP appeared against an item on the agenda we all relaxed as it meant it would not get done as Ron could never make his mind up and so would always defer to Roy.'

Tucker, however, was always at pains to bring Plummer into discussions on any new scheme, saying he greatly appreciated Plummer's mental input. He was less forthcoming with other, even senior colleagues, keeping much secret and producing one of two stock responses to any question he did not want to answer: 'There are factors you are not aware of' or 'It's all been agreed'. The result of this superior attitude combined with his intellectual dominance was that few of those at meetings with Tucker dared to ask questions for fear of showing ignorance. They would nod in agreement and afterwards check with one of the other senior participants, such as Gardner.

One of those closely involved in the formation of Rossminster described what was behind the subterfuge over Tucker's real role.

The plan was that the new company would build itself up profitwise and then float its shares. Flotation would require repute. Tucker would stay outside the organisation and use his tax expertise to bring high income on the finance which the bank, as a separate entity, would provide to his venture. His high-yielding financial facility would be an income sweetener. The Rossminster Group would substantially carry on orthodox operations. Without that it would never be treated as a bank and there would be no flotation. There would be three safeguards: a QC would be chairman; Plummer stated expressly that the bank would be 'whiter than white in the matter of taxation, only doing such things as educational policies for children'; and Tucker would remain extramural.

Rossminster Group, the first of three Rossminster parent companies, was incorporated on 12 July 1973 with offices at 19–24 St George Street, Mayfair. From the beginning Rossminster's ownership was located offshore. The share capital was £12,500, divided into 50,000 shares of which 47,499 were allotted to Torteval, a nominee company run by John Glauser in Guernsey, and the balance to Plummer (2500), with one share set aside for Don Coles, a Guernsey business associate of Glauser.

While running the Slater, Walker operation in Guernsey, Glauser had been active in the administration of two Tucker tax schemes. These were the version of CIP that involved the Deprived Children's Aid Fund, and the Trust Takeover Capital Loss scheme to avoid capital gains tax, which had been sold in 1973. Glauser received a slice of the profits through a Manx company. He intended to form his own trust company: his friend Coles had already established Marchwood which he was eager to expand. Glauser was attracted by the opportunity of joining forces with Plummer, so generating trust business for his own company, which could provide the offshore fulcrum Plummer and Tucker wanted for their new venture. To this end Rocquaine Trust had been formed in May 1973.

Torteval was the shield behind which Tucker and Plummer's control of Rossminster could be hidden. Its registered office was that of Glauser's advocates Carey, Langlois in St Peter Port. Behind Torteval lay two Manx companies, behind them a battery of Guernsey discretionary trusts, and behind the trusts the Tucker and Plummer families. The trusts were to control 90 per cent of Rossminster – Miller and Gardner sharing the balance – until Benyon and Trotman, the junior partners, realised their promised shared 5 per cent stake.

The Manx companies which held Tucker's and Plummer's controlling interest were Kerrowfoot and Bryde, both of which predated the Rossminster Group, having been formed on 16 February 1973. The arrangement of directors and shareholders of both companies followed the pattern that was to become the Rossminster hallmark in structuring its offshore operations for maximum flexibility and minimum disclosure: namely, a Manx-registered company with directors resident on the tiny Channel Island of Sark but instructed by an administrator resident on Guernsey, with the shares held in a Guernsey nominee company.

Following the creation of the Trumpet and Ridge trusts three more trusts were established at about the same time as Rossminster itself – the Keith Number One Settlement, and the Ulysses and Leander trusts. The Keith trust was settled by Keith Tucker, Roy's chartered surveyor brother. Two years later, after he had moved to Belgium, the Number Two and Number Three settlements were created. According to one of those involved, Tucker and Plummer produced their own trust deeds and informed the trustees these would be disclosed to the Revenue as having no income but a possible future capital benefit.

Keith Number One was settled with £6000 from the £126,000 in the

Trumpet Trust, closely linked with Roy Tucker in the Exempt Debt Scheme. The funds available in the Trumpet Trust indicate how successful Roy Tucker had been even before the formation of Rossminster. The beneficiaries were to be the descendants of the two brothers' father, Clifford Tucker, including Roy but excluding Keith Tucker and his wife. Keith Tucker subsequently informed the trustees, Rocquaine, in a letter of wishes, that they should look to his brother Roy for advice on the running of the trust and the use of its funds. Certainly Roy Tucker, rather than his brother, gave instructions to the trustees: indeed on two occasions he gave instructions for the trustees to be changed, which suggested that this trust, like Keith Number Two, was for his or his family's eventual benefit. Roy Tucker also received the monthly statements of trust assets from the Guernsey trustees. Furthermore, the first asset acquired by the Keith Number One trust was the ownership of Kerrowfoot, which then took a 45 per cent holding in the Rossminster Group. This trust was later to own other significant Manx companies – Hartopp, Peroneus and Cambury – through which the ownership of Rossminster and other related assets was to filter.

Keith Number Two was settled with £80,000 from the Trumpet Trust. However, because of exchange control regulations, this money was held in a blocked bank account in Guernsey until 1979, after Keith Tucker emigrated. The funds were loaned to a Guernsey subsidiary of the trust, Adana Investments, which invested the money in government securities, and the interest was paid into an external bank account in Keith Tucker's name. However, Keith Tucker admitted on one occasion that he merely deducted $10 and passed on the remainder to his brother, who anyway received a monthly statement of the trust's assets as well as instructing the trustees.

Keith Number Three was settled with £40,000, also from the Trumpet Trust, and was, like the other two, for the benefit of the Tucker family. However, Roy Tucker indicated to the trustees that Plummer was also to be a potential beneficiary as a 'moral dependant' of Keith Tucker. Plummer himself appeared to confirm this interest when he wrote to the trustees in 1977 to say that 'It is of course the Number Three Settlement that I am concerned with.'[4] He also received a monthly statement of affairs on both this trust and its Guernsey subsidiary, Bolney Investments.

The Plummer interest in Rossminster was effectively held by the Leander and Ulysses trusts. Leander was settled by his wife Jean but instructions to the trustees came from Plummer, who also received the monthly statement. Its first acquisition was a half interest in the Manx company Bryde – the other half being owned by the Ulysses Trust, of which Plummer himself was the settlor. Later the two trusts acquired other Manx companies – Nadine, Deal Investments and Lamond – through which ownership of Rossminster and other assets passed.

Because of the trusts' ownership of Kerrowfoot and Bryde, both Tucker and Plummer could maintain, if challenged by the Inland Revenue, that they should not be assessed on the assets owned by the trusts under Section 478 since the trustees received no income but relied purely on making capital gains, none of which had been realised, or the repayment of loans. In fact capital gains were realised but through subsidiaries or sub-subsidiaries of the trusts. However, because they had settled the Leander and Ulysses trusts and were UK residents, unlike Keith Tucker, the Plummers faced a potential capital transfer tax liability which Plummer either uncharacteristically overlooked or intended to deal with at a later date – which is exactly what he did, albeit in a most unusual manner.

The creation of the trusts and their interlocking Guernsey and Manx companies emphasised the vital importance to the whole Rossminster operation from the beginning of the opportunities provided by Britain's two home-grown tax havens. Through his work at Slater, Walker – he had been a director of Slater, Walker Consultancy (Channel Islands) – Plummer had tapped a rich seam of local expertise both in Guernsey, through John Glauser, and in the Isle of Man, where Slater, Walker's man Charles Cain, a future member of the local parliament, the House of Keys, proved a useful ally. Through Glauser, Plummer had connections to Carey, Langlois, one of the leading firms of advocates in Guernsey. They could provide valuable advice and perform the necessary mechanics to get companies incorporated. Cain provided introductions, similar advice and assistance in the Isle of Man. Hundreds of companies were to be formed in the next six years.

A whole industry has been created on the basis of the medieval or Elizabethan treaties under which Jersey, Guernsey and the Isle of Man retain self-government. Escaping tax is a multibillion-pound business, costing the Treasury hundreds of millions of pounds in lost revenue each year.

Bankers, lawyers and accountants of the highest repute, including the associates of British banks and the branches of British legal and accountancy practices, vie to lend themselves knowingly to transactions involving UK residents which at the very least involve tax avoidance. Their excuse is that UK tax law is no concern of theirs but of their clients. In doing so, they take their cue from local government officials. 'That is a problem for the UK authorities, not us,' William Dawson, then the Manx Government Treasurer, replied privately when asked about the use of the Isle of Man to evade tax. For political reasons the authorities in the Channel Islands and the Isle of Man will not repeat such blatant statements publicly for fear that the UK government might otherwise end their cosy, one-way relationship. The phenomenal growth since the Labour Government of 1964 in bank deposits and locally registered companies which do no local business proves just who gained and who lost. Between 1964 and 1979 13,000 Manx companies were formed compared with only 1300 in the previous forty years or more. In Guernsey the total number of active registered companies grew from a few hundred to 3600 by 1974, and between then and 1979 another 4700 companies were incorporated. In Jersey in 1964 there were just 60 corporation tax companies doing no local business. By 1979 that figure was 5500.

The revenue and employment generated from being a tax haven has become very important to all three islands. Jersey, the first and most advanced, saw its bank deposits of sterling grow from just £62 million in 1964 to £3500 million fifteen years later. By 1979 Guernsey's sterling bank deposits had risen to over £1000 million from £160 million since 1972. The Isle of Man did not start to license banks until 1975, but in four years had attracted more than £500 million.

Jersey's income from the corporation tax on companies which did not trade on the island had reached £1,500,000 by 1979, almost four times the level of only five years before. Guernsey's income from the same source was only £9000 in 1964, but by 1979 it was £520,000. The Manx Treasury received £311,000 that year from its equivalent tax.[5]

In 1973 a nonresident corporation tax company could be formed in the Isle of Man for just £200 a year. The fee in Guernsey was £350. Adding fees for nominee directors, secretarial charges and formation costs pushed the figures up to £775 and £950. Trusts were even less expensive, requiring an annual fee of £300 and as little as £10 to form the settlement.

In Rossminster's first year Tucker and Plummer surveyed the world's tax havens in looking for the best deal. As well as the Channel Islands and the Isle of Man they went to Gibraltar, a British colony with similar tax and other advantages to the tax havens nearer home. There they formed the Victor Trustee company and several other companies under the aegis of one of the Rock's prominent lawyers, Louis Triay. They visited Liechtenstein and acquired several *Anstalts* – the Rolls Royces for escaping tax: companies without share capital whose true ownership is virtually detection-proof and protected by one of Europe's most stringent secrecy laws. The leading *Anstalt* administrator Dr Herbert Batliner provided his services. Also recruited were the services of the Luxembourg-based international accountant Francis Hoogewerf. Further afield, the Bermuda attorneys Appleby, Spurling & Kempe and Cox & Williamson were brought in.

But the nub of the Rossminster empire was in that northerly version of the Bermuda Triangle formed between the Isle of Man, Guernsey and the most colourful of the Channel Islands, Sark.

One of Europe's last feudal fiefdoms, Sark has been self-governing since it was granted by Elizabeth I to a Norman nobleman, Helier de Carteret, in 1565. Though part of the bailiwick of Guernsey, Sark has its own parliament, the Chief Pleas, and its own ruler, Helier de Carteret's successor as Seigneur. Its relationship to Guernsey within the bailiwick is a microcosm of the Channel Islands' relationship to Britain – and Guernsey laws do not apply there.

Sark offered unrivalled attractions to the tax-avoidance industry. There was no company or income taxation: nor was there any company law, which meant that no companies could actually be formed on Sark. But that did not matter because the island had something much more valuable and unique – a plentiful supply of local residents, prepared to do what they were told, who would become 'stooge' directors of Guernsey, Jersey or Manx companies for a mere £50 to £100 a year. All they were required to do in return was to hold any necessary 'board meetings' for the purposes of rubber-stamping what had already been decided by the real directors, usually nine miles away on Guernsey, on instruction from the real owners, usually in Britain.

Such meetings could take place anywhere. 'You can have a meeting when you're washing up in the kitchen,' said the Guernsey company administrator John Lipscombe, who handled much of Rossminster's administration there in the early days. 'That is why if you have directors from the same family it makes matters so much easier.' Or, as a company administrator commented with a smile, 'You just have to be careful not to spill coffee over the papers.' Failing families, there were always the neighbours. After all, as another Sark 'director' put it, 'You can meet in one another's homes. It takes thirty minutes to an hour at least six times a year for one company. In a week it can take one day out of seven if you have a number of companies.' Meetings can take place over a drink in a relaxed, cosy atmosphere, after which the board minutes or any other documents can be duly signed confirming the already taken decisions. It is, said one of the busiest practitioners, 'a profitable sideline. The extra money is useful. It enables you to spend more on the island, use more electricity, employ a gardener.'

It did not matter that such directors were mere puppets, nor did they need to worry about the true purpose of certain of the companies. The directors were not liable for any of the company's activities, as they would have been under British law, so these were not a cause for concern. Under most companies' articles of association the directors were totally indemnified from responsibility for its actions. Rossminster's busy nominee company Abbeville was a typical Guernsey company, and its articles stated:

The directors, auditors, secretary and other officers or servants or agents for the time being of the company shall be indemnified out of the assets of the company from and against all actions, costs, charges, losses, damages and expenses which they or any of them shall or may incur or sustain by reason of any contract entered into or any act done, concurred in or omitted, in or about the execution of their duty or supposed duty or in relation thereto except . . . through their own wilful act, neglect or default.

In the Isle of Man the form was only slightly different. The articles of what was to be Rossminster's ultimate parent company stated that:

no director shall be liable for any loss, damage or misfortune which may happen to or be incurred by the company in the execution of the duties of his office.

Sark directors were therefore perfectly happy to do as directed by the all-important third director – the Guernsey or Manx administrator who might visit the island but more likely would simply send the documents across by the regular launch, weather permitting, from St Peter Port. There was no penalty in being a 'stooge', only rewards. With most of the 500 population retired and with time to spare, trust companies and banks in Guernsey found no shortage of volunteers for the 'Sark lark'. Each had its own house favourites dotted around the picturesque island, three miles long and one and a half miles wide, which the author and Sark resident Mervyn Peake called 'a long, wasp-waisted rock'.

The ornithologist and author Frank Rountree and his wife Diana lived at La Perronerie, an impressive mansion on the northwest corner of the island. In more modest surroundings, three quarters of a mile away to the south at Le Petit Dixcart, were the lady pig farmers, the Canadian Patricia Falle, separated from her Sarkee husband, and her companions, first a studio potter, Diana Hope-Norris, and then Mary-Ann Collins. Both houses were among the forty feudal properties which carry a hereditary vote in the island's parliament.

The more modern Dixcart Cottage nearby was the home of a former Royal Navy commander, Palliser Alfred Milbanke Hudson, known locally as 'Boffin'. At La Mer, on the island's northern tip – almost a mile away by bicycle along the High Street and through the leafy lanes with their low stone walls – was his usual partner, a former actor and part-time bank manager, John York.

Martin and Barbara Joyner at Clos du Moulin ran the local photographic shop and were another popular duo, especially with Rossminster. So too were two late arrivals on the rent-a-director scene, the former travel agent Douglas Dawe and his wife Pamela at Pres du Creux, overlooking the tiny harbour.

As many as eighty Sark residents hired themselves out as directors. Whatever their backgrounds, all of them tended to assume the grand if totally misleading title of 'financial consultant' once they had joined this corporate circus. Even so, the rent-a-directors were a reticent lot when it came to discussing their activities. 'Tax for Sark residents is done by guesswork, so if you throw your money about you pay more, so it's a good practice not to discuss business affairs,' one veteran of this unique cottage industry put it. A recent suggestion that those participating in the 'Sark lark' might contribute 5 per cent of their income to an island trust was dismissed in the local parliament as 'idealistic'.

And even 'stooges', it seems, have a code of confidentiality preventing discussion of the companies whose boards they so silently grace. But then silence on Sark is most certainly golden. Two Sarkees can handle fifty or more 'directorships', earning a very welcome and undemanding £2500 or more a year taxfree.

The advantage of such a transparent arrangement to those involved in the tax-avoidance industry was that it enabled them to set up a cheap but highly effective corporate structure which was nominally controlled on Sark but which could be run just as if it were based in London, which of course in reality it was.

The vanishing act could be best achieved by forming a company in the Isle of Man (cost £200 a year) with its administrator and one director in Guernsey (cost £100 a year) but the majority of the three-director board on Sark (cost £100 a year). The company did no business on any of the three islands, and so paid no local taxes. But, even more importantly, if there were any queries from the Manx, Guernsey or British authorities it could be claimed that the control of the company lay on Sark. No one therefore had jurisdiction.

The whole edifice was palpably unreal. No one – least of all the Inland Revenue or the offshore authorities – believed that the hundreds of companies concerned were really controlled by the Sark directors. Everyone realised they were puppets of the paymasters in Guernsey or beyond. Asked what would happen if a Sark director refused to act as instructed, John Lipscombe replied, 'That would be very interesting but it has never happened.'

But demonstrating the unreality of the Sark directors' role was a different matter. As the board minutes indicated, Sark was where the decisions were officially taken, with the result that the island which Helier de Carteret had colonised to prevent pirates from raiding the ships that plied between Jersey and Guernsey became a base for modern-day pillagers of the Treasury, responsible for the disappearance of untold millions in tax.

Although the trusts which Tucker and Plummer had created remained hidden from public view, Rossminster very quickly surfaced publicly in Guernsey under the guidance of John Glauser. On 24 July 1973 Rossminster Holdings (Channel Islands) was formed, to be followed on 11 September by Rossminster Financial Services. However, Tucker's and Plummer's plans suffered an unexpected rebuff when they sought to establish a bank. The Channel Islands authorities, jealous of Jersey and Guernsey's expanding potential possibilities as a banking centre for nonresident deposits, were not prepared to issue banking licences as freely as other tax havens had done to their cost. Guernsey officials did not feel that Rossminster met their criteria, and so rejected the application. Tucker and Plummer turned instead to the Isle of Man, which was just starting to flex its muscles in the offshore financial marketplace and was anxious to attract the same type of banking business as Jersey and Guernsey – an overeager approach which was later to result in several banking collapses. The Manx requirements were far less stringent, since at the time the island had no banking legislation. The fact that Rossminster had no banking experience was no obstacle to their doing banking business in the Isle of Man, and Rossminster Finance was incorporated there on 5 September 1973.

All the pieces were now in place for marketing Tucker's next range of tax schemes before the end of the 1973–74 tax year. It already promised to be a bumper year – for a general election looked increasingly probable, leading to a likely Labour victory, and Shadow Chancellor Denis Healey had left the rich in little doubt what that would mean in terms of taxation.

THE PIPS START TO SQUEAK

'I warn you, there are going to be howls of anguish from the 80,000 rich people.' Denis Healey's pronouncement at the party conference on 1 October 1973 gave fair warning of what was to be expected if Labour won the coming election. In particular he focused on property developers – a pet Labour hate – who had made some of the biggest financial killings as a result of the boom of the previous three years. 'I will squeeze them until the pips squeak,' Healey declared.

The Heath government's defeat over the miners' strike brought forward the general election to 28 February 1974. The Labour Party's expected if narrow victory – which had been preceded by the collapse of the stock and property markets – and the imminent approach of the first Healey budget combined to accelerate vastly the demand for tax-avoidance schemes before the end of the 1973–4 tax year. The rush was on for Tucker's and Rossminster's services.

Denis Healey did not disappoint his opponents. In the budget on 26 March he announced that the top rate of income tax was going up from 75 per cent to an unprecedented 83 per cent; in addition, investment income of more than £2000 a year would have a further surcharge of 15 per cent. This meant that someone paying the top rate of tax on his earned income and who also had an unearned income of more than £2000 would now be left with just 2p in every extra pound. This was the price to be paid for obtaining trade-union support for pay restraint.

The rich pips did not just squeak or howl in anguish. They first cried with rage, and then set about finding ways of getting out of Chancellor Healey's vicelike embrace. Many, especially in show business, decided to emigrate and become tax exiles. Others decided that however high their charges might be, Tucker and his rivals suddenly seemed a very attract-ive proposition, in that they left a good deal more to enjoy than the Inland Revenue. Tucker and Plummer became alternative Chancellors of the Exchequer. Denis Healey wanted 98 per cent; they would settle for, at most, 20 per cent.

The peak tax-scheme months of February and March were more than ordinarily busy that spring. Clients were queuing on the stairs outside and in the reception areas of Tucker's offices in North Audley Street and Rossminster's in St George Street. 'It was like a supermarket dealing in money,' said the Tyneside property man George Miller, who was one of those in the queue. 'People were queuing up down the street, we could not turn them away,' recalls Tom Benyon.

Tucker and Rossminster were well prepared to meet the rush. Already available were the latest versions of such tried and tested Tucker favourites as the Capital Income Plan. Also an offer was the newer Trust Takeover Capital Loss Scheme, which had been introduced the year before to avoid capital gains tax.[1] If you earned more than £25,000 a year or your company had made profits or capital gains of more than £100,000, then Roy Tucker was interested in hearing from you. The Rossminster framework now in place in London consisted of the Rossminster Acceptances bank, which had been formed on 17 July 1973, five days after Rossminster itself, backed by its flotilla of finance companies; while offshore in Guernsey and the Isle of Man were Rossminster Finance, Rossminster Financial Services, and Rocquaine Trust with its accompanying supply of off-the-shelf trusts and companies.

Tucker had also developed some new ideas which were ready for marketing. 'Roy could take a piece of legislation and come up with a tax-avoidance idea in ten minutes,' says Richard Gardner. Tucker's latest idea took advantage of the loophole in the tax legislation provided by the relief granted on bank interest charges, which could be offset against income for individuals or profits for companies.

John Glauser claimed to have drawn to Tucker's attention the possi-bilities of exploiting this loophole. The neat step Tucker thought of was to generate a sufficient interest charge in one year to wipe out the entire tax liability. This was done by making a one-, two- or five-year interest payment entirely in advance on a Rossminster-provided loan instead of, as is usual, at quarterly or other regular intervals. The loan would thereby create a fee for Tucker, interest for the Rossminster bank and a tax loss for the client. The Advance Interest Scheme was Tucker's and Rossminster's first big success together and as a result brought both to the attention of the Inland Revenue and, though not for another two years, of the Press as well.

The first version of the scheme was the Five Year Note model, which appeared in 1973. This involved borrowing from Rossminster Acceptances and investing the proceeds in a five-year promissory note from the Tucker-controlled finance company Hallpark Financiers, which had been formed in March 1973. Its directors were Tucker, Plummer and one of their earliest recruits, June Hallas, who administered Tucker's personal tax affairs. Interest on the Rossminister loan was paid in advance covering the first year plus seven days, and was paid from the loan. The interest on the promissory note was allowed to accrue. After the year and seven days the promissory note was sold for the amount equal to the outstanding loan, which was then repaid. The loan interest paid to Rossminster Acceptances was to be deductible against income tax, and the profit on selling the promissory note was to be taxfree. The accrued interest on the note would cancel out the bank interest charged and would also be taxfree as the note was cashed before it was repayable. The cost to the client was 20 per cent of the tax he was trying so hard not to pay.

Later in 1973 Tucker further refined the note scheme into the Five Year Deposit version, again involving Rossminster Acceptances and Hallpark, but this time using deposits which moved between the two rather than a promissory note. The client would open a bank account with Rossminster Acceptances with a loan equal to the advance interest due on a five-year-plus-seven-days loan which he then received. The interest was due on Day One for the first period of one year plus seven days, and was effectively paid from the loan. The amount of the loan – less a 20 per cent deduction for the fee – was then deposited with Hallpark for five years plus fourteen days at a 1 per cent higher interest rate. After one year plus six days the client assigned his right to repayment of the Hallpark deposit to Rossminster Acceptances in settlement of the loan which was achieved by the repayment of the principal and accrued interest by Hallpark. Again the advance interest paid would be deducted from the client's income for tax purposes. Rossminster received its money back, plus the fee.

Both these Tucker creations were countered by Treasury amendments to the Finance Act late in 1973. So, early in 1974, the Advance Interest concept was even further refined to produce the One Year High Income or Non-Deposit Scheme. This reduced the loan period to one year and introduced a third party to the deposit transaction – a Tucker-associated finance company, Boreton, to whom the loan would be novated, i.e. to whom the liability to repay was transferred. The notional advantage of acquiring such a liability was the use of the loan proceeds until repayment. The taxpayer would sell the loan to Boreton at a discount on the amount outstanding. This notional profit was to cancel out the interest charge. Boreton had been formed on 23 November 1972 with Tucker and Simon Cardale as nominee shareholders for Smallfold, whose address was Tucker's office. Boreton did a certain amount of business in 1973, but nothing like the frenetic activity it was about to indulge in. Its role was to acquire the Tucker client's debt to Rossminster Acceptances after the first year's interest had been paid. The original plan had been for a recognised, independent bank or stockbroker to make the loan, but the banking crisis of the spring of 1974 ruled that out – there was now no demand for unusual banking business – with the result that the Rossminster bank was used as before. Boreton then repaid Rossminster Acceptances with its own money.

The Non-Deposit Scheme proved a runaway success, marketed as it was just in time for the Labour victory at the polls and ahead of the feared Healey budget. 'I sold a lot of that,' admits Colin Emson. 'It was the best of them all, a beautiful clean scheme.' According to Tucker:

It just came to me in the bath. I had been turning legislation around. Suddenly things came together. The hardest part of the job was not thinking them up; it was putting them into practice on a practical level. That is where the real contribution to tax avoidance lies.[2]

Clever though these schemes were, Rossminster faced two particular problems. Rossminster Acceptances was not recognised as a bank by the Inland Revenue because it was little more than six months old. This created a risk that the advance interest payments made to a nonrecognised bank would not be accepted by the Revenue as tax-deductible. This was crucial, as was the acceptance of the advance payments as 'annual' interest even though they were paid on day one. Only 'annual' interest payments were tax-deductible. To confirm that the loan interest could be claimed as 'annual' and not 'short' interest, Tucker elicited three legal opinions. The first, from Charles Potter QC and Denis Carey, was given in November 1973. Carey had been used on the Trust Takeover Capital Loss Scheme while Potter was to become a regular opinion-giver. But the crucial confirmation of this key point came from Peter Rees in an opinion for the

Non-Deposit Scheme early in 1974. Already a prominent member of the Revenue Bar, Rees had entered Parliament as the Conservative MP for Dover and Deal in 1970. His opinion on the Non-Deposit Scheme was the first of several helpful legal opinions this MP and future Treasury minister was to provide for Tucker's tax-avoidance schemes over the next three years. He was also the first of four Conservative MPs, three of them later to become ministers in the Thatcher government, who would feature in the Rossminster story.

The other and more basic problem with the Advance Interest schemes was how to finance them, given that Rossminster Acceptances, unlike a long-established bank, did not have other people's millions to lend. This was a more difficult problem to solve, but the answer was not long in coming. It was simplicity itself. As the loan would go back to Rossminster Acceptances after a year and would never leave the charmed Rossminster circle, all that was needed was to create the impression that the money had been there for the relevant period – no more than the length of the completion meeting, during which the cheques went round the table. The figures on those cheques could be a big as you liked, so long as at the end of the meeting they cancelled each other out, which they would do once Hallpark had paid the taxpayer's cheque, drawn on his Rossminster Acceptances account, into its own account at Rossminster Acceptances.

However, at this early stage in its development even the precocious Rossminster bank could hardly claim to be lending out multimillions in real, as distinct from Monopoly, money. So it was necessary to introduce into the equation a replacement for the Slater, Walker banks which had served Plummer so loyally in the past. The replacement was provided through another old friend.

Malcolm Horsman had been the most successful of Jim Slater's protégés at Slater, Walker. He had left to go his own way with a Slater, Walker satellite, Ralli International. In the boom years of the early seventies this had grown Topsy-like until it had effectively taken over the paper giant Bowater, with Horsman becoming managing director. In 1973 Bowater joined forces with the rich Cayzer family of the shipping group British & Commonwealth to enter the banking field. The vehicle was the jointly owned St Mary Axe Finance, then a small company in the Cayzer camp. By the end of 1973 the bank had deposits of £14 million and was looking for new business.

An accountant himself, Malcolm Horsman become a personal client of

Rossminster. Their close links are illustrated by Classfirst, a share-dealing company formed for Horsman in May 1974. Rossminster was involved in Classfirst from its earliest days. In May 1975 Horsman left the company, which had not traded, and it became a significant member of the Tucker-Plummer empire. 'Classfirst was acquired for a particular transaction but the transaction did not come off,' says Horsman. 'I did not do anything with the company and Rossminster picked it up.'

Through Horsman, Rossminster became a banking client of St Mary Axe Finance, which agreed to provide the services of an account through which Rossminster Acceptances could issue the cheques necessary for the Non-Deposit Scheme as used by individuals. James Heyworth-Dunne, then the bank's managing director, explained how the arrangement worked:

They had a bank account, more than one account. There were debits and credits which cancelled each other out. The interest on the debits was ⅛ per cent higher. No money was advanced to Rossminster and there was never any credit limit. Rossminster were not a borrowing customer. They just paid for a facility. No cheques were drawn which did not involve their own money. The bank itself was not at risk.

St Mary Axe Finance was hardly likely to put itself at risk financing the tax schemes. Its chairman had made it clear that the bank's policy would be 'to consider new lending propositions with the utmost care' – for in the spring of 1974 the 'fringe' banking crisis was at its peak, with banks collapsing or tottering as a result of poor loans. This, however, was not how the relationship appeared from the outside, where it seemed as if Rossminster Acceptances had millions to lend through its account at St Mary Axe Finance. The fact that it was all the usual Tucker currency, circular Monopoly money, with the only real money being injected by the clients to pay his and Rossminster's fees, was well disguised, not only from the clients but also from the Inland Revenue. This was essential. For just as the scheme could fail if the interest was not allowable, so it could fail even faster if there was no actual loan, because Rossminster Acceptances had no money to lend. Even artificial tax schemes rely on there being real money on the table.

The first enthusiastic users of the latest Non-Deposit Scheme model were Rossminster insiders – a pattern that was to be repeated in the years to come. After all, who better to know a good tax scheme when they saw one, especially when it came at a discount? Both Tucker and Rossminster adopted a policy of rewarding their staff with bonuses instead of increased salaries. These were geared to the success or anticipated success in each tax season.

A friend of Tucker's wife's, William Cairns, then twenty-five, had worked for a paint company before he joined Roy Tucker & Co. in 1973 as Richard Gardner's assistant. He was soon a director of 160 'mechanical' companies, essential components in the tax schemes. In February 1974 Tucker informed him that he was to receive a £5000 bonus. Both men were determined – 'as a matter of professional pride', as Lord Justice Donaldson put it in the Court of Appeal – that this should be taxfree. So, on 1 March, Cairns engaged in a two-year version of the Non-Deposit Scheme. He borrowed £37,740 from Rossminster Acceptances for two years at 13.25 per cent payable in advance – equal to interest of £5000.55 a year – paying that first instalment with his own cheque for £5000, which was then repaid from the loan. Four days later he paid the balance of the loan – £32,740 – to Boreton, of which he had become a director on 14 February: in return Boreton took over his liability to repay Rossminster in two years' time. This way Cairns hoped he had established a tax deduction against his income of the £5000 advance interest payment, which would mean his receiving his bonus taxfree.

The great majority of the 150 to 200 clients for the Non-Deposit Scheme were, however, outside clients who feared the effects of the impending Healey squeeze. One of these was George Miller, a thirty-six-year-old Newcastle businessman and probably Rossminster's first big client.

Miller's business background was in textiles. He had been chairman of West Cumberland Silk Mills and managing director of the Pringle of Scotland knitwear company. Inspired by the easy money being made in the heady days of the property boom, he had acquired the Little Benton estate, 101 acres of undeveloped land within sight of the Tyneside shipyards. Most of the site was farming land, the rest was occupied by Imperial Tobacco and a motley collection of small engineering, building and scrap-metal businesses. The site had cost Miller about £300,000 but by autumn 1973 he was negotiating to sell it for about £1 million to Moorgate Properties, part of the burgeoning Wilstar property empire of William Stern, then the biggest name in property and the most acquisitive.

Miller had stood to make a profit of some £700,000, but with the arrival of the Labour government it looked as though he would lose almost all of it in tax. All but £2000 of the profit stood to be taxed as unearned income at the top rate of 98 per cent which would have left little more than £14,000 at the end of the day. Were the deal to go through a company, this would first of all involve paying corporation tax on the profit, then capital gains tax, and finally the top rate on the remainder, which would have to be paid out as a dividend – all of which could mean as little as £5000 being left. Such doleful arithmetic made a tax-avoidance scheme extremely attractive. 'I was not unhappy to pay tax on the profit,' says Miller,

but the tax structure at that time was punitive. It would have wiped out all of the profit and one of the things I was quite anxious to do was to finance some research at Newcastle University which was going to cost in the order of £120,000. It would have been quite impossible to do this if I had been subjected to the punitive tax rates at that time.

Miller had decided to form a partnership with another Newcastle businessman, Michael Harris, whose computer bureau he was backing, and that the profits from the Little Benton sale would be shared between them. The deal was to be channelled through a joint company, Harmill.

Miller's accountant, David Armstrong, had met Ronald Plummer twice, most recently when he had lunched at Slater, Walker while working for Coopers & Lybrand on the audit. He first decided to seek Rossminster's help in October 1973. Miller and Harris travelled with him to London in late October to meet Plummer and Tom Benyon. Miller later recalled that first meeting: 'They stressed the business of the punitive rates of tax. Benyon was a personable character, he seemed to be the front man, the salesman, but the brains appeared to be Plummer.' Miller was very impressed by Benyon's presentation of the scheme they proposed, the Five Year Note version: 'His role was really that of a contact man, in America they would say he was in the people business, pulling in as much business as possible and selling the schemes. He was a very presentable person and also a good talker, very persuasive.'[3] Benyon informed them that Rossminster would want £140,000 to do the scheme – 20 per cent of the anticipated £700,000 profit. But they would be prepared to take only half of the fee on completion with the rest as an overdraft to be repaid in a year, a measure of the eagerness to hook Rossminster's first big catch. After a successful meeting at Rossminster, Miller and Harris accompanied Benyon to Tucker's office across Mayfair in North Audley Street to meet Richard Gardner.

Miller and Harris were hooked, not just by the tax that would be saved and the fee arrangement, but by what was probably the greatest marketing asset Rossminster had to offer – Tucker's guarantee to fight at his own expense a legal test case at least to the High Court if the scheme were challenged by the Inland Revenue. 'It is intended that the guarantee will cover the costs of solicitors and counsel in doing all necessary work for rebutting any Revenue claims before the courts,' Gardner confirmed in his follow-up letter[4] – which amounted to putting aside £35,000 out of the profits from the scheme. Tucker was the first tax-scheme promoter to offer such an after-sales service. Even the thorough Bradman had never thought of that. It proved to be a winner – so much so that all Tucker's rivals had to copy it.

By 31 October 1973 Miller and Harris were ready to proceed. All they needed was that Stern should sign the contract for the purchase of Little Benton. But, unknown to them, Wilstar's bankers were becoming reluctant to provide further finance, despite an orgy of lending which had resulted in Stern providing, and the banks accepting, personal guarantees in excess of £100 million. So as a highly unusual part of the deal Stern asked Miller and Harris to lend back to him £600,000 of the £1 million purchase price over ten years. This way Stern only had to find £400,000 to buy the land. As the price was so good, Miller and Harris agreed.

A meeting was arranged for 5 December, at which Miller and Harris would enter into the tax scheme, which had now been switched from the Five Year Promissory Note to the Five Year Deposit version. Rossminster's enthusiasm to have them as clients had resulted in a cut in the fee to £120,000, of which £50,000 would be lent to them by Rossminster, repayable in a year. The only real, i.e. non-Rossminster, money in the deal would be the £70,000 part-fee payment which Miller and Harris were to provide.

Everybody was ready to do the deal except Stern, who continued to stall. By now his empire was cracking under the pressure of the property crash which had begun in November 1973 with the sudden rise in the Minimum Lending Rate to 13 per cent and a tough minibudget. This had sparked off the 'fringe' banking crisis, and was making Stern's bankers increasingly nervous.

Nevertheless the Little Benton contract was finally exchanged in late January 1974 for completion the following month. Moorgate Properties was to pay a total of £1,014,000, giving Miller and Harris a £676,000 profit, but only £400,000 of the purchase price was to be received in cash: the balance was translated into a ten-year loan guaranteed by Stern and his company, Metropolitan Property Holdings. This was to prove a fatal misjudgement on the part of Miller and Harris. However, their confidence in the loan was encouraged by assurances from one of Stern's bankers that he was in good financial shape. Despite having signed the contract, Stern delayed again, as the banking and property crises deepened. All the 'fringe' banks had lent extensively to property companies, and their frantic efforts to have loans repaid resulted in forced sales of properties, which in turn drove down values, making bank loans look even more exposed and so prompting further attempted sales. With Labour now in power and an early budget expected, Miller was anxious to complete the deal before the end of the tax year on 5 April. Moorgate Properties were put under notice to complete on 12 March. It was agreed to enter into the tax scheme at a completion meeting which was to take place in Roy Tucker's offices on 19 March – one week before the budget. By now the tax scheme proposed for Miller and Harris had changed once again, this time to the One Year High Income version. Gardner wrote to them setting out the details. He also had reassuring news on whether the advance interest to be paid would be tax-deductible: 'Since the interest paid should be regarded as annual interest, the scheme will be unaffected and Mr Peter Rees QC, who has been instructed in this matter, has confirmed this.'[5]

Rossminster Acceptances would lend each of them £2,125,000 for 370 days at 16 per cent a year payable in advance on Day One. Each interest payment was £344,658. This was to be paid by means of a banker's draft from a clearing bank which Miller and Harris were to bring to the completion meeting. From the Rossminster loan £1,844,942 was the same day to be deposited with Hallpark. This left £280,058, which would be used in part to repay the banker's draft. As Gardner explained:

At the end of Day One you would each normally be out of pocket to the amount of £64,600 which is the difference between the loan interest payable out of your personal funds and the balance of the Hallpark Financiers deposit on which you are free to draw or leave to earn interest . . . This deficit represents the costs of operating the scheme of £60,000 each and the remaining £4600 each will be paid to you in due course . . . as interest due on your deposit.[6]

All that was happening was a circular movement of the funds represented by the banker's drafts, which in the end went back to where they had started, less the Rossminster fee, still the only real money in the transaction. The other loans and deposits were purely book entries.

To make the deal even more attractive to its first major client, Rossminster arranged that only £40,000 of the £120,000 fee was payable on completion. Another £40,000 would be due in six months and the £40,000 balance would be treated as a twelve-month loan. In effect Miller and Harris were being lent their own money which they had brought to the deal through the banker's drafts.

One third of the nonrefundable 20 per cent Rossminster fee was paid to David Armstrong for the introduction, a fact known to Miller and Harris. Such generous commissions were a powerful incentive to steer business Rossminster's way – still more so since the introducers would often surrender one third of their commission to the client's professional adviser, their accountant or solicitor. This generous commission arrangement was central to the success of the network of contacts Rossminster began to build; it represented a potential conflict of interest which was probably unrealised by many other Rossminster clients, who may not have been aware that their trusted accountant or lawyer stood to collect perhaps 3 per cent of the tax to be saved for advising the Tucker scheme. It was obvious that the introducers stood to collect a commission as they made no charge to the client. But the position with the professional advisers is less certain: some told their clients, others did not.

On 19 March Miller, Harris, Armstrong and the local Barclays Bank manager travelled to London to complete the arrangements. After further attempts at delay, Stern had finally completed the deal. Miller and Harris had received £400,000, and Harmill had lent Moorgate £600,000 with repayment on demand possible after five years. First they went to Rossminster's offices in St George Street to sign the loan agreement with Rossminster Acceptances. Present at that meeting were Gardner representing the scheme's promoter and manager, Roy Tucker & Co., and Plummer, Benyon and Trotman representing the scheme's financier, Rossminster.

Rossminster Acceptances agreed to lend Miller and Harris each £2,125,000. for a year plus five days, together with a further loan of £40,000 each. The second loan was to be repaid £10,000 in seven days and £30,000 due on 24 March 1975 like the major loan. This was to provide the £80,000 balance of the Rossminster fee replacing the earlier arrangement to repay £40,000 after six months.

However, Rossminster's first big client almost pulled out at the last moment. Miller was unhappy at being asked to indemnify Rossminster against any action by the Inland Revenue if the test case failed and the scheme did not work: 'I almost refused to do the scheme, my hand was literally upon the door to walk out of their offices. I finally gave in and went ahead with it, but I came within an ace of not doing it at all.' That crisis over, and armed with the signed loan agreements, Miller and Harris then made the five-minute journey through Mayfair to Roy Tucker's offices at Audley House for the completion meeting. Miller recalled the scene on his arrival. 'Lots of people queuing up, going in and taking these bank drafts. I remember remarking that it was rather like the Lavender Hill Mob because there was a man who looked rather like a large pugilist with a rollneck sweater and a fancy lavender suit on. It was like a money shop dealing in rather peculiar bank drafts.'[7]

Present at the completion meeting were Gardner and Benyon together with June Hallas and Barry Pilkington representing Hallpark, with whom the loan was to be deposited. Miller and Harris were presented with a form letter from Roy Tucker & Co. setting out the terms of the One Year High Income Scheme. Two points in particular were significant.

Although we have every reason to believe that the scheme is soundly based in law and the documents give proper effect thereto, there is no guarantee that the anticipated tax relief will result from the implementation of the scheme. Neither we nor the Rossminster Group nor any of their subsidiary companies nor the other parties to the scheme can accept any responsibility or liability whatsoever for any expense or loss incurred as a result of the scheme being embarked upon.

We have your undertaking to the effect that you will not divulge any details of the scheme in any way without our prior consent unless required to do so by law.

Miller and Harris signed their copy of that letter, and the paper chase began.

Miller and Harris were each given a cheque for £2,125,000. 'These were rather staggering amounts, to be quite honest,' says Miller.

I'd never held a cheque in my hand for £2,125,000 and neither had my colleague. We jokingly said that we would take off with these cheques. I must say there was great consternation on the faces of the Rossminster people when we said this. But it was only a joke. They were handed straight back. We held them, I suppose, for all of about thirty seconds. This was the loan they made to us on which we paid the interest to mitigate the tax situation on the profit arrived at from the sale of the land.[8]

The joke over, they both handed over the banker's drafts for £344,658 from Barclays Bank. The Rossminster cheques were then deposited on one day notice with Hallpark, which guaranteed the loan to Rossminster, while Miller and Harris in turn indemnified Hallpark over that guarantee. Both then opened bank accounts at Rossminster, and Trotman confirmed the opening of the accounts. Miller and Harris then signed a letter to Hallpark requesting the withdrawal of £280,048 from the £2,125,000 deposit, a draft for which was then drawn up and the amount paid into each account at Rossminster. They then gave drafts for a similar amount drawn on those accounts to the Barclays Bank man to take back to Newcastle. The paper chase was over.

Rossminster Acceptances' £4,250,000 had gone round the table, and £3,689,906 had ended up at Hallpark but pledged back to Rossminster as security. The remaining £580,000 had gone to Barclays, but this money had effectively come from the two drafts for £689,316 with which Miller and Harris had sat down at the table: these too had gone round the table, largely ending up back where they started, in the bank manager's pocket. 'The paper money flying about took a matter of a few minutes,' Miller estimated later.[9] But at the end of those few minutes he hoped and believed that all tax liability had been removed on the £680,000 profit on the Little Benton deal. The cost had been the non-refundable fee, payable whether or not the scheme succeeded, of £40,000 down and £80,000 to pay – £20,000 in a month and the rest in a year – under the easy terms offered and accepted.

Seven days later, the Boreton part of the scheme was activated. Miller and Harris signed an agreement with Boreton whereby it assumed the liability to Rossminster Acceptances of £1,844,942 each, in return for receiving a cheque for that amount withdrawn from Hallpark, which was removed from its guarantee. Boreton then repaid the Rossminster loan. Ten pounds was left in the accounts at Hallpark and £5 in those at Rossminster so that they could be maintained until after 5 April in order to prove the commerciality of the whole transaction.

Just how unreal the performance had been was illustrated by something the significance of which escaped both Miller and Harris at the time, their sight no doubt blurred as much by the speed with which the papers passed round the table as by the tax-free riches about to come their way. The two £2,125,000 cheques were not in fact Rossminster cheques at all, but had been drawn on the Rossminster Acceptances account at St Mary Axe Finance. This was because, although they described themselves as 'private bankers', Rossminster Acceptances were not recognised as a bank by the Inland Revenue. The St Mary Axe Finance cheques had been immediately credited to Miller's and Harris's accounts at Rossminster and then paid on the Hallpark, which deducted the £280,000 with which Barclays were to be repaid and held the rest as security for the loan until it was paid on to Boreton a week later. As everyone in the room except Miller and Harris knew, the cheques were designed to be presented in the normal way, but had that happened they would not have been met – which explains the consternation and weak smiles which greeted Miller's joke about leaving with his cheque. The 'private bankers' did not have £4,250,000 to lend – indeed no overdrafts were allowed to Rossminster Acceptances clients, and no cheque for over £1000 could be issued without notice. Nor could St Mary Axe Finance have made a real loan of more than £4 million, for at the end of December 1973 its total customer loans had been only £5,400,000, while its current or readily realisable assets, such as cash or short-term loans, amounted to only £16 million. It was in no position to lend 25 per cent of these funds on one deal, especially at a time of banking crisis. As its chairman, Malcolm Horsman, admitted, 'It would be quite inconceivable that St Mary Axe Finance would be involved in multimillion transactions.'

Of course the truth was that the two cheques were written with no intention of their ever being presented in isolation from the matching cheques from Hallpark and the clients' own drafts. At the end of the banking day on 19 March they would have been presented at the same time that the cheques from Hallpark and – more importantly, because this was real money – the Barclays drafts were paid in. No overdraft facility or loan was required; the debits and credits would cancel each other out, leaving St Mary Axe Finance with a ⅛ per cent fee on the debit items for providing this facility.

Rossminster Acceptances had lent £4,250,000, which it did not have and which did not, in any real cash sense, exist. Had it come out, this alone would probably have doomed the tax scheme, for to be effective it was essential that the transactions should not be a sham, yet what could be more of a sham than to lend and collect interest on effectually nonexistent money? This point, however, was never tested in court.

Roy Tucker was well aware that the Inland Revenue were unlikely to accept the scheme without a challenge, which was one reason for clients being encouraged to divulge nothing. On 23 May 1974 Tucker wrote to all the clients who had done the scheme:

You will recall that we have undertaken to draft replies to any queries which may be received from the Inland Revenue in connection with the scheme, and it is of course absolutely essential that any information be submitted in a manner approved by us.

In view of the current climate of government opinion on tax matters, there must be a danger, however small, that the premature leakage of any details could affect the provisions of the Finance Bill currently being considered before Parliament.

Would you please therefore ensure that any queries that are received on the scheme be sent to us . . .

It follows therefore that telephone conversations, and in particular personal discussions with the Inland Revenue, should be avoided.

No clearer indication could be given of how much the Tucker style of tax avoidance relied on secrecy and nondisclosure. This was re-emphasised on 14 June, when Tucker again wrote to all participants confirming that £35,000 had been deposited at Rossminster Acceptances in an account controlled by him and Patrick Roney to cover the legal costs of negotiating or fighting a test case – if necessary to the House of Lords – on the One Year High Income Scheme. Tucker would select the case to fight, on the condition of 'the acceptance by you of our advice at all times as to the manner of reply to any letters or communications received from the Inland Revenue.'

The undertaking to fight the test case, which Tucker had now extended from the High Court to the Lords, was good for up to fifteen years. As an extra incentive Tucker's firm also agreed to provide, free of charge, 'all reasonable assistance of a general nature in dealing with correspondence with the Inland Revenue in connection with the scheme'. This was an offer no client could sensibly afford to ignore, especially as the price was merely to leave the Revenue to Tucker, which most of them would be only too happy to do. And they could continue to use the tax money.

Tucker reminded clients again of the need for secrecy in another letter on 22 November:

Although details of the loan taken are now with various Inspectors of Taxes, to the best of our knowledge the Revenue is not yet aware of the essential ingredients of the scheme. Without unreasonably withholding information we wish to defer as long as possible the Revenue learning of the details . . .

As a means of preventing countervailing action by the Revenue this tactic was a failure. The advance interest loophole for individuals was closed by the Finance Act 1974, which restricted tax-deductibility to loans for business purposes only.

By now, however, Miller and Harris were less concerned with the inspector of taxes than with William Stern and their £600,000 loan. For in early May Wilstar Securities, after struggling to survive since March with the aid of new loans, had crashed, first into receivership and then, a month later, into liquidation. Wilstar owed its bankers £180 million, £110 million of which had been personally guaranteed by Stern. With property values now down to 20 per cent of their peak a year before, unsecured creditors like Harmill stood to lose everything. When the first £60,000 repayment was not made in March 1975, Harmill – which had the dubious distinction of being Stern's largest unsecured creditor – tried to obtain repayment of the entire loan from Moorgate Properties, but without success.

Miller and Harris now had two problems. They still owed £60,000 to Rossminster Acceptances, which was to have been funded by the Stern repayment, and £240,000 to the First National Bank of Chicago, major creditors of Stern, who had financed Harmill in return for assignment of the Moorgate Properties loan. The bank now refused to provide further funds.

On 24 March 1975 Rossminster Acceptances demanded repayment of the £60,000 one-year loan which represented the unpaid half of the fee for the now redundant tax scheme. Loan or fee, Rossminster claimed repayment of the £60,000 plus £33,907 interest. Unable to pay because of Stern's collapse, Miller and Harris stalled. Threatened with legal action in January 1976, Harris claimed that the loan was not a loan at all but a fee. The loan, he told Rossminster's solicitors, was 'a euphemism for a series of bookkeeping entries, as no money has actually been lent'. He suggested Rossminster should 'exercise the same patience as ourselves', especially as they had 'been amply rewarded, in the interim, some £60,000 relating to a transaction which is not yet completed'. Rossminster gave them more time.

The way in which the £60,000 claim against Miller and Harris was handled after 1976 suggests that Rossminster was anxious not to have the issue of St Mary Axe Finance and the tax scheme it made possible aired in public, and that aspect of the scheme was never tested before the courts. In July 1976, however, its participants were informed that the Inland Revenue did not agree with Peter Rees and intended to take a test case before the Special Commissioners. Where tax relief had been granted it was withdrawn and tax assessments were issued. But it was another three years before the Revenue actually challenged the advance interest before the Commissioners, using the variant of the scheme adopted by William

Cairns. The Revenue contended that the advance interest he paid to remove the tax liability on his £5000 bonus was not interest, but that if it was it was it was 'short' not 'annual' interest and had to be paid to a recognised bank, which Rossminster Acceptances was not. By this time Peter Rees was a Treasury minister in the Conservative government.

In 1974, however, the Non-Deposit Scheme represented Tucker's biggest success to date. Tucker and Plummer later estimated that 200 individuals – from 'City businessmen and pop stars to sports champions'[10] – with taxable income of £10 million took part in it. Confirmation of the scale of the scheme can be seen in the Boreton accounts, which had £58 million deposited at Rossminster Acceptances in July 1974. This was just part of the £100 million Rossminster provided as loans to Tucker clients who bought the Non-Deposit Scheme. The scheme only produced a profit of £25,000 for Boreton. A year later, with the scheme now inactive, Boreton's income was just £2753. Although it was nominally owned outside the group by Smallfold, the Boreton profits still belonged to Rossminster. A minute of a 1974 internal meeting between Tucker, Plummer and Glauser records: 'The whole of the assets of Boreton and Smallfold to be regarded as at the disposal of the group – whatever the legal ownership of the shares.'[11]

Thanks to the One Year High Income Scheme and Denis Healey and the Labour government, Rossminster's first year had been an outstanding success. The gross profit on that one scheme was estimated by Tucker and Plummer at £1 million before deducting introductory commissions of at least £500,000 net: the Inland Revenue, on the other hand, stood to lose £7 million. For the year ending in July 1974 Rossminster Group made a pretax profit of £362,509. Most of this had been earned by Rossminster Acceptances, which turned in £266,717. Despite having deposits at the year end of only £3,800,000, the bank showed advances made during the year of £14 million, as well as promissory notes issued for a further £4,400,000. But then most of that 'paper' lending was netted off by matching payments in. Rossminster believed in putting its money to work, even if it just went round and round in circles. For, as banking manager, Michael Coysh, later admitted to the Special Commissioners, there was no limit to the sums Rossminster could make available for the Non-Deposit Scheme – so long as the money paid out to participants came back to Rossminster in the form of deposits.

No dividend was paid to the shareholders, but they and their associates did not exactly go without. Plummer paid himself as managing director £63,167, while Benyon and Trotman received between £27,500 and £37,500.

But this was just the visible onshore profit. Invisibly and offshore, much larger hoards of cash were already accumulating in the discretionary trusts and their related company satellites, or 'profit centres' as they were called internally. Each scheme had an offshore profit centre to which cash from the scheme proceeds was directed. At a meeting with John Glauser on 29 October 1974 Tucker and Plummer discussed some of these sources of offshore cash. Some £20,000 had been provided in a Manx company, Ballakewin, to cover test-case guarantees in the Trust Takeover Capital Loss Scheme. As Rossminster had provided for this onshore this was now no longer required, so the £20,000 was to be paid to a new offshore trust via the Tucker-linked Trumpet Trust. Another £6500 remained in Boreton and Smallfold from the pre-Rossminster scheme involving promissory notes. Half of this money was split between the Trumpet Trust and the Plummer-linked Pandora Trust. A new trust, codenamed Ajaxene II, was to be set up by Keith Tucker. The meeting minute records how this was to be done.

The trust was to be set up with 'beneficiaries capable of including all individuals and companies in the world'. However, Keith Tucker was to separately appoint his brother and Plummer as appointees. From an earlier trust £300,000 was to be appointed to the new trust via a company in the Rossminster group. Of this, £100,000 – 'the agreed distribution as at 31 May 1974' – was to be appointed to two other trusts named as Trumpet II and Pandora II, the beneficiaries of last resort were to be the Institute of Chartered Accountants. These trusts were also to be set up by Keith Tucker 'on similar terms to the existing Trumpet I and Pandora I'. These are probable references to what became the Keith Number Two and Three trusts.

Tucker and Plummer did not only think of themselves: Rossminster also gave £200 to the Conservative Party. Benyon had fought but lost as the Conservative candidate in Harold Wilson's Huyton constituency in the February election. His reward was to be selected to fight another Labour stronghold, Wood Green in north London, in the forthcoming October election. The Rossminster director may not have been advancing his ambition of becoming a Member of Parliament, but he was making the kind of political contacts that came in useful.

Tucker and Plummer also established the Rossminster Foundation on 30 July 1974 as a charitable trust with the gift of shares in Hallpark Financiers, valued at £5000. The Foundation's objects were 'the benefit of such charities or charitable purposes . . . as the trustees in their absolute discretion think fit'. The trustees were Plummer and Trotman. In its first year the Foundation had an income of £44,986, of which it donated precisely £520 to charity.

External evidence of Rossminster's growing status was its move in the autumn of 1974 to much plusher accommodation and a more prestigious address at Vogue House, 1 Hanover Square. The problem of the Inland Revenue's continued nonrecognition of Rossminster Acceptances was also solved in June 1974 by acquiring from Grindlays Bank for £300,000 its dormant subsidiary Grindlays (London) Finance, which already held Revenue recognition. It was promptly renamed First London Securities.

After the sweeping Labour victory in October 1974, Tucker and Plummer believed there was going to be a lot of money to be made before the avoidance was legislated out of existence and Rossminster was all set to make the most of that opportunity. Appropriately enough, Roy Tucker & Co.'s new telex answer-back code became BORVER – REV(enue) ROB spelled backwards.

HOW TO LEND £700 MILLION

The increase in corporation tax for most companies to a record 52 per cent in the Healey budget created a rush of corporate customers for tax-avoidance schemes. Until 1974 the demand had largely been from either individuals with big income-tax problems or the owners of tightly held private companies who faced a similar burden as a result of having to distribute after-tax profits as dividends – a source of income which could now bear tax at a penal 98 per cent. But with more than half their profits likely to go to the Chancellor, companies both large and small suddenly discovered the attractions of what Rossminster and Roy Tucker had to offer.

Tucker and Plummer had foreseen this, and planned accordingly. The advance-interest concept could be applied to companies just as well as to individuals. Interest on bank loans was equally deductible from profits before tax and from incomes. It just required larger loans – much larger loans.

It also required a bank which had already been recognised by the Inland Revenue so that there would be no delays in implementing the schemes in time for the financial year end. Companies, unlike individuals, do not all make up their tax returns to the 5 April deadline: their financial year can end on any date. For the tax-scheme promoter this meant that business continued all the year round instead of being bunched into February and March. Another attraction was the bigger fees corporate clients could be charged, since the tax saved would be that much greater. Once it had First London Securities and its Revenue recognition, Rossminster was all set to market the Advance Interest Scheme – corporation tax version.

In addition to First London Securities – the directors of which were

Plummer, Trotman and John Tillotson, another chartered accountant – the players in the Rossminster team for the first version of the company scheme were Hallpark Financiers, Ashleymore, a finance company formed in June 1974, and Brindonian, a £100 finance company formed in July 1974, with Tucker and Barry Pilkington as its directors and activated in October that year.

The Tucker client took a thirteen-month loan from First London Securities at an interest rate which created an interest payment, due on Day One, that was sufficient either to reduce or entirely wipe out the taxable profits of the company. Once the loan had been received and the interest paid, the client's company sold the loan to Hallpark, or bought promissory notes from Ashleymore. It then transferred the obligation to repay the FLS loan from these funds to Brindonian in return for a fee. The right to the loan funds was sold at a profit sufficient at least to wipe out the advance interest charge. Brindonian held either the funds as deposits at Hallpark or Ashleymore promissory notes as security. These were pledged to FLS. The client company then withdrew, leaving Brindonian to receive the Hallpark deposit or the Ashleymore notes and transfer either of them to FLS in settlement of the loan. This way the Monopoly money would have gone round in a circle, with only the fee to Brindonian, paid by the client, representing real money. This would mainly represent the fee to Tucker for use of the scheme. Rossminster, through FLS, would collect fees, and interest too.

The first loan Brindonian took over was for the relatively modest amount of £667,000, on 30 October. A month later, on 29 November, the £100 company, which had a paid-up capital of only £6, took over the obligations for repaying two loans for £62,813,000 and £58,407,309 owed to two Rossminster companies by Boreton. These represented the money lent to individuals who had bought the Non-Deposit Scheme and then novated the loans to Boreton. Boreton paid Brindonian with a draft for £112,765,000 but the same day also received a cheque for £120,401,483 from Hallpark representing the deposits made with those loans. Plummer later admitted that Rossminster would not have had sufficient resources to honour the £112 million bank draft unless a corresponding credit was received the same day.

Another nine loans were taken over in December, bringing to £142,000,000 the obligations Brindonian had assumed. Activity gathered pace as the popular 31 March financial year end neared. Thirty-six loans, totalling some £273 million, were taken over in that first three-month period from as little as £60,000 to £32 million. As many as seven deals were done in one day – 27 March – for £24,500,000.

After a final fling in April, in which twelve loan transactions on 14 April were followed by two giant loans for £20,530,000 and £46,116,000, Brindonian stepped off the stage to be replaced by the appropriately named Richstock. It returned to participate in five more loan transactions in March 1976, one alone of which was for £34,270,000, and then retired.

In the seventeen months of this pantomime performance Brindonian had entered into eighty transactions linked to tax-avoidance clients of Rossminster. The amount involved in all these deals totalled £415 million, yet Brindonian's paid-up capital was still only £6. It is difficult to calculate the amount of corporation tax these transactions were designed to save, but an informed estimate is up to £40 million, which must have generated for Tucker and Rossminster at least £2 million.

These fees represented real money and so, for a time, did the tax savings. But just how real the activities of Brindonian were which made both possible is illustrated by its own accounts for the period October 1974 to September 1976. It had received interest of £42,781,000 on the FLS 'loans' it had taken over during this period. But the cost of acquiring these, mainly the payments made to Rossminster clients, totalled £42,460,000, leaving only £321,000. The profit generated by all this hyperactivity was just £85,877, producing a dividend of a mere £28,000. But the real profit to the scheme promoters was taken at a much earlier stage, and directed elsewhere than into taxable dividend income in the UK.

Richstock was created on 27 February 1975 following the phenomenal success of Brindonian. Its directors were Tucker and two of his staff, the office manager Duncan Hackforth – previously a director with Tucker of Brindonian – and a secretary, Clare Colvin.

Its first loan transaction was undertaken on 14 April involving £660,000. Six weeks later, on 27 May, it took over a £20,500,000 transaction. Richstock's activities were not concentrated in frenetic bouts like Brindonian's but proceeded at a regular pace throughout the year. By the end of September it had taken part in thirty-one loans involving £67,700,000. Three months later the numbers had risen to sixty-two loans and £198 million, the two biggest transactions involving sums of £60 million and £32 million.

As the in-house legal expert at Roy Tucker & Co. who dealt with the clients, Brian Gautrey was involved in many of these transactions as well as in the other circular money schemes. 'We would start passing cheques at 8 am and continue until 5.30 pm,' he recalled. 'We would stand at the counter of the National Westminster in North Audley Street passing over cheque after cheque.' According to another Rossminster insider, 'At one time we were clearing cheques through National Westminster at the rate of £35 million a day.' The recycling of this Monopoly money went on into 1976: twenty-one transactions took place in January, including one for £60 million, until by the month's end the total loans participated in by Richstock, a company with a paid-up capital of precisely £100, had reached £292,509,000, potentially costing the Inland Revenue up to £30 million in lost tax and earning Tucker and Rossminster at least £1,500,000. From 27 February 1975 to 11 January 1977 Richstock received interest on its loans of £45,102,000 but paid out £45,076,800 to get them, leaving a 'profit' of £24,300. According to the balance sheet all this activity was made possible from two loans of £5 million and £60 million.

This money-go-round would probably have continued, and the sums involved would have spiralled up towards £1000 million but for disclosure of the Advance Interest Scheme by two newspapers and surprisingly swift government action to plug the loophole.

The whistle was blown in the first week of June 1976 by a front page article in the *Guardian* written by Stewart Mansell, followed by further front-page revelations on 5 June that £500 million had been 'lent to tax avoiders' by Rossminster. The *Guardian* revelations were expanded the next day in a more substantial article – the first to be devoted to Rossminster and Roy Tucker – by the *Sunday Times* financial journalist Lorana Sullivan, who had been looking into Rossminster for some weeks. An American who had arrived in Britain in the early 1970s to work for the *Wall Street Journal*, Lorana Sullivan, although not an accountant, is a highly regarded investigative reporter with a reputation for unravelling complex financial dealings.

'I received a call from a contact at Companies House [the companies registry] who was mystified by all the mortgages being filed by Brindonian and Richstock,' she recalls. When she checked the company records she made another discovery. As a veteran of investigating Slater, Walker, she noticed that the typing on certain of the Rossminster company documents looked familiar – indeed Plummer's secretary had taken her typewriter with her from Slater, Walker. Armed with this and other information Lorana Sullivan went to see Plummer. She was subsequently somewhat upset by the *Guardian* revelations as she felt that Plummer had not completely explained Brindonian's and Richstock's activities. But then Roy Tucker, who had cut short his holiday to return home and defend the scheme, was not exuding information either: 'All I can say is that some of these arrangements involve the borrowing of money and if large sums are borrowed there is obviously a charge on the register. I am not prepared to explain further to anyone except someone who wants to set up a scheme and then only in confidence.'[1]

On 6 June Lorana Sullivan wrote the first of what were to be a long-running series of exposés of Rossminster. The article detailed how the scheme worked and the roles of Brindonian and Richstock, suggesting that the potential loss to the Revenue could be as high as £60 million.

It was not good news. The official, robust Rossminster line was that all that mattered was that 'the schemes must be within the law'.[2] Benyon, the would-be politician's schooling already evident, sought to defuse and dissemble. He described Rossminster's role as

providing sophisticated tax advice in the corporate sphere. It involves restructuring and company doctoring, which is not a euphemism. The aim is to maximise profits and minimise the tax payable on profits. But we are not involved in devising tax-avoidance schemes where these comprise a series of actions basically unconnected with the company's trade or business.[3]

The last part of this statement was true – but was not the whole truth. The schemes were not devised by Rossminster but by its unseen North Audley Street alter ego and joint controlling shareholder, Roy Tucker. And few companies were in a position to borrow up to £60 million and, having done so, fewer still were able to relieve themselves of the liability to repay that loan within days and in such a painless fashion.

Much more astute and aware of the thin ice on which he and Rossminster were standing, Tucker adopted the high moral stance of a public benefactor with which he was to defend his and Rossminster's activities. 'On philosophical and moral grounds we would defend what we do very strongly,' he told the *Guardian*:

I feel quite strongly that with the overall burden of taxation so high we provide a necessary service for the taxpayer. Quite frankly we act as a safety valve against evasion . . . and emigration. We've stopped many very wealthy people leaving the country.

The government believes in redeploying wealth and we think too much wealth is concentrated in the government.[4]

All Conservative and Liberal voters, and even those *Guardian*-reading Labour supporters who earned over £20,000 a year and faced paying the 83 per cent top rate of income tax, could sympathise with such sentiments. However, facts to support the claim that Tucker and Rossminster were backing Britain by preventing evasion and the 'brain drain' were harder to come by. Given the criminal penalties for evasion and the disruption involved in emigration it would have been very surprising if that many of Tucker's clients had opted for either rather than paying 52 per cent corporation tax.

Certainly the Labour government was not convinced. For the first time the Treasury and the Inland Revenue realised that they faced a new threat. The repercussions for the Treasury of the mass marketing of tax-avoidance schemes were extremely serious. Within two days the Treasury minister Denzil Davies told the House of Commons that the Inland Revenue would challenge the effectiveness of the schemes and add a clause in the 1976 Finance Bill to counter such artificial avoidance measures.[5] This immediately threatened those clients who had bought the scheme with receiving no relief for the advance interest payments against their corporation tax – proof of just how much the Tucker advantage depended on secrecy.

Some 160 clients had bought the Advance Interest Scheme by June 1976, to avoid at least £40 million in corporation tax. Now Tucker would have to honour his guarantee to fight a test case. Tucker and Rossminster, however, could afford to be relaxed about the position. Their fees were nonrefundable, win, lose or draw in the courts. Government legislation was closing the stable door two years too late. Whether the clients felt as relaxed is less certain, especially as since 1975 interest on tax demanded would continue to accrue even if there was a test case.

But not everybody inside the Rossminster circle was happy with the way matters had developed even before the embarrassment caused by the publicity over the Advance Interest Scheme. The first doubters emerged in 1974 as a result of the success of the One Year High Income Scheme. The lawyer Henry Scrope had joined Roy Tucker & Co. in 1973 as the in-house legal adviser on drafting tax-scheme documents. Scrope wrote the instructions to counsel designed to elicit the legal opinions that 'sold' the schemes. Despite its acceptance by prominent tax counsel, he had become concerned about the concept of 'circular money', which was integral to almost every Tucker tax scheme but might not be considered real money as required by the statutes, and by the growing scale of the Rossminster operations, which increased the possibility of something going wrong.

By autumn 1974 Scrope had decided to resign. He was replaced by another tax-law specialist, Brian Gautrey, who came from the City lawyers Berwin Leighton, well known to Godfrey Bradman. Although not a qualified solicitor, Gautrey had fifteen years' experience in handling tax affairs.

Scrope's exit was followed in January 1975 by that of the Rossminster auditors, Deloitte, who notified Plummer that they no longer wanted to act for the company. This was a bombshell. Informed of the decision by the Jersey branch of the firm, who also resigned as auditors of the Guernsey companies, John Glauser wrote to Plummer in late January, 'This will have local repercussions on our board and local accountants. Careful thought is necessary.'

Deloitte's departure, however, passed without exciting any public comment. Eventually – after certainly two other leading firms had been approached – they were replaced by another member of the 'Big Eight', Coopers & Lybrand. Coopers were well known to Plummer through their role as auditors to Slater, Walker – themselves no strangers to unusual accounting techniques – and to Trotman, who had qualified with them.

Even so, Deloitte's departure, like that of Henry Scrope, was very significant, echoing the doubts held by tax experts with a close knowledge of the inner workings of Tucker's schemes that the schemes would ultimately survive examination by the courts. Because of such reservations Deloitte, firmly part of the City Establishment, felt sensitive about its association with Rossminster. A year before Deloitte had informed Rossminster that they would not wish to continue acting as auditors if financing tax schemes rather than conventional banking was to become the predominant part of the business. They were assured that this would not be so. Deloitte felt that undertaking had been breached so they decided to resign as auditors. This decision was further influenced by some partners' concern at the 'way out' nature of certain of the schemes and the questionable morality of Rossminster's activities. Accounting for the movement of huge sums of Monopoly money as if it were real posed a dilemma for any auditor required to produce a clean audit certificate attesting that the accounts presented a 'true and fair view of the state of affairs and of the profit for the period', as required by law. This problem was reflected in a letter written in January 1975 from Glauser to Plummer, then visiting Guernsey, about Deloitte's replacement by Coopers & Lybrand. He warned Plummer, on the basis of Coopers' role as auditors to the local Slater, Walker companies, that there could be difficulties in having them as auditors to any of the 'mechanical' companies used to make the tax scheme work:

If . . . any new auditor is to take over the audits of the R Group's offshore subsidiaries, it is most strongly recommended that R. F. Ltd [Rossminster Finance] be liquidated so that he is not obliged to concern himself with that company. You will recall that it has played a significant part in the arrangements with Gades Ltd known as TTLS [Trust Takeover Loss Scheme] . . . The size of the figures which have passed through its books have caused comment . . . It is understood that most of the present directors would prefer not to be called upon to act in any resumption of activity of similar size.

Glauser's warning proved unnecessary. Coopers & Lybrand did not see the same difficulties as Deloitte.

However, Rossminster's lawyers in Guernsey proved harder to satisfy. On 16 May 1974 Glauser had advised Tucker on the sensitivity of de Vic Carey and John Langlois to the type of business Rossminster intended putting through Rocquaine Trust, of which they were both directors as well as being the company's advocates. Langlois had informed Glauser that as far as the trust business introduced by Rossminster to Rocquaine was concerned the two advocates 'would still like to look at the trust cases before acceptance and be given some idea of what lay behind the trust'. Glauser explained, 'His purpose is really to see that he and his fellow advocate are not involved in any controversial schemes such as might attract publicity in the UK press.' Asked by Tucker for his comments on Glauser's letter, Plummer scribbled a note saying, 'This seems a reasonable request for a director of the company to make.'

A Labour Government, unlike a Conservative one, might well consider taking legislative action and so kill the golden tax-haven goose if it was proved that Jersey and Guernsey were abusing their relationship with the UK. On 30 September 1974 Glauser wrote to Richard Gardner:

We have for some time been aware that . . . it would be necessary to face up to the new tax situation in the UK and find nonprovocative solutions . . . The Guernsey directors of Rocquaine Trust would not wish the company to be involved in schemes . . . we shall have to examine any proposal on its merits to see that there is no likely reflection upon Rocquaine, which is anxious to maintain the best possible image.

This unease was increased by Deloitte's resignation and Rossminster's decision to form the Beauvais Trust company, to be owned by Rocquaine, to handle new clients' business from the UK. On 7 April 1975 John Langlois wrote to Glauser informing him that he and Carey were reluctant to be trustees of the new company. Carey considered 'that as trustees we could be under very great pressure from the UK tax authorities if ever we were called upon to comply with the terms of the new [Capital Transfer Tax] Act'. Glauser spoke to Carey, but was unable to change his mind. As he told Langlois in a letter on 11 April, he was worried that 'publicity might one day result from some case relating to the avoidance of tax through the use of a trust, for instance in connection with the avoidance of Capital Transfer Tax'.

The Guernsey attorney-general's reluctance was not surprising given Glauser's frankness about the risks and Beauvais's likely business:

One cannot guarantee that at some future time a perfectly normal trust will not come under fire from the UK Revenue, especially taking into account their new and aggressive attitude towards overseas discretionary trusts. Furthermore, the legal avoidance of the new capital transfer tax will certainly form a part of the activities of all leading solicitors in the UK in the future, who will we hope seek the assistance of Beauvais Trust.

To mollify Carey and keep his firm as advocates Glauser proposed that the Rocquaine Trust would now 'concern itself exclusively with non-UK clients, to the extent that these can be found'. UK clients would all go to the Beauvais Trust, which was to be owned by a charitable trust with two in-house companies as trustees.

That was sufficient. Langlois wrote back on 5 May agreeing that Carey, Langlois would continue to act as advocates, although no member of the firm would serve as a director or trustee of either Rocquaine or Beauvais.

Similar concerns about what Langlois called 'the aggressive attitude of the UK tax authorities' had already resulted in the retreat as shareholders of record, in certain Rossminster companies in the Isle of Man, of Charles Cain and David Moorhouse who had helped set up operations there.

The cracks, however, had only been papered over in Guernsey. Growing concern about the unexpected and worrisome direction Rossminster was taking decided not only Carey, Langlois but also John Glauser to leave. This decision may have been influenced in part by the sudden departure of Brian Gautrey in January 1976. Although Tucker claimed that he had fired Gautrey, Gautrey's version is that he left because of doubts about the way in which a version of the Non-Deposit Scheme involving commodity trading – sold to individuals to reduce their income-tax liability – was carried out.[6] In particular, he was concerned that every commodity purchase was matched by a sale and vice versa, designed to limit if not entirely eliminate any risk of a real loss to the scheme promoters, as distinct from the 'paper' loss to be generated for the client. Like Henry Scrope with 'circular money', Gautrey felt this artificiality could jeopardise the chances of the scheme succeeding in law. If there was no real risk there was no real trading, and if there was no real trading there could be no real tax-deductible loss. The counsel's opinion for the scheme assumed genuine trading financed by borrowings from FLS, the interest on which was used to reduce taxable income. Gautrey raised the issue with Tucker and Plummer on the grounds that by ignoring the artificiality of the scheme, clients were being misled as to its likely success. Not surprisingly they did not agree.

Whether his departure was seen as a red light in Guernsey, as Gautrey claims, is not certain. It was, however, a factor; still more so was the fact that Rossminster had not developed along the lines that had been envisaged in 1973. The 'fringe' banking crisis had forced the abandonment of any plans for a stock-market flotation unless Tucker and Plummer were prepared to offer the shares very cheaply. 'It seems that a decision was taken in favour of 'jam today' instead of flotation tomorrow,' says one insider. Also the increasing importance of the tax-related business as distinct from the orthodox banking business had created a growing gap between London and Guernsey. 'The offshore trust business was in any case almost static with London no longer assisting or introducing. The London parent became progressively more remote. The Channel Island subsidiaries felt increasingly irrelevant and out of touch and their executives had to start reassessing their position,' is how one of those involved saw it. This view is confirmed by John Glauser:

I began to sense a bigger business going on elsewhere about which I did not know enough. Rocquaine was not originally started to do merely tax work – on the contrary. Originally it was started to be an orthodox trust business. The original intentions were not adhered to and it was not developing along the lines we wanted. Not enough orthodox bank trust business was developing in London.

Carey, Langlois took a policy decision to resign because of the increasing dominance of Roy Tucker and his tax-avoidance activities over Plummer's original plans. 'Things had changed, we preferred the old regime,' said John Langlois. On 13 February 1976 Glauser and Carey, Langlois resigned from all the Rossminster companies in Guernsey and the Isle of Man.

What had changed was perhaps that Plummer's ambition to become a banker and run an orthodox trust business in Guernsey had been submerged by his and Tucker's realisation of the potential in tax avoidance and their aim to exploit that to the full while it lasted. It was not surprising that Tucker and Plummer had lost interest in orthodox banking and trust business, for the profits to be made out of tax avoidance were incomparably bigger and rising year by year. Not only were there big money-spinners like the Advance Interest Scheme, but the returns from selling smaller schemes could be equally attractive. The Deferred Purchase Capital Loss Scheme was reckoned to be capable of earning £300,000 net in commissions from creating £6 million in artificial tax losses. It was marketed by a Guernsey company, Marchwood, owned by the March Trust set up for the benefit of Rossminster Financial Services. Glauser's friend Don Coles was the trustee and was also – as recorded by the minutes of a May 1974 meeting in Liechtenstein between Tucker, Plummer and Glauser – to remain 'optically' the owner of Marchwood. 'Optically' was a favourite Tucker and Plummer euphemism for the external appearance, arrangements that cloaked in secrecy the true ownership of companies they controlled. The bespectacled accountants liked to control what the outside world could see of their activities.

In 1975 Rossminster Acceptances more than trebled its pretax profits to £864,500 – not that there was any tax to pay. That was seen to by creating artificial losses in a subsidiary, which were passed on under the accounting process of group election, whereby subsidiary companies can opt to pass profits upwards to the parent company as dividends so that the parent alone is taxed. Losses can also be passed on to be used as a tax credit. Otherwise corporation tax of £460,000 would have been payable.

First London Securities had an even better first year under the Rossminster banner. Profits for the period from December 1973 to July 1975 were £154,000. But this figure was greatly understated as a result of FLS itself taking advantage of the Advance Interest Scheme, Brindonian version. In fact its profits were nearer £1,700,000, helped by £1,103,500 in fees from Advance Interest clients. As a result of what Coopers & Lybrand coyly termed 'certain transactions' producing losses, £850,000 in corporation tax was avoided. These 'transactions' included generating an interest charge of £31,514,314 to other Rossminster group companies, which reduced the profit available for taxation, and there were even losses of £2,900,000 to be carried forward into future years as a tax offset. Neither the 'certain transactions' and their effects nor the fact that FLS listed its advances to customers at £375,500,000, all but £5,900,000 of which had been accounted for by equally unreal deposits from other group companies, appeared to disturb the auditors. But Coopers & Lybrand were to become used to big numbers: for the next year, which ended in March 1976, Ashleymore, the Rossminster company with which Richstock made deposits, showed amounts due from other group companies of no less than £589 million, with £509 million due to group companies, and earned £2,467,000 profit on interest paid on these staggering amounts of £45,900,000, less interest it paid out of £37 million. The Rossminster Group itself disclosed profits up from £367,500 to £2,246,600. Once again there was no tax charge, assuming those 'certain transactions' and the accompanying counsel's opinions had done their stuff. If not, there could be a tax bill of up to £2 million. The group could again afford to give £200 to the Conservative Party.

Never ones to disdain the opportunities Tucker had created for others, the Rossminster Group's directors – Miller, Plummer, Benyon and Trotman – joined Tucker, Gardner and certain other executives in taking advantage of the Advance Interest Scheme to reduce their own personal tax liabilities. This was done through Middlelane Investments. Formed on 23 October 1973, Middlelane's directors were Nicholas Pilbrow, Gardner and Brian Mepham. It was a subsidiary of a Manx company, Ogbourne Investments, whose board had been made up of Glauser plus either the Rountrees or York and Hudson on Sark. Ogbourne had been very active in the Capital Income Plan schemes. Middlelane borrowed £3,765,000 from Rossminster Acceptances, to be repaid in 1978, which it invested in annuities and shares in an associate company, Mandeville. In the year to July 1975 the four Rossminster directors and the others each guaranteed a portion of the annual interest payable to Rossminster Acceptances and made 'payments' to discharge that obligation. The four directors personally guaranteed and paid £2,312,100 of the loan. Plummer's share was £1,323,000, Benyon's £403,000, Trotman's £352,000 and Miller's

£233,100. The interest charge on this was available as a tax offset against their incomes, ensuring that these could be taxfree. Miller and Plummer paid themselves £36,785 that year – Miller's salary going up from £1500 and Plummer's down from £63,000 – so both would have seen much of that taxed at the highest rates. Once the interest had been paid, they assigned the liability for the guarantee of the Middlelane loan to Brindonian at a discount, thereby creating a taxfree profit to cancel out the interest charge.[7]

But some of the gilt had been taken off the profit performance by the desertions in Guernsey and the ripples they had caused, and by the adverse publicity surrounding the Advance Interest Scheme. Tucker and Plummer were now determined to keep a low profile. They feared attracting more of the Labour government's legislative lightning, which could put them out of business at any time. But Rossminster had in mid-1976 embarked on a halcyon period which was to continue unchecked for the next two years.

ROY TUCKER GOES TO THE THEATRE

An elegant Victorian church of imaginative and unusual design, St George's, Tufnell Park, stands today in north London like a ship stranded by an unexpected, outgoing tide, deserted by its former congregation of professional people and City men who could not afford the grander addresses of Highgate and Hampstead. The Tufnell Park Estate is now a relatively quiet island, surrounded by inner-city decay and the heavy traffic which crosses this part of Holloway. St George's was long ago replaced as the local landmark by the nearby women's prison.

By the early seventies this stylish, round church with its high, vaulted dome was deserted and destined for demolition, little more than a century after it had been built by George Truefitt, one of the more eccentric Victorian church architects. It was then that the actor George Murcell discovered St George's and saw in it a possibile home for his long-nurtured project to produce Shakespeare in the round. A veteran of Old Vic productions and small parts – usually as a villain – in countless British films, the burly, bearded Murcell had been pursuing his dream since 1967; so, in 1973, he and a seven-man group of fellow actors and theatre lovers – including Peter Sellars, Christopher Plummer and Eric Porter – raised £27,500, bought the freehold of the church and set about turning it into an Elizabethan theatre. But Murcell was still a long way from putting on his first Shakespeare play: to convert and equip the church and fund the first season of plays he needed at least a further £250,000.

Few seemed to share his enthusiasm for Shakespeare in the round. The Arts Council, the Greater London Council and the local Islington council all rejected applications for grants, and with no prospect of subsidised backing it looked as though his dream would remain unrealised. Then, early in 1974, Murcell met Roy Tucker at a party: 'He asked me what I did and I said, well, I'm trying to build a theatre. We talked about it. He thought it was very interesting and he liked the whole concept. I think that genuinely caught his interest and from there on he was instrumental in helping us bring it about.'[1]

Tucker himself explained his enthusiasm as follows: 'I am interested in the arts generally and attracted to things which might be lasting and of quality.'[2] For once this was not public relations. Tucker was genuinely interested in not only the theatre but opera, ballet and films. As Murcell confirmed, 'Tucker is one of the few people I've met in the business world that actually are artistic.' That much was clear from his tax schemes. His partners in Rossminster, however, only shared his interest in tax and money.

'First of all, he gave us a lot of good advice on how to go about funding the theatre,' says Murcell. Tucker's initial suggestion was that the theatre should raise capital by a share issue on the stock market, placing shares with private investors, but this plan was stillborn as a result of the continuing stock-market collapse throughout 1974. Then Tucker, already an expert on charities through Home and Overseas Voluntary Aid Services and the Deprived Children's Aid Fund, turned his attention to the fact that the theatre was already registered as a charity 'to promote, improve, maintain and advance education particularly by the production and presentation of educational plays and the encouragement of the arts'. Tucker suggested that the theatre might like to follow HOVAS and DCAF down the annuity trail, but the theatre company had no funds with which to purchase annuities, in April 1975 their liabilities exceeded their assets by £12,000, and its directors were opposed to the idea of borrowing.

Tucker then came up with a proposal that proved acceptable. The charity would be used to take over private companies which had done a particular corporation tax avoidance scheme Tucker had devised. It was necessary for these companies to be taken over so that Tucker and Rossminster could realise their profit taxfree. According to Murcell, 'I don't really understand it now. I knew that he was a fairly clever accountant and that there were schemes big companies use to try and save their tax bills.'[3] He says he saw several legal opinions on the scheme, including one from Robert Wright QC, a prominent company law expert, all of which confirmed that the scheme would work and that there was no objection to the charity being involved.

Tucker had cast St George's for the leading role in his latest and most popular financial pantomime, the Company Purchase Scheme. A version of this had been given its premiere in 1973 and had continued to run successfully, though in a modest trial fashion, off the tax-avoidance Broadway. Now with the possibilities St George's offered there was potential for a new version that would prove a runaway success involving feats of scripting and presentation of which any playwright would be proud.

At the heart of the St George's version of the Company Purchase Scheme was the unique tax-exempt status of a registered charity, which meant it paid tax on neither its income nor its capital gains. Any profits realised through such a charity would avoid all tax. To this concept was added two other vital ingredients from the tax laws. First, a subsidiary's right to choose to pay its profits as a dividend to its parent company taxfree on the group election principle whereby only the parent company is taxed; and secondly the opportunity, if the parent company was a registered charity, to take these profit payments not as dividends but as uncovenanted donations, thereby avoiding the need to retain any provision for future corporation tax. Such, in outline, was the St George's scheme – to put together a group of companies of which the parent was a charity, which would then receive all those subsidiary companies' profits as un-covenanted donations free of both corporation tax and advance corporation tax. The charity would be financed by Rossminster to acquire companies owned by Tucker's clients; the profit to Tucker and Rossminster would be in buying those companies' profits at a substantial discount, as well as in interest charges and fees. The charity would be left with a small contribution to a worthy cause.

By 1975 Tucker and Plummer were charity experts. They had formed not only HOVAS and the DCAF but also the Rossminster Foundation which had donated £37,000 to charity in its first two years, mainly from the income on its shares in Hallpark Financiers. And then there were the Tucker and Plummer Charitable Settlements. Plummer's trust was for the 'benefit of such charitable purposes as the trustees in their absolute discretion think fit', and Tucker's settlement had similarly worded objects. Both had been set up in 1975 with £10 and £510 from the Rossminster Foundation. Four years later the Roy Tucker Charitable Settlement had grown to £20,000, but had given only £4000 to charity. The Ronald Plummer Charitable Settlement was much more active, largely thanks to a

£60,000 interestfree loan from the Leander Trust. It took shares in and made loans to two companies associated with friends of Plummer: some £85,000 went into Dunsland, which converted property into residential accommodation for single people, while another £3000 went into the Ascension Lift company, which developed special lifts for the disabled. Real charities received somewhat less. The Rossminster Foundation also donated £5000 each to charitable settlements for both Benyon and Trotman, which were set up in 1976. The Trotman settlement made a number of small donations, as did the Benyon settlement – which also spent £3000 on six paintings, a diamond brooch and a silver salver, trumpet and jug.

Although it relied on probably the most complex series of arrangements even Roy Tucker had devised in order to work its alchemy of making corporation tax disappear, the Company Purchase Scheme was in itself simple.

A private company (Company A) had profits of £100,000 on which it would have to pay £52,000 in corporation tax, leaving net assets of £48,000. A 'mechanical' company (Company B), owed by St George's, agreed to buy Company A for £74,000 – the net assets plus half the tax due to be paid. Finance for the purchase was put up by a Rossminster bank. The vendor of Company A was £26,000 better off than if he had paid the tax. Now the trick was to realise the £100,000 profits in Company A which Company B had bought for £74,000 without also having to pay tax.

To do that both companies entered into a tax scheme that would remove that tax liability, so leaving the £100,000 free to be passed on to St George's. Once this was done, Company A paid on £96,000 taxfree to Company B, utilising the group election principle. Tucker was paid £4000 for use of the scheme. On the basis of a counsel-approved tax scheme having removed its tax liability, Company B then paid that £96,000 on to its parent company, the charity, by way of an uncovenanted donation. Because it was paid to the charity and because of the previous tax scheme there was no need to retain any part of the profit to cover advance corporation tax. Emptied of their profits, Company A and Company B could be wound up after a year or so. The registered charity had received £96,000 but it owed £74,000 to the Rossminster bank plus interest and other charges which resulted in the total cost of the purchase being £94,000. The charity was therefore left with a taxfree £2000 as its reward. Rossminster and Tucker shared £24,000; the vendors were £26,000 better off; only the Revenue had lost out, to the tune of £52,000. That, at least, was the theory.

The classic example of the illusionist's art whereby Tucker aimed to make the corporation tax liability of Company A disappear was the Gross Annuity Scheme or GAS. A sophisticated form of pass-the-parcel played for very high stakes, GAS involved buying and selling the rights to receive and pay four yearly annuity payments, which were shuttled between UK- and Manx-registered companies controlled in Sark or Bermuda. The money in the system to buy and pay the annuities came from First London Securities or Rossminster Acceptances (IoM), the new Manx bank, which needless to say received it all back at the end of the performance. In the time it took for the necessary documents to be signed, Company A removed its corporation tax liability by making an equivalent capital loss.

It achieved this vanishing trick in essence through being paid by an offshore company to take over the obligation to make four annual pay-ments to another UK company then merely making one tax-deductible payment before paying another offshore company to take over the obliga-tion to make the three further payments. It had by so doing established a relief against tax equal to the amount of that first annuity payment. But it required some twenty-one steps taken over a period of five days to complete this version of the Gross Annuity Scheme, known as internal GAS, used by the St George's charity (external GAS was used by client companies to avoid corporation tax without going through the Company Purchase Scheme). Most of these steps involved the initial creation and switching of annuity payments and obligations between Guernsey- and Bermuda-controlled Manx companies[4] or Guernsey- and Sark-controlled Manx companies. The companies were to be resident in Bermuda for tax but in the Isle of Man for exchange control as Bermuda was outside the sterling area and funds could not be sent there freely. Only when this structure of matching payments and receipts had been estab-lished was it expanded onshore to bring in the UK-registered T (for taxpayer) and S (for scheme) companies controlled by Rossminster.

The first four steps, involving the exchange of promissory notes, due for payment 4 days, 369 days, 734 days and 1099 days hence, between three Manx companies took place on Day One, usually a Wednesday. The notes all had slightly different values depending on the view taken of interest rates in the future. The first annuity, between two Manx companies, was arranged with FLS funds. Another five moves were made on Day Two and the rights and obligations under the promissory notes were switched among the Manx companies, one of which then agreed to pay an annuity to an s company onshore. On Day Three four more steps brought in the tax-bearing T company which was paid by the Manx company to take over its obligation to pay the annuity to the s company. The latter also agreed to make a matching annuity payment to the one it was due to receive from the T company to another of the Manx companies. On Day Four, usually a Monday, the annuity payments were made. On Day Five the T company paid the Manx company a similar amount (thereby cancelling out the capital 'profit' represented by the initial payment received) to resume its obligation to make the other three payments to s. For the taxpayer the game was now over: he paid the fee to Tucker and Rossminster, and departed a wealthier if not a wiser man.[5]

One of the few to understand GAS fully was Richard Gardner, the organiser of all its seventeen different but equally opaque forms. 'I feel like one of the only three men who understood the Schleswig-Holstein question,' he says.

Once again there was no real money in the GAS system, because what FLS or Rossminster Acceptances (IoM) put in moved round between the accounts at the bank for the relevant companies. The banks never lost control of the money, which was never at risk. Everything relied on that old Tucker favourite, circular money. Once again the stamp of approval was forthcoming from leading tax counsel, including Peter Rees. He advised that it was within the law for the T company to establish a loss by paying an annuity to another UK company, which in turn paid this on to an offshore company. However, it was essential that the initial payment to the T company should come from offshore income. In reality the money was always controlled onshore and often came from FLS in Hanover Square. Whether that crucial part of the GAS structure was made clear to Peter Rees is uncertain.

Armed with this ingenious device and three or four legal opinions to go with it – these included what was, perhaps, for Tucker and Plummer the most important opinion of all, namely that it was acceptable for a company's directors to rely on counsel's opinion, and so not make any future provision for the payment of tax on the assumption that the preceding tax scheme succeeded in law – GAS was slotted into place behind charitable status, group election and uncovenanted donations to complete the Company Purchase Scheme, Roy Tucker's most potent creation. The play was all set to begin. By the time the performance ended, four years later, £91 million in taxable profits had disappeared behind the curtain at the St George's Elizabethan Theatre in Tufnell Park.

The earlier, more modest tryout of this exercise in financial farce – but lacking the crucial charitable ingredient – involved Meadclose, formed in March 1972. Meadclose began trading in August 1973 with two of Plummer's friends – Peter Webster and Eiddon Morgan, another ex-Slater, Walker alumnus – as directors. The company was controlled by Kingsmuir Investments, a Manx company linked to John Glauser. Later in 1973 Meadclose acquired three companies for £284,000 as part of a corporation tax scheme. This activity was greatly stepped up in the period from May 1974 to December 1975, just as Tucker was discovering the attractions of Tufnell Park. During this period the ownership of Meadclose came onshore to a company called Duncandale, run by a chartered accountant friend of Plummer's, Bernard Cue, to avoid Meadclose being classed as a 'close' company (controlled by five or fewer participants or its directors) and therefore subject to Section 461 d(2) of the Income and Corporation Taxes Act. As a 'close' company Meadclose would have had to pay out as dividends all its profits, involving the payment of not only corporation tax but also income tax at the top rate plus capital gains tax if any of the companies acquired were sold. This was avoided by conferring 'open' status on Meadclose so making it 'd(2) proof' by inserting a parent company, Duncandale, which had enough shareholders, twenty-two, to be classed as 'open'. The subscribers to Duncandale in August 1974 included such friends of Tucker and Plummer as Brian Mepham from HOVAS, Colin Emson, the leading introducer of business, the Yugoslav ballet dancer Jelko Yuresha and George Murcell.

Still earlier, Dilnow, a Manx company, had participated in a version of the Company Purchase Scheme until September 1974. This had been set up in 1972 with first eleven and then fourteen shareholders, several of them well-known players in the Rossminster game, such as the Gibraltar lawyer Louis Triay and the Luxembourg accountants Kurt Sanne and Guy Urbin. Glauser's company Kingsmuir Investments also became a shareholder.

Up to December 1975 Meadclose bought another eight companies at a cost of £9 million, the money being provided by FLS. These were mainly property and investment dealing companies, including a subsidiary of Sphere Investment Trust, part of the Touche Remnant investment management group headed by Lord Remnant. Rossminster was becoming acceptable in the City. The purchase cost was largely refinanced by the dividends the companies then declared – £7,900,000 – and the return of share capital from a company that was wound up. Any corporation tax liability was removed by the Advance Interest Scheme so the dividends could be paid taxfree to Meadclose. Duncandale received a dividend of £10,000 but the real profit was made through FLS by Rossminster which pocketed most of the discount between the purchase price and the value of the assets acquired.

Meadclose disappeared from the stage a little faster perhaps than expected as a result of the resignations of Webster and Morgan in January 1976, three months after St George's became operational. 'We both resigned to do other things,' says Morgan, who became a picture restorer.[6] They parted on 'perfectly amicable' terms which included £10,000 for loss of office. It may well have suited Tucker and Plummer to wind down Meadclose as the curtain went up in Tufnell Park. However, some Rossminster insiders believed Webster and Morgan had become concerned about Meadclose's activities.

Backed by £250,000 from Tucker and Rossminster, George Murcell's dream slowly took shape during 1975 as builders converted the Victorian church into a 490-seat Elizabethan theatre. Although the theatre itself did not open until April 1976, the tax avoidance performance opened earlier, once the necessary change in the theatre's memorandum of association was approved at a meeting on 29 October. This allowed the charity to 'sell, let, manage, mortgage, dispose of or turn to account all of the property or assets of the company as may be thought expedient'. The theatre could now begin acquiring companies and so provide the finance the arts establishment and local council refused to give. The cost to the government would have been less than 5 per cent of what St George's Elizabethan Theatre now proceeded to cost the Inland Revenue. George Murcell freely admits that he did not understand the workings of what the charity referred to as its 'substantial new method of raising funds'.

The lights went on at London's first Elizabethan theatre to open in four hundred years on 23 April 1976, Shakespeare's supposed birthday, with a performance of *Twelfth Night* starring Eric Porter. It was followed by *Romeo and Juliet* and *Richard III*. Despite critical acclaim, attendances did not reach the 60 per cent break-even point. In its first year the box office brought in only £117,000 towards the theatre's £284,000 running costs.

Tucker had agreed to underwrite the anticipated first-year loss, but this guarantee was not really required as a result of the donations which poured into the theatre charity from its behind-the-scenes activity. From October 1975 to February 1977 the theatre received £52,984,000 in uncovenanted donations from the companies it acquired through the Company Purchase Scheme. Repayment of loans to Rossminster banks cost £51,833,000, plus interest of £875,000, leaving the charity with just £276,585 for its services – a lot more than the £67 received in donations the previous year. All this guaranteed that the theatre would open for a second Shakespeare season in 1977.

Just what kind of fantasy lay behind this performance is illustrated by the accounts of the St George's subsidiary Beachpage, a property company. It did an Advance Interest Scheme to the tune of a £96,950,000 interest 'payment' and a £96,855,000 'receipt' for passing on the future liability to repay in order to offset its own and other subsidiaries' tax liabilities. When the Advance Interest Scheme was killed off by the Labour government in June 1976, the Company Purchase Scheme became entirely GAS-powered.

However, cracks were starting to appear in the theatre façade. As well as putting up £198,000 to pay for the conversion of the church, Tucker had agreed to cover the first-year losses up to £100,000 and those for the second year up to £125,000. However, as the theatre still proved unable to match its success as a tax-avoidance vehicle, the pressure increased for Tucker and Rossminster to have a bigger say in the running of the company – making for tensions with Murcell, who began to feel he should know more about the tax side.

Tucker had already taken a close personal interest in a project to film the Shakespeare plays and sell them on video cassettes for educational purposes, and possibly to television in Britain and the USA. He was joined in Television and Educational Classics by an American TV producer Paul Bosner and Alexander de Grunwald, the son of a film director. But the videos were of indifferent quality and any hope of making TV sales disappeared in 1977 when the BBC announced it was to film all Shakespeare's plays. Only one video – of *Romeo and Juliet* – was made, but £150,000 had been lost by the time the project collapsed in mid-1977. The Tucker family trusts, through Hartopp, a Manx company, had loaned the video company £125,000 interestfree.

With so many deals going through the charity Murcell began to realise how little he knew about them. Furthermore, he was not encouraged to ask any questions. Murcell consulted his lawyers who advised him that as he was a director he was liable for the company's activities, and so it was in his interest to know more about what was happening outside the theatre. The lawyers' advice was that he should ask to see the company accounts. If he did not get this information he was advised to resign. Murcell put this request to his codirector William Halliwell, who represented Tucker and Rossminster on the board of the charity – Tucker was a director of the video company and the theatre production company, but not of the charity itself. According to Murcell the response was far from enthusiastic: 'I just said I must have access to all the accounts, not only the accounts that affect the theatre but that affect the company and that was the end of that really. I was removed from the board.'[7] George Murcell was forced out of the company he had founded on 25 August 1977. His replacement was Halliwell's partner in the dozens of companies which used the Company Purchase Scheme, Nigel Bruce-Watt.

The result of the row and the theatre's continued poor performance at the box office was to bring the curtain down on Shakespeare in the round. The theatre closed for eighteen months.

But it was still business as usual on the tax-avoidance side. Companies continued to pass through the doors of the St George's charity and then on to a charitable trust, the St George's Trust in Guernsey. From February 1977 to July 1978 donations of taxfreed profits totalling £30,900,000 passed through the books of a charity whose principal objects were supposed to be 'the promotion of artistic, theatrical and educational activities'. The outcome for the charity was a payment of £559,000.

The theatre did not reopen until April 1979. By then the involvement of Tucker and Rossminster was effectively over. The year to July 1979 saw further donations of £7,499,000 pass through the books but the payment to the charity was a mere £47,000. After that, St George's run in Roy Tucker's theatre of the absurd came to an end.

By then George Murcell had regained control of his creation. After his removal Murcell took his case to the Industrial Tribunal alleging unfair dismissal, and two years later he settled the case out of court. He was paid £58,000, including £48,000 for his shares in the theatre production company. That sum was then paid to Tucker for his shares in the company which owned the theatre. The Tucker link severed, a new charity, St George's Theatrical Productions, was formed in June 1978 and took over at the theatre.[8] Tucker's last link with the theatre, his £200,000 loan, was repaid in 1980.

Well before their problems with Murcell, Tucker and Plummer had initiated a second and less publicly visible charity to share St George's role in the Company Purchase Scheme. Like the theatre, Blessingwell was an unusual corporate creation in that it was a company limited by guarantee rather than with a share capital. It had been formed in December 1975, but did not become active until November 1976. Its initial trustees were Halliwell and his wife Susan.

Blessingwell's registered office, and the registered office of the myriad companies it proceeded to acquire – which included the original Rossminster Group and its two banks – was 55 Wynn Road, Tankerton, an undistinguished, semidetached terrace house on the Kent coast near Whitstable. This was the home of Halliwell's widowed mother-in-law, Mrs Rose Gill. Visitors to Wynn Road quickly realised this was no ordinary registered office. A small woman in her sixties, Mrs Gill appeared very apprehensive of callers, only opening the door a fraction. 'It's nothing to do with me. You must apply to Hanover Square,' was all she would say.

Blessingwell's objects were 'the relief of poverty, the advancement of education, the advancement of religion and such other purposes beneficial to the community as are charitable at law'. As far as education was concerned there was to be 'particular reference to the production and promotion of stage and theatrical works'. Since, unlike the theatre, it was a custom-built charity, its articles enabled it engage in such activities as buying and selling property, investing and borrowing, which were essential to its role as the maw into which the denizens of the Company Purchase Scheme would, as far as the Inland Revenue were concerned, disappear.

In its first year as a charity Blessingwell's only significant charitable deed was to help finance a production of *Hamlet* at the St George's theatre with the aid of a £10,000 donation received from Kemforth, a Rossminster associate. This was insufficient to cover the loss at the box office, which was almost double the donation. However, from September 1977 Blessingwell came into its own as a tax-avoidance vehicle.

In the year ending March 1979 Blessingwell paid £47,580,000 for companies (including Rossminster Acceptances and First London Securities) which in turn paid on uncovenanted donations of taxfree profits totalling £45,826,000. The balance was made up from a loan. As a charity Blessingwell distributed £321,000, mainly to the St George's theatre but also to the English Music Theatre, the London Festival Ballet and the Young Musicians Symphony Orchestra. By March 1980 Blessingwell had acquired 103 companies, spending a further £18,870,000 to receive donations of £19,068,000. The same four charities together with others, like the British Ski Club for the Disabled, shared £267,000. The following year the hand-out to charities was curtailed at only £74,000. That year, though, a further £4,771,000 was spent on buying another ten companies, producing donations of £4,063,000. By March 1981, 77 of the 113 companies Blessingwell had acquired were in voluntary liquidation, including the original Rossminster Group and all its subsidiaries.[9]

Profits paid taxfree as donations to the two charities totalled £160 million, indicating a possible corporation tax liability of up to £83 million. For providing that loophole the two charities received just under £1,500,000 – less than 1p in the pound – for objects 'beneficial to the community'.

The exploitation of St George's Elizabethan Theatre and Blessingwell exposed the impotence of the Charity Commission when it comes to overseeing the 150,000 registered charities; but then the Charities Act never envisaged the use of charities for retailing tax schemes. Ironically, the only query raised about either charity prior to 1979 was by the Inland Revenue, which back in 1967 was concerned about St George's original articles of association because they could allow too much commercial activity and so compromise its charitable status. Blessingwell was registered without query by either the Revenue or the Charity Commissioners.

As guardians of the Charities Act, the Commissioners were not equipped either to understand or control what was being done in the name of charity. At that time only two of its 300 staff were engaged in investigations, and these were mostly the result of external criticism rather than internal vigilance. 'We are totally reactive,' says the secretary, David Forrest. 'We were unaware of what was happening.' This lack of awareness was helped by the failure of either charity to file its accounts within the one-year deadline requested by the Commissioners. The first St George's accounts were not provided until January 1979, and those of Blessingwell not until August 1980, both were two years later than required, and by then both had served their real purposes. Charities do not have to produce accounts unless required by law to do so, which was not the case with the Rossminster charities. The Charity Commissioners can request accounts but if these are not forthcoming the only sanction is to obtain approval from the attorney-general, which is rarely given, to go to court. Tucker and Plummer subsequently denied that they had ever abused charitable status for tax purposes. But it is difficult to see how the activities of St George's Elizabethan Theatre and Blessingwell can be viewed as anything but abuse of charitable status. Artistic and educational charities had been provided with money which might not otherwise have come their way – a cynical penny-in-the-pound sop in exchange for at least £5 million, the fortune each man had earned largely through exploiting the charitable loophole.

GO TO ISLE OF MAN,
COLLECT £7 MILLION

To the first-time visitor, the Isle of Man is like a land that time forgot, for ever frozen in the Britain of the 1950s. With its shabby seafront of small hotels and boarding houses with holidaymakers sitting outside during the summer, its nondescript shops and restaurants, its uninviting amusement arcades and pubs, and its hoardings advertising little-known or elsewhere long-forgotten entertainers, Douglas is an unlikely financial centre. But ever since the first Wilson government in 1964 the Isle of Man has boomed as a tax haven, under an hour's flying time from London and even less from Manchester.

The Manx authorities deliberately set out to rival Jersey and Guernsey – which were longer established, more expensive and more selective – in attracting those who wanted to get their money away from the Inland Revenue and a socialist-run Britain. As part of the British Isles but not part of the UK, the Isle of Man, like the Channel Islands, shares all the advantages but none of the disadvantages, such as high tax rates or value added tax. Since the 1860s it has been self-governing. Tax is only 20 per cent for residents and zero for locally registered companies who do no local business.

Forming such companies was and is no problem, with the local authorities only too willing to cooperate. Permission is only needed for the choice of name. Once formed, there is effectively no supervision and no onerous disclosure requirements. There is no need even for local directors. The local lawyers and accountants whose offices jostle each other along Athol Street, the financial heart of the island known locally as the Street of Thieves, are ever eager to help. Few questions are asked about the reasons for the formation of a company or even its real owners so long as the formation fees and annual £200 tax is paid. 'It is not a Manx concern if UK tax is being evaded' was the view of the Government Treasurer William Dawson. All that seemed to concern Manx officials during the boom years of the 1960s, and 1970s was that the number of banks and companies formed on the island should go on rising, along with the earnings from them; and they did.

Until 1960 it was rare for more than forty companies to be formed in a year. Over 1600 companies were formed in 1973, ahead of the expected return of a Labour government in Britain. During the life of that government a further 8300 companies came into being, and by 1979 company formations were running at 2500 a year. The majority of these companies were formed for UK taxpayers intending to avoid or evade tax.

By 1980 the revenue from the £200 a year 'road tax' required for each of the corporate tax-avoidance vehicles had grown sevenfold to an annual £300,000. It was part of the all-important financial services sector's contribution which now represented more than a quarter of the island's income. The earnings from banking, insurance and related financial activities grew tenfold to £37 million in the ten years to 1979.

For Tucker and Plummer, the Isle of Man was a magnet whose pull, once discovered, became irresistible. As the authorities in Guernsey became suspicious and uncooperative after the exit of Glauser and Carey, Langlois, the Isle of Man became Rossminster's offshore fulcrum. Instructions still emanated from London. The offshore management and ownership, through the trusts, remained in Guernsey. But the companies through which the deals were done and the fortunes were filtered were increasingly Manx-registered, usually equipped with two Sark directors manipulated by Rossminster's man in Guernsey.

Rossminster formed at least 130 companies in the Isle of Man, three times the number registered in Guernsey. Most were formed during one year, 1976, either under the auspices of David Moorhouse and Edward Ardern at the local Anglo-Manx Bank, owned by financier Alan Lewis, or later through its former employee Alexander Thompson who left to start Commercial and Trust Management. Rossminster had been put in touch with Anglo-Manx through the Slater, Walker network and Charles Cain. Almost all these companies were initially formed by John Hilditch, a retired bank manager:

A young man contacted me from the bank and said that there was a job going registering companies with some part-time work as a company secretary. It was just being a glorified clerk, really. I would form companies to be on the shelf as the Isle of Man is a tax haven. I would be involved with them for one day or until they started to trade and then resign. I would collect the company registration forms from Anglo-Manx Bank, take them home and fill them in, then take them back to the bank. I possibly formed 300 companies over two years, the most was twelve in one day. When they were sold I would sign blank transfers for the shares, charge a £120 fee for the minute book and company seal, and resign. I didn't know who bought the companies.

The first companies Rossminster formed in the Isle of Man were key players in the convoluted chain of command designed to obscure the group's real ownership. Most were formed in 1976, as Tucker and Plummer set about realising part of the wealth they had generated in the previous three years. By spring 1976 Rossminster was enjoying a record-breaking third year. After only six months, profits were more than the £2,200,000 earned in the previous year. It was decided to reorganise so as to enable the proceeds from this progress to be realised offshore, tax free.

The first stage in the two-part move which would free more than £3,500,000 for distribution to the shareholders was a change in the ownership of the U K companies. On 31 March the Rossminster Group was taken over by a recently formed company, Fulcrome. The price was £3,504,400 paid in deferred and ordinary shares and £3,500,000 of loan stock. The shares and loan stock went to the two Manx companies which owned the original Rossminster parent company, Bryde and Kerrowfoot. These were controlled by the Leander and Ulysses and Keith Number One trusts. In July Fulcrome changed its name to Rossminster Group, and the original company of that name became Rossminster Group Holdings.

By the beginning of September the stage was set for the second phase in what Tucker termed the 'cash extraction' plan whereby Rossminster's owners would be able to pay themselves part of the profits Rossminster had earned without paying any tax or reducing their shareholding. The key element in this was the £3,500,000 loan stock which was to be repaid out of U K profits. Fulcrome had no assets except its share in the profitable Rossminster subsidiaries. They therefore paid up those profits as dividends without any withholding of tax, under the group election principle. These profits were then used to repay the loan stock. Because they represented a repayment of loan capital, such payments did not attract tax in the hands of the recipients. This way £3,500,000 in U K taxable profits became a taxfree offshore pay-out. Had the same amount been paid as a dividend to the Rossminster shareholders it would have been highly taxed.

The plan went into action on 15 September when Bryde and Kerrowfoot were sold to another Manx company, Camlet, controlled in-house. Payment was delayed pending other events due to occur on or by 30 September, the day the Fulcrome loan stock was to be redeemed. The loan stock itself was sold to a Rossminster group company, Avongrange, on 16 September for £3,500,000, plus £105,000 due in accrued interest. Then on D-Day, 30 September, the loan-stock interest was paid and the loan stock immediately redeemed from £3,825,000 Fulcrome received in dividends. This gave Bryde and Kerrowfoot £1,885,000 each. They then repaid £330,000 to the Pericles Trust, linked to Tucker and Plummer interests, which had earlier financed the buying out of Miller's and Gardner's 5 per cent in Bryde and Kerrowfoot. Miller had received £150,000 and Gardner £180,000. Bryde now sold its half-interest in Rossminster to its new Manx parent company, Nadine. This company had been registered on 13 July by John Hilditch and was owned, like Bryde, by the Leander and Ulysses trusts. Its shares, however, were in the name of the Appian Trust company and the directors were Martin and Barbara Joyner on Sark plus Arthur Lewis-Grey, Rossminster's new man in Guernsey. The two trusts received Nadine shares for their shares in Bryde. Kerrowfoot sold its Rossminster half-interest to its new Manx parent, Hartopp. Registered on the same day as Nadine and with identical shareholders and directors, Hartopp was owned by the Keith Number One trust, which swapped Kerrowfoot shares for shares in Hartopp. Bryde and Kerrowfoot were then put into voluntary liquidation which enabled the companies to pay out all their assets to Nadine and Hartopp. The cash and Rossminster shares that had been in Bryde and Kerrowfoot were now in Nadine and Hartopp. But on the way £3,605,000 in cash had been made available for taxfree distribution through the redemption of the Fulcrome loan stock, while the £1,600,000 cash held in each of Bryde's and Kerrowfoot's bank accounts, generated from the offshore 'profit centres' set up for each tax scheme, had also been distributed as the proceeds of their liquidation. Nothing onshore had changed, but offshore Rossminster's owners had now doubled their amount of cash.

All these events had to be carried out to a rigid timetable, as it was necessary for Camlet to use the funds arriving in Bryde and Kerrowfoot from redemption of the loan stock to pay Nadine and Hartopp. So, although the resolutions to put the Manx companies into liquidation only took place at 10 am, the liquidator had to be persuaded to take the unusual step of making an immediate cash distribution to the shareholders

(Camlet) of all but £500 of the assets. Bryde had £1,668,200 in the bank and received £1,750,000 from the Fulcrome loan stock, enabling it to make a distribution to Camlet of £3,414,400 which then found its way to Nadine. Similarly, Kerrowfoot had £1,635,900 in the bank, plus the £1,750,000, and so made a distribution of £3,382,100 to Camlet and then on to Hartopp. The two new Manx companies had to pay £250,000 to the offshore trust interests of Tucker and Plummer's four colleagues who were also to participate in the 'cash extraction'.

At the beginning of 30 September 1976 the Tucker and Plummer trusts had £3,304,000 in the bank, their investment in the Fulcrome loan stock and the shares in Rossminster. By the end of the day they had just under £6,800,000 in cash and still held their shares in Rossminster. It was all done discreetly, and was tax free. Few even inside Rossminster were aware of the slight of hand which had confirmed Tucker and Plummer as offshore multimillionaires.

The reorganisation of Rossminster coincided with reshuffles in the offshore arrangements through which they exercised their control. Initially all roads had lead through Bryde and Kerrowfoot to the Leander, Ulysses and Keith trusts. But in 1975 the Keith Number Two trust had been established, when Keith Tucker emigrated to Belgium. This had been followed by the Keith Number Three trust, of which Plummer had been nominated as a potential beneficiary, as a 'moral dependant' of Roy Tucker's brother.

Each trust soon became the owner of a litter of Manx companies which started out owning the shares in Rossminster but went on to own Tucker's and Plummer's homes, certain of their contents, and a variety of investments. Hartopp controlled Cambury, Peroneus and Darmas, which were all formed between March 1977 and March 1978. Cambury bought Tucker's home, Nettlestead Place near Maidstone in Kent. Nettlestead is an impressive manor house set in 400 acres of land. It was acquired in October 1977 for £425,000 and let to Tucker rentfree for five years in return for certain improvements being made.[1] A year later Cambury spent a further £94,000 on the Chisholme estate near Hawick, Roxburghshire. Antiques worth £70,000 were bought for Nettlestead Place at a sale in Kent. One visitor described the house as possessing 'more Madonnas on the wall than most foreign cathedrals'.[2] Other *objets d'art* included a table which formed part of Marie de Medici's dowry on her marriage to Henry of Navarre.[3]

The directors of Cambury – Keith and Angela Tucker and Lewis-Grey – were rarely consulted on the purchases. But then Tucker's brother and his wife were hardly readily available for board meetings, and became even less available when, in 1978, they moved from Belgium to Venezuela. Through Cambury Roy Tucker was able to live rentfree as lord of the manor, secure in the knowledge that his home and a large part of its contents were owned offshore, safe from the Inland Revenue or any other creditor. Just how independent Cambury was is illustrated by Tucker's instructions that the rent for the farm, 'be as low as possible' to avoid any UK tax problem for Cambury. This was done by imposing 'maximum repairing obligations on the tenant', Tucker.

An even more extensive network of Manx companies spread out beneath the umbrella of the Leander and Ulysses trusts. All were notionally controlled on Sark but control, via Lewis-Grey, lay in London with Plummer. Nadine financed Deal Investments which came to hold the 41.5 per cent Plummer interest in Rossminster. Lamond in 1978 acquired the Plummer family home in Bayswater, a modern town house with two garages just off Hyde Park, for £110,000. Tucker and Plummer also set up a series of trusts for the benefit of non-UK residents, thereby excluding themselves unless they left Britain. This was to put the trusts outside Section 478, which taxes the income received by foreign trustees acting for UK residents following a transfer of assets abroad.

The Magnum Trust owned a Manx company of the same name. An option to acquire this company was held by a UK trust, the Third Parliamentary Trust, of which Tucker and his wife were trustees. This would have enabled Tucker to breach the trust if necessary and acquire its assets. This option was never exercised and the quaintly titled Parliamentary Trust remained dormant. The Magnum Trust was also trustee for the Iota Trust in Guernsey. Described as 'a black hole trust' because its ownership appeared impossible to ascertain, Iota controlled the Manx company, Forwood, which was used by Tucker as the vehicle for his extensive commodity dealings and later for his bid to be a film financier. The initial funds in Iota had come from the Pericles Trust, which had received profits on certain early Tucker schemes. These were passed on to Magus and, on its liquidation, to Forwood, which was formed in February 1977. Later Forwood received a share of the offshore profits directly.

The arrangements for Plummer were identical, with only the names changed. For Third read Fourth Parliamentary Trust, for Magnum read

Serin, for Iota read Omega, and for Forwood read Perdon and Rasklith. Omega had also been funded from Pericles via Magus. Perdon and Rasklith were used by Plummer for his private investments which were, typically, less flamboyant than his partner's.

After the 1976 'cash extraction', the final piece in the Rossminster ownership jigsaw fell into place about a year later as part of an exercise designed to place control of the Rossminster group publicly offshore and, on the way, protect the profits earned in 1976 and 1977 from tax. Until the summer of 1977 Rossminster appeared to be, and indeed was, a UK-based concern. The parent company, the Rossminster Group, was UK-registered and its shares were held by nominee companies at the address of Vogue House. The only suggestion of offshore involvement was the former presence as shareholders of Torteval, the Guernsey nominee company. The reality was that the ownership of the latest Rossminster Group, like that of the first, resided firmly offshore in the Guernsey trusts. Now, with a defensive network of supposedly Sark-controlled Manx companies erected ahead of the trusts and behind the nominee companies, the obfuscation was sufficiently complete for a new offshore parent company to appear. Established on the Isle of Man, it would control an appropriately three-legged Rossminster based on banks in London (Rossminster Limited) and Douglas (Rossminster Acceptances) and the Rossminster Trust company in St Peter Port.

The first step was the formation of Rossminster Holdings. This was formed by Commercial and Trust Management on 28 July 1977. But immediately there were problems in Guernsey, where Lewis-Grey was coordinating the exercise. Tucker and Plummer wanted a strong-seeming board rather than the normal Sark stooges in order to give the new parent company an impression of independent respectability, essential now that Rossminster was to be seen as being controlled from a tax haven. That would dissuade speculation about the identity of the real owners, which would certainly be encouraged if the directors were transparent nominees. The problem was that there was no rush of candidates.

The group's Guernsey advocates, Roger Perrot and Nicholas van Leuven, declared the position to be too sensitive. Michael Beaumont, the Seigneur of Sark, displayed some interest – so much that Lewis-Grey put him on the board, only to remove his name when he changed his mind three days later. Although he presides over an island on which a large number of his subjects earn their living as rent-a-directors, the Seigneur sees this as a sensitive subject and refuses to discuss his role in Sark's only export. Eventually, just twenty-four hours before the first board meeting of the new company, Lewis-Grey recruited Julian Clyde-Smith, a young Jersey lawyer, to join himelf and Desmond Miller, now retired from the Bar but still living in London.

For the next year, by which time Miller had moved to Guernsey, Rossminster Holdings, the parent company of the entire group, held its board meetings in the lounge at Dinard airport in France. This was considered the most convenient and tax-effective location from which the master company could conduct its complex affairs. The reason was that the company could not have meetings in London as it would be liable to UK tax, and it faced the 20 per cent tax rate in Jersey or Guernsey if it held meetings there. Miller tended to avoid these board meetings if possible on the grounds that he disliked the small aircraft which took them from Guernsey or Jersey to Dinard. So Rossminster Holdings' affairs – comprising two banks, a trust company and all the corporate paraphernalia of the largest and most complex tax-avoidance operation ever – were left to Rossminster's employee Lewis-Grey and Clyde-Smith, a lawyer who knew very little at that time about the group. Fortunately for both of them, they merely had to do as they were told from London.

Rossminster Holdings had an issued share capital of £100,000. The shares were all in the name of Guernroy, the Royal Bank of Canada nominee company in Guernsey. Behind Guernroy were two more Manx veils leading back to Hartopp and Deal Investments which held Tucker and Plummer's controlling share stake for the Keith, Leander and Ulysses trusts.

Rossminster was further capitalised in November 1977 by an issue of debentures totalling £5,465,000. The funds for this originated from the 1976 'cash extraction' and a repeat version the next year which involved the sale of the Rossminster Group and its most profitable subsidiaries to Blessingwell by way of the Company Purchase Scheme.[4] After this deal in October 1977 the two former Rossminster Groups disappeared. The first became Firstwatch, and its successor Ironshire. This was all part of the cosmetics which presented a clean public face but made it very difficult to discover what was happening behind it.

The Blessingwell transaction also allowed the two smallest minority shareholders, Benyon and Trotman, formally if discreetly to claim their 5 per cent interest. Their own names too were to be hidden behind the Manx and Guernsey veils. It had always been intended that Benyon and Trotman would have shares in Rossminster. Miller had been a public shareholder from the start, as had Plummer–Miller with a 5 per cent interest, as opposed to Plummer's 45 per cent. Gardner was an undisclosed shareholder with a 5 per cent stake. The rest was held by Tucker, whose presence was also not disclosed. The Miller and Gardner shares had been purchased for £330,000 ahead of the 'cash extraction', but it was intended that they should return as shareholders in Rossminster Holdings. It was understood that Benyon and Trotman would also become shareholders at a future date. From 1975 this intended interest was represented through their shareholding in Dawnfern Finance, in which they held 250 shares each while Miller and Gardner held 100 each. In October 1976, following the 'cash extraction', Dawnfern was acquired by a Manx company, Jingate, which was intended to take a 17 per cent stake in Rossminster.

The problem for Gardner, Benyon and Trotman was that their shares were held in the UK, so any capital gain would be taxable. Miller intended to deal with this problem by emigrating to Guernsey. Gardner says that his interest was held partly in his and his wife's names, and partly in a family trust offshore for his children. When it was decided to form Rossminster Holdings and sell the Rossminster Group to Blessingwell, it was also decided to transfer this Gardner stake, plus Benyon and Trotman's interests, offshore via Jingate. In March 1977 Jingate sold Dawnfern Finance to the Rossminster Group for shares, putting 17 per cent of Rossminster into the Manx company then controlled by the four small shareholders. What followed was of necessity labyrinthine in order to avoid a substantial capital gains tax liability following the purchase of the Rossminster Group by Blessingwell while at the same time providing the funds to finance Rossminster Holdings through subscribing for its debentures, while all the time satisfying the Inland Revenue that what was actually happening was not in fact happening. The problem was that unless the four minority shareholders could receive most of their capital gain on the sale to Blessingwell taxfree, they would not be able to pay for their share of the debentures and so maintain their interest in the new Rossminster parent company. This is how the problem was solved.

Dacron, a Manx company, made a bid below their real value for the shares in Jingate held by the four shareholders. The low valuation could be justified by the fact that each shareholder had only a minority stake in a company which held only a minority interest in the Rossminster Group. So although Jingate's 17 per cent was worth more than £1 million, Gardner, Benyon and Trotman sold their Jingate shares for just £260,000 – £140,000 to Gardner and £60,000 each for the other two. Miller retained his Jingate shares. Jingate now entered into an option agreement, exercisable after 5 April 1978 – by which time Miller would have moved to Guernsey – to sell its 17 per cent of Rossminster Group to Blessingwell for about £1,300,000.

Jingate borrowed £870,000 which it invested through another Manx company, Azure, in three more Manx companies, Armon, Regstane and Newel. These were owned by the Archimedes, Socrates and Pythagoras trusts – Rossminster was very fond of classical allusions for its trusts – whose beneficiaries included the Gardner, Benyon and Trotman families. With this money Armon, Regstane and Newel purchased debentures in Rossminster Holdings – £330,000 for Gardner, £137,000 for each of the others – as well as their respective shares in Dacron to give them back control of Jingate.

Blessingwell acquired the majority of the Rossminster Group from the Tucker and Plummer trusts in October 1977. The valuation put on the group was just over £7 million – twice the price for the purposes of the March 1976 deal, and an indication of the profits Rossminster was making.

From August 1975 to February 1976 the declared group profits were £3,225,450, and in the year to February 1977 they were £2,702,200.[5] Rossminster had over £3,825,000 available for a dividend after February 1977, which was why it was necessary to utilise the Company Purchase Scheme in order to extract that money taxfree. Blessingwell exercised its option to buy Jingate's Rossminster Group shares on 6 April 1978, paying £1,300,000 for them. Dacron was then liquidated, distributing to the Gardner, Benyon and Trotman interests their share of this cash – enabling repayment of the loans Armon, Regstane and Newel had invested in their Rossminster debentures.

At the end of the exercise Gardner had received only £140,000 in the UK that was taxable, but Armon had collected £330,000 tax-free, which had been invested in the Rossminster debentures. This saved tax of £100,000 on the real value of his Rossminster Group investment. Benyon and Trotman both received £60,000 in the UK that was taxable, but saved £40,000 in capital gains tax as a result of Regstane and Newel acquiring the £137,000 each, which went into the Rossminster debentures. Miller had £330,000 in the debentures and £142,000 in offshore bank accounts. They also had their Rossminster Holdings shares offshore: Miller and Gardner had a 6 per cent interest each, while Benyon and Trotman had their 2.5 per cent each, all held through offshore trusts.

The final piece of the jigsaw involved the creation of a new trustee company which would be interspersed between those trusts and the outside world. Tucker and Plummer had always paid close attention to the public holders of record of the shares in the Rossminster Group and Rossminster Holdings, even though they were only nominees. Until the March 1976 reorganisation, the trustees had been the Rossminster-controlled Rocquaine Trust, which held the shares through Torteval on behalf of the Tucker and Plummer trusts. But while planning the 'cash extraction' Tucker and Plummer decided it would be advantageous if the trustees were not a 'close' company like Rocquaine but an 'open' company which did not have to distribute all underlying profits, even those it held in trust, as dividends and at the highest tax rate. It was therefore decided to find a friendly, independent trustee.

The answer was provided by David Pearl, an accountant friend of Benyon's who was running a small public company, Meru Group – a one-time tin-mining company in Malaysia but now an investment company with leisure interests. His father had been a leading figure in Conservative politics in London – a property millionaire, Leonard Pearl was a former Lord Mayor of Westminster while Pearl's brother Simon was a school friend of Prince Charles. As a public company with more than fifty shareholders, any subsidiary of Meru which acted as trustee would automatically have 'open' status, which would apply to the underlying assets it held for others, thereby avoiding the dividend distribution trap of 'close' company status. In March 1976 Meru therefore acquired the recently formed Manx company Appian Trust. Tucker and Plummer agreed to pay excess trust fees of some £3000 a year, which Appian would pay on to Meru as a dividend or fee. Appian was merely a 'bare' trustee. The decisions still came from Tucker and Plummer in London.

The potential problems posed by 'close' company status had earlier caused them to execute another neat little sidestep by making Bryde and Kerrowfoot – the original Manx holders of their shares in the Rossminster Group – into 'open' companies. On 27 February 1975 – just before the reorganisation – both companies issued 350 14 per cent noncumulative preference shares to Classfirst, the company they had acquired from

Malcolm Horsman. As in certain circumstances, such as winding up, the 350 preference shares carried votes, they could be held to be able to outvote the 250 ordinary voting shares in each company held first by Torteval and then by the Appian Trust and so control both Bryde and Kerrowfoot. Similarly Classfirst itself had been made 'open' by the issue of 250 noncumulative preference shares to a subsidiary of the publicly owned Investment Trust of Guernsey, which could outvote the 100 ordinary shares in Classfirst held by Pinelake, a Tucker–Plummer associate. Like Classfirst, Bryde and Kerrowfoot now became 'open' companies for tax purposes. This was vital as they were about to receive almost £4 million from selling the old Rossminster Group to its successor, after which Classfirst served a similar useful purpose for Nadine and Hartopp, being allotted 250 preference shares in each on 20 September 1976.

However, the Meru manoeuvre ran into an unexpected hitch on 30 September 1976 when its Stock Exchange quotation was suspended pending its takeover of a US company. This automatically removed the 'open' status conveyed via Appian, which now held the ordinary shares in Hartopp and Nadine. However, it was some time before this event – with its potential tax consequences for Tucker and Plummer – was realised. It was then decided, in March 1977, to create a whole new in-house trustee structure which could be kept under closer control but which would still avoid the 'close' company dividend trap.

One reason for this decision was David Pearl's reluctance to have Meru continue its involvement, on the grounds that its auditors advised against it. For the same reason he turned down Benyon's invitations to use Tucker's tax schemes for the company.

At the centre of the new arrangement was Dreadnought, another Manx company formed on 7 March by John Hilditch after paying one of his frequent visits to the Companies Registry. Hilditch was back again on 30 March to form its subisidary, Trust and Mercantile Management.

Initially Tucker and Plummer wanted Dreadnought and its trust company to be set up in Guernsey, but the authorities there refused permission on the grounds that they suspected the companies might assist the avoidance of UK tax. The Manx authorities were not so particular.

Avoiding tax was indeed Dreadnought's *raison d'être*: it was to own Trust and Mercantile, conveying 'open' status on the trust company and so on the entire Rossminster group. It would do this as the holder, on behalf of the Guernsey trusts, of the shares in the Manx companies which were the shareholders of Rossminster Holdings. Trust and Mercantile would be an 'open' company by the device of ensuring that its own shares were held by a company which would itself be classed as 'open' on the grounds of its having a wide enough number of shareholders. This meant finding more than a dozen trusted friends and associates of Tucker and Plummer to take up shares in Dreadnought.

Although a Manx company, Dreadnought was run from Guernsey and had as its directors Rossminster's local advocates Perrot and van Leuven. Ten shares each were allotted to seventeen individuals, including Tucker, Plummer, Lewis-Grey and his secretary. At a meeting in Lewis-Grey's office they selected who the other shareholders should be: a neighbour of Tucker at his home in Ireland; a woman who lived in a flat at Tucker's Westbourne Park, Paddington home; Tucker's ballet-dancing friend, Jelko Yuresha; Plummer's old accountancy colleague, Brian Mepham; another Slater, Walker alumnus, Simon Raynaud; Ian Livingstone, the husband of an associate of Simon Cardale; a company owned by Bernard Cue, another old Plummer friend; Ann Dolan, who had once worked for Tucker but now lived in Ireland. With four other men and one woman they made up the crew of Dreadnought, designed to protect Tucker and Plummer's empire from attack by the Inland Revenue.

Once established, Dreadnought, like Trust and Mercantile, did very little. The trust company replaced Appian in Hartopp and Nadine and also became trustee of the St George's Trust in Guernsey, part of the Company Purchase Scheme which made use of the theatre. But instructions continued to flow as before from London. So careful and attentive to detail were Tucker and Plummer – because of the vital role Trust and Mercantile played in their defences – that they ensured that the trust fees were paid not only in advance but in excess, so that there would always be enough for a dividend to be paid to Dreadnought. Thus there could never be any outstanding creditors of the trust company – such as one of the shareholders – who could jeopardise that crucial 'open' status. The excess fees were quietly recycled back to the trusts after Dreadnought had received its dividend.

As part of this offshore reshuffle, another new company was also brought in to replace Classfirst as the preference shareholder used to reinforce 'open' status on Rossminster Holdings. This was Treblejet, also owned by Pinelake, whose registered office was that of Rossminster's lawyer Patrick Roney. Treblejet used the same device as Classfirst to establish its own 'open' status. It issued 1000 14 percent cumulative preference shares to a public investment trust, British Empire Securities and General Trust. The investment trust was brought in to Rossminster by William Fossick, another ex-Slater, Walker colleague of Plummer who had joined the Rossminster bank in London. His family had links with British Empire Securities, which was looking for investments offering a high income. This could be provided by the preference shares issued by the Rossminster-linked companies. So in April 1977 Treblejet replaced Classfirst in Hartopp and Nadine, the first of many Tucker and Plummer companies in which it was to appear.

The defensive structure that Tucker and Plummer had erected to protect them and their fast-growing fortune from the eyes and grasp of the Inland Revenue was as close to perfection as it could be. The web of discretionary trusts and offshore companies was as impenetrably opaque as the *Anstalts* and *Stiftungs* of Liechtenstein with their matching Swiss numbered bank-account accessories. And it would probably have remained so had not the man who kept its secrets changed sides.

OUR MAN IN SARK – THE OFFSHORE
ODYSSEY OF ARTHUR LEWIS-GREY

Arthur Lewis-Grey had never intended to be either a barrister or a tax expert. After leaving Sedburgh school in Yorkshire he briefly considered an army career, but an abbreviated encounter at Warminster staff college convinced him and the army that they were not made for each other. 'Tactlessly argumentative' was the military assessment. He then thought that the open-air life of a farmer might be the answer and enrolled at Nottingham University to study agriculture. After a year he had learned a lot about managing a 500-acre farm he could not afford, but nothing about the everyday practicalities of being a small farmer, so he switched to agricultural economics. By the end of his degree course, he had decided on accountancy as the way ahead.

But he was interviewed by a large commodity-trading company and did well enough to be short-listed for a second interview over two days in Geneva. Unsure about commodity trading but certain about the attractions of two days in Geneva, he went, and ended up staying three years advising the commodity company on the effects of E E C entry on the British agri-business.

In 1973 his parents' deaths left Lewis-Grey with a small amount of money. 'I decided to invest it in myself. People had commented on the fact that I had a legal-type brain so I decided to take myself off to Lincoln's Inn and become a barrister.' He was called to the Bar in July 1975. Already twenty-seven years old and with a wife and two children to support, Lewis-Grey soon found the idea of spending his five-year pupillage learning about irrelevant subjects like crime and divorce both frustrating and financially unrewarding. Then in October 1975 he spotted an advertisement in a Sunday newspaper seeking a barrister with tax experience and offering £30,000 a year. 'I rang up the recruitment consultants and said, 'I'm not sure I'm worth £30,000 a year but I am a barrister and I did do well in my tax paper in the final examinations.' They were impressed enough to arrange an interview with Roy Tucker, who gave Lewis-Grey the job.

So in November 1975 Lewis-Grey went to work for Roy Tucker & Co. in North Audley Street. To begin with, he worked on what became the Commodity Carry Scheme, because of his knowledge of commodity trading, and helped Brian Gautrey to develop capital transfer tax schemes, since he had taken a particular interest in the new tax. Gautrey had been encouraged to set up a bespoke tax consultancy to be run in London alongside the 'off-the-peg' schemes he was selling – not least by John Glauser, who was eager to develop an orthodox, non-Rossminster trust business in Guernsey. However, in the New Year Gautrey left, with Tucker citing 'differences of personality'. Lewis-Grey was asked by Tucker to take over Gautrey's work and wind it up. This he endeavoured to do despite a very limited knowledge of tax planning. Then one evening, as he was working late at Audley House, he received a telephone call from Tucker in Stratford-upon-Avon where he and Plummer had gone for a three-day planning session:

Tucker told me that Glauser would have to go. Would I take over for a year? An immediate anwer was required. I replied that I would be interested, subject to certain conditions such as my wife agreeing to move to Guernsey, and to a verbal assurance from him that there were no skeletons in the cupboard. Tucker swore that as far as he knew there were none.

The basis for Glauser's departure was said to be his refusal to become involved in the 'cash extraction' plan. An Anglo-Swiss who liked to emulate a Swiss bank manager in both dress and correctness, Glauser had expressed a strong distaste for the proposed Rossminster reorganisation involving the payment offshore of £3,500,000 in UK profits via the Fulcrome loan stock. The scheme had been approved by counsel, but Glauser was still unhappy at the way the scheme was to be executed by companies of which he was a director. He was concerned about the exchange-control implications. Guernsey was sensitive to its position in the Sterling Area and its relationship with the Bank of England. When Tucker and Plummer insisted on going ahead, an already disenchanted Glauser quit.

The morning after Tucker's surprise telephone call from Stratford,

Lewis-Grey found himself on a private plane with Roy Tucker heading for Guernsey. Tucker had chosen to go by private plane to make sure that he didn't miss that evening's episode of Wagner's 'Ring' cycle at Covent Garden. Armed with a copy of *Butterworths*, the tax lawyer's bible, Tucker gave his new man in Guernsey a crash course in the relevant sections of the Income and Corporation Taxes Act and the Taxes Management Act.

At the Rocquaine offices Tucker and Lewis-Grey discovered 'a pile of files on the floor and the complete absence of Glauser and his secretary': both had retreated to Glauser's home on the island, from where he planned to return to orthodox trust business. Tucker and Lewis-Grey soon learned that not only did Rossminster now have no local managing director but it faced the loss of its local lawyers and its Sark resident directors. All had followed John Glauser's lead and resigned. So 'Tucker and I took a boat to Sark that same day to try to undo the damage.' It was to be the first of more than a hundred visits Lewis-Grey was to pay to the island home of the rent-a-director business:

It was a source of considerable amusement to me. As we walked the half a mile up the hill from the landing jetty to the main street, I mused on how many tax barristers who suggested the use of Sark directors in the sophisticated London world of tax planning had ever seen this place or considered the intellectual or practical abilities of the Sark directors and whether it would ever be possible to convince the Revenue that the companies were controlled here in truth.

The purpose of the Sark mission was to persuade Glauser's two teams of Sark directors – John York and 'Boffin' Hudson, and the ornithologist Frank Rountree and his wife – to stay with Rossminster. York was the part-time manager of the island's only bank. 'The meeting was held in the back office at the bank with York periodically breaking off to attend to a customer. The meeting was a failure. What they had heard about Rossminster from Glauser had put them off. They were resigning from all the Rossminster-related companies.'

Tucker and Lewis-Grey took the launch back to Guernsey and the private plane back to London, and shortly afterwards Lewis-Grey returned to Guernsey to take up the position as managing director of the Rocquaine Trust. The offer of his new job opened Lewis-Grey's eyes to the true nature of the relationship between Tucker and Rossminster, as well as to who really owned Rossminster.

It was at this point that I realised that the relationship between Roy Tucker and

Rossminster was less than arm's length. Here was I being asked by my employer – Tucker – to leave his employment and become a Rossminster employee. But my employment negotiations were still with Tucker. Indeed, throughout the time I was in Guernsey he communicated to me what my salary and other terms of employment were. I had assumed that Rocquaine Trust was a subsidiary of the UK group. Far from it. I discovered that the companies of which I became a director actually owned the Rossminster group.

Lewis-Grey was catapulted into the trust business without any experience, and suddenly found himself on the boards of fifty companies despite never having been a company director before:

There was a very simple explanation to all of this and that was that I was not supposed to worry myself about what the companies I was a director of were up to. I simply had to sign all the letters and other documentation that was put in front of me. It was not necessary for the proper performance of my duties that I should understand the transactions. Possibly the overriding reason for my selection for this post, apart from my availability, was one of trustfulness. It quickly became apparent that whoever was in charge of the trust company in Guernsey was also in charge of numerous investment holding companies and indeed the companies that owned the trust companies. The person in charge of Guernsey legally owned everything effectively on a single-signature basis. Hence the need to select someone who would not run off with their money. After all, there was no way they could legally claim redress. The whole edifice had been constructed on the basis of tax deniability. That translated into a complete lack of legal control.

On arriving in Guernsey, Lewis-Grey set about rebuilding Rossminster's vital offshore outpost. He felt extremely isolated: he knew no one, and he had to counter the vibrations his predecessor had sent round the small community of lawyers, accountants and bankers who serviced the tax haven. Through persistence and a 'liberal application of Rossminster's money' he succeeded. On Sark he increased the going rate for 'stooge' directors. Martin and Barbara Joyner, distant relatives of Barry Pilkington, were brought in. Michael Bennett, a friend of Tom Benyon's, introduced Patricia Falle and her fellow pig farmers who were already acting for other trust companies. Bennett, a director of the local Slater, Walker insurance company, also agreed to be a director of certain companies.

As the pace and scale of the offshore work increased, Lewis-Grey had to increase the staff in Guernsey well beyond the one-man-and-a-secretary level Glauser had found adequate. Michael Marshall, an affable Royal Navy Reserve officer and assistant banker, was brought in as office manager and multidirector, and Ian McMillan, a retired publican from

Liverpool who had come to Guernsey to avoid tax, was also recruited. Whereas in London there was one individual in charge of each scheme, in Guernsey there was only Lewis-Grey. Almost as soon as he took over, the tempo of work began to rise – not only because of the Rossminster reorganisation, but because the start of the tax-scheme peak season brought with it all Tucker's latest offerings. Immensely complicated documents involving dozens of companies arrived by every post. Lewis-Grey was starting life as he continued to live it for the next two and a half years.

When a company was registered in Guernsey the local advocates handling the formation had to fill in a questionnaire for the Commercial Relations Office which asked, among other things, for details of the beneficial owners or the persons for whose ultimate benefit the company would be operated. They were also asked if the company was to be used for the avoidance of UK tax, but this did not present too high a hurdle to Lewis-Grey. 'Circumlocutions' regarding the nature of their intended business

invariably resulted in the companies being formed. The Guernsey officials were satisfied and they in turn could reassure the Home Office that the island was not abusing its status. In truth Guernsey is a tax haven, though it is extremely bad form so to describe it to Guernsey officials. They insisted on calling it a financial centre. They also claim that Guernsey serves non-UK clients. Genuine non-UK clients were thin on the ground.

The Guernsey authorities were unenthusiastic about the renewed proposal that Rossminster should open a local bank, but suggested that it might instead like to take over a small existing bank, Barnett Christie. This was not welcomed by Rossminster, but before any decision could be taken, Barnett Christie had collapsed.[1] After that narrow escape, and with the Guernsey authorities now even more cautious, it was decided to try and open the new bank in the Isle of Man. 'Without hesitation they said "yes". It was embarrassingly simple,' recalls Lewis-Grey. Rossminster Acceptances (IoM) was set up in July 1977, replacing Rossminster Finance, with Ian Callow as the local manager. The Manx bank could now be used for the circular money transactions which were a crucial ingredient of many Tucker schemes, in particular the all-important Gross Annuity Scheme.

Very soon Lewis-Grey was at the thriving centre of Guernsey's booming tax-haven business in offshore trusts and companies:

Virtually every day successful entrepreneurs came to see me. They were attempting to transfer all or part of their companies or other assets into the hands of offshore trustees. They came over and made a day of it, usually with solicitors. The cost must have been tremendous. Often structures were set up and the anticipated profit never arose. Generally the clients were out of their depth. Some big names were involved. Other trust company managers sometimes hinted at their clientele. I now often reflect that virtually the entire Establishment of England is in offshore trust-company files.

Even with his limited but fast-expanding knowledge of trust business it was clear to Lewis-Grey that it was all very 'low tech' in terms of legal principles and concepts:

All the trust companies use discretionary trusts which the client shelters behind. The trust company managers know who the client is but as far as the documentation is concerned charities are named as beneficiaries. Very rarely if at all did these charities ever receive anything for having their names used in this way. Once such a trust had been set up it was simplicity itself to transfer assets into it from the UK, thereby out of the grasp of the Inland Revenue. A variety of techniques can be used – reinvoicing, holding investments which quickly appreciate, providing services. None of these were new and for many years there has been good anti-avoidance legislation to deal with it. Evidence is the crucial part.

Because of the differing requirements of the corporation tax and Company Purchase schemes that Tucker sold and Rossminster financed year round to fit in with differing financial year ends, Lewis-Grey and his staff were kept busy from January to December, but the peak was still in February, March and April. 'Then we would be handling ten cases a day. The documentation would have made a pile four feet high, and each document would have to be read, checked, the correct figures, such as for the loan-interest or annuity payments, entered, signed and photocopied.' Board meetings were needed to ratify all the intermeshing transactions which made up each scheme. Meetings on trust-company business could be held in Guernsey, as no tax liability would arise, but if they involved Guernsey companies or companies with a majority of Guernsey directors they had to be convened off the island so as to avoid the local 20 per cent tax – if five companies were in the deal, and all had to pay the local tax, then the entire profit would have been eaten up.

To prevent this problem from arising, Lewis-Grey embarked on a regular shuttle from Guernsey to Sark or to Dinard 60 miles away on the Brittany coast, holding what pass in the tax world for board meetings in kitchens and airport lounges. The requirements for the meetings in Sark or Dinard were increasingly dictated by the short time scale of schemes, such as GAS, in which transactions had to be carried out, and ratified by the relevant company directors, on the first, fourth and seventh day of the scheme's cycle. And as Day One for one client could be Day Four for another and Day Seven for a third, various meetings could be carried out at the same time, but since the schemes started on different days of the week, this meant that meetings outside Guernsey had to be held without ceasing, especially in the peak period. 'I was perpetually in motion. It was a great logistical exercise. I would manage one takeoff and landing every day for ninety days,' Lewis-Grey recalls. In his office at Weighbridge House he kept a pair of walking boots, jeans and an anorak specifically for the forty-minute trip by launch across the nine miles of the English Channel to Sark. At least twice weekly, Lewis-Grey would clamber up the steep hill or ride on the tractor-pulled trailer to the cycle-hire shop and then set off on his rounds, first along the main street to the Joyners at the camera shop, then onto Patricia Falle at Le Petit Dixcart or the Rountrees at La Perronerie, a rambling old house next door to the Seigneur. He took with him the board minutes which the Sark directors were required to sign. There was little or no discussion of the transactions involved or consideration of the documents – but of course the directors were only being asked to ratify decisions which had already been taken by Lewis-Grey on instruction from London. So concerned was Lewis-Grey about the transparency of what the Sark directors were doing that he felt he should go to the island rather than just send the papers to be signed, so that at least he could say that there had been a board meeting of the three directors. Such thoughts never troubled the locals. 'I never knew a question to be asked,' says Lewis-Grey. Given their level of financial sophistication and tax expertise, the Sark directors would have had some difficulty anyway in understanding what was involved in the transactions they were blithely authorising, quite apart from which their silent compliance was expected in return for the £100 fee.

Board meetings were held 20 minutes' flying time away in Dinard, not just to get round the problem of Guernsey tax but also 'to speed up the service and get more into a day' by holding meetings for many different companies. According to Lewis-Grey:

This had the advantage that we could use the Guernsey-based directors. However, we had to prove that the meetings did take place and so, sometimes twice a day, Marshall or McMillan and myself would charter a plane to fly us to Dinard. Much to the amusement of the French officials, we would progress no further than the airport bar where the briefcases would disgorge reams of documents and innumerable company seals. Within half an hour, all the documents duly signed and sealed and the board meetings minuted, the papers would go back in the briefcases and we would be back on the plane to Guernsey. Sometimes it was first thing in the morning, sometimes it was last thing at night. We became well known to the French immigration officials. 'Ah, they said, you have come to sign the documents, yes?' Frequently we met colleagues from other trust companies on similar excursions. They seemed to behave slightly more casually and always seemed to fit in a meal. Keenness and pressure of work made our excursions brief. We were a very peripatetic board.

On their return from Dinard or Sark, telexed instructions had to be given to the relevant Guernsey or Manx banks to pay the sums involved in all the transactions that had now been ratified. This was a very complex and time-consuming exercise since the banks insisted on the instructions being coded.

Lewis-Grey's dealings with the local bank managers in Guernsey, where all the major British high street, overseas and merchant banks are represented, gave him an insight into how this essential part of the tax-haven fabric functions: 'Sometimes I would have to explain to local bank managers why millions of pounds were flowing through their accounts but not staying there. They were worried about the ebb and flow of large sums of cash and whether their banks were facilitating the politically sensitive business of tax avoidance.' This decided Rossminster to take its business elsewhere, to the local branches of the Royal Bank of Canada and the Bank of Bermuda, who were more accommodating and much less inquisitive. But if the local branches of the British clearing banks were particular about the business they handled, the same could not be said, according to Lewis-Grey, for their subsidiaries engaged in trust business.

At the end of his first year in Guernsey Lewis-Grey had no complaints or doubts about what he was being asked to do. His only criticism of his life there was the impossibility of separating work and social life, 'since a small, closely populated island meant that one's friends at work were also one's social acquaintances'. This social claustrophobia was to prove a factor in his subsequent disenchantment – as it does with many tax exiles once they have tired of the endless rounds on the golf course and the cocktail-party circuit.

Until June 1977 Lewis-Grey was paid by the Rocquaine Trust, after which he became an employee, at £20,000 a year of the Rossminster Trust. But he regarded Tucker and Plummer as his employers, because all discussions regarding his employment were carried out with them and they referred to him as their employee:

I would constantly receive instructions from Tucker and Plummer regarding transactions to be entered into by the offshore companies. Frequently they would visit Guernsey to discuss matters with me and give instructions. If I had disobeyed them in any way, quite simply, I would have been dismissed. I was constantly aware of this fact. I can think of no direct order that I disobeyed. In fact, towards the end of my time in Guernsey, when the workload was extreme, I didn't even have time to enquire into the rationale for the underlying transactions, so an objection by me would have been even less likely. The mere existence of a legal pathway whereby Tucker and Plummer could have secured my dismissal caused me to comply with their wishes.

A considerable part of Lewis-Grey's time was spent organising and running trusts and settlements not only for Tucker and Plummer or the other four individuals he had come to see as his employers but also for a number of other members of the Rossminster circle as well as outside clients. He was involved in over fifty trusts with colourful names like Paddy, Calm, Donkey, Eerie, Tennessee and Uganda or historical names such as Gladstone and Disraeli. Such names were often chosen by Lewis-Grey as a private joke. For example, a trust established for the Australian lawyer John Elmgreen was called the Mackenzie Trust after the *Private Eye* cartoon character Barry Mackenzie, the archetypal Aussie. Tim Nicholas was allotted the Crystal Trust, reflecting his love of expensive champagne.

In his role as trustee, protector and ringmaster, Lewis-Grey became used to carrying out the instructions of those whom he considered to be the true owners of the trust's assets, whether he agreed or with them or not. One about which he had several disagreements was the Alpha Trust, established for the benefit of Tom Benyon and his family.

The Alpha Trust was set up in 1977 at the time of the Jingate deal, in the course of which Benyon and Trotman emerged as fully fledged shareholders in the ultimate offshore parent company, Rossminster Holdings. The settlor of the trust, with £50 to £100, was Kingsmuir Investments, the Manx company run by Glauser, which had about fifty such trusts on its shelf. The named beneficiaries were charities but the trustees, Rossminster companies, had the power to appoint the trust funds to any beneficiary they chose. 'Benyon knew of and approved of the existence of this trust,' says Lewis-Grey. 'I looked to him for guidance concerning the investment of the trust's funds. At no time did I or any company of which I

was a director take any independent decision concerning the trust funds.'
In the event of his death, Benyon wrote to Lewis-Grey, the trustees were to
take instructions from his brother-in-law.

In September 1977 the Alpha Trust received between £70,000 and
£80,000 from Rossminster sources. This was kept in an account at the
Royal Bank of Canada. Periodically Lewis-Grey received telephone
requests from Benyon for sums of between £2000 and £3000 to be
brought to him in London. 'One of my colleagues would phone the Royal
Bank of Canada and ask for some English pound notes to be available for
collection. These would then be put in a brown envelope, a receipt would
be typed up and myself or one of my colleagues would take the money to
London and physically hand it to Benyon.'[2] Only once did Benyon say why
he required the cash – to pay the builder working on his swimming pool.
On one occasion Lewis-Grey had to leave £2000 for Benyon at the
Customs at Jersey airport – receiving a receipt for 'one brown envelope' – to
avoid breaching exchange control regulations by taking the money to
Dinard. Lewis-Grey collected it on his way back to London.

Lewis-Grey says that he frequently warned Benyon of the risky nature
of delivering these envelopes stuffed with cash: 'I regarded them as risky
because they could identify Benyon in the eyes of the Inland Revenue as
the true beneficiary of the trust. He seemed oblivious of these risks.' This
view was shared by Richard Gardner when he heard of the payments.
According to Lewis-Grey, Gardner 'felt that it prejudiced his own
position. He felt that if any of the shareholders identified themselves with
their trust then the others would be similarly regarded by the Revenue.'

Over a period of two years Lewis-Grey ferried to Benyon £27,000 in
anonymous envelopes delivered in London. To protect himself and the
trust company he insisted that Benyon signed a receipt for each delivery,
which was filed with the trust's accounts. The bookkeepers treated the
payments as loans, although Lewis-Grey never discussed any rate of
interest or proposals for repayment or security.

Problems with a flat in Lennox Gardens, near Harrods, spawned the
Alpha II Trust. In 1977 Lewis-Grey was asked to buy Benyon's half-share
in the flat for £11,500. The flat was occupied by an American commodity-
dealer friend and was in his name. Lewis-Grey became concerned that
there could have been a breach of exchange control regulations by Benyon
lending the American the money with which to buy his half-interest in the
flat. He discussed the problem with Bank of England officials when they

visited Guernsey. They accepted that if the £11,500 was paid to Benyon in the UK and the flat then registered in the trust's name there would be no further problem. The Alpha II Trust therefore became the legal owner. Next year the trust acquired the other half-interest and sold the flat, making a substantial profit. Lewis-Grey switched the flat into a separate trust so that the Bank of England would not discover the existence of the other assets in the original Alpha Trust.

His dealings with Benyon illustrated what Lewis-Grey came to see as a worrying fiction about the trusts he administered for the Rossminster insiders.

A Rossminster trust was almost an abuse of the term trust. I would assert that I didn't have any independence of operation in my capacity as trustee. No judgement was required to act as a trustee for Rossminster. At no time did I or any company of which I was a director ever take an independent decision concerning the administration of trust assets. Invariably the interested parties were asked for directions concerning the administration of the funds. From my legal knowledge and training, my status in the Rossminster organisation could only be described as that of a bare trustee. In short, the monies contained in the trusts were not in practice owned by the trustees. Always the funds were regarded as being in the direct ownership of Tucker, Plummer, Trotman, Benyon, Gardner and Miller.

As a result of his crucial central role in the Rossminster reorganisations of 1976 and 1977, Lewis-Grey developed a detailed inside knowledge of Rossminster and its ownership structure. He is in no doubt what that showed: 'I reviewed all the documents and correspondence leading to the setting up of the Keith, Leander and Ulysses trusts which owned the entire outfit. Clearly Rossminster was owned by Tucker and Plummer, though the Revenue would be powerless to prove it. I was there just to provide a front.'

A SCHEME FOR ALL REASONS

'I used to say to clients that it could all be ended by the stroke of a pen,' recalls Colin Emson, who introduced more clients to Tucker and Rossminster than most. 'All that was required was one line in the Finance Bill saying that any transaction for which the "main purpose" was the avoidance of tax would not be effective.'

Tucker and Plummer too never believed that the tax-avoidance boom would survive the second and convincing Labour election victory in October 197₄. No doubt this was a factor in the decisions to cash in through the 'extraction' exercises of 1976 and 1977. They openly voiced opinions to colleagues that Denis Healey was certain to close up most of the loopholes or possibly bring in the type of blanket anti-avoidance legislation already existing in other countries. That would allow the Inland Revenue simply to 'look through' any arrangement or offshore company structure if the main purpose was the avoidance of tax.

But to their surprise, such fears proved unjustified. No revolutionary measures were taken by Healey; instead, the Labour government, like others before it, chose to adapt the stable-door approach, legislating against a discovered abuse millions of pounds in lost tax too late. The government gave more power to the Revenue to deal with tax evasion and avoidance but it stopped short of giving it the wide discretionary powers to decide when the 'main purpose' of a transaction was tax avoidance.

Three factors persuaded the Labour government against such a move. The Inland Revenue were not in favour of being given wide-ranging powers which might not command broad public support. The result could be an unacceptable burden of test cases which, given the Tomlin doctrine then prevailing among the Law Lords, the Revenue seemed likely to lose.

The Inland Revenue was also far from convinced that the Australian anti-avoidance measures had proved successful. There was also opposition from within the Labour Party to granting extra powers to the judges to decide who should be taxed. Judges were seen as too elite a group, selected from too narrow a section of society and one not renowned for Labour sympathies.

Despite such objections a proposal for broad anti-avoidance legislation was discussed but rejected during 1976. Also discussed was the possibility of extending the Inland Revenue's jurisdiction to the Channel Islands and the Isle of Man. Supported by the Revenue and the Treasury, this was vigorously opposed by the Home Office, who declared that such a move was not allowed under the treaties with the British government and that, if imposed, it could encourage the three island tax havens to declare a form of unilateral independence. The proposal did not go any further.

So Labour stuck with the old-fashioned way of dealing with this new-fashioned threat, which was just what the tax-scheme promoters wanted. It meant that they could still spot the loopholes and rush as many clients as possible through them as fast and as discreetly as possible, before the Inland Revenue finally woke up and acted. And as long as the courts continued to be guided by Lords Clyde and Tomlin, any subsequent legal challenge was unlikely to succeed.

By 1976 tax avoidance was rapidly seeping down from the very rich to permeate the entire business community as well as an increasing number of individuals who found the tax charge on their incomes unacceptable. Peers, judges and politicians joined pop stars, property dealers and casino owners in the Tucker waiting room. In the corporate world major City banks and large public companies were joined by well-known privately owned companies and small, family-owned concerns. Companies carried out corporation tax or capital gains tax schemes, while their directors would undertake individual schemes to avoid their personal tax. Many returned year after year to repeat the ritual.

At one stage Tucker even came up with a scheme which made it possible to avoid levying PAYE on employees – a modern version of the Duke of Westminster's ploy, using his and Tucker's favourite tax-avoidance instrument, the annuity. But it was never marketed. 'You must not attack the root of the system,' Tucker is said to have explained in what was a rare moment of self-restraint and public-spiritedness.

One client who illustrates how acceptable tax avoidance had become by the midseventies was Sir Robert Bellinger, who for five years from 1970 had been chairman of the National Savings Committee, a small savers' movement which by 1974 had attracted over £10,000 million into government coffers. He was well known in the City as a former Lord Mayor of London and as an active company director, being chairman of the Kinloch grocery chain and a director of the Rank Organisation and Arsenal Football Club. In 1975 Bellinger resigned from the National Savings Committee in protest at the Labour government's inflationary economic policies. That year Kinloch was taken over, and not long afterwards he took part in a Tucker/Rossminster scheme designed to avoid capital gains tax on about £100,000. He saw no contradiction between this and his former role of assisting government finances. 'The two things are different. It depends what you are trying to achieve,' he says. Tax avoidance was 'a financial opportunity' and he describes himself as 'alert to financial opportunities'. He would not discuss the details of the scheme or why he did it except to say, 'It was all within the law and the tax rates then were not taxation but extortion.' And, as he pointed out, certain National Savings issues have always offered a government-approved form of limited tax avoidance for the top-rate taxpayer.

The former Conservative minister 'Ernie' Marples became a Rossminster client after he left politics in 1974 with a peerage. He was the epitome of the self-made man, and was hailed in a 1960 profile by the *Observer* as 'the star alumnus of the Opportunity State' not long after he became transport minister in 1959. Marples had built up substantial residential property interests in London, and Rossminster was brought in to advise him on his tangled tax affairs. He was being pressed for some thirty years' back tax relating to his house in Belgravia and also capital gains tax on certain of his properties. Not even Tucker and Plummer were able to help. Three days before the end of the tax year in April 1975 Lord Marples, without waiting to pack all his bags, left for France. Tucker's and Plummer's relationship with the exiled peer ended with a dispute over unpaid fees.

Tax avoidance was not, however, the preserve of Conservatives alone. The leading Liberal peer, Lord Tanlaw, a member of the wealthy Inchcape family, also became a Rossminster client and carried out a scheme to avoid tax on a £200,000 capital gain. Lord Tanlaw did not respond to a request to discuss his dealings with Rossminster.

A much more recent entrant to the Lords whose path inadvertently crossed that of Rossminster was Lord Young, an influential member of Mrs Thatcher's Cabinet and among her inner circle of advisers. Qualified as a solicitor, David Young launched on a career in property. In 1970 he sold his successful industrial-estates company Eldonwall to Town and City Properties. Shortly after this, in 1972, when Town and City became a shareholder in a small developer, City Securities, run by a London-based South African, Dennis Mosselson, Young became a director though not a shareholder. Through an oversight he remained a director, although he was under the impression he had resigned, even after he left Town and City in 1975 to become the property adviser to a leading American bank, Manufacturers Hanover Trust. By 1978 City Securities had assets of more than £1 million.

By this time, however, David Young was more involved in politics than property. He had joined the Centre for Policy Studies, set up by Sir Keith Joseph in 1977 to advise the Conservative Party from a right-wing standpoint. In 1979 he became the Centre's director and, after the Conservatives' election victory, adviser to the Department of Industry and then special adviser to the industry minister, Sir Keith Joseph, on the privatisation programme. In 1982 Young moved to take over at the Manpower Services Commission and two years later joined the cabinet as a life peer and minister without portfolio with responsibility for solving unemployment.

Like Young, City Securities was moving ahead, and early in March 1979 it entered into a scheme, involving Rossminster, to avoid £330,000 in corporation tax. On 1 March 1979 City Securities subscribed for 300 preference shares in Townwright, a company in the Blessingwell stable. Though allotted, these shares could subsequently be renounced. The 100 ordinary shares in Townwright were held by a nominee company, Major-wise, although one share was in the name of Roy Tucker. This kind of arrangement usually involved the exploitation of tax losses generated in the Tucker/Rossminster associate by the holder of the preference shares whose voting rights in certain circumstances, such as winding up, enabled it to claim the company as a subsidiary – because it would have 75 per cent of the votes. Once it could do this then losses, by the process of group election, could be passed on upwards to the parent company who had profits to shelter from corporation tax. The loss passed on, the client company could then renounce its shares in the Tucker/Rossminster associate, which would be wound up.

Mosselson recalls he was 'sold' on the scheme by his accountants, who were no strangers to Rossminster. 'We had such doubts but the senior partner said, "I do them myself, we do it for our own property transactions." The pressures were considerable. You would go to a party and everyone would be talking about the schemes and say how clever they were. There were counsels' opinions by the reams. Everybody said it's OK and everybody's doing it. It was a whole social thing.'

But Mosselson still remained less than totally convinced despite going ahead with the scheme. 'We made provision for the tax just in case.' This proved a wise precaution. City Securities was to be engaged in a battle with the Inland Revenue over its claim for tax relief regarding 'certain arrangements which were intended to mitigate the impact of taxation' in the period from March 1978 to September 1980. The matter was still unresolved when David Young discovered he was still a director and resigned in January 1983. However, by June 1984 City Securities had withdrawn its claim for relief and agreed to pay £489,000 in tax and interest. 'When you turned around everyone was gone,' Mosselson says bitterly about all those who had encouraged and promoted tax schemes.

Just what losses Townwright made is unclear for the company was placed in voluntary liquidation in July 1980 and no accounts have been published for the period after July 1978. When the liquidation was finally completed in 1985 the company still faced unresolved tax assessments. Lord Young says that although he was still technically a director he had no knowledge of City Securities' activities after 1975.

Confirmation of Rossminster's City acceptability came in 1976 when Hambros, the merchant bank, bought Tucker's biggest tax scheme to date to eliminate a £6,200,000 corporation tax liability created by the successful development and sale of one of the City's largest office blocks. In the midsixties Hambros, the property developer Felix Fenston and the Prudential Assurance had joined forces to redevelop the Ethelburga site at the corner of Bishopsgate and Wormwood Street, and in 1972 Bishopsgate Developments was formed to undertake the project and lease the 320-foot-high building. The building, 99 Bishopsgate, was completed in spring 1976. Bishopsgate Developments then negotiated the sale of the lease to the building's main tenant, the Hong Kong & Shanghai Banking Corporation, for £32,350,000. This created a £6 million plus tax bill on the £24,641,000 capital profit. Enter Roy Tucker and the Gross Annuity Scheme, external version.

On 14 October 1976 Bishopsgate Developments was acquired by Sandplume, a corporate conduit via which companies passed on their way through the Company Purchase Scheme, then playing at St George's Elizabethan Theatre. The Berkeley Hambro and Fenston representatives were replaced on the board by William Halliwell and – for one day only, but the day on which the crucial tax scheme deal would be approved – by Gordon Taylor, who served as a director for a day on many scheme companies where Rossminster did not want two of its own making up the board. His role fulfilled, Taylor was replaced by Halliwell's constant companion in over 300 boardrooms, Nigel Bruce-Watt.

Bishopsgate Developments relied on External GAS to remove both the capital gain and its trading profits from taxation. Because the profits were so large, the numbers in the scheme needed to be equally impressive. For taking over an obligation to make five annuity payments of £15 million each, Bishopsgate received from an offshore company controlled by Rossminster a payment of £61,500,000. It made one £15 million payment to another Rossminster entity. Then, in order to escape the liability for making the other four payments, Bishopsgate paid £47,596,000 to yet another offshore Rossminster vassal company, leaving a surplus of £13,904,000. The benefit from External GAS was that while the annuity payment was allowable against tax the surplus resulting from the disposal of the annuity liability was a capital item and so not taxable. The net result therefore was that the bulk of the proceeds from the sale of 99 Bishopsgate were available to be paid over to St George's on the other side of the Company Purchase Scheme. Before expenses the charity received a donation of £25,940,000 – the largest it was ever paid.

The Berkeley Hambro and Fenston interests sold Bishopsgate Developments to St George's for £24,600,000, its profit on the property, realising a profit on their investment of £18 million on which tax at a maximum of 18 per cent instead of 52 per cent was paid. Tucker's fee would have been at least 10 per cent of the tax saved – £600,000. In addition he and Rossminster now had a slice of the £7,750,000 left from the £32,350,000 sale proceeds of the building, which was taken in fees, bank charges and interest, leaving a modest amount for the charity whose tax-exempt status had made the whole exercise possible.

The Inland Revenue, however, was not impressed by this disappearing trick. It slapped in an assessment for corporation tax on profits of £10 million. The company appealed against the estimated assessment. Relying on the legal opinions in the Tucker package it declared: 'In the opinion of the directors on the basis of leading tax counsel's opinion and on the basis of legislation in force at the time the transactions were effected . . . there will be no liability to corporation tax.' They and Tucker were wrong. In September 1982 Bishopsgate Developments was put into liquidation on the grounds of tax liabilities totalling £6,246,000, against which it had assets of precisely £947.

The leading Lloyd's insurance group Minet were another prestigious City customer. They engaged in a Tucker/Rossminster scheme during 1977 to remove the corporation tax liability on profits of £6 million, from the sale of certain investments. Once again External GAS was used. Once again the Inland Revenue were not persuaded and put in an assessment for corporation tax on the £6 million. For four years Minet resisted on the basis of the legal advice which came with the scheme, but in 1981 it conceded defeat and provided for a tax payment of £2,387,000.

Minet was not Rossminster's only Lloyd's client. Brookgate Investments was the holding company for the Lloyd's agencies run by the underwriters Raymond Brooks and Terence Dooley who acted for 700 'names' with money in their underwriting syndicates. Unknown to the 'names' whose money backed the syndicates' insurance activities, Brooks and Dooley had set up an offshore reinsurance company in Bermuda, Fidentia Marine Insurance, into which they channelled highly profitable reinsurance business. By 1978 Fidentia controlled assets worth over £7 million created from the premium income siphoned away into it. Rossminster were at all times unaware of the purpose to which Brooks and Dooley were putting Fidentia.

Brooks and Dooley decided to sell Fidentia below the market valuation, to reduce their liability for UK tax, and then secretly repurchase it through a Bermuda discretionary trust of which their families would be the beneficiaries. Brookgate sold Fidentia to a subsidiary of Bermuda Fire & Marine Insurance, with which it carried out a lot of reinsurance business, for £895,500 in March 1978 realising a £858,000 profit. To avoid £300,000 in UK tax it had previously issued 4000 7½ per cent redeemable participating preference shares to Senatering, a Rossminster nominee company. As there were only 1000 Brookgate ordinary shares it could now be claimed that Brookgate was a Senatering subsidiary and so was part of the St George's charity. Brookgate and Senatering would then avoid the tax liability by way of group election, with the latter making an un-covenanted donation of its profits to the parent company, the charity, which was tax-exempt.

Now that UK tax had been avoided, Brooks and Dooley secretly repurchased Fidentia. It continued to have the benefit of the 'names'' money until 1982, by which time it had received more than £6 million. When this was discovered in 1982, Lloyd's ordered an investigation which resulted, two years later, in Brooks being expelled and Dooley suspended.[1] Nor did Brookgate avoid paying the £300,000 it owed in tax: challenged by the Inland Revenue in 1982, it admitted defeat and provided for the payment.

The company used for the Minet tax scheme, Miltonworth, was one of the scheme companies which ended up being owned by Kemforth, which had been set up in May 1976 and was controlled by Rossminster's in-house multidirector, William Halliwell. It featured in several of the bigger tax schemes involving well-known corporate clients. Some insiders linked these deals with Godfrey Bradman, who, when his banking and property ventures suffered after the 1973–4 crash, returned – discreetly – to selling tax schemes. While keeping a low profile with the Inland Revenue, he steered clients to Tucker and Rossminster.[2] Tucker had always acknowledged Bradman's innovative genius. According to some who saw the two tax gurus together, Tucker was in awe of Bradman, whom he considered his only intellectual superior, crediting him with spotting the charity loophole. Others were less impressed. One Tucker associate complained of the ritual which had to be observed at a meeting with Bradman. 'Bradman just sat there with his hands clasped as if praying. You had to type your name on a piece of paper each time you went to see him. You couldn't smoke. You couldn't eat meat.'

But Roy Tucker was only too happy to accept Bradman's clients and assistance in return for a slice of a larger than average fee. Bradman would provide a scheme of his own for the client as the 'front end', transferring the tax liability to a Bradman-controlled company. Tucker's role would be to come up with the 'back end', to take over that Bradman company and wash out the tax liability. This usually meant using the Company Purchase Scheme and External GAS. Tucker and Bradman split the fees equally but some on Tucker's side felt Bradman was doing too little for too much, especially as it was Tucker who was left with the clients' 'dirty washing'. But just how lucrative this alliance of erstwhile rivals could be was evidenced when Bradman and Tucker teamed up on the biggest tax scheme Rossminster ever handled.

During 1976 the Institute of Chartered Accountants changed the basis on which it recommended that long-term civil-engineering contracts should be treated in company accounts. The ICA advised that auditors should now ensure that companies took credit for part of the expected profit less any allowance for losses in each year that work was in progress on the contract. This meant that in the first year of this change in accounting policy it would also be necessary to adjust previous years' figures to reflect the new policy.

When George Wimpey, one of the largest international contracting groups, came to apply this new approach to its 1976 accounts they had to make adjustments to prior years' profits of £21,700,000 which was then added to reserves. But the Inland Revenue informed Wimpey that it considered these profits to be taxable in that year even though the profit had not yet been received by the company. Wimpey found this suggestion unacceptable but offered to pay tax on the amount spread over five years. The Revenue refused this offer. With the end of its financial year in December 1976 fast approaching, Wimpey turned to its auditors, Deloitte Haskins & Sells.

Two weeks before end of the year Colin Emson was contacted to see if he could come up with a solution. As speed was of the essence and he wanted to avoid a competiton for the enormous fee at stake, Emson decided to use both Tucker and Bradman, but for different reasons. 'Tucker was the best for concepts but Bradman was the best for paperwork. Roy's documents always looked like the nineteenth photocopy of the nineteenth photocopy whereas Godfrey's were on parchment-style best-quality paper.' According to Tom Benyon, Rossminster were not too sure about becoming involved in the Wimpey scheme and confronting the Inland Revenue head-on over such a large amount of tax. 'But you couldn't turn down a £1 million fee.'

The scheme Tucker and Bradman devised involved the use of GAS applied to a dormant Wimpey subsidiary which could then pass on the tax loss the scheme generated for the benefit of its parent company. The company chosen was Wimpey Laing Esfahan. The scheme went into effect on 23 December 1976, eight days before the end of Wimpey's financial year and nine days after Colin Emson had first been approached.

First, Wimpey Laing Esfahan purchased an annuity contract from Hamme Investments, a very active Wimpey subsidiary, for £35,154,000 which it paid with the aid of a bank loan. Six days later W L E, now owned by Kemforth, received a £35 million payment as an annuity from Hamme. The £35 million annuity payment was tax-deductible so Wimpey now had a £35 million charge against its profits which would produce corporation tax relief of £18,200,000. The cost of the exercise to Wimpey, including all expenses, was £2,800,000, paid to Cortongreen Financial Services, part of Bradman's London Mercantile group. The fee worked out at £2,300,000 gross or £1,800,000 net and would have been split equally between Tucker/Rossminster, Bradman/London Mercantile and Emson, but Tucker was so impressed that, over colleagues' objections, he renegotiated the fee split more in Bradman's favour. The fee paid and the tax supposedly saved, Rossminster and Kemforth were left to unscramble the annuity contract between W L E, soon renamed Farmost, and Hamme. It did this by entering into another similar G A S arrangement, this time with a Rossminster associate offshore.

Buttressed by the legal opinions which came with G A S and the as yet undiminished reputations of Bradman and Tucker as tax gurus, Wimpey were confident that all this paper-shuffling would result in saving the company £18 million in tax. 'As a result of transactions during the year, the directors are hopeful that a tax benefit, equivalent to the greater part of the 1976 charge for taxation, may become available,' stated the company's accounts sent to shareholders in May 1977. Wimpey were reassured by the fact that Bradman had agreed to pay the costs of a test case up to £30,000 plus up to another £30,000 to pursue appeals. However, Wimpey's confidence did not extend to discussing the workings or merits of the Tucker/Bradman scheme with outsiders. At the *Sunday Times* Lorana Sullivan, alerted by an anonymous telephone caller to the significance of the small note in Wimpey's accounts, contacted their finance director Harry Norris, who confined himself to saying that the arrangements were 'singularly complex'. A few days later she was contacted again, this time to arrange a meeting with her anonymous informant. At the meeting Lorana Sullivan was handed a package of documents by an intermediary repre-senting a lawyer who had acted for Bradman. 'It was a simple grudge. He was owed money,' she explains. The documents were copies of those setting out the Wimpey scheme. Harry Norris once again declined to discuss the transactions – 'it would be against the interests of our shareholders.' Lorana Sullivan published the outline of the £18 million scheme in the *Sunday Times* on 27 May 1977.

In a note referring to the scheme, Wimpey had informed shareholders: 'As a matter of prudence no credit has been taken in these accounts.' This proved very prudent indeed.

For a major company like Wimpey, a relaxed relationship with the Inland Revenue is important. Accounting for every item of expenditure, especially overseas, is impossible – yet that is what the Revenue could require before accepting such expenditure as allowable against tax. Wimpey suddenly found the Revenue very lacking in understanding when it was revealed that they had done the Tucker/Bradman scheme, in particular over the granting of exemptions from collecting the tax due on payments made to its self-employed labour force. Wimpey soon got the message, but so did the Revenue. It could avoid the lengthy process of litigating to collect the £18 million if it would accept that the tax would be paid over a number of years, as Wimpey had initially suggested, as the profits on which it was based were received. Within a year a deal had been done and Wimpey agreed to drop its claim for the tax relief generated by the Tucker/Bradman scheme. Not only had Wimpey obtained the Revenue's agreement to a phased payment of the tax due on the change in accountancy practice but by the use of accepted tax reliefs, such as stock relief and capital allowances, it had removed much of even that tax liability.[3]

The use of artificial tax avoidance by a major public company like Wimpey made the Inland Revenue worry that other household names could follow suit. Clients of the calibre of Wimpey gave tax-scheme promoters like Tucker respectability. Tom Benyon for one believes that the Wimpey deal marked the point where the Revenue decided that Rossminster had gone too far.

Wimpey were not the only captains of industry who availed themselves of Tucker's brand of tax avoidance. The Salmon and Gluckstein families, founders of the food and catering group J. Lyons, had substantial property interests through a private company, Group Houses, which became a customer for the Advanced Interest Scheme. Group Houses entered into the Company Purchase Scheme and was acquired by St George's in March 1976.[4]

From the beginning, small public companies had been quick to become Rossminster clients. Among these were the SGB building-materials group; Mercantile Credit; the hotel and electronics group AVP Industries, run by the millionaire Harold Poster (it did two schemes, each to avoid tax on about £400,000 in profits); the clothing company Helene of London; the Midlands engineers Deritend Stamping; the furniture makers Restmor; and Hampson Industries and Hill & Smith, engineering firms headed by the Midlands millionaire Tom Silk, vice chairman of West Bromwich Albion football club, who did schemes to avoid over £200,000 in tax.

However, the experience of the housebuilders Alfred Walker & Son illustrates how tax schemes solved some short-term problems but in the longer term created others. The Birmingham company became a client of Rossminster in 1975, introduced by its auditors, Bloomer Heaven, and did three Tucker schemes – Advanced Interest, Reverse Annuity and one involving an increase in the base value of its assets. The tax saving was to be £300,000 but none of the schemes was accepted by the Revenue and by 1980 the potential exposure, including interest, was approaching £500,000, a figure the company could not pay without 'severe cash flow problems'. It was able to negotiate a deal with the Inland Revenue involving the payment of just £67,000 in development land and corporation tax, and £13,000 in expenses. Like Wimpey, Walker was able to use up other, acceptable tax deductions for the rest.

Not surprisingly, Rossminster found a ready audience among Plummer's fellow alumni from the Slater, Walker academy of financial science, especially for the individual income tax schemes. Chitfield Enterprises, whose directors included Slater's former assistant Charles Harris, was a participant in the Company Purchase Scheme. One of the earliest clients, from 1973, was Slater protégé Michael Buckley, whose company Dundee, Perth and London Securities owned most of the Falkland Islands at one time. Buckley's relationship with Tucker and Rossminster caused some internal dissension and subsequently considerable public embarrassment for Buckley. The final accolade came when Jim Slater himself became a client. After he quit Slater, Walker in 1975 Slater, backed by several of his fellow City financiers such as James (now Lord) Hanson, 'Tiny' Rowland and Oliver Jessel, went into property dealing. Twice companies linked to the self-described 'minus millionaire' – Bripalm Properties and Kentshourne Properties, both subsidiaries of Slater's company Strongmead – became clients for Tucker schemes, in 1977 and 1979.

Rossminster also found favour with two of Tucker's and Plummer's fellow graduates of the Arthur Andersen academy – Christopher Bailey and Brian Duffy. Bailey and Duffy had introduced clients through their company Trinity Professional Services; then in 1976 they took over a little-known Lancashire building company, Brown & Jackson, and turned it into one of the stock market's high flyers of the late seventies. By 1979 its profits had grown to almost £5 million, helped by an aggressive acquisition policy and the lavish use of tax-avoidance schemes, especially those involving 'losses' generated through commodity dealing. For that one year alone no fewer than three schemes were used to avoid tax totalling £1,038,000.[5]

But the greatest inroads made by Rossminster and Tucker were among the ranks of successful private companies, where the impact of 52 per cent corporation tax on profits plus 98 per cent income tax on dividends, together with Capital Gains Tax and Development Land Tax, were felt most keenly. As 'close' companies they had to pay out most of their net profits.

National Car Parks is one of Britain's biggest postwar business success stories. It was started by Donald Gosling and Ronald Hobson with £200 on a rented bomb site in central London. By 1974 profits had passed the £1 million mark and NCP was the largest company of its kind in Europe. The more extrovert of the two partners, Don Gosling, had friends in the Labour Party and was knighted in the 1976 resignation honours of Harold Wilson. By the time of his knighthood NCP was already seeking substantially to avoid paying taxes the Labour government had imposed. During 1976 and 1977 NCP sought to avoid £1,200,000 in corporation tax through using Tucker's Gross Annuity Scheme.

From 1975 onwards a string of highly successful family-owned companies entered the Rossminster portals in Hanover Square. Among these were John Swire, the old-established Far East trading group who control Cathay Pacific Airlines; Underwoods, the high-street chemist chain; and the Olympus camera distributors David Williams. Sir John Betjeman's son-in-law Rupert Lycett-Green, owner of Blades, the Savile Row tailors, was involved in a company which sought to avoid tax on a Yorkshire land deal. By coincidence Betjeman had once been inspired to write a poem by St George's church, in the days before it became a vehicle for tax avoidance.

In 1975 Arthur Fenton Hill held the highly lucrative franchises for the dutyfree shops at Heathrow airport, but these were to expire the following year. Far from certain of renewing these gold mines, Hill was concerned to preserve as much as possible of his profit. His lawyer was Jerrold Moser, who had worked with Tucker and Plummer on the Exempt Debt Scheme and resumed his links with them after Tom Benyon had informed him of Rossminster's creation and asked if he had any potential clients. As a result, in 1975 Hill did two Advance Interest schemes. The Inland Revenue, however, did not accept the claim for tax relief. With the Heathrow leases gone Hill chose to fight, relying on Tucker's legal opinions. By 1979 the Revenue were claiming a total of £2,050,000 in tax and interest. In 1982 Hill surrendered and paid £1,003,00. Not paying an original £720,000 corporation tax bill had proved a very expensive decision.

Helene of London had a similar experience. A 1976 bid to save £620,000 ended up by 1983 costing £1,100,00 including interest.

Rossminster also attracted others who were no slouches at exploiting tax loopholes. Maritime Fruit Carriers had been built up by the Israelis Yaacov Meridor and Mila Brener, using the incentives offered by Britain and other countries in the early seventies to obtain orders for their depressed shipbuilding industries. MFC would then sell the vessels or their tax benefits to companies wanting to reduce their own tax bills. By 1976 the shipping market had collapsed and the incentives had been considerably reduced by legislation. MFC could only survive by selling its remaining operating vessels, but this created a tax liability the near bankrupt company could not meet. In 1977 Meridor and Brener came to Rossminster to take advantage of the Company Purchase Scheme. Three MFC companies – Chichester Shipping Lines, Savannah Shipping, and Elsden Shipping Lines – steamed off to Blessingwell with corporation tax assessments for £10 million. These were still unresolved when the companies were put into voluntary liquidation in July 1980.[6]

But the most bountiful source of business for Rossminster was from the world of property. The 1973–74 property collapse and the subsequent Labour tax rates convinced those property developers and dealers who still had profits to cash them in as it seemed most unlikely that there would be similar money to be made in the future. This produced the first wave of clients for Tucker and Rossminster in 1974 and 1975. But once the crisis had passed, the Bank of England lifeboat had been launched and interest rates had fallen, it became possible to make money in property as before, and there was a steady stream of developers and dealers looking to avoid capital gains tax and the new development land tax introduced in 1976.

One of the most unusual of the property men who became a client was Kenneth Frampton, a London property developer and accountant who had discovered evangelical Christianity in his fifties. He had donated money and a home to a variety of controversial sects and formed a religious charity. Frampton had once owned the site of the Post Office Tower in London. Between December 1975 and March 1976 he sold three property companies to St George's. The companies faced tax assessments on profits of £8,500,000.[7]

Trevor Osborne had been a council chartered surveyor and had gone into property development in the Thames Valley with just £100 of capital during the late sixties. He had founded the Speyhawk group in 1973 and attracted considerable publicity when, at thirty-four, he bought the entire picturesque Cornish fishing village of Porthleven for £400,000 in 1977 to redevelop it. 'I'm a hard-working businessman, not a philanthropic society,' he declared in response to criticism of his plans. 'It's a great shame and sadness to me that there is envy today towards a man with ambition and a man who has achieved his ambition. Yes, wealth is still possible. It's just a little harder.' That's where Rossminster came in. Osborne, active in local Conservative politics, became a client in February 1978 when one of his companies faced a tax bill for at least £350,000.[8]

Rossminster mirrored the Britain of the seventies – all business life was there, united by the common purpose of seeking to avoid tax. One of the boom businesses of the years from 1975 onwards were the gambling casinos, especially those in the West End. Prevented by the civil war in Lebanon from gambling in Beirut, Arabs carrying millions in petrodollars flocked to London, making it Europe's most profitable gambling centre attracting over £750 million a year.

The Victoria Sporting Club was one of the first and largest London casinos, earning more than £1 million a year. Since 1970 it had been run and half-owned by Cyril Levan. The VSC was a banking client of First London Securities, depositing large sums from the previous night's gambling at the bank in Hanover Square, so it was not surprising that Levan should turn to Rossminster when he had a tax problem over a property company he and his solicitor owned. What was surprising was that Rossminster should agree to take him as a client, for in November 1978 the VSC had been raided by officers from Scotland Yard's Serious Crimes Squad and Gaming Board officials. Levan was subsequently charged with theft and Gaming Act offences relating to the alleged underdeclaration or 'skimming' of more than £1 million in casino takings. In March 1979, while Levan was on bail, Tucker and Rossminster arranged a Company Purchase Scheme tax deal for the property company. Levan was acquitted at the Old Bailey in 1981.

All these and dozens of other clients were brought to Tucker and Rossminster by a wide circle of so-called introducers and beyond them what became a nationwide network of professional advisers, some lawyers but mostly accountants. The introducers consisted of self-described tax specialists, financial consultants, insurance and investment advisers whose ranks had been swelling throughout the sixties and seventies as more and more individuals entered the market for life insurance, pension plans, custom-built investment packages and, from 1974 onwards, tax avoidance. Most of these experts were little more than upgraded insurance salesmen. Most indeed had started out as insurance brokers selling high-commission, unit-trust-linked insurance policies which had been mass-marketed from the late sixties on the back of the rising stock market and inflation. Some were professionally qualified accountants; many were qualified by little more than the right background (public school, army officer), the right accent, a personable approach and the right West End address. Either professionally or socially they were plugged into innumerable potential sources of business. It was a small step from discussing life insurance with its built-in tax advantages to discussing the clients' whole business or personal financial situation and requirements, especially when their motivation for taking out large insurance or pension policies was to avoid tax.

A handful of these tax planners and financial or investment consultants were Tucker's and Rossminster's main source of business – men like Simon Cardale, Tim Nicholas, who had joined forces with John Arthur to form Centrespur, and Colin Emson of Emson & Dudley (introduced to Tucker and Plummer by Cardale when he was marketing the Reverse Annuity Scheme). There were also the commission-hungry salesmen of more prestigious rivals like Towry Law, Antony Gibbs and Lowndes Lambert. Cardale was so successful he ended up buying the Company Purchase Scheme for his own company. John Arthur and an ex-Slater, Walker colleague, Peter Berry, took over a public company, London Investment Trust.

Colin Emson was probably the most successful of all the introducers, earning more than £500,000 on top of the £600,000 he took from the Wimpey deal. Of the 600 clients whom he advised to do tax schemes, at least half went to Tucker and Rossminster. Between 1971 and 1978 he put clients into most of Roy Tucker's schemes. He even bought two Tucker schemes for his own personal use. 'We were only dealing with the froth on the top of the pint of beer. We weren't touching the body,' he explains in justification.

Rossminster were also assisted by the support of some of the larger major accountancy firms. Thornton Baker, whose senior tax partner Philip Hardman was a regular BBC voice on tax matters, had sixty offices around the country. 'To suitable clients who had sufficient profits we said "these schemes are available". We did not recommend the schemes merely told of their existence. If we did not tell the clients other firms would,' Hardman explains. He passed on a similar message when contacted by other accountants from smaller firms.

These formed part of the most potent sales force for Rossminster, the network of local professional advisers, the accountants and lawyers in the London suburbs, the Midlands and the north of England on whom many of Britain's family businesses relied for advice. Once word spread along that professional grapevine of the Saviour of North Audley Street and the miracles he was working Rossminster was ensured of a stream of eager believers.

The Tucker gospel was propagated by word of mouth among friends and business acquaintances, golfing partners and drinking companions as well as wherever professional advisers met. Within a year or two every accountant knew someone whose client had done 'an awfully clever tax scheme' which probably came out of the Tucker stable. The introducers hawked their Tucker wares in advertisements and at seminars, wherever the word could be spread.

For those facing Healey's confiscatory tax rates the Tucker alternative did not take much selling, especially when it was presented by smooth salesmen in impressively plush offices, giftwrapped in a slick package that included the reassurance of legal opinions from eminent QCs and Roy Tucker's fighting fund to take on the Revenue in a test case. To most clients it was irresistible. 'He played on people's greed,' says one accountant, several of whose clients did business with Tucker and Rossminister but came to regret it.

THERE'S NO BUSINESS LIKE
SHOW BUSINESS

The seventies was the decade in which the record industry became a worldwide megabuck business. Elvis Presley, the Beatles and the Rolling Stones had been among the first pop millionaires. New rock stars and teenybopper idols immediately had a multimillion-pound earning capacity from record sales, concerts and films.

The British members of this largely ephemeral elite were quickly faced by substantial tax problems. Some, like Mick Jagger and John Lennon, solved these by living abroad; others set up company structures offshore to mitigate the effects. Those who remained in Britain could keep very little of their earnings to finance the obligatory life in the fast lane. Furthermore, fashions in music are as fickle as any public taste – life at the top of the pop charts could be very lucrative but very brief, and the champagne and Rolls-Royces would soon disappear unless the earnings from the golden days had been preserved. All too many pop stars had already ended up being bankrupted by the Inland Revenue for tax that was never paid because they had believed that the music and the cash would never stop.

The pop world proved a receptive audience for Rossminster's proposals for minimising tax on high incomes and preserving capital. One of the first to take the Rossminster road was a record company, Arcade Records, a small independent outfit without particular big names. It was the first company to use TV extensively to advertise its records – especially its cut-price collections of recent hits or hits from the fifties and sixties. Its auditors were Wilson, Wright, a City firm with a large show-business clientele, many of whom it put into Tucker tax schemes. It also acted for many of the companies which were put through the Company Purchase Scheme.

Another Wilson, Wright client to be put into a Tucker tax scheme was the singer and songwriter Gilbert O'Sullivan, managed by Management Agency & Music, which also handled the singers Tom Jones and Engelbert Humperdinck. MAM's finance director Bill Smith was a former partner in Wilson, Wright, and several MAM artists and senior executives became Tucker clients.

In 1973 Gilbert O'Sullivan at twenty-six was one of the world's top pop stars after hits like 'Clare', 'Alone Again' and 'Get Down'. That year he was advised to do the Advanced Interest Scheme in order to avoid tax of more than £400,000.

By the time it became clear that the Advanced Interest Scheme might not work, O'Sullivan no longer had the cash to pay the tax that the Inland Revenue were demanding. Independently advised by new accountants, O'Sullivan negotiated an unusual deal with the taxman – he agreed to pay the tax and the Inland Revenue agreed to await the outcome of a civil action he had commenced against MAM challenging the terms of his contract and seeking a greater slice of more than £14 million in record royalties. In March 1985 O'Sullivan received £2 million in an out-of-court settlement, and paid the Inland Revenue an estimated £600,000 including £170,000 in interest plus some minor penalties. Without the legal windfall he would have had to sell assets in order to meet the tax debt the Tucker scheme was supposed to have removed. That matter resolved, Gilbert O'Sullivan joined the tax exiles in Jersey.

A superstar whom Rossminster claimed to have enlisted as a client was the ex-Beatle George Harrison. He was said to have done a personal income tax scheme to save £100,000 for 1977/78. Tom Benyon and Barry Pilkington were only too pleased to boast about their new client while the secretaries in North Audley Street waxed lyrical about the quiet multi-millionaire. 'I learned somewhere over the past twenty years to close my eyes and sign cheques and not end up in the slammer' is how Harrison describes his way with money.[1] In fact his finances are handled through top-class accountants and professional advisers; the introduction to Rossminster was said to have come through a firm of City lawyers.

The biggest tax-scheme client to emerge from the megamillionaires of pop was Led Zeppelin, four British rock musicians who, without releasing singles, had sold 20 million LPs in the twelve years from 1968 to 1980 and consistently played to capacity crowds at concerts around the world. The lead singer Robert Plant and the guitarist Jimmy Page wrote most of the group's music and so had two bites at the royalty cherry. Another big – 20 per cent – bite was taken by their manager Peter Grant. Like most entertainers, each member of Led Zeppelin had formed a service company through which he received royalties and other income in order to substitute corporation tax for income tax. Corporation tax would be payable at the lower rate on profits considerably reduced by their salaries as directors plus expenses; income tax would be paid only on the salary and would be much less than if paid on the gross income of the company. In both 1976 and 1977 Jimmy Page earned £180,000 while Robert Plant's earnings exceeded £90,000; over the two years Peter Grant earned £243,000; and the two other group members, the bass guitarist John Paul Jones and the drummer John Bonham, each earned more than £100,000.

Despite the service companies and a period as tax exiles, Led Zeppelin faced a huge tax problem in realising the royalty income accumulating in the companies. This totalled £3,668,000 at the start of 1978 – Page's share alone was almost £1 million; Plant's and Grant's over £700,000 each. Ahead of the end of the 1977/78 tax year Led Zeppelin decided to tackle the problem with the aid of the classical music-loving Roy Tucker. Between 23 March and 4 April 1978, the four musicians and their manager resigned as directors following the purchase of the companies by St George's. Jimmy Page Enterprises, More Luck than Judgement (formerly Robert Plant Enterprises), Peer Grant, Dormouse Music (Jones) and Things That Go Bump in the Night (Bonham) made un-covenanted donations to St George's totalling £3,830,000, representing anticipated royalty income. These donations included a potential 24 per cent profit to Rossminster plus 2 per cent for the charity – the discount at which the cash assets had been purchased.

Shortly afterwards tax assessments on profits of £1 million were placed on both the Page and Grant companies. In total the Revenue claimed corporation tax on £2,270,000 from the five companies.

The wrangling between the Inland Revenue and Led Zeppelin's advisers, who did not now include Rossminster, continued until 1984 before an agreement was reached. The total settlement made was in the region of £2,400,000, including not just the corporation tax they had sought to avoid (£1,300,000) but also overdue PAYE income tax on their director's salaries. It was one of the largest settlements ever made by the Inland Revenue. Page, Plant and Grant all agreed to pay £500,000 to £750,000 each. (Bonham died in 1980.) They avoided having to pay interest as all but Grant had at an early stage purchased tax certificates which could then be used to meet the tax bill. All they had obtained from Tucker and Rossminster in the end was a six-year delay in meeting that bill.

In 1978 Roy Tucker recruited the services of the film star Roger Moore, better known as James Bond, to help solve a pressing Rossminster tax problem in return for helping 007 escape from the taxman's clutches. For this Tucker had his personal solicitor John Stutter, who also acted for Roger Moore, to thank.

In 1964 Moore, then best known from TV's *The Saint*, set up a UK service company, R. M. Enterprises, 'to exploit for all purposes the name and reputation of Roger Moore by any medium in any part of the world'. The company was owned by Moore, his wife, his brother and his agent David Greenwood. Roger Moore's career took off from 1973 when he took over as James Bond. Although Moore lived abroad, R. M. Enterprises continued in business, its profits healthy but unspectacular – for 1977 they were only £44,000. But in the year to December 1978 profits were expected to exceed £400,000, heralding an expensive tax problem.

Tucker and Plummer, too, had an unexpected tax problem building up in their Manx bank, Rossminster Acceptances (IOM). The bank had had a very successful year but its profits would have to be paid as a dividend to its parent company Rossminster Holdings. Under Section 478 of the Income and Corporation Taxes Act – designed to stop the transfer of assets abroad by UK residents to avoid tax – the Revenue could tax either the UK settler or the UK beneficiary of a foreign trust on any income it received. To date the Keith, Leander and Ulysses trusts in Guernsey had avoided Section 478's net by ensuring that the trusts only received and disclosed capital profits which, unlike income, were not assessable for tax. But with the inception of Rossminster Holdings, owned by the trusts, and the impending need for Rossminster Acceptances to pay over its profits as a dividend, this defence could be breached – and the Inland Revenue could assess Tucker, Plummer or their families for those profits.

James Bond to the rescue. Tucker and Rossminster agreed with Roger Moore's advisers a deal which would solve all their problems: R. M. Enterprises would buy Rossminster Acceptances with its profits and then speedily sell the bank to Eureka Productions, a film company controlled by Tucker and Moore's lawyer John Stutter, David Greenwood's widow and Moore's agent Dennis van Thal, Eureka would equally speedily sell

Top Ronald Plummer and Roy Tucker ended six years of subterfuge with this 1979 photograph and the admission that their family trusts jointly controlled Rossminster. *Photo: Financial Times. Bottom Left* Tom Benyon, whose role as a junior partner in Rossminster cost him his career as a Conservative M P. *Photo: Universal Pictorial Press and Agency Ltd. Bottom right* Tax barrister Desmond Miller became Rossminster's chairman, describing as 'boy scout morality' criticisms of its activities. *Photo: Brian J. Green.*

Opposite top This unremarkable semi-detached house in a quiet street of Tankerton, Kent was home for dozens of companies at the end of their journey through a Tucker tax scheme. *Opposite bottom* Nettlestead Place, the Kent manor house which is still home for the now bankrupt Tucker, even though he does not own it. *Above* The Bayswater town house near Hyde Park provided for Plummer by a generous offshore company.

Top left Property developer George Miller, who became Rossminster's first big client. *Photo: Granada Television. Top right* Chartered accountant Godfrey Bradman, most successful and far-sighted of the tax-avoidance gurus. *Photo: Universal Pictorial Press and Agency Ltd. Bottom* Cartoonist Michael Heath helped the *Sunday Times* in 1976 to explain the essentials of Tucker's Advance Interest tax scheme.

Three for the 'Sark Lark'. *Top left* John York, part-time manager of the island's only bank. *Photo: Guernsey Evening Press.* *Top right* Martin Joyner receiving a telephone call at his camera shop from Rossminster in Guernsey to warn him that he is about to appear in a 1980 *World in Action* documentary about Rossminster. *Left* Patricia Falle had ordered the film crew off her farm a little earlier, before alerting Rossminster to their presence on the island. *Photos: Granada Television.*

Top left Inland Revenue Chairman Sir William Pile who gave the go-ahead for the Rossminster raids. *Top right* Rossminster's man in Guernsey Arthur Lewis-Grey whose 'whistle blowing' resulted in the raids. *Photo: Granada Television. Bottom* The hole-in-the-wall at Lower Little Pollet, St Peter Port into which vanished 55 packing cases filled with Rossminster documents from London. *Photo: Granada Television.*

Top left A very relieved Tucker outside the High Court after escaping with a £1000 fine following the disappearance of his vital desk diaries. *Photo: Jack Mainwaring. Top right* Tucker's secretary Lynette Binks whose efficiency caused Tucker's vital desk diaries to disappear. *Photo: Jack Mainwaring. Bottom* Rossminster P.R. man William Taylor, who preferred fiction to facts. *Photo: Syndication International.*

Three lawyers with very different views of Tucker's tax schemes. *Top left* Peter Rees QC, the Conservative MP, who said they worked and defended them in Parliament. *Photo: Universal Pictorial Press and Agency Ltd. Top right* Lord Templeman, the judge who consistently ruled against artificial schemes from the High Court to the House of Lords. *Photo: Press Association. Left* Lord Wilberforce, the senior tax Law Lord who provided their death knell. *Photo: Camera Press Ltd.*

Rossminster Acceptances and its profits back to Rossminster Holdings; in addition both R. M. Enterprises and Eureka would be acquired by Blessingwell through the Company Purchase Scheme. This way Rossminster would realise the profit in the bank not as income but as a capital gain and so dodge Section 478. The vendors of R. M. and Eureka would end up with 74 per cent of their net asset value instead of 48 per cent.

This clever deal slipped into operation in December 1978 when R. M. Enterprises, with the aid of a £193,000 bank loan, probably from Rossminster, bought Rossminster Acceptances (IOM) for £675,000. The valuation seems to have been based on the £500,000 share capital plus £175,000 in profits. Three days later, on 18 December, the shares in R. M. Enterprises were acquired by Blessingwell. The next day R. M. sold Rossminster Acceptances to Eureka for the price it had paid – £675,000. Eureka needed a £436,000 bank loan to afford the purchase. Twenty-four hours later Eureka too was inside Blessingwell; another twenty-four hours and Eureka had passed the Rossminster Acceptances parcel back to its original owner, once again for £675,000, the same price as six days before. Neither R. M. nor Eureka had seemingly made any gain from these transactions – indeed it had cost then £15,000 in loan commitment fees, possibly to Rossminster. The potential reward to R. M. and Eureka lay on the other side of the transaction once the GAS-powered Company Purchase Scheme had done its job. This had to be put into effect before the companies' financial years ended on 31 December. R. M. expected profits of £450,000, on which there would be a corporation tax liability of £234,000. Selling to Blessingwell for around £330,000 could leave the vendors £115,000 better off. A similar process happened with Eureka, whose profits were expected to be about £250,000.

By 31 December, just sixteen days after the clockwork operation began, it was over, with all parties assuming they could look forward to a much more profitable new year. But the Inland Revenue, as in all cases where it discovered the Company Purchase Scheme at work, challenged the annuity arrangements entered into by both companies, and slapped a corporation tax assessment on R. M. for profits of £600,000 and on Eureka for £350,000. Both companies appealed, but with assets of just £11,000 to meet a potential liability of £312,000, R. M. opted for voluntary liquidation in July 1980. The tax assessments still remain unresolved. Eureka was forced into a creditors' compulsory liquidation in July 1981 as a result of its potential tax liability of £144,000 against which it had assets of only £4000, and that too remains unresolved.

It could prove easier for James Bond to escape the attentions of his assorted villainous antagonists than for Roger Moore to outwit the Inland Revenue. Since neither R. M. Enterprises nor Eureka Productions is in a position to pay the corporation tax claimed, the Revenue is expected to apportion the tax liability among the previous and present owners of the company. This has been the tough approach adopted with many of the family-owned private companies that bought the Company Purchase Scheme.

Another leading figure from the British film industry who became involved with Rossminster, not in a personal tax scheme but to resolve a highly complex land deal, was Bryan Forbes, well known first as an actor and then as a writer, director and studio executive.

In the late fifties, a local solicitor Robert Mew and two partners bought 136 acres of land at Hurstwood Park, Waterlooville, just outside Portsmouth. Some 32 acres of the site had planning permission for development but the remainder did not. By December 1972 Mew and his partners had still not obtained planning permission, so they were extremely interested when a group of investors offered to buy them out even though they would have to wait until the planning issue could be solved and/or the land sold before they received the very nice agreed price of £1,350,000. The four-man investor group was headed by the barrister reckoned to be the leading legal authority on town planning and development, Kenneth Bagnall. Bagnall – who was to become a QC in 1973 and a crown court recorder three years later – was considered to have the legal expertise to break the stalemate over Hurstwood Park and allow development to begin. Bagnall, like Forbes, lived in the exclusive Surrey village of Virginia Water. The other two partners were both friends of Forbes – a local garage owner Edwin Bowlby and London property man Sidney Kaye.

By 1978 the land's value had risen to £4 million but now the Bagnall/ Forbes group faced two new problems. One was Development Land Tax. The second and more pressing problem was that after waiting six years for their money the Mew group were pressing to be bought out.

Rossminster agreed to finance the buying-out of the Mew group in Hurstwood Timber, the company formed to develop the site. Tim Nicholas and John Arthur – then running their own mini-Rossminster,

Centrespur, out of Audley House – also became involved through their company Optann Investments. For both Rossminster and Centrespur it looked like a potentially good deal since Hurstwood Timber was on the verge of selling all but 22 acres of the Waterlooville land for £3,200,000, making a profit of £2,645,000. A complex series of deals went ahead, starting on 27 March 1979. The A shareholders finally received their £1,350,000; the Bagnall Forbes group then sold Hurstwood Timber to Optann for £2,350,000. Optann sold Hurstwood Timber to St George's.

Forbes and friends put in £1 million of the cash received for Hurstwood into a new company, Zestime, and borrowed £3 million from Rossminster to take over Hurstwood's land-sale contracts. In order finally to realise the profit they had been anticipating for seven years, the Bagnall/Forbes group needed to obtain planning permission for the rump of the Waterlooville land and be able to sell it for an amount in excess of the net borrowings from Rossminster – but this they were not able to do. In October 1981 Rossminster appointed a receiver to Zestime, and it was wound up two years later.

Everyone but Bryan Forbes and his little league of gentleman investors had made money out of the Waterlooville acres. 'There was never any pay-out, just pay-in. I ended up considerably out of pocket,' Forbes says sourly. He estimated his loss at £6000–£7000.

Roy Tucker's involvement with the British film industry became far greater than his tangential role in the affairs of Roger Moore and Bryan Forbes. He and Rossminster became substantial backers of feature films. At least in the beginning this was as much a product of Tucker's interest in the arts as of Rossminster's search for new forms of tax scheme and the clients to buy them.

In 1976 Tucker met Don Boyd, a 28-year-old independent film director who was just completing his second, necessarily low-budget film. Boyd was introduced to Tucker by Tim Nicholas, whom he knew socially. Boyd's father had wanted him to be an accountant. Tucker was genuinely interested in films and became friendly enough with Boyd to ask if he would carry out an evaluation of the St George's theatre venture, with which Tucker was increasingly unhappy. 'He wanted a professional's view to confirm his own suspicions,' is how Boyd puts it. Boyd was withering in his criticism of the pilot video of *Romeo and Juliet* – 'It was amateurish, poorly filmed and had cost far too much.' Shortly after Tucker received Boyd's report, the video project was cancelled.

Tucker quizzed Boyd extensively about the way in which films were financed. Like all independent filmmakers, Boyd was always looking for backers, and when Tucker offered to put up finance both personally and through Rossminster for Boyd's company Kendon Films, this was especially welcome because Boyd's second feature film, *East of Elephant Rock*, received a mauling from the critics when it opened in January 1978. 'If any industry creditor had wanted to foreclose I would have had it financially,' Boyd says candidly. Through the family trusts in Guernsey and via the Manx company Hartopp, Tucker agreed to put up more than £100,000 for Kendon in return for a 49 per cent interest in a new company, Minbourne, which acquired all Boyd's interests for £700,000 in October 1978. First London Securities lent £30,000. This money was earmarked for Boyd's next project, *Sweet William*, written by Beryl Bainbridge, for which he had obtained the American actor Sam Waterston and the British actress Jenny Agutter. The new money went on the script and the actors.

Boyd still says that he believes Tucker's interest in films was very much a personal one – 'He told me he was winding down his tax activities.' However, it was not long before the tax-avoidance possibilities offered by film finance came to the fore. According to Don Boyd, the man responsible for this was not Tucker but Tim Nicholas, then running his Rossminster clone Centrespur. Nicholas suggested that if Tucker would produce a tax scheme he would market it, mainly through a new company, Audley House Consultants. He was supported in this by Barry Pilkington who owned that company with another Rossminster alumnus, the Australian lawyer John Elmgreen. Tom Benyon too was very interested in marketing a tax scheme via a new Rossminster spin-off, Manx-owned NAS Financial Services. Pilkington Elmgreen and Benyon had been the chief presenters of Tucker's schemes to clients.

Nicholas was not coming up with anything new. Like several of Tucker's tax schemes, this was an adaptation of someone else's idea. This idea, like the use of commodity dealing, had originated across the Atlantic. Using film finance as a tax shelter vehicle had been common in the United States for some years. Partnerships were marketed to provide finance for Hollywood in the same way as for oil or gas wells, with guaranteed tax deductions and the possibility of worthwhile profits. Other tax scheme promoters had already spotted the opportunities this offered.

One of these was Colin Emson, who in late 1977 began marketing limited partnerships in films to be made by the London company South Street Films and sold by the Manx-registered General Film Company. The promoters of this very successful tax shelter were the solicitor Alan Joelson together with John Daly and Derek Dawson of the Hemdale Group.[2]

It was soon seen that there could be a considerable market for a Tucker-hallmarked scheme to high income earners seeking equally high tax relief. Tucker did not take much persuading and Boyd did not need any persuading at all to agree to produce the package of films that was talked about as being financed by the clients of Audley House Consultants and the Rossminster bank. From dealing with a budget of £90,000 Don Boyd found himself presented with the opportunity to make five films costing £3 million.

The attraction of the film scheme relied on the peculiarities of the law relating to partnerships and the vagaries of film finance. Boyd through Kendon agreed to make five feature films for a fixed cost of £3 million – this money to be guaranteed by the Tucker and Plummer family trusts. Plummer was brought in strictly for the business opportunity – he showed little or no interest in the artistic side. The backing was to come from the Rossminster bank in London against these guarantees. A partnership was then formed·to produce each film, with Boyd or his wife Hilary as the general or managing partner in each one. Limited partnership interests were then sold to high income earners who would rather pay a 20 per cent fee to Audley House or NAS than 83 per cent to the Inland Revenue. The aim was to sell up to eighteen (the maximum number of partners allowed) partnerships – limited in liability to the extent of the investment each partner made – to provide 25 per cent of the production cost of each film, based on a figure guaranteed by Kendon. If the film ran over budget – as films usually do – Kendon, via the Tucker and Plummer trusts, would pick up the extra cost. Rossminster would provide the other 75 per cent of the film's budget against the Tucker and Plummer guarantees.

The reason films were an attractive tax shelter to the high income earner was that he would not just be able to write off his initial investment against his tax liability but four times that figure, as if the partnership had financed not 25 per cent but 100 per cent of the film's cost. The reason for this was a quirk in the law regarding partnership accounts. When the film was completed but before it was released to cinemas, the only asset of the partnership was the can of film which had cost, in the case of *Sweet*

William, £1 million to produce but which had no definable value. At that moment the partnership could close its books and draw up its first accounts, showing a loss of £1 million including the £750,000 owed to Rossminster. Each limited partner would have a pro rata share of that £1 million loss even though together they had only invested £250,000, because Rossminster was not a partner. So the £1 million loss could be claimed by the limited partners on the basis of four times their investment – a taxpayer who invested £25,000 would be able to claim relief of £100,000 against his income.

Once the loss had been established, the limited partners would be encouraged to sell all but a tiny residual interest in the partnership at about cost to Forwood, a Tucker-associated Manx company, or another offshore company controlled by the scheme promoters. Any profits from the film would then flow offshore. At the same time the Boyds would cease to be general partners, being replaced by an offshore-controlled UK company with directors in Bermuda and shareholders in the Isle of Man. The scheme promoters and the Tucker/Plummer interests would therefore expect to share any profits taxfree. The taxpayer would have made no gain on his investment but a threefold gain in tax relief, and by retaining a small interest in the partnership he could claim that the aim of the scheme was tax deferral, not tax avoidance, and that it was a commercial as distinct from an entirely artificial device. Rossminster would earn substantial fees and interest payments. The marketing companies would take a share of the 20 per cent fee along with the scheme promoters. And Don Boyd got to make five feature films at 25 per cent less than they would otherwise have cost in borrowed funds and stood to make a small profit as general partner. As ever, only the Inland Revenue stood to lose.

In addition to *Sweet William* the films Don Boyd was to make with the Inland Revenue's and Rossminster's assistance were *Scum*, a brutal story of life inside a Borstal which had been made as a TV play for the BBC but banned; *Hussy*, a vehicle for Helen Mirren as a nightclub hostess who becomes involved in a story of drugs and murder; Derek Jarman's version of *The Tempest* with the pop singer Toyah Wilcox; and *Blue Suede Shoes*, a semidocumentary about rock and roll in Britain. The total actual production cost was budgeted at £1,500,000 before adding on the financing, marketing and administrative costs.

Sweet William was by far the most expensive and ambitious. Nicholas,

Pilkington and Benyon began selling limited partnerships in Berwick Street Films in August 1978. Rossminster put up £710,000 for Kendon Films secured on the film print. By the end of March 1979 eighteen limited partners had joined, investing £251,000. A last-minute entrant on 15 March was Michael Orr, managing director of Colt Cars which imported Mitsubishi cars into Britain. Orr owned 51 per cent of Colt and had a substantial income as a result of its success. He invested £17,000. Orr said much about 'being patriotic' and that Colt paid '£50,000 a day in tax'. He and the other partners all retired from the partnership on 22 March to claim their tax deductions.

To help finance *Scum*, which was to cost about £250,000, limited partnerships were sold in the Berwick Street Films (A) partnership. Ten investors put in £86,000 between November 1978 and March 1979; the balance came from Rossminster. One of the first in was Barry Pilkington himself. The former England soccer star Terry Venables, then manager of Crystal Palace, invested £12,500, joined by the son of the Crystal Palace chairman. But the most celebrated and largest limited partner in the backing of *Scum* was the ace Lloyd's underwriter Ian Posgate, known as 'Goldfinger' because of his legendary successes in making money from underwriting marine insurance risks. Posgate ran the biggest insurance syndicate at Lloyd's. His own company had been acquired in 1970 by the Alexander Howden broking group and his earnings as a Howden director, including bonuses, had risen from £45,000 in 1977 to £165,000 in 1979. He was estimated to earn almost as much again from his other Lloyd's interests and investments in syndicates. Posgate was not only the highest earner in Lloyd's but one of the highest-paid people in Britain. Such success presented Posgate with a massive tax bill of at least £2000 a week, most of his Howden income being taxed at 83 per cent and his other, unearned income at 98 per cent. For the high-living, public-school educated Ian Posgate, *Scum* was a wonderful opportunity to lighten that load. He invested £31,250 with the prospect of collecting a tax relief worth £125,000. Michael Denby, his partner in the Posgate & Denby underwriting agency, invested £18,750.[3]

After being in the partnership for at most a month the limited partners in *Scum* left the stage on 6 April, establishing a tax loss for both the 1978/79 and 1979/80 tax years. By investing in one year and disinvesting in the next a taxpayer could spread the loss over the two years. A Forwood-owned company became general partner and later in 1979 the control was switched to another Manx company, Financial Enterprises, although the directors remained in Bermuda.

For *The Tempest* the Berwick Street Films (C) partnership was formed in January 1979. This time a Forwood-owned company was general partner from the start. An early limited partner was Nicholas Samuel, the accountant son of the City banker Peter Samuel, the brother of Viscount Bearsted and a director of the merchant bankers Hill, Samuel. He invested £15,000. At least £35,000 was raised towards the film's £180,000 budget. All the limited partners had stepped aside by May 1979 and control of the general partner passed to Financial Enterprises.

The Berwick Street Films (B) partnership was formed to make *Blue Suede Shoes*, which, at £150,000 was to be the least expensive of the five films. This partnership was also formed in January 1979 for the 1978/79 tax year. However, no limited partnerships appear to have been sold in that or in the Berwick Street Films *Hussy* partnership launched the following month to help raise its £300,000 cost. By July 1979 Rossminster was owed £1,100,000 by Kendon Films for advances against the five films which it held as security. These loans were covered by further security of deposits made with Rossminster by Financial Enterprises representing the Tucker and/or Plummer interests.

Scum opened in London in September 1979. It was the one undisputed success, well received both critically and at the box office, grossing £133,000 in a four-month run at one cinema. *Sweet William* lasted just one week in the West End in April 1980, and the takings were only £1700. *The Tempest* opened a week later and fared much better. *Hussy* followed a week later but proved a disappointment. *Blue Suede Shoes* was never released.

'Overall we broke even on the £1,500,000 production cost,' says Don Boyd. *Scum* he estimates made three times its cost. '*Sweet William*', he says, 'cost too much, was poorly distributed and will never recover its cost.' *The Tempest* 'will not cover its cost', and neither will *Hussy* – 'very disappointing'. But one in five was a success and that, says Don Boyd, is about the industry average. After producing a tiny £3000 profit on a £1,200,000 turnover in 1979, his own company, Minbourne, plunged to a £319,000 loss the following year.

Boyd himself says of his brief encounter with Roy Tucker and Rossminster, 'It enabled me to make my reputation.' But he was not helped in raising finance for his own subsequent films by his previous links with Tucker. 'The City was suspicious about the Rossminster link.' Boyd finally severed his links with Roy Tucker in 1984. The debentures issued to Hartopp were repaid and the 49 per cent interest in Minbourne was bought out. 'I still owe him a moral debt,' Boyd says.

The limited partners – none of whom Don Boyd ever met – have yet to discover whether the film-partnership scheme will survive the courts. So far, the signs are hopeful. In May 1986 the Law Lords ruled against the Inland Revenue over its challenge to the South Street Films partnerships.[4]

Don Boyd estimates that Tucker and Plummer, through their family trusts, lost money on the film venture since they had to cover all the bank guarantees and make up what was not earned at the box office. But the trusts did own the bank, so it was perhaps more a loss of profit than a genuine loss.

Artificiality, not art, was Roy Tucker's strength. His flop as a film financier illustrated that, unlike his hero Godfrey Bradman, he could conceptualise but not commercialise. Tax avoidance was one thing, business was another – as the House of Lords was to remind him.

A SHORT-LIVED DREAM

Although Tucker and Plummer would never concede that tax avoidance Rossminster style was anything less than respectable, they realised that, despite their ever more glittering clientele and the multimillion-pound banking transactions, Rossminster still lacked City status. There was after all much more to being a bank than just possessing a Section 123 licence and using it for 'funny money' deals. City banks acted for outside clients, raising finance, advising on takeovers; they acted as principals, making investments in companies on their own behalf and that of clients. With his background at Samuel Montagu and Slater, Walker, Plummer was particularly attracted by the image of Rossminster as a merchant bank engaging in corporate finance deals. Such business was not only lucrative but offered the prestige that would never come from being seen as just a promoter of ever-so-clever tax schemes. Godfrey Bradman had already made this transition with London Mercantile. Banking also offered a longer life for Rossminster than promoting tax avoidance under the threat of a government-enforced close-down.

So Rossminster Corporate Services was set up to be run by two aspiring bankers specifically recruited to realise this new ambition. Michael Preston was, like Roy Tucker, a product of St Paul's School and accountancy but with Oxford in between. After qualifying with Price, Waterhouse he had gone to work for First National Finance Corporation, the largest survivor of the 'fringe' banking crisis. Frustrated by the lack of dealmaking opportunities while FNFC was in intensive care, he was immediately attracted by the offer to join Rossminster. His friend and partner Julian Walter knew both Plummer and Benyon from their days at Slater, Walker. Walter and Preston were convinced by Plummer that Rossminster was genuinely eager to establish a corporate finance business like the City merchant banks and that this would be given a high priority and the necessary resources. Preston and Walter were joined at Rossminster Corporate Services by Eugene Gomeche, a former tax adviser to the CBI.

RCS was incorporated in November 1974. The entire Rossminster staff at that time consisted of Plummer, Benyon, Trotman, the bank manager Michael Coysh and three secretaries. The first corporate deals attracted little or no attention. But Rossminster's involvement in Talbex, a 'penny stock' company engaged in making soap and aerosols and running hairdressing salons, brought it into both the public eye and *Private Eye*. The reason was the participation in the Talbex deal of the leading Conservative Peter Walker.

Talbex had run into disturbing losses and internal dissension during 1974 as a result of a disastrous move into hire-purchase finance. A substantial interest in the company, controlled by the former chairman Fred Stebbing and certain associates, was up for sale and came to the attention of Tim Price, Peter Walker's political assistant. Price discussed the possibilities of buying the Stebbing shares with his predecessor Tim Yeo, who was now a fund manager running a small unit-trust group. They agreed that if the business could be turned around it was a good investment opportunity, and decided to approach Walker, ask him to join them and, more importantly, to arrange the £250,000 finance required. Walker was reluctant to finance the deal himself but he agreed to propose it to Plummer whom he knew from Slater, Walker. Price and Yeo already had contacts at Rossminster in Benyon and Trotman.

Walker approached Plummer with the Talbex deal in August 1975. Plummer turned it over to Preston for evaluation. Preston felt it was an unattractive proposition for Rossminster even though only a small sum was involved, but Plummer did not want to disappoint Walker, so Preston agreed to Rossminster buying the Talbex stake but with Walker, Price and Yeo having an option to buy most of Rossminster's shares at any time up to March 1977. If they did not exercise that option, Rossminster had an option to make them buy all its shares at the same price. To strengthen Rossminster's position Preston asked Peter Walker to put up his Worcestershire farm as collateral.

'The part I played in the transaction was to put up all the collateral that was required in return for which I was offered an option on a proportion of the shares,' Walker explained later.[1] The MP and his associates would be able to buy 80 per cent of the shareholding in Talbex at Rossminster's cost price plus interest and less any dividends received. Each had an option on just under 7 per cent of Talbex.

On 1 October 1975 Merestock, a Rossminster subsidiary, disclosed it had bought 26 per cent of Talbex – 4,780,000 shares at fractionally over 5p a share, an investment of £243,000. Yeo went on the Talbex board as its representative. Peter Walker's involvement had already surfaced in two newspaper reports, but the convoluted nature of that involvement was not known.

To begin with it seemed that Talbex would indeed turn out to be the deal all concerned hoped it would be. Within a month the share price had almost doubled to 9¾p and the company reported a return to profitability. But by mid-1976 the picture had changed for the worse: profits started to slip and an acquisition, approved by Yeo but opposed by Preston, went sour, costing Talbex £130,000. By October 1976 the share price was down to 3¾p. Walker, Price and Yeo were uninterested in taking up shares at the previously agreed price as it was then well above the stock-market price, and it was decided to renegotiate the option, extending it by a year from May 1977. The number of Rossminster-owned shares under option was reduced to 70 per cent of a holding which had itself been slimmed to 21 per cent by the sale of 5 per cent at 6p a share to Locana (UK), the Canadian-owned company which had taken over Yeo's unit-trust management concern. Walker, Price and Yeo now had an option on just over 4 per cent of Talbex each. More collateral for Rossminster's investment was also required.

Although the trading results improved and Talbex returned to profitability, Rossminster was not interested in remaining as an investor. It was therefore agreed in November 1977 that its shares should be placed. Yeo undertook to place the shares he and the others held under option; Preston indicated that he would be interested in purchasing the rest. Yeo informed Preston that Locana would take up his shares and that those of Walker and Price were to be sold to Artoc Bank and Trust on behalf of its clients, the Iranian Investment Company. 'At the time my advice to Peter Walker, and he would have told Tim Price, was to hold on to the shares as a recovery situation,' says Yeo. 'But they wanted to sell as they had been in a long time. They just wanted to avoid a loss or make a small profit. They asked me to place the shares so I found Artoc.'

The Artoc deal went through on 18 November. Artoc was an Arabbacked, Bahamian-based bank run by Peter de Savary, a colourful oil broker turned would-be banker who was on the lookout for propositions. Walker and Price sold their 9 per cent of Talbex to Locana at about 6½p a share, giving them a more ¼p profit after two years. 'There was a very small profit after meeting the costs involved,' Walker says.[2] Yeo's partners were unaware that he intended to sell their shares to Artoc. 'Their shares were sold on at the same price, there was no profit to me,' Yeo declares.

Walker and Price, however, were not pleased when, almost three weeks later, on 13 December, Yeo sold the 1,790,000 Talbex shares held by Locana to Artoc's clients at 10p a share. Their unhappiness grew apace when the Talbex price went rushing ahead to 25p on news of this 10 per cent purchase and further purchases taking the Artoc stake to 29 per cent. Tim Price was so displeased that he had to be dissuaded, because of the adverse publicity for Walker, from taking legal action against Yeo over the 4p-a-share profit he and the MP had lost and Locana had found. 'There was no row with Peter Walker but Tim Price or his solicitor wrote to me after the Locana sale. I reminded him of my letter advising them to hold the shares,' recalls Yeo, himself now a Conservative MP.

Rossminster too had made very little out of Talbex. Preston had agreed to buy the balance of its Talbex shares at 6¾p; he offered shares to other Rossminster executives but only Benyon accepted.

Rossminster did slightly better with the deal Preston and Walter did two days after the purchase of the Talbex shares. On 3 October 1975 Rossminster bought the W. W. Drinkwater group, which had interests in aggregates, road haulage and industrial waste disposal, for £3,600,000 as part of a Company Purchase Scheme to enable the Drinkwater family to realise a large capital gain on land the company owned in West London. Normally the family would have bought back the trading assets as Rossminster had no interest or expertise in management, but in this case Plummer agreed to Preston and Walter retaining the waste-disposal business. A week after it bought the Drinkwater group, Rossminster sold the rest of it to an associated company, Riverflow, as part of the Company Purchase Scheme for £4,700,000. Only £119,000 of this profit was realised in cash; the rest remained in the company as a £927,000 interestfree loan from First London Securities, secured on the remaining assets, including the head office in north London, which were valued at up to £850,000.

Preston and Walter were unable to turn Drinkwater into a profit-making business, so the industrial waste-disposal companies were sold, via St George's, for £325,000 in 1977. The freehold property was sold the next year for £440,000. Had Rossminster been able to stem Drinkwater's losses, one option considered was to realise its profit by injecting the waste-disposal interests into yet another Preston/Walter acquisition, Jacksons Bourne End.

Jacksons was a sleepy little company earning unexciting profits from making millboard for the motor and shoe industries, but it was sitting on a gold mine in rural Buckinghamshire. It owned some 30 acres located just off the M4 motorway and ripe for housing or industrial redevelopment. The land had last been valued in 1927 but almost fifty years later was estimated to be worth over £2,000,000. Rossminster had not been the first to spot Jacksons' potential: the merchant bankers Guinness Mahon had already built up a 32 per cent shareholding but had made no moves to unlock the company's assets.

Rossminster began to amass a share stake and by July 1975 had bought just under 10 per cent of the company at a cost of only £42,000 – such was the lack of perception of Jacksons' potential. In December Rossminster disclosed that it held 229,000 shares – 22 per cent – through its UK subsidiary Dawngrange. This represented an investment of £93,400.

But Jacksons could not persuade the local planning authorities to release more of the land for development, so after three years Tucker and Plummer decided to try and break the deadlock. In February 1979 Rossminster Holdings bought out the Guinness Mahon holding for £1 a share – £312,000 – and made an offer for the 42 per cent of Jacksons it still did not own, after further purchases by Dawngrange. The Jacksons directors were unappreciative of the bid, terming it inadequate. They proved their point and the correctness of Rossminster's initial evaluation by revealing that the land at Bourne End had been revalued at £1,750,000; if the local council allowed development it could be worth 'significantly more'. Together with the business and another 20 acres in Leicestershire they estimated the company's assets at £2,530,000 or 238p a share. Not surprisingly, the Rossminster takeover failed. But it was now firmly in control at Jacksons with, after other small purchases, 60 per cent of the shares, and so stood to benefit most from any realisation of the assets' real value. This the company now began to do, slowly obtaining planning approval for small parcels of land. Within two years the land was valued at £3,400,000.

Realising the full potential in Jacksons Bourne End was to take more than ten years, but for money in a hurry the last deal Michael Preston put together at RCS takes a lot of beating by any City bank.

At an early stage Preston and Walter had been interested in property deals. Property values had been hit hard by the secondary banking crisis. There was no shortage of property on offer from banks who had once outbid each other for the honour of making the biggest loan. For a new bank which bore no scars from that crash and had money to lend, there were good deals to be done.

If Britain ever had a rival to Howard Hughes, in mystery if not in millions, it was Sir John Ellerman. From the day in 1933 when he inherited his father's £40 million fortune (£18 million went in death duties) at the age of twenty-three he all but disappeared from public view. Only a few old and unauthorised photographs ever existed. Following one of his father's three rules – the others were save money and avoid extravagance – he avoided all publicity, hid his business and private activities and was mentioned by newspapers only when there was speculation about his position among the world's richest men. He devoted his life, outside business, to his two great interests; the study of rodents and Gilbert and Sullivan operas.

Sir John Ellerman's father, the son of a German consular official who began as a clerk in an accountant's office, made his fortune out of shipping, owning one of the largest fleets in the world. But he had also been an early devotee of property, buying up a substantial slice of central London. He bought all of Great Portland Street and part of Oxford Street from Lord Howard de Walden and the freehold of the Drury Lane Theatre from the Duke of Bedford. Ellerman spotted that as income-tax rates rose there was a great saving and substantial profit to the very rich in sacrificing immediate income for future capital profits by acquiring commercial or shop properties which would yield much higher rentals and capital values once the existing leases expired. Since such capital gains were untaxed, the benefit was considerable to those who could afford to wait ten or fifteen years.

The Ellerman fleet suffered heavy losses during the Second World War but by the sixties it had been rebuilt, and the Ellerman interests now included two breweries and significant share stakes in a large number of major public companies, such as the International Publishing Corporation, owners of the *Daily Mirror*, and the Savoy Hotel group, as well as four large investment trusts. The property holdings had also been expanded so that Ellerman owned not only much of the area bordered by Great Portland Street, Tottenham Court Road and Oxford Street but also other sites in Soho and Holborn as well as the Waldorf and Rembrandt hotels and the Sun Wharf on the Thames.

Sir John Ellerman died, as much an enigma as when he had succeeded his father forty years before, in July 1973 at the age of sixty-three. He left an estate valued at more than £60 million, of which the Inland Revenue took £37 million and the remainder went to his widow. The shipping fleet was owned by charitable trusts and a Luxembourg company to avoid the threat of a forced piecemeal sell-off on his death.[3] The property interests had been maintained separately in the Ellerman Property Trust. In 1976 Malcolm Fraser, a friend of Preston, offered Rossminster the opportunity to buy the entire property portfolio.

The properties were valued in the Ellerman accounts at £1,800,000 but were worth considerably more – Rossminster agreed to pay £3,600,000 cash for the properties and other assets, mainly cash.

Rossminster set up a company structure that would ensure discretion for both vendor and purchaser. The Ellerman trustees had insisted that after the sale the Ellerman name should disappear; and instead of being bought by Rossminster itself the Ellerman Property Trust was acquired by the six ultimate owners or their offshore family trusts. This was done through a new company, Hillcoll, which on 10 June 1976 acquired 58 per cent of Alanvale Securities. A week later Alanvale acquired the Ellerman Property Trust financed by a £3,660,000 loan from a Rossminster bank. The other shares in Alanvale were held by Preston, Fraser and the two individuals who had negotiated the initial agreement with the Ellerman trustees, Louis Mautner and Michael Sack. The shares in Hillcoll were held in identical proportions to those in Rossminster, with 83 per cent held by the Tucker/Plummer interests and the balance split between Miller, Gardner, Benyon and Trotman.

By June 1977 all the properties had been sold, yielding a £1,680,000 profit above the £2,900,000 at which they had been estimated for the purposes of the deal. Because almost all the properties had been held since before 1939, there was a maximum tax charge on the profit of 20 per cent. Such liabilities were soon dealt with via the Gross Annuity Scheme and group election. This enabled the Alanvale Property Trust, as the Ellerman company was now called, to pay a £5,190,000 dividend, representing its entire assets, to its parent company Alanvale Securities. A much larger Gross Annuity Scheme was then deployed to remove the tax liability on Alanvale's profit which, after repaying the Rossminster loan, was £1,925,000. After buying out the non-Rossminster shareholders, Hillcoll then sold Alanvale to a nominee for St George's, realising a £1,100,000 profit; it then made its GAS-powered way into the Company Purchase Scheme and the St George's charity.

Before the sale to St George's took place, however, there were some subtle cosmetic changes in the ownership of the Hillcoll shares. Certain of the insiders, such as Benyon, held their shares personally in the UK. The anticipated profit on the sale of Hillcoll to St George's generated a potentially large tax liability. It was therefore decided that prior to the sale of Hillcoll those owning the shares onshore would sell them to an offshore buyer, a family trust. In the first half of 1977 Benyon sold his 2½ per cent of Hillcoll to Matula, a Manx company formed in September 1976. Matula had Martin and Barbara Joyner on Sark as its directors and the Rossminster nominee company Abbeville as its shareholder, but it was owned by the Benyon family trust. Because the interest in Hillcoll was a small minority one it could be sold at considerably less than its share of the market value of the whole, a formula often used when Rossminster assets changed hands among the owners. It would therefore be Matula which reaped the bulk of the profit taxfree when, shortly after this sale, Hillcoll itself was sold.

The Rossminster insiders and their interests realised a £1 million taxfree offshore profit from the Ellerman deal plus the fees earned by Rossminster itself for financing the purchase.[4]

By the time the Ellerman deal was completed in June 1977 both Michael Preston and Julian Walter had left Rossminster: Walter in September 1976, Preston six months later. Throughout 1976 both had become increasingly disillusioned about Plummer's commitment to merchant banking, which seemed to have declined in proportion to the realisation of the far greater profits to be made from tax schemes. 'Ron and Roy were very democratic, they would only do what everyone agreed to,' says Tom Benyon. 'Not everyone wanted to be a merchant bank so we did not do it.'

The expansion of the tax-avoidance side also placed two substantial obstacles in the way of further development by Rossminster Corporate Services. Less and less money was available for corporate finance deals, unless, like Ellerman, they were in-house. The funds available, via First

London Securities and Rossminster Acceptances, were increasingly needed for the Company Purchase Scheme; and the profits generated by deals like Ellerman did not stay inside the group but went offshore and so were not available to finance new business.

The concentration of the two banks on tax business had produced a potential £2 million tax liability. Even though Rossminster claimed this would not be payable, clients were put off by the fear that Rossminster might suddenly need to find the money to meet this tax bill. It also showed that the banks did not carry on normal banking business – an impression confirmed by the Revenue's refusal to accept Rossminster Acceptances as a bank.

Preston had also become concerned at the increasingly blatant style of tax avoidance in which Rossminster was engaging. He felt that it would soon produce a backlash from both the Revenue and the Labour government. It was clear to Preston by the start of 1977 that, after only three years, the dream of Rossminster as a merchant bank had died. From now on as long as the good times lasted there would be no attempt at depicting Rossminster to the City or anyone else as anything but what it was. But, while Preston and others in the City might wish to distance themselves from such an image, it was proving no obstacle at all to Rossminster's winning influential friends where it really mattered – in politics.

THE MINISTERS FOR ROSSMINSTER

'Cut taxes' has long been a battle cry of the Conservative Party. Initiative, hard work and excellence among entrepreneurs and managers should be rewarded by dropping the high level of personal taxation favoured by Labour and even some Conservative governments. These sentiments were shared in the Tory heartland of the county shires where large landowners and family-business proprietors bewailed such Labour creations as Capital Gains, Developmental Land and Capital Transfer Tax.

To many Conservatives, therefore, Bradman, Tucker and their imitators were almost latter-day Robin Hoods, especially after the tax on unearned incomes rose to leave just 2p in the pound. The fact that the tax avoiders were effectively robbing the poor PAYE-payer to keep the self-employed rich in the style to which they wished to remain accustomed went not so much unnoticed as unaccepted. The Tory line on tax avoidance was honestly – if embarrassingly for the Chancellor, Sir Geoffrey Howe – voiced by the party chairman Lord Thorneycroft when the Vesteys' tax-avoidance excesses were made public in 1980. 'I wouldn't criticise the Vestey family. I know absolutely nothing about the Vestey tax arrangements. I don't know how he does it – I wish I could find out,' he declared.

In fact Lord Thorneycroft was no stranger to tax-avoidance arrangements: he had personally participated in a sophisticated tax scheme, linked to an offshore insurance company, which at that time was being challenged by the Inland Revenue.[1]

Tucker and Plummer were not themselves political. Unlike Bradman, with his ill-judged attempt to buy off the miners in 1974 and so save the Heath government, they had made no public impression outside a

167

narrow financial context. However, they spoke the language of many Conservatives.

Rossminster contributed to party funds – encouraged by fundraisers like Jock (now Lord) Bruce-Gardyne – and entertained prominent Conservatives like Sir Geoffrey Howe, Peter Walker and David Howell. Tom Benyon says, 'The Conservatives knew what we were doing. We had lots of people in to lunch and told them.' Rossminster's acceptability within the Conservative Party on philosophical grounds increased markedly with the swing to the Right that accompanied the decline and defeat of the Heath government. The electoral reversal swept not only Edward Heath but also the traditional, quasi-paternalist 'Conservatism with a human face' from control of the party. In its place during 1975 came Margaret Thatcher and her highly personal interpretation of Victorian values: hard work, self-help, the profit motive and materialism but without compassion, charity or social conscience. Mrs Thatcher's band of self-made followers, largely drawn from the ranks of the small businessman and the professional second eleven, soon dominated the higher echelons of the party, replacing first the Heath men like Peter Walker and then undermining the representatives of the Tory Old Guard like William (now Lord) Whitelaw and Francis Pym.

The new mood was summed up by Mrs Thatcher's slogan 'A capitalist in every home'. The aim was the generation of wealth by those who either did not have any or did not have very much. High tax rates were an obstacle to the explosion of incentive and energy these new Tories intended to release in order to revitalise Britain. State intervention and controls were to be dismantled. The Civil Service was to be pruned sharply – which meant that Revenue manpower would be cut. Public spending was to be slashed, so the taxation requirement could be reduced. Private enterprise was to be given its head. The law of the market place was to predominate.

The taxman on the other hand had few if any friends. When in 1976 the Labour government gave the Inland Revenue enhanced powers, including the right to enter and search offices and homes, with which to combat tax evasion – already costing more than £2000 million a year in lost revenue – the Conservatives attacked the measures as excessive and unnecessary. Lobbyists for vested interests, like the National Federation of the Self Employed and Small Businesses, alleged intrusion into privacy and talked of 'Gestapo tactics'. Their cries of self-interest were soon heard in the House of Commons and echoed by Conservative spokesmen; indeed, an early pledge of the Thatcher government was to investigate – i.e. reduce – the Inland Revenue's powers, a promise it redeemed by appointing the Keith Committee in July 1980 to 'enquire into the tax enforcement powers of the Board of Inland Revenue and the Board of Customs and Excise . . . to consider whether these powers are suited to their purposes having regard both to the need to ensure compliance with the law and to avoid excessive burdens upon taxpayers'.

The new Tories were a ripe and ready audience for the Rossminster philosophy. They too had little time for 'Boy Scout morality' where tax was concerned. Many of them would have merited the description of 'fiscal psychopaths' given to Tucker and Plummer by one of their closest colleagues. And as this change in Conservative politics and policies began to take place in 1975, Rossminster already had a foot firmly planted in the Commons door through the former insurance salesman Tom Benyon, at that time a very junior partner at Vogue House but already a veteran of two unsuccessful bids for Parliament. Ironically, he was a man whose political views were more in tune with those of Edward Heath and Peter Walker than their successors.

Benyon was to many of those who came into contact with Rossminster the most likeable as well as the most lightweight, possibly because he was neither an accountant nor a lawyer but a salesman with a somewhat greater knowledge of the world beyond the taxes acts. He was articulate, smooth, an ex-public school, ex-Guards officer, ideal for the role Rossminster needed to fill. Like a 'greeter' in a casino or the 'warm-up' man on a TV show, Benyon could make the clients feel relaxed. He would not (could not) overwhelm them with technical detail about the schemes, but he could give them the sales pitch, appealing to their greed and fears, which would make them 'hot' for the Tucker/Rossminster package. As a 1977 Rossminster brochure put it, Benyon had 'special responsibility for public relations, communications and marketing'.[2] The others were obsessed by tax but Benyon, perhaps because of his background, had a different attitude – 'Tax was very boring, silly, but you could make a lot of money.' He was much more interested in politics and already well advanced with putting his plausibility to work politically. A Bow Group member, in December 1973 he was rewarded with nomination as the Conservative candidate for the upcoming general election in Huyton, the Merseyside constituency of the Labour leader Harold Wilson, who had a 21,000 majority.[3]

Benyon did well enough at Huyton – clipping Wilson's majority by 6000 – to be given a second chance later that year, this time in the slightly more winnable north London seat of Haringey, Wood Green, held by Labour's Joyce Butler with a 7500 majority.

Benyon did not win Wood Green, in fact the Labour majority was slightly increased. He regrouped his resources and decided on the long haul of the local politics and good works route to a safe seat. He moved to Adstock near Oxford and became a member of the Aylesbury Vale District Council in 1976, a member of the Buckinghamshire County Health Council and vice-chairman of the Buckingham Conservative Association. He also became active in charity work for the mentally handicapped and the young.

In March 1979, with a general election due later in the year, Airey Neave, the MP for Abingdon and Conservative spokesman on Northern Ireland, was assassinated by a car bomb planted by Irish terrorists. Benyon was short-listed for selection as candidate in this Tory stronghold – but he had a very strong rival, none other than Tim Yeo, Peter Walker's assistant and Rossminster's partner in the Talbex deal. Yeo was four years younger and had more impressive Conservative credentials; he had been personal assistant to Shadow Minister Patrick Jenkin. Yeo too had stood in the 1974 election, against a future Labour leader, Neil Kinnock, in the South Wales stronghold of Bedwellty.

Benyon was resigned to awaiting his chance at the following general election and had agreed to assist John Nott in his St Ives constituency. However, suddenly Yeo withdrew from the selection contest. The local constituency association learned that he had been criticised by the Stock Exchange early in 1978 over the sale of shares in an engineering company from his Security Selection company to the unit trusts it managed. The Stock Exchange felt sufficiently strongly to report its findings to the Department of Trade which licensed Yeo's company. Yeo repaid the profit to the unit trusts and no further action was taken. Just how the local selection committee became aware of this matter was never known but it created an embarrassment for Yeo which encouraged his decision to step down.[4] Tom Benyon was quickly nominated as the Conservative candidate for Abingdon and was elected with a more than doubled majority of 22,000 in May 1979.

Because so much of Tucker and Plummer's activities and plans could be affected by government policy and legislation, in particular the closing of tax loopholes or the opening of new ones, it was vital to have eyes and ears at Westminster. Benyon's political ambitions and contacts made him an ideal means of obtaining influential introductions, as did Rossminster's annual £5000 political contributions.

Peter Walker, although a self-made man who had made his money in the City and a strong believer in lower taxes as carrot to incentive, did not subscribe to the Thatcher themes of abolishing state controls and encouraging business at all costs. In a 1973 speech Trade and Industry Secretary Walker had declared, 'Captalism should not be regarded as the means for a few to get rich without regard to the needs and hopes of the majority of people. The government must see that commercial activities are fair, open and just.' Such criteria could hardly be met by tax avoidance, Rossminster style, which relied heavily on hiding from the Revenue the reality of what was happening in order to benefit the few who could pay Tucker's fees against the interests of the many.

In January 1976 Walker was dropped from the Shadow Cabinet and turned his attentions once again to business. By then he owned two farms and had directorships with his old insurance broking business, Walker, Young, and an engineering company in his Worcester constituency. He had received some £350,000 from selling his Slater, Walker shares which financed these and other interests.

According Nigel Tutt in *The Tax Raiders*, Walker attended a cocktail party in 1973 celebrating Rossminster's launch and subsequently 'used the company for corporate finance advice,' becoming a 'regular visitor'.[5] This, however, is strenuously denied by Walker himself: 'I received no corporate finance advice from Rossminster or any other form of tax or financial advice. From memory I knew Mr Plummer. I do not remember attending the initial cocktail party but may well have done so. On a couple of occasions I lunched there.'[6]

Some of his friends, though, were interested. Bernard Myers predated Jim Slater as a business associate of Walker's by several years. His son Sefton had met Walker while they were doing their National Service. He later invited Walker to become a director of the family property company, Rodwell. Bernard Myers owned the Walton Manor estate in Buckinghamshire and had spent at least £500,000 on it. He all at once found himself sitting on a six-figure windfall when the Labour government decided to build the new town of Milton Keynes and compulsorily acquired his home and its 320 acres in 1970. After a long legal battle Myers was finally awarded £636,000 in 1974. Three years later one of his companies used a Tucker tax scheme.

Tucker and Plummer also made influential contacts among the new Tory hierarchy, thanks to Desmond Miller. As a member of the Bar Council and a leading tax counsel, Miller was a useful point of reference for anyone approached on behalf of Rossminster. He was well known in Conservative circles, where the worlds of taxation and politics often meet in an interchange of information and mutual interest, irrespective of which party is in power. The views of tax counsel are often sought by shadow Tory ministers and backbench MPs alike. Certain of Miller's barrister colleagues, both past and present, were also to be found earning a more modest second income as Members of Parliament. One of these was John Nott, a former junior Treasury minister in the Heath government but in 1975 merely the MP for St Ives.

Like Tom Benyon, Nott had chosen the army as his career before becoming interested in politics. The son of a rice broker, he served with the Gurkha regiments in Malaya before resigning to read law and economics at Cambridge, where he was president of the Union in 1959. Nott was called to the Bar as a member of the Inner Temple where Miller was a leading light, but instead of the law Nott chose the City, joining the merchant bankers S. G. Warburg. For six years before entering Parliament in 1966 he worked at the bank, rising to become a general manager. After he left office in 1974 Nott did not make the ritual return to the City. Instead, while remaining an Opposition Front Bench Treasury spokesman, he became a business consultant. Late in 1975, through Miller, whom he had met on a party finance subcommittee when he was a junior Treasury minister, he was introduced to Rossminster as available for consultancy work.

The MP for St Ives was one of the new Tories who spoke the language Tucker and Plummer wanted to hear. He had attacked the new Capital Transfer Tax in a January 1975 speech, warning that 'the Saving Classes' would withhold taxes because of 'penal and objectionable' tax legislation. In a February 1975 *Daily Telegraph* article he wrote in similar vein attacking the Finance Bill's 'wholly unacceptable extension of the Inland Revenue's powers to snoop into the private affairs of individual citizens by requiring professional advisers and banks to spy on their clients'.[7] He praised entrepreneurial talent and those who chose the 'challenge and rewards of independence'. In another article for the *Daily Telegraph* decrying 'the myth of the rich, top people', Nott wrote in November 1975: 'It is hard to discover any country in the Western world where the incentive to strive for improvement, the urge to acquire skills and the natural desire to perpetuate the continuity of the family by inheritance have been so consistently under attack.'[8] In particular he singled out 'the crippling rate of marginal taxation on high income families':

That a businessman striving all his life to build up a business can be taxed at more than the total value of that business when he transfers it to his son – these are the real scandals of our society ... The real question, which will increasingly have to be considered in the next few years, is not whether the present distribution of income and wealth is unfair, but whether the differentials are not now so narrow, compared with other countries, that incentive, savings and effort are being hopelessly restricted to the long-term detriment of the whole community.

Such words were music in Rossminster ears. Nott was an attractive catch: as an Opposition Treasury spokesman he was ideally placed to serve as an early warning system on Labour legislation or advise on government intentions; he had banking and industrial expertise which Rossminster, still playing at merchant banking, felt it needed; and he could be a source of new business as well as an influential representative. Before the end of 1975 John Nott had signed on as a paid consultant and adviser. This soon started to pay off politically. In December 1975, soon after his appointment as shadow Chancellor, Sir Geoffrey Howe was brought along by Nott to meet Plummer at a Rossminster lunch.

Nott was paid at the rate of £6000 a year through Rossminster Corporate Services. On one occasion he protested jokingly that he was 'getting the money under false pretences', but there was never any protest on the Rossminster side. On the contrary, there was considerable satisfaction with the MP's contribution, which took up quite a lot of his time. Benyon in particular was keen to have Nott involved. The view of other Rossminster insiders was that with three children to educate, a farm to run and no lucrative directorships, Nott welcomed the money.

Most of John Nott's time at Rossminster was taken up with E. Bailey, the sugar brokers. In December 1975 Rossminster had bought 49 per cent of Bailey from the Canadian group Brascan for £522,664 with an option on the balance for £100.

Bailey by then was already a crucial participant in the tax schemes Rossminster was marketing involving commodity dealing. But there were much bigger plans to use a tax scheme exploiting the possibilities in generating artificial losses on commodities. The scheme involved a massive 'book entry' turnover of matched purchases and sales where a mistake could be very costly for Rossminster, should it be caught out by a sudden rise or fall in the price of the commodity involved, this made it essential that Bailey functioned efficiently. Nott told the *Sunday Times* some years later that he had been put in to 'watch the risky commodity business with a banker's eye'.[9]

At the time he was seen as more of a management consultant cleaning up and improving the Bailey administration, even investigating the background of its commodity dealers.

Nott also told the *Sunday Times* that he was not then aware of Bailey's crucial role in tax-avoidance schemes. However, as a frequent visitor to the Rossminster offices he would have been hard pressed not to become aware of its main business. Certainly he was aware of the true position when in 1977 Rossminster bought the rest of E. Bailey, for at that time the ruling authorities in the London sugar market insisted that the dealing subsidiary E. Bailey Sugar should be owned separately from Rossminster. (Such sensitivity is ironic since one of the largest sugar brokers, E. D. & F. Mann, had been a Tucker client.) The shares were put in the names of Glyn Evans (80 per cent), Nott (10 per cent) and former banker John Phillimore who had represented Brascan (10 per cent). The profits were paid to Rossminster via a management charge. Nott said that he only agreed to hold the shares 'on condition that the company undertook to do no more tax planning dealing'.[10] By that time Rossminster's involvement with commodities was waning anyway. Another Rossminster executive confirms that Nott advised Tucker and Plummer to give up certain of these activities. He also warned about the possible government backlash following publicity over the Wimpey tax scheme.

Although hired primarily to advise on corporate finance, Nott did not shrink from Rossminster's mainstream business. For example, he attended a 1978 meeting with Miller and Plummer to discuss using Tucker schemes in Ireland in association with a firm of Dublin accountants. A former Tucker associate recalls discussing with Nott whether a tax scheme would help resolve a personal tax problem stemming from an inheritance. Nott was also a source of potential clients. One possible deal he suggested involved the former chief executive of Burmah Oil, Nicky Williams, well known in Conservative circles through Denis Thatcher's position as Burmah's director of planning and control. Williams's whiz-kid status had been cancelled when Burmah all but collapsed on New Year's Eve 1974 after serious overexpansion. RCS turned down the Williams deal. They also rejected another deal Nott brought in, to finance a company of which he had agreed to be chairman, Andrew Hydraulics International.

In 1975 an engineer, Trevor Andrew, had the idea of setting up a company to exploit various patents, trademarks and technical expertise in the sphere of crimping – a process then used in the production of man-made fibres – held by his American friend James Mason. The American agreed to give Andrew access to 'the results of my experience', but the engineer still needed to raise the finance to produce the equipment. For this he turned to another friend, John Nott, whom he had known since the MP first entered Parliament. Nott knew not a little about hydraulics from his time at Warburgs and had been chairman of Imperial Eastman (UK) which made hydraulic equipment.

Nott put up the suggestion that Rossminster should back Andrew's company but the proposal was rejected by Michael Preston on the grounds that the shareholding offered in return was too small. Rossminster was looking for quick profits, not venture capital situations where money would be tied up for years and the return meanwhile would be either small or nonexistent. Undeterred, Nott managed to interest the Scottish merchant bank Noble Grossart. Andrew Hydraulics was launched in August 1975 with a small factory in Bedford making hose and couplings. Nott agreed to be chairman and was given 7000 shares; his three children received 1000 each. Trevor Andrew described this as a 'finder's fee' in return for the MP bringing in Noble Grossart.

Rossminster later became involved in Andrew Hydraulics, in its more usual role as a provider of the means to avoid tax, establishing an offshore discretionary trust in which the royalties payable to Mason for his trademarks and know-how could be sheltered. According to Trevor Andrew, it was Mason, not Nott, who was responsible for the approach to Rossminster, on the advice of the accountants Arthur Andersen. The James Mason Settlement was created about the time Andrew Hydraulics began to trade. Andrew, Mason, Nott and the company secretary visited Guernsey. One reason for the visit was that the trust would involve cash being paid offshore and, according to one participant in that meeting, Nott was 'particularly careful' to ensure there was no exchange control problem. The arrangements were agreed by the Bank of England on the basis –

confirmed by a firm of London solicitors – that the trust had been set up by a nonresident.

As a further part of the Rossminster-administered arrangements, a dozen UK patents held by the Mason trust were applied for in the name of Abbeville, a Rossminster nominee company. According to Andrew, Abbeville held the rights for the use of these patents worldwide.

Just who were the intended beneficiaries of the Mason settlement is a matter of dispute. According to one former Rossminster executive, the trustees wrote a minute stating that, when there was money to be distributed from royalties received, this should go to the Andrew Hydraulics shareholders on a pro rata basis. However, Andrew denies that John Nott was ever a beneficiary although admitting that both he and Mason could have been. In fact, Andrew Hydraulics was never in a position to pay any royalties: it lost more than £100,000 in three years. In April 1979, just before the general election which resulted in his becoming first trade secretary and then defence secretary, John Nott resigned from the company. He had never been very active as chairman, according to Trevor Andrew, merely attending board meetings. Andrew claims he bought the 10,000 shares back but will not say at what price; it would be surprising if this was more than the nominal value of £5000. The company went into liquidation in 1982. (Nott declined to be interviewed about his involvement with Rossminster.)

Tucker's involvement with Peter Rees, who on the Conservative election victory had been appointed minister of state at the Treasury responsible for casework and policy at the Inland Revenue, did not become known until Rossminster itself became a political issue. The embarrassment Rees's appointment created for the Inland Revenue, by then well into its investigation of Rossminster, exemplified the situation the Revenue often found itself in when challenging the Tucker tax schemes. Time and time again it discovered that a particular counsel could be unsuitable because he had previously advised Tucker or Rossminster, for by the late seventies few if any of the top names at the tax Bar had not taken the Tucker shilling at one time or another. When it came to challenge the Advance Interest Scheme used by the Rossminster and Tucker insiders, the Revenue employed as its counsel in the Cairns case Charles Potter QC, who had advised Tucker on a similar scheme sold to companies which had also been challenged by the Revenue. Many at the tax Bar were held in low esteem by the Revenue as a result of their links to Tucker, and the

Revenue would not use their services. Indeed one senior Revenue official had demonstrated his distaste by resigning from the Bar over the attitude of some of his colleagues.

With Tucker's busy, year-round schedule of marketing at least one income tax, corporation tax and capital gains tax scheme a year, he was a regular and substantial caller upon the tax Bar's services. According to Richard Gardner, who attended many of the legal conferences, Tucker would never accept what counsel said if it was negative or unhelpful. 'He would always argue points. He always believed he knew better.' As a result his schemes were sold backed up by or carrying the imprimatur of opinions from prominent tax and company law QCs such as Charles Beattie (a particular Tucker favourite), Peter Curry, Michael Jump, Andrew Park, Barry Pinson, Charles Potter, Leolin Price, Rex Bretten, Robert Wright and Michael Wheeler as well as Peter Rees.

According to a lawyer who instructed some of these on Tucker's behalf, the tax barristers were divided into two groups. A minority took what might be called the Lord Denning approach towards the civil law in general. They would look through the mechanics of the scheme and say it would not work because the result – the avoidance of tax – was not what Parliament intended. This view was championed from the midseventies by Lord Templeman, then a High Court judge. But the majority did not subscribe to this more principled than legalistic view; they looked only at the words of the statute. 'They would accept a possible interpretation so long as it was not specifically disallowed,' says the former Rossminster lawyer. Peter Rees was of that school and as a result became one of the tax QCs most favoured by Roy Tucker.

Like Miller and Nott, Peter Rees was a member of the Inner Temple. He was the son of an Indian Army major-general, and had been called to the Bar in 1953; when Tucker came on the scene twenty years later Rees was one of the top tax experts. From 1970 onwards he had combined this role with being the Conservative MP for Dover, after three failures elsewhere. Rees was a small, round man with a bustling and somewhat aggressive manner, marked out early as minister potential because of his tax expertise. Within two years he was Parliamentary Private Secretary to Sir Geoffrey Howe, then the solicitor-general. According to former Rossminster insiders, Rees was one of the first tax counsel to be consulted by Tucker. He subsequently provided legal opinions on the early Non-Deposit Scheme and several later schemes, until 1977. One Tucker associate says that he was used because he was among the most sympathetic of the tax QCs towards the Tucker approach. 'He was very robust,' recalls Tom Benyon, using the legal fraternity's euphemism for a barrister who relies as much on rhetoric as reason. 'He did not look at anything but the law. Tucker used him a lot because he got opinions. Rees always gave an opinion.' That is not to say, however, that Rees simply nodded through whatever Tucker suggested; on two or three occasions he advised against a Tucker proposal on the grounds that it would not work.

Peter Rees's approach to the Healey tax rates was predictable. Once he was elevated to the position of an Opposition Front Bench spokesman, he accused the Labour government of stifling enterprise, penalising hard work and putting an increasing burden on the taxpayer. He proposed exempting the Channel Islands and the Isle of Man from the provisions of Capital Transfer Tax. In a speech on the 1977 Finance Bill he declared, 'With the tax structure and the rates of taxation that exist at present . . . there is a pressure to avoid and I am afraid that at the margin there is pressure to evade right throughout the country . . . I am afraid it is a sad commentary on human nature.'[11]

Peter Rees will not say how many legal opinions he gave for Tucker schemes and will not discuss any of those opinions on the grounds of professional ethics. He was aware that his written opinions were used to market the schemes – 'You had a pretty shrewd idea from the way the instructions were phrased.' Explaining his position he says, 'As a QC you're just asked about the law. The questions are always very carefully phrased. You're not asked if it's good to do it or if it's in the public interest or moral.' Yet in a speech he made to an audience of accountants in December 1979, just seven months after taking office, Rees recognised the relevance of such issues: 'There are great risks if major tax avoidance passes unchecked. Schemes which are devised purely for tax advantages and which have no commercial justification at all cannot be allowed to pass unchallenged . . . Not to do so would probably lead inevitably to a justifiable loss of confidence in the fairness of the tax system.' A Labour Chancellor could not have put it better. Explaining this dichotomy, Rees says simply, 'As a minister you're interested in other issues.'

On 3 December 1977 Peter Rees, along with Jeff Rooker, the Labour MP for Birmingham, Perry Barr, who was to become a persistent hammer of Rossminster, appeared on a London Weekend Television programme concerning Tucker's activities.[12] This edition of *The London Programme* featured some of the Tucker/Rossminster schemes and interviewed Tucker, who defended their legality and explained the demand for his services by pointing to the high tax rates. (Tucker felt he came out of the programme well but this view was not shared by other, more astute Rossminster insiders, who were dismayed by his insensitivity to the moral issues the programme was raising.)

The final portion of the programme consisted of a studio discussion between Rooker and Rees, who was there as both a tax expert and a front-bench spokesman. Rees later tried to play down his appearance on what he termed 'not a particularly significant programme'. But it was significant that Rees showed no sympathy for the activities of Tucker and Rossminster. 'No one in public life can responsibly be enthusiastic about quite such stark schemes,' he said, talking about the Advance Interest Scheme. 'The people who engage in them are not really engaged on what I call productive work.' Rees even supported the introduction of general anti-avoidance legislation. But what he did not say was that he had provided legal opinions for a variant of the same scheme or that he had continued to advise Tucker until as recently as earlier that year.

Rees's explanation for this omission is that he was precluded from doing so by professional ethics and Bar rules. 'It is a matter of strict convention of the Bar that a barrister does not disclose whom he advises professionally or what advice he has given,' he says. But it might have seemed candid to have intimated to Rooker and the audience, even in the most general terms, that he had more than a passing knowledge or involvement with Tucker and his type of highly artificial schemes rather than to be seen as taking a principled stand criticising those from whom he had accepted fees. But then the Conservative MP had made it clear that he did not want to debate the moral issues involved in tax avoidance: 'I don't think I want to get drawn into the moral aspects of this, we can all say we disapprove.' Jeff Rooker at least felt that Rees had been less than straightforward. 'Peter Rees made no disclosure of the Rossminster link before, during or after the debate,' said the angry Labour MP, who learned of that connection almost two years later through an article in *Private Eye*. Rees's response was to say that 'it was generally known that he advised on tax matters'.

This information would most certainly not have been known to most viewers of the programme just as his intimate knowledge of the Tucker scheme concerned was not appreciated by his fellow MPs when some months later Peter Rees stood up to address the Commons on the evils of the retrospective legislation proposed by the Labour government to deal with it. This scheme brought together in key roles three of the four Members of Parliament whose names were linked to Rossminster and Roy Tucker.

CARRIED AWAY

Tucker and Plummer had always been fascinated with commodity dealing and the profits which could be made in that esoteric world of 'spot' and 'futures' markets through being 'long' of coffee or cocoa and 'short' of copper or tin, without ever possessing so much as a bean or an ounce. For the speculator, commodities is the ultimate gamble, played on a world stage with the spoils going to the quick and the brave. The development of the concept of 'futures' – contracts to buy or sell a commodity at today's price but in one, three, six or twelve months' time – made it a game which could be played by any wealthy investor, not just the end users of commodities such as food or metalworking companies.

A speculator can gamble by putting up just 10 per cent of the face value of the contract, aiming to sell it well before it would be necessary to take delivery of the commodity concerned and so pay the 90 per cent balance. If a sufficiently large quantity of the commodity is bought even a small rise in its price can represent a disproportionately much greater profit – or loss. By putting up £250,000 an investor could take a position in £2,500,000 worth of coffee. Once the price of coffee rises by 10 per cent, that contract is worth £2,750,000, and the £250,000 profit repays the initial investment. Any further rise is all profit.

The conjuring of profits almost out of the air with limited or no need for capital was an alchemy which attracted Tucker and Plummer, men who at a stroke of several pens were able to make taxable profits disappear. Tucker in particular was a commodity speculator of long standing; indeed, his and Plummer's fondness for commodity speculation were a source of some concern to certain of the other Rossminster principals who did not share their confidence in their ability to beat the market – especially after one incident in which Tucker and Plummer got it wrong and cost the company £200,000.

Tucker and Plummer were not only attracted as investors, they saw in commodities an opportunity that could be developed for tax-scheme purposes. At an early stage a version of the Non-Deposit Scheme had been marketed involving commodity dealing as the tax-deductible business purpose for which the loan was required. Like film finance, commodity investment as a tax shelter was not new and had been recently developed in the United States to produce tax-allowable losses.[1] Tucker refined the American concept into a package which could be offered to those in Britain seeking to avoid either income or corporation tax.

The impact was to go far beyond anything either he or Plummer could have foreseen. The Labour Government's response not only killed the scheme, once exposed, but dealt a mortal blow to all artificial tax avoidance. The repercussions from the marketing of the Commodity Carry Scheme marked a watershed in both political and legal opinion over the type of off-the-peg, highly artificial avoidance schemes that Rossminster had made its own. It convinced the Inland Revenue that Roy Tucker and Rossminster had to be stopped.

To produce his scheme Tucker combined two unrelated concepts: the 'straddle' tactic used in commodity dealing and the accounting peculiarities of partnerships. The 'straddle' is a means of covering a gamble in a commodity by matching a contract to buy forward with a contract to sell. It can be used to speculate not only in the price of the commodity but also in the differential between the prices for different dealing months. This has less risk but also less reward, though the profits can still be worthwhile.

The investor buys a contract for a forward purchase of coffee, cocoa or sugar in a particular month and at the same time buys one to sell the same amount of the commodity for delivery in that month. He then buys two more contracts which enable him to do the exact reverse. The prices of these contracts, if the months are selected carefully, will usually move roughly parallel, maintaining a similar differential. The potential risk could therefore be calculated and limited. For as little as £500 to £2000 an investor could buy a 'straddle' position in 50 tons of sugar or five tons of coffee. He could then, depending on the price movements, sell all contracts simultaneously or sell the ones which are unprofitable and continue to run the ones that promise most profit.

If such deals were done through a partnership, it would be open to the partners to decide when the accounts covering that trading should be made up. A partnership that remains unchanged produces its accounts at the end of each twelve-month period, but if a partner leaves, then the old partnership is terminated and its accounts can be made up to that date. The new partnership then continues with different partners.

Tucker's idea was to devise a series of partnerships in which clients would be temporary partners and so, by astute use of commodity 'straddles', be able to generate on one side artificial losses which could be claimed for tax purposes and on the other matching profits which would not only protect Rossminster's position as the financier but could also be realised offshore when the taxpayer was replaced in the partnership by a Tucker/Plummer-controlled entity. This was the basis of the Commodity Carry Scheme.

In order to make the CCS work and avoid the risk of wiping out Rossminster and with it a large part of the wealth they had already amassed, Tucker and Plummer needed the expertise of E. Bailey and its managing director Glyn Evans. While the scheme would generate considerable commissions for Bailey, it was essential that the genuine, risk-filled trading should be limited in order to protect Rossminster against loss. An independent broker might not have been keen to undertake such a welter of 'paper' business, and would know far too much about the essential artificiality of the dealings underlying the scheme. And Tucker and Plummer were never ones to give commissions to others if they could keep or at least share them.

In December 1975 Rossminster purchased effective control of Bailey. By this point Tucker was almost ready to launch the CCS. He had already consulted Peter Rees and another top tax counsel, Barry Pinson, for their opinions on two versions of the scheme, one for individuals seeking to avoid income tax and the other for companies seeking to avoid corporation tax. He approached the MP for Dover first.

On 7 November 1975 Rees was sent details of the workings of the CCS by Tucker's solicitors Roney, Vincent. Rees was merely asked about the company version and given an example of a client seeking to obtain a £45,000 relief against corporation tax. A company 'owned by the promoters' which was trading as a commodity dealer would form a partnership with the client's company. The Rossminster company to be used for this would be Valleymark, which was set up in September 1975 with Trotman, Benyon and John Tillotson as directors. Tillotson, a chartered accountant, had a penchant for commodity dealing and later left Rossminster to set up his own commodity company with the Rossminster executive who handled the CCS business with Bailey. The Tillotson view of commodities was that 'you have to have your greedy glands under control'.[2]

The profits and losses of the Valleymark partnership would be split 90:10 in favour of the client's company, which would put up £900 of the £1000 share capital. On the first day of trading the partnership would enter into a number of 'straddle' contracts in sugar.

The contracts would be designed to produce a loss and a profit on each leg of the 'straddle' of at least £50,000 within fourteen days. First London Securities would finance the partnership to purchase these contracts. As soon as the loss on one side of the 'straddle' reached £50,000 it would be frozen by closing the 'long' or 'short' positions. After that the aggregate of the profits less losses would equal £50,000. On day fourteen any lossmaking contract would be closed but those showing profits above the £50,000 required to balance the loss would be kept open, while those producing profits of less than £50,000 would be closed. This would leave the excess profits to run on into the next accounting period so they could be realised on day fifteen or at any later date.

So on day fourteen the partnership would show realised losses of some £50,000 plus unrealised profits of £52,000 which after commissions to Bailey (£1000) and interest to FLS (£250) would leave a net unrealised profit of £750. For accounting purposes only the realised loss would count, the profit being carried forward into the next or a subsequent accounting period. At this point the Tucker client would sell his 90 per cent of the partnership to another company 'connected with the promoters' for no payment. In return for the tax advantage it hoped to achieve by taking a credit for the 90 per cent of the £50,000 loss the client would pay to have its share of the Valleymark partnership taken away. The fee would be 10 per cent of the tax saved less the initial investment and the residual value of the unrealised net profit. In the example quoted to Rees, the Tucker client would have paid £2925 net for his £45,000 corporation tax deduction. The partnership, now controlled entirely by Rossminster, would then continue trading for several months in order to realise the net profit.

Peter Rees gave his opinion on the nine points raised by Roney, Vincent on the legality and effectiveness of Tucker's ingenious scheme at a conference in his chambers at New Square, Lincoln's Inn, on 13 November. He confirmed them in a written opinion on 27 January 1976, which began by giving some advice for Tucker to follow:

I think that it would be advisable for the partnership, if it wishes to establish a trade for tax purposes, to embark on a series of transactions – preferably in the same commodity – and to prolong these transactions, even though the identity of the partners may change, over several accounting periods.

He confirmed that it would be acceptable to make up the partnerships accounts on the basis of only realised losses: 'On this basis there will be a realised loss but an unrealised profit, so that account should be taken of the former but not of the latter for tax purposes.' Rees then drew attention to a way round an earlier tax case in which it had been held that a transaction whose primary objective was not commercial but to extract an advantage from the tax system would not be regarded as a trading transaction and so would not provide any relief for tax purposes:

I consider, however, that it would be difficult for the Revenue to distinguish between partners on the basis of their different objectives – particularly since, for the purposes of assessment, a partnership is to be treated as a single entity. Consequently, if a partnership were conducted on a proper commercial basis and if the motives of one or two of the partners were clearly commercial, then the partnership profits should be assessable to tax and its losses available for relief.

Rees did, however, point to a potentially more serious obstacle. Section 170 of the Income and Corporation Taxes Act required that any trade for which a loss was claimed must be carried out on a commercial basis with a view to making profits. This went to the heart of the Commodity Carry Scheme, which was designed purely to create a loss for the taxpayer, who was in the partnership solely for the resulting tax relief. 'It might, however, be argued by the Revenue, if all the facts were appreciated, that the trade was not being carried on with a view to the realisation of profits in the first accounting period.' However, the secretive way in which Tucker and all the other tax-avoidance promoters worked meant that the Inland Revenue would almost certainly not be able to appreciate all the facts until and unless the claim for tax relief was challenged. By his admission of what the effect would be 'if all the facts were appreciated' Peter Rees indicated the highly artificial nature of the Commodity Carry Scheme, and that its success relied not on its merits but on the Revenue not finding out. Despite this, the future Treasury minister was still prepared to give his legal blessing to the Tucker scheme. He even drew Tucker's attention to a possible loophole in Section 170: 'It seems to me that it could be demonstrated that each transaction undertaken by the partnership was designed to, and would very likely, realise a profit, although not necessarily in each accounting period.' Rees did, however, advise against the client paying to be taken out of the partnership in case that 'provoked' the Revenue to challenge the scheme through the client claiming for the resulting loss.

Rees also advised against Tucker's proposal of an option agreement to limit the client's potential loss on disposal. This, the QC wrote, indicating his awareness of the true nature of the Commodity Carry Scheme, 'would heighten the artificiality of this scheme and might, notwithstanding the entirely commercial motives of the continuing partner, provoke the Revenue to argue that the partnership was not in fact carrying on a trade but merely some fiscal device.' But essentially a 'fiscal device' is exactly what the Commodity Carry Scheme was.

Within a little more than three years of writing his opinion, which became essential to Tucker's marketing of the scheme and which revealed his awareness of the Revenue's likely reaction to it, Peter Rees was the Treasury minister responsible for tax policy. 'I would look at the Commodity Carry Scheme differently as a QC than as a minister,' says Rees. But it is not surprising when they read his opinion that some senior Inland Revenue officials felt that Peter Rees was more on the side of the poacher than the gamekeeper.

By the time Tucker received Peter Rees's helpful opinion, in January 1976, the scheme was all set to be sold. Tucker had already received a second legal green light from Barry Pinson QC, also in Rees's chambers. Pinson had been asked on 8 December by Roney, Vincent to advise on what was then called the Copper Carry Scheme, designed for sale only to individuals. The essential scheme differed very little from the company version put to Rees in November. In their instructions to Pinson, Roney, Vincent admitted that the scheme would enable the Tucker client to 'obtain a considerable tax advantage and this is his admitted principal purpose of entering into the partnership'. However, the dealing company was there to make 'commercial profits'. The solicitors also admitted the essential artificiality of the client's 'loss':

For tax purposes there would be a loss, although there would not be a real commercial loss, and in the following accounting period for tax purposes there would be a technical profit not equivalent to an actual commercial profit. In other words, for tax purposes profits are 'straddled forward' because of the valuation rules thereby giving rise to a loss in one period over and above the real commercial result, and an equal profit in the succeeding period over and above the real commercial result . . . the profit in the following accounting period arises to other persons.

The price of the tax advantage was to be double that charged for companies – 20 per cent of the tax saved. Pinson came back very quickly, in ten days, with an opinion approving the Tucker scheme. He saw no legal objections.

The Commodity Carry and Copper Carry schemes were both marketed during 1976 but towards the end of that year and in anticipation of the 1977 tax season, Tucker decided to drop the Copper Carry version, refine the Commodity Carry model by increasing the number of partners first from two to three, then to four, and to market it only to individuals. He put his new proposals, via Roney Vincent, to Rees and Pinson on 7 February 1977. Both were asked to confirm that the additional partner would produce no 'adverse consequences' and that there had been no changes in the law since the date of their previous legal opinions. Pinson again replied first, on 15 February, confirming that all was still well. Rees replied on 22 February in a similar vein. Tucker also obtained a favourable opinion on other legal aspects of the scheme from a third eminent and much used QC, Charles Beattie.

In time for the usual March rush, Barry Pilkington, the one-time Revenue official, drew up an explanatory package of material. He re-assured potential clients that they would be able to claim 90 per cent of the losses to be made by the bigger partnerships, stressed that 'no overall commercial loss' would be suffered and estimated that even given the undoubted risks of commodity investment, 'Following the careful advice of the commodity brokers, commercial losses to the partnership will not exceed 7 per cent of the loss required.' As before, Valleymark was to be the managing partner and put in 5 per cent on the initial capital. It was joined in the partnership by Goldcog, which had been set up in March 1976 with Plummer and Trotman among its directors but owned by the parallel Rossminster group, Thornwright. Like Valleymark it was run from Vogue House. Goldcog was to have 4 per cent of the partnership; another 1 per cent was to held by Tom Benyon, who had been a Valleymark director until February 1977, when Plummer had also resigned from Goldcog. Benyon was initially unenthusiastic about his role in the scheme because of its high profile and his future political ambitions, but eventually agreed.

The client would put in 90 per cent of the capital which would equal 30 per cent of the loss it was hoped to create. First London Securities would then grant the partnership a facility equal to four times that loss. Some time after five days from when the partnership started trading, the looked-for loss would be established by use of 'straddle' deals. The client would then assign his 90 per cent interest to Coltpearl, which had been formed on 1 March 1977 and was controlled by a Manx company, Algrave Investments, associated with the Tucker/Plummer trusts. Halliwell was one of Algrave's directors and its registered office was with a firm of London accountants in nearby Manchester Square often used by Rossminster. The fee paid to Coltpearl, by way of an effective discount on the assets of the partnership, was 13 per cent. Tucker was to be paid 7 per cent of the tax saved. For an individual looking to save £50,000 off his income tax the cost would have been £10,280 before deducting a share of the anticipated £3000 dealing profits. But without a tax scheme the same individual would have had to pay £36,000 in tax on earned income and £43,000 if it was unearned.

Those Tucker clients who were offered the new scheme were sworn to secrecy about the details. The introductory letter from Roy Tucker & Co. made that crystal-clear: 'Details of the scheme are revealed to you on the strict understanding that you will not divulge any such details to any person in any way without our prior consent, unless required to do so by law.'

A similar warning came with the package of explanatory material, legal opinions and blank agreements sent out by the firm to professional advisers. A covering note advised:

These papers are given to you on the strict understanding that you will regard them as confidential in relation to your client for purposes of perusal either personally or with your own colleagues on a similar confidential basis. They should not be copied and they should be returned to us as soon as possible, whether or not your client wishes to proceed with the scheme.

The prime consideration at the initial stage of marketing the scheme was to prevent rivals from stealing the idea and the potential customers, but it was best, even at the initial stage, to keep the Revenue from knowing that a new scheme was being marketed. Early warning could result in legislation that would reduce the profit for everyone.

No word of the Commodity Carry Scheme leaked out and Tucker anticipated a further selling season for the tax year ending in April 1978.

By now it had been decided to reintroduce the corporation tax version, and for this purpose an outside commodity dealing company to replace Valleymark was required. In May 1977 John Tillotson bought control of Bambella Trading and went on the board with Nigel Bruce-Watt.[3] As the managing partner in the corporation tax version of CCS, Bambella joined forces with Goldcog and Benyon plus the client. By the end of June 1977 Bambella's turnover had more than doubled at £6,850,000. It had, however, made a £5000 loss against a previous £79,000 profit.

Tucker and Plummer soon discovered that running the Commodity Carry Scheme in practice went a lot less smoothly than the description provided to Rees and Pinson suggested. Even they could not predict all the vagaries of the commodity markets. According to Richard Gardner, on a number of occasions clients had to stay in the partnerships much longer than the minimum period because the necessary loss had not been achieved. This increased costs and cut the promoters' profit. There were also unexpected problems created by Bailey. Bailey was supposed to take positions on behalf of a pool of Rossminster and client money, with the profits and losses of that pool allocated by Tucker to the relevant clients, to each according to their tax need, but on one occasion the Rossminster pool was hit by an unexpected loss of around £11,000 at the end of the month.

The wider the marketing of the Commodity Carry Scheme, the more Tucker's security arrangements were in danger of breaking down, as more and more accountants and solicitors were sent the helpful package of explanatory documents and legal opinions. In September 1977 one of these professional advisers or their clients for unknown reasons made an unauthorised distribution of the Commodity Carry Scheme documents. They were sent anonymously to the *Sunday Times*. The package was quickly passed to the newspaper's resident Rossminster watcher, Lorana Sullivan, with a hastily scribbled note from the City editor asking, 'Does anything in this capture your imagination?' It certainly did. Described on the cover as 'Commodity Carry Scheme 1977 – Description and Principal Documents', the package contained copies of all the agreements between the client and the other partners, draft minutes and letters, bank mandates and all other necessary agreements and confirmations and an outline of the way the scheme worked with examples. What had been put together in order to sell the Commodity Carry Scheme to clients was now put to work just as effectively to bring it to an end.

By her assiduous study of Rossminster documents and company

accounts plus a little inside help, Lorana Sullivan had already made Tucker and Plummer so uncomfortable with her disclosures that she was known in Vogue House as 'Piranha' Sullivan. At that time she probably knew more about Rossminster than any outsider apart from the Inland Revenue. On this occasion Lorana Sullivan knew more than even the Revenue, as she discovered when she contacted a senior official there to discuss the contents of the anonymous package. He quickly rushed round to the *Sunday Times* and, in return for a copy of the documents, explained just how the scheme worked. The result of this cooperation was published on 9 October. The effect was instant and, for Tucker and Plummer, traumatic.

In the course of the article, under the headline 'Carrying a tax loss away', Lorana Sullivan made a comment which was to prove the focal point of the actions and reactions her exposure of the Commodity Carry Scheme sparked. 'The Tucker–Rossminster team's success arises from its ability to press yet another scheme into service as soon as the Inland Revenue squelches its current effort.' That indeed had been the case, with the comforting result for Tucker and his clients that the taxman was always bolting empty stable doors. Those already through the loophole were safe.

The Commodity Carry Scheme changed all that. The Revenue's reaction to the scheme was far stronger than before, for two reasons: the scheme was the apogee of artificiality, claiming tax relief for a nonexistent loss; and the concept was so wide ranging that if it was allowed to pass unchallenged then the potential loss to the Revenue in tax from the Tucker scheme alone could be at least £15 million. Armed with these arguments senior Inland Revenue officials went to see the chief secretary of the Treasury, Joel (now Lord) Barnett, himself an accountant. They proposed a highly unusual and inevitably controversial response – to kill off the Commodity Carry Scheme immediately by bringing in retrospective legislation disallowing any claim for tax relief made under it. 'Although the Inland Revenue proposed retrospective legislation they did not expect it to be agreed,' Barnett recalls. The reason was political. Retrospective legislation is always unpopular in Parliament on the grounds that it is unjust and attacks individual rights. The law, as judges constantly remind the public, must be certain. If a course of action is taken on the basis of a legal loophole which exists at the time, that action should not, except in rare circumstances, be made illegal on the basis of what the law should have been but was not. It was for this reason that the Revenue's proposal ran into internal opposition within the Treasury and from Barnett's political colleagues. But Barnett himself was convinced by the Revenue's case:

It was the only way to stop what I consider to be a quite repugnant system that was being used deliberately against the interest of every single taxpayer in the country and there was no way in my view in which it could be stopped without retrospective legislation. At that time when I saw this becoming a very big operation of hundreds of millions of pounds, to me I had to take a balance as between one's abhorrence of retrospective legislation and one's abhorrence of people literally taking hundreds of millions of pounds away from every other taxpayer who is having tax deducted from them. It was vital to kill the mass marketing of tax schemes once and for all. I felt it would close down a large part of the tax-avoidance industry.[4]

Barnett estimated that Commodity Carry style schemes could cost the Revenue at least £200 million a year in lost tax simply on the limited information already available. This equalled the total loss from tax avoidance in the years from 1973 to 1976. A Labour government struggling to fight inflation by controlling public expenditure could not afford to see these amounts disappearing from government coffers, especially through such blatant devices. Barnett and the Inland Revenue carried the day. The Commodity Carry Scheme would be outlawed retrospectively.

The first hint of the bombshell came in a written parliamentary answer given in the Commons on 25 November 1977. Barnett disclosed that the 1978 Finance Bill would contain legislation to ban the scheme, and went on to declare that the Chancellor 'will be considering from what date legislation against a claim to loss relief contrived in this kind of way should be effective'.

This was something that neither Tucker and Plummer nor anyone else in the tax-avoidance industry had ever considered likely or politically possible. Tucker and Plummer had assumed that any move by the Labour government against tax avoidance would be blanket legislation modelled on the Australian variety where by the onus would be on the taxpayer to prove that he had not taken part in an artificial avoidance scheme but had established a tax loss legitimately by a commercial transaction. For three years the taxman had been plodding after the fleet-footed scheme promoters. Suddenly he had caught up.

Until November 1977 Tucker could always advise a client that whatever happened when the tax scheme was discovered by the Revenue and legislated against, until then his tax relief should be safe, assuming the blinkered courts with their concentration on minutiae ruled in its favour in the test case which would be fought. Retrospective legislation made any test case redundant and threatened immediately to cancel the tax advantage a client had already paid a nonrefundable fee to obtain. The future of artificial tax avoidance looked extremely problematical, for once retrospective legislation was introduced it could happen again. At a stroke of the pen, as Colin Emson had predicted, the government had changed the rules. Now it was a very different game and one that Tucker and Plummer no longer relished. 'We all realised the writing was on the wall, that the Rossminster type of tax avoidance was over,' says Tom Benyon.

Just how drastic the government intended to be over the Commodity Carry Scheme and how severe a warning it intended to give the tax-avoidance industry was made clear by Chancellor Denis Healey in his April 1978 budget speech. Healey declared:

Tax avoidance . . . has emerged recently in a new form which involves marketing a succession of highly artificial schemes – when one is detected the next is immediately sold – and is accompanied by a level of secrecy which amounts almost to conspiracy to mislead. The time has come not only to stop the particular schemes we know about but to ensure that no schemes of a similar nature can be marketed in the future. So the provisions I shall be introducing this year to deal with artificial avoidance by certain partnerships dealing in commodity futures will go back to 6 April 1976.[5]

The government's determination was further demonstrated during the debate the following day by Joel Barnett: 'We can show those concerned that for the future the game is just not worth the risk. I propose that we should legislate in each case as it comes to our attention in such a way as to remove all tax advantage of a scheme from the outset'.[6] He reiterated his warning during the debate on the second reading of the Finance Bill. 'I hope to persuade the House to legislate to ensure that it will not be possible in the future for those industries to continue.'[7] The Conservatives were appalled – retrospective legislation was particularly unacceptable in tax matters. Their attack on the proposal was lead by the shadow Chancellor, Sir Geoffrey Howe, backed up by the new boy on the Opposition front bench, Peter Rees.

Howe was sympathetic to the government's aim of stamping out artificial tax avoidance. 'There is a point when avoidance can be regarded as improper and unacceptable . . . deserving to be stopped up because it amounts to a defiance of or an escape from the underlying intention of the legislature,' he declared.[8] And he had little time for the scheme marketed and financed by his erstwhile luncheon hosts terming it an 'unmeritorious provision'. He was determined that the Conservatives should not be seen as 'the friends of improper and mischievous tax avoiders'.[9] But he was totally opposed to the use of retrospective legislation against them. He made his position clear when Barnett sounded him out prior to the budget, and in the post-budget debate he spelled out why: 'Although I understand the difficulties . . . to march down the road of introducing retrospective legislation is to make a very fundamental and important change of principle . . . This is a serious path down which to march and we shall challenge the Government on it because it is dangerous to overturn this principle.'[10]

Peter Rees made his mark at an early stage in the debate. On 13 April he pressed the junior Treasury minister Denzil Davies for an explanation of why it was necessary to give retrospective effect to the Commodity Carry Scheme clause. As the Conservatives' tax expert, Rees wound up the budget debate. He quickly came to the proposal for dealing with the Tucker scheme. Tax avoidance, he pointed out, was not a 'clear-cut area'. Unlike Sir Geoffrey Howe, Rees was in no way sympathetic to the government – Rossminster and its imitators was a problem of their own making:

We must draw a sharp distinction between avoidance and evasion, although both are a phenomenon of a high tax rate system . . . Labour Members must face the fact that if they are to use the tax system as a sharp political weapon, people will respond in kind. If they can get advice which enables them to order their affairs so as to keep the rate of tax on their income or their capital down to what they regard as reasonable – and these matters must be subjective – it is only to be expected that they will do so . . . We have to carry the general body of taxpayers with us. They will tell us ultimately what is a fair rate and what is not. Some of them will do it by moonlighting, by flitting, by evasion. Others, perhaps the more sophisticated, and . . . those who have access to better advice, will do it perhaps by avoidance. Neither phenomenon is attractive. We all recognise that.[11]

The QC then turned his attention to the Commodity Carry Scheme in particular:

This is the first time that I have been able to discover that [the Labour government] have chosen to legislate without prior warning at all – subject to one point. This is why I think that their position is even more discreditable than has yet been revealed . . . If the scheme is not soundly based in law, what need to legislate back to 1976? If it is soundly based in law, we can consider in Committee – no doubt taking a robust view – what measures are appropriate . . . The measure proposed . . . is utterly repugnant to every constitutional principle which we on this side hold dear.

Rees resumed his attack during the committee stage of the Finance Bill on 6 June. He spelled out what became known as the 'Rees rules' which a government should follow before introducing restrospective legislation.

The MP for Dover and Deal was also to the fore in the final July debate on the measure, winding up for the Conservatives. While indicating, if somewhat less fulsomely than Sir Geoffrey Howe, a lack of enthusiasm for the scheme, Rees blamed the Inland Revenue. He told the Commons, 'The Revenue does not come to this problem entirely with clean hands.'[12] However, the scheme was defended against one of the government's main accusations: 'I do not think that [it is] hedged around with a secrecy which amounts to a conspiracy of silence.' A curious statement, given the admission in Rees's opinion of the danger 'if all the facts were appreciated'.

Taxpayers and their advisers were entitled to rely on the statutes. 'Those outside this House are not required to look into our minds or even required to study very closely the speeches we make in our debates. They are concerned only with the finished articles and the statutes which reach the statute book.' Taunting Barnett he declared, 'I am not entirely persuaded that the chief secretary has understood the dimensions of the problem.' Rees even questioned the chief secretary's knowledge of the scheme. As if to prove his own, in comparison not inconsiderable, inside knowledge the Conservative MP declared definitively, 'The House should know at once that the scheme at which this clause is aimed could be undertaken only by an individual.'

This, however, was incorrect, for the retrospective legislation would have hit also at the corporation tax version of the scheme sold the year before. Rees must have forgotten or overlooked that he had advised on such a version in November 1976. His instructions from Roney, Vincent had declared, 'It is thought that the scheme applies equally for individuals or for companies.'

At no time during these speeches did Peter Rees MP make any disclosure that among the 'better advice' that had been offered to Roy Tucker and his clients had been that of Peter Rees QC or that in questioning whether it was 'soundly based in law' the government were challenging that very advice given by the lawyer MP for Dover. He did feel it necessary to 'declare a personal interest as a lawyer' in the final debate,[13] but that was the limit of his disclosure. In comparison, the Liberal spokesman John Pardoe felt it necessary to declare, 'I am a member of the London Metal Exchange'.[14]

It is not possible to say precisely what is and what is not a declarable interest for an MP and when or if it should be disclosed, despite the clarifications and rules forced upon the House of Commons in the wake of the scandal surrounding the corrupt architect John Poulson in the early seventies. Whereas the principle of declaring any personal pecuniary interest before proposing legislation or voting in the Commons was clear, the position when it comes to speaking in a debate was and is much less clearly defined. After Poulson and the election of the Labour government the House of Commons introduced a register of Members' interests and in May 1974 voted in favour of a new rule governing the declaration of an interest by an MP:

In any debate or proceedings of the house or its committees or transactions or communications which a Member may have with other Members or with Ministers or servants of the Crown, he shall disclose any relevant, pecuniary interest or benefit of whatever nature, whether direct or indirect, that he may have had, may have or may be expecting to have.[15]

The question is therefore whether the fees Peter Rees received from Roy Tucker for providing legal opinions on the Commodity Carry Scheme counted as a 'relevant pecuniary interest or benefit' and therefore should have been declared in that April 1978 debate.

Peter Rees's position is unambiguous. Despite receiving the fees, he says he did not have a 'direct, financial interest' and was 'precluded from declaring that he had advised on the Commodity Carry Scheme by professional ethics'. According to Rees, he would have had a direct interest only if he had been paid on a contingency fee basis (allowed in the United States but not in Britain) or if he had personally done a scheme. But as he had simply advised for a fee he no longer had any direct interest to declare. Pressed on this point, Rees replied, 'It's a matter of strict convention of the Bar that a barrister does not disclose – even in the House of Commons – whom he advises or what advice he has given.' So the MP felt he was 'unable to admit that he had advised on that scheme or had advised Roy Tucker'. It was in any event, Rees maintained, 'generally known that he advised on tax matters'. There would thus seem to be a complete contradiction, affecting those MPs who are barristers, between the rules of the House of Commons and the rules of the Bar.

Rees also maintained that there was no need to make any declaration of interest in the Commodity Carry Scheme because he was not discussing the legal merits of the Tucker scheme but the constitutional issue of retrospective legislation. 'I do not accept that any ruling of the House required declaring an interest and it was not possible for me not to speak as the tax expert on the front bench', was Rees's typically pugnacious and uncompromising response.

However, other MPs who are also barristers are less certain. Denzil Davies, a Labour Treasury minister who spoke in the 1978 budget debate, is also a former tax counsel. He feels Peter Rees should have either made a declaration of his past involvement or not spoken in the debate. 'That would have been the right thing to do. More frank. I would be very reluctant to comment on a matter in which I advised.' Rees, he says, could have simply declared that he had given advice on the scheme without identifying his client.

A similar critical view is taken by another former Labour Treasury minister and barrister, Dick Taverne, now the Social Democrat director of the Institute of Fiscal Studies. He considered Rees's nondisclosure 'a mistake'. 'I would have thought some declaration was necessary,' he says. 'My instinct would have been to mention it.' Rees, Taverne felt, could have resolved the ethical problem simply by saying that he had advised an unidentified client who might be affected by the government decision, but it would have been 'politic' to disclose that he had been consulted.

Peter Rees himself was sufficiently conscious of the rules on declaration of interest to feel that it was necessary during the 1977 budget debate to make not one but two declarations: one total, one partial – neither substantial. When referring to proposals regarding retirement annuities for the self-employed, Rees prefaced his speech by saying, 'I must here declare a special and personal interest in that I am self-employed.'[16] Later in that same April 1977 debate, when chiding Joel Barnett for advising on tax avoidance when he was in practice as an accountant, Rees referred, rather modestly, to his own 'slight professional acquaintance with these matters'. He also felt it necessary to declare his interest as an investor in a 1976 Finance Bill debate on woodlands.

On a more substantial matter such as the debate on the Commodity Carry Scheme it is hard to see why Peter Rees did not feel that parliamentary convention and fair dealing with his fellow MPs should not override Bar rules and that it would be less than frank not to make at least some partial disclosure. For it is at the very least arguable that by receiving fees from Roy Tucker on the Commodity Carry Scheme in 1975–77 Peter Rees came within the 1974 definition laid down by Parliament of a 'relevant, pecuniary interest or benefit of whatever nature, whether direct or indirect'.

By his nondeclaration Peter Rees also fell short of the more simple criterion emphasised by Mr Speaker King in 1969 that 'it is a good thing for an honourable Member to declare his interest'.[17] The background to that convention is set out in Erskine May, the bible of parliamentary procedure: 'The origin of this convention was at its inception more in the nature of a courtesy, or prudent precaution.'[18]

Rees's predecessor as the Treasury number two, Joel Barnett, was not impressed by his arguments for nondisclosure and described Rees's stance as 'a bogus point of view based on a very narrow definition of the rules'. Speaking as an accountant, Barnett said there would have been no question of having to disclose clients' affairs: 'If I were involved as Chief Secretary and there was a former client of mine whose case or type of case we were discussing, I would certainly want to tell the House of my previous involvement'.[19]

But just then, when the government was making a determined move against artificial tax avoidance by hitting a blatant example which could cost the country millions in lost revenue, it was perhaps not the best time for a Conservative front bench spokesman publicly to admit his own crucial involvement in trying to help that tax revenue disappear. The electorate was unlikely to be sympathetic to arcane arguments about Bar ethics, especially when, as Rees himself admitted, the scheme's very success depended on the Inland Revenue not finding out the truth. Peter Rees declared in his final speech, 'It will be for the House and for the country outside to judge who has leaned over backwards to observe the constitutional proprieties.'[20]

The *Sunday Times*'s disclosures and Joel Barnett's quick response brought an unexpectedly sudden end to the marketing of the Commodity Carry Scheme, but it had been very profitable while it lasted. Goldcog in its first year handled commodity deals worth £1,600,000 that produced a profit of £73,000 and a £30,000 dividend to Thornwright – after the now obligatory use of the Gross Annuity Scheme. Between November 1977 and July 1978 its commodity dealings more than doubled to £3,750,000, producing a lower profit but enabling a £95,000 Thornwright loan to be repaid. Coltpearl, to whom clients assigned their interest in the partnerships, was spectacularly successful: in the twelve months to March 1978 it earned a profit of £2,021,000.[21] Bambella was less productive. In the year to June 1978 it made a profit of only £3500 on deals worth £600,000. All four companies – Valleymark, Goldcog, Coltpearl and Bambella – did little or no trading after 1978 and were all wound up with substantial but unagreed tax liabilities in 1980 and 1981.

E. Bailey benefited substantially from its involvement in the Commodity Carry Scheme. In the year to July 1977 its income soared from just under £900,000 to a record £3,100,000; about £340,000 came from Rossminster group commissions. Another £155,000 had come from the same source in the period to July 1976 following Rossminster's purchase of a near half-interest.

Rossminster bought out the rest of E. Bailey during 1977. With the Commodity Carry Scheme banned, Tucker's and Plummer's interest in commodity dealing waned. Although it never equalled the £2,400,000 it earned in 1976–77, Bailey continued to be very profitable. In both the following years profits exceeded £1 million. Very little of this Bailey profit went in corporation tax due to tax losses generated in the traditional Rossminster way. In 1979 it was decided to sell Bailey, and a new company, E. Bailey Commodities, acquired the business for £2,825,000, more than five times the value put on it by Brascan less than four years before. Another £1,300,000 was left in the old Bailey company in cash. The shareholders in the new Bailey company, with the exception of Glyn Evans, who had a tiny percentage, were the offshore interests of the six Rossminster principals. Only Miller appeared in his own name – he was now nonresident for UK tax. The others were represented by five Manx companies – Darmas, Valen, Kallow, Pectineus and Tanror Investments. The first two companies were associated with the Tucker and Plummer trusts respectively. Kallow was associated with the Gardner interests and Pectineus and Tanror with Benyon and Trotman.[22]

On 24 September 1979 E. Bailey Commodities was sold to London Investment Trust, run by John Arthur, who partnered Tucker's former associate Tim Nicholas in the Rossminster clone Centrespur. The price was £2 million – £1,025,000 in cash and the balance in 6,500,000 LIT shares. LIT's brokers acquired 2,500,000 of these from the Bailey vendors for £375,000. As the LIT share price raced up to 34p during 1980 from that 15p placing price, the 4 million shares became worth £1,360,000.[23] A further £500,000 in LIT shares was issued to the Bailey vendors in March 1982. Bailey proved one of the best Rossminster deals: an investment of some £523,000 returned nearly £3,500,000.

The Tucker clients who paid to buy the Commodity Carry Scheme had less to celebrate from their brief introduction to the mysteries of commodity dealing – the tax reliefs they had paid up to 20 per cent to achieve were worthless. But then success was never guaranteed, despite the reassuring statement in the pro forma Tucker letter to potential clients that 'we have every reason to believe that the scheme is soundly based in law'. And it had also been made clear that Tucker accepted no responsibility or liability and that the fees charged were not refundable – win, lose or draw. Even the tax-avoidance apologists were silenced by the totally artificial nature of the latest Tucker masterpiece. Tax avoidance Rossminster style was starting to appear antisocial and not just to those on the Left. The undeclared war between the Inland Revenue and Tucker and Plummer had begun, in private but in earnest. That change in the political and legal climate presented the Inland Revenue with an unexpected ally.

ONE PIECE OF PAPER

By 1976 the sheer scale of the problem posed by Rossminster's ever expanding clientele made it necessary for the Inland Revenue to take the initiative. The Revenue were now faced by single schemes which could cost up to £100 million if successful.

A year before Denis Moorcraft had been appointed under secretary in charge of anti-avoidance operations, by now a top priority. A career Revenue man, then in his midfifties, Moorcraft had become a tax officer straight from grammar school just before the outbreak of the Second World War. Highly regarded by those who worked for him, Moorcraft had immediately made his mark by setting up the Special Offices to target specific areas of tax evasion and crack down on identified offenders. Equipped with the wide new powers of search provided in the 1976 Finance Act – themselves evidence of the urgency with which evasion was now being treated – the Special Offices soon proved highly effective. Areas of rampant evasion such as North Sea oil-field workers, meat porters at Smithfield market, Fleet Street casual print workers, the publishers of pornographic magazines and the sex shops that sold them were targeted one by one, and the amounts of tax recovered were spectacular.

The creation of the Special Offices had been made necessary by the boom in the black economy encouraged by escalating inflation, the introduction of VAT and high tax rates which combined in a mutually beneficial conspiracy those who wanted a job done for less with those who wanted to take home more from the job they did. Tax evasion was costing ten times what it was estimated was lost through tax avoidance schemes, but shortage of manpower meant only glaring examples were tackled. The campaign against the tax avoiders was, however, a very different one to that against the tax evaders – fought with different weapons and with a different type of Revenue official, dictated by the nature of the opponent. Revenue investigators had to use the 'softly, softly' approach rather than the Flying Squad tactics sometimes favoured by the Enquiry Branch, which handled most cases of evasion.

The Rossminster investigation was given to the T2 or Special Investigation Section of the Revenue's Technical Division which dealt with tax avoidance. (One of the changes Denis Moorcraft had made was to change the name of T2 from Legal Avoidance Section, which he felt gave the wrong impression, one almost of acceptance.) It was put under the control of assistant director William Dermit, a small, stocky, grey-haired, quietly spoken man in his fifties who looked like a retired army colonel rather than an investigator. The appearance was deceiving, however – 'He would have made a very good policeman,' said one admiring former colleague. Dermit had taken over the SIS in 1976 when, for him, 'Rossminster was just a small cloud'. From an office on the third floor of Melbourne House, one of those anonymous office buildings so beloved by the Inland Revenue, just opposite its Somerset House headquarters, 'Bill' Dermit began to track not just the activities of Rossminster but, more significantly, the personal tax affairs of its owners, in particular Tucker and Plummer. 'The most complex investigation the Inland Revenue has ever handled', was how he described it.

A key element in the Revenue's suspicions was the secrecy which surrounded the schemes. 'We always knew about Tucker and Rossminster but the problem was secrecy', explained a former senior Revenue official. 'There was a long time lag before we discovered that a scheme had been mass marketed'. This was because clients were instructed to answer no Revenue queries without consulting Tucker and information was withheld by Tucker until the last legal moment. The Revenue's response to these tactics is made clear by Sir William Pile, then its head: 'We were to be kept in the dark and I think this is a furtive way of behaving. I think the secrecy of these schemes is itself evidence that the purveyors knew that if the facts were known Parliament may well step in and declare them illegal.'[1] However, it was not just the Revenue that Tucker was afraid of, as Arthur Lewis-Grey makes clear: 'Ideas are actually in very short supply so it's in the interest of the tax-avoidance industry to allow a scheme to run for as long as possible, say two or three years, so they're desperately concerned that a new idea does not leak out too quickly.'[2] Tucker saw this as being 'businesslike'.[3] Dermit and his fellow investigators preferred quoting Dr Johnson's statement that where there was secrecy, roguery was close behind.

They were somewhat unevenly matched opponents. Dermit, the cautious, correct civil servant nearing retirement with an abiding distaste for artificial tax avoidance, versus the high-powered, inventive intellect of Tucker and the methodically efficient Plummer. Both were almost young enough to be his sons and both were prepared to do anything the tax laws did not specifically disallow. On his side Dermit had the not inconsiderable resources of the Inland Revenue. But facing him and his team of skilled investigators was the moat of the English Channel and four hundred years of Channel Islands independence, beyond which lay Rossminster's offshore operations and the all-important controlling discretionary trusts. Unless that moat could be bridged it would be impossible to unravel the secret of Rossminster's ownership and the ultimate beneficiaries of the multimillion proceeds from marketing and financing Tucker's tax schemes.

Sitting smugly onshore, in homes owned offshore, Tucker and Plummer were confident that, try as they might, the Revenue would not be able to pierce that defence. Moorcraft, Dermit and the SIS team knew the problems but felt that the schemes at least were not invulnerable. 'We believed we could win as long as we could get the full facts out,' recalls one of the SIS investigators. 'Filling in forms and signing documents is not reality.' What was required was simply a 'hard investigation'.

The Revenue began probing the Rossminster empire at as many points as possible, looking for a disgruntled employee or dissatisfied client. The order went out to local inspectors of taxes to inform Melbourne House of any Tucker scheme they encountered. Any such scheme was to be challenged and no relief given.

Word spread along the tax grapevine that the Revenue was moving against Tucker and Rossminster on a broad front and anyone who got in the way by doing business with them could fall under Melbourne House suspicion and merit similar treatment. Former Rossminster employees found their tax affairs taken over by the SIS from their local inspector and were quizzed at length about any claim for tax relief. The Revenue's aim was to find any crack in the solid façade presented by Vogue House and Audley House which would reveal what really did go on in the offshore companies and trusts into which the control of Rossminster disappeared.

What the Revenue desperately needed was an inside informant, but its shaking of the Rossminster tree produced not a single informative apple.

In a surprising and unparalleled move which illustrated the seriousness with which the Rossminster threat was viewed inside the Inland Revenue, Denis Moorcraft, in the wake of the Commodity Carry Scheme, accepted an invitation to be interviewed for the *London Programme* on Rossminster. For the first time a senior Revenue official was seen making the case against Roy Tucker and his tax schemes. 'We don't just consider it a serious problem, it's one of the gravest problems I think we have today,' Moorcraft declared. Moorcraft did not ask for permission to appear on the programme, broadcast on 3 December 1977. He did, however, inform the chairman of the Board of Inland Revenue of his intention. The anti-avoidance chief thought it essential to get the Revenue point of view across to the public since it was losing the publicity war. After the programme Moorcraft felt his performance was ineffective in comparison with Tucker's, but it was far too effective for his political bosses at the Treasury. Ministers let it be known that that they did not want to see their officials discussing policy on such sensitive subjects. Neither Moorcraft nor any other Revenue official appeared on T V again.

Inland Revenue traditionalists too believed – and still believe – that the public interest was best served by their remaining grey, faceless and, most of all, silent. Moorcraft's decision was seen as the right step, however, by those who realised that Tucker and Rossminster could not be handled by this antiquated approach, especially since Tucker would go on T V and speak to newspapers about how everything he did was legal and how tax avoidance was a safety valve from the frustrations caused by penal taxation and so he prevented Britain's best and brightest from emigrating or closing down their businesses. The fact that he and Plummer had moved control of Rossminster out of the country, and with it most of the wealth they had created, naturally went unmentioned. Against the Revenue's silence, Tucker and Rossminster seemed to have all the best tunes. And who loved the taxman anyway?

Denis Moorcraft's high-profile response had one powerful backer: the recently appointed chairman of the Board of Inland Revenue, Sir William Pile. A tall commanding figure with the stern bearing and precise manner of a headmaster, Pile came to the Revenue towards the end of a distinguished thirty-year career at the top levels of Whitehall. After two years as director general of the prison service and six as permanent under-secretary at the Department of Education and Science, he arrived at the Inland Revenue in 1976, just as it began to embark on its offensive against avoidance and the black economy. Not sharing the inhibitions of those whose lives had been spent within Somerset House, he was willing to back new initiatives. Like Moorcraft, Dermit and others engaged in the Rossminster investigation, Pile felt a sense of moral distaste bordering on outrage over the cosy injustice perpetrated on the more than 20-million-strong army of involuntary PAYE taxpayers by the increasingly blatant operations of Rossminster and its imitators. 'Our view was that the Rossminster schemes were unacceptable because they were making tax that was legitimately collectable uncollectable. They were creating devices whereby tax was not paid though Rossminster and the Revenue knew that it should.'[4] Before long the drive against avoidance in general and Rossminster and Roy Tucker in particular began to assume the character of a crusade for certain of those most closely involved.

Early in 1978 Tucker realised a measure of the hard line the Inland Revenue under Pile was taking when, somewhat belatedly, he tried to do a Bradman-type deal with the Revenue, offering to stop marketing tax schemes in return for immunity from further pursuit. After the decision to bring in retrospective legislation against the Commodity Carry Scheme Tucker had in any case all but decided to withdraw from the tax-avoidance business. In exchange for his retirement Tucker wanted the Revenue to let existing schemes go through or return to the previous system of contesting each scheme via a test case and to drop its wide-ranging opposition to Rossminster. At a meeting, Moorcraft and Dermit made it clear that the time for doing such deals was past.

The reason was that for the Revenue the cloak of secrecy which surrounded everything, in particular the ownership of Rossminster itself, the nature of its relationship with Roy Tucker and the fate of its escalating profits from his schemes, raised questions of possible tax evasion on a massive scale. Once the Revenue had discovered that Rossminster effectively shared in the tax saved by Tucker's schemes, it looked to see whether this appeared in the individuals' tax returns. Of course it did not. 'How could Tucker and Plummer make so much money and not pay tax? If it was that easy we'd all be doing it,' one SIS man commented. If it could be shown that Tucker, Plummer and the others, rather than the offshore trusts, could benefit from Rossminster's profits, either in income or capital, or had done so since 1973, then it was no longer a matter of unravelling the byzantine intricacies of tax avoidance but the more direct task of proving what the Revenue convinced themselves was tax evasion and fraud. But without inside information, it was impossible to penetrate the Manx and Guernsey fortresses. And after more than a year of challenging, probing and questioning – including two days of interviews with Tucker early in 1978 – no such information had been forthcoming. Then in January 1979 the Inland Revenue received a telephone call from a most unlikely source.

After more than two years in Guernsey Arthur Lewis-Grey had begun to become disenchanted both with the Channel Islands and with Rossminster. Like his predecessor John Glauser he had started to chafe at the limitations placed on his role by Tucker and Plummer. He was interested in developing an orthodox trust business with outside, non-Rossminster clients but this was not of interest to the Rossminster kingpins. They wanted the Guernsey office to concentrate on Rossminster and their affairs, and they wanted to keep a tight control over its management.

Lewis-Grey's frustration and disenchantment increased when Desmond Miller took up residence in Guernsey in April 1978, having acquired a £70,000 house in St Peter Port the previous year. Lewis-Grey saw a limited role developing for himself – 'I foresaw that I was becoming surplus to requirements.' At thirty-two he was not tempted to settle for the luxury of a life in a pleasant but somewhat claustrophobic tax-haven retirement home, so he began to consider the prospects for either leaving Rossminster or returning to England. Such thoughts were encouraged by the mounting pressure of work as Rossminster endeavoured to squeeze the last drop out of the tax-avoidance boom.

These developments coincided with a crisis in his own private life, the near break-up of his marriage. But Lewis-Grey had also started to question the whole basis of the Rossminster operation. Like all tax barristers, Lewis-Grey had never devoted much time to the morality of tax avoidance – legality was all that mattered. Now he began to dwell on the reality of Rossminster's offshore operations and of the discretionary trusts which he had had under his control since February 1976.

Lewis-Grey was not the first Rossminster insider to become disenchanted: there had been Glauser, Preston and more recently William Fossick, who had been largely responsible for the Rossminster banks, and the company secretary Martin Feeney. Yet another Slater, Walker alumnus, Fossick, during monthly visits to Guernsey expressed concern that if certain tax schemes failed, First London Securities could be insolvent. He resigned to join a firm of City solicitors used by Rossminster. Feeney, also a lawyer, returned to private practice, too. 'I could not control it so I left. The burden of work was too great. I was unable to check it all.'

Other events also disturbed Lewis-Grey. At an early stage he had pointed out to Plummer that he risked a potential capital transfer tax problem over the Leander and Ulysses trusts because they were administered by nonresident trustees in Guernsey. This could result in an ultimate charge on Plummer and his wife as settlors of the trusts, and any distribution of assets by the trust could create a CTT liability. Ensuring that valuations of the trusts' assets were kept to a minimum in returns to the Inland Revenue was only a stopgap answer.

Then, in 1977, Lewis-Grey began to receive a number of calls from Plummer asking about the legal definition of residency for Guernsey tax purposes. Lewis-Grey feared that Plummer intended to join Miller and Cairns in Guernsey, thereby making his own position as managing director largely redundant. He discovered that Plummer was instead proposing that his mother should go to live in Guernsey and that the trusts' assets could then be distributed to her. When it was pointed out that this could create a local tax liability, as the trusts specifically excluded Guernsey-resident beneficiaries, Plummer replied that his mother would first stop off in Jersey and take delivery of the trusts' assets there, this way avoiding both UK and Guernsey tax.

Plummer asked to be kept informed about the availability of suitable homes locally, and in January 1978 Plummer's wife Jean and his mother, Rose Plummer, visited Guernsey to view various houses. Lewis-Grey describes Rose Plummer as a likeable but unsophisticated woman whose greatest concern was the Guernsey climate because she suffered from bronchitis. She explained that she was moving from Pinner to Guernsey because Plummer intended to move there. There was no mention of tax advantages. The possibility was discussed of buying a boarding house for her to provide both an income and company, since she knew no one in Guernsey. 'Ron is sending his mummy to join his money' was the joke in the Rossminster office after the Plummers returned to London.

Plummer continued to discuss becoming a nonresident with Miller. One suggested advantage was that it would make it easier to negotiate a deal with the Revenue once both taxpayer and funds were outside UK jurisdiction. In March 1979 a home was bought for Rose Plummer just above the harbour at St Peter Port for £215,000; Plummer himself took up residence in Guernsey the following year.

A report prepared by Roy Tucker on the position at 5 April 1978 indicated the house cleaning that Tucker and Rossminster were undertaking after the Commodity Carry Scheme storm and his failure to negotiate a deal with the Inland Revenue. The report set out the 'provisions for the future' as Rossminster was discreetly wound down. It estimated that the cost of administering 1200 companies until liquidation in two and a half years' time would require £650,000. Another £200,000 was budgeted to cover the cost of 'Roy Tucker & Co. client relationship work' for the next four and a half years. Halliwell and Bruce-Watt's costs for running the Company Purchase Scheme companies was put at £200,000. Tax work on the Rossminster companies was expected to cost £150,000. The fund to fight test cases on the tax schemes earmarked a further £280,000. All this had been provided 'in cash and in discreet funds'. Redundancy costs were budgeted at £100,000. The total sum estimated to be required was £2,030,000.

AJR Financial Services was established to take over much of the secretarial and administrative work for the 1200 companies in the Rossminster group, and be responsible for dealing with the legal work associated with the Revenue challenges to the various schemes. Formed in April 1978, AJR was owned by three former Rossminster employees – Arthur Piercy (Benyon's one-time boss at Slater, Walker Insurance), John Bottomley and Richard Hallas – who had handled accounting and tax matters at Vogue House. Hartopp, controlled by the Tucker trusts, provided £10,000 for Lewis-Grey to subscribe for preference shares, which gave Rossminster voting control of the company, which operated out of Rossminster's former offices in St George Street.

The Tucker report set out what the switch to AJR was designed to achieve – paying most of the remaining UK funds to the offshore Rossminster owners. The various groups of internal and scheme companies were to be billed from offshore for the necessary administrative, tax and legal services required until they were liquidated. These companies were mainly grouped under Kemforth and Shareworker together with the Company Purchase Scheme companies resting in St George's and Blessingwell and the Rossminster and Tucker/Plummer trust companies. All were to be invoiced a total of £480,000, to be paid in advance – it was 'an urgent matter', said the report, to establish that these companies had the money to pay. In case UK funds were not immediately available substantial reserve funds had been accumulated offshore in a company codenamed Yellowhammer, specifically set aside to meet Roy Tucker & Co.'s costs over the next five years – perhaps £250,000. It was hoped that this would, like the other costs, be met instead from future income, and all the Yellowhammer funds, together with the £480,000 provided for administrative costs and the £280,000 in the Tucker fighting fund, would become freely available to the offshore owners.

These arrangements were activated throughout the summer of 1978 and were ready to be put into practice by August. The key to it all was a Manx company, Vercot Services, which had been formed in late July with Cairns and Marshall from Rossminster in Guernsey as directors. They were later joined by Plummer's friend Simon Raynaud, a shareholder in Dreadnought, through which the Tucker and Plummer trusts exercised control of Rossminster. Miller and Lewis-Grey also joined the board. Vercot was a subsidiary of a Guernsey company, Victory Holdings, which had Bermuda-based directors, Gordon and Maureen Copley, and was controlled by the Victory Trust.

In an *aide-mémoire* dated 19 May Desmond Miller stated that Victory 'has been stripped of its assets other than £107,000 in cash'. Victory and the Victory Trust were to be the repository of the Yellowhammer reserve funds. At a Victory board meeting on 2 August at Dinard airport the arrangements between Vercot, AJR and the UK companies were set out and approved. Having entered into contracts to supply secretarial services for ten years to Blessingwell, St George's, Thornwright, Kemforth, Shareworker and all their subsidiaries in return for a lump payment, Vercot then subcontracted these services to AJR.

Because of the way the deal was structured, no VAT would be payable by the Rossminster companies as the contract was with an offshore company. More significantly, control of a large quantity of crucial internal Rossminster documents would now lie outside the UK and beyond the Inland Revenue's jurisdiction. Lewis-Grey expressed some reservations about this but was assured by Miller that it was perfectly legal. Indeed, counsel's opinions had been obtained from Peter Curry QC and, three years before, from Michael Wheeler QC.

Soon afterwards fifty-five packing cases arrived in Guernsey, containing highly sensitive material relating to the roles in many internal group and mechanical 'scheme' companies of the Rossminster directors and key executives of both the company and Tucker's firm. The files in London had been sifted in accordance with the Miller *aide-mémoire*. Under the heading 'Security', Miller wrote, 'It has to be ascertained that there are no documents on these [head office] files other than those which in the sense indicated should be there.' He went on to warn, 'All ex-main Board Directors should now consider what information is in their hands, what should be retained and what is unnecessary or embarrassing.'

The Rossminster insiders were battening down the hatches before the storm they feared was coming.

Such a large number of files could not be accommodated inside the small Rossminster Trust offices at Weighbridge House, and it was necessary to find a location that was convenient, discreet and secure. One hundred yards up the narrow, cobbled street from Weighbridge House, Langlois, a firm of furniture retailers, had a large – 10 feet by 10 feet – cellar cut into the wall which ran along one side of Lower Little Pollet. The cellar was used as a storage room and was divided by a steel grille a few feet behind the solid green wooden doors of the nondescript entrance. It was decided to put all the packing cases there.

As a further precaution Rossminster established what Tucker, in his report on the situation at 5 April 1978, very candidly termed the 'Staff Disaster Fund'. His report said, 'This fund is designed to protect staff who will possibly be exposed to substantial financial liabilities arising out of matters undertaken in the course of their duties.' The report listed who the beneficiaries of the fund were to be and why:

[Plummer, Trotman, Piercy]: These persons have (accidentally and ? negligently) paid up dividends out of profits which were not there except on the basis of certain tax arrangements.

[Benyon]: he has been involved as partner in sundry commodity dealing partnerships.

[Gardner, Pilkington, Cairns, Nicholas]: These individuals have all been directors of companies which entered transactions which would have been impossible had the tax schemes not worked.

[Colin Knox]: He has taken on auditships at short notice and in difficult situations.

Tucker went on to describe just how the Disaster Fund would work:

It was decided that the company would contribute £50,000 to any 'disaster claim' but no more. The £50,000 could at the individual's option be paid to him in the UK or be paid into a trust fund abroad. At that individual's option, it could be paid before the

Category I cont

Banking Dept	£35,000 +
RT/CO (Fickling/Matthews?)	£35,000 —
Sundry	£30,000 +

100   10(

CATEGORY J

Staff Disaster Fund.

This fund is designed to protect staff who will possibly
be exposed to substantial financial liabilities arising
out of matters undertaken in the course of their duties.
The persons involved appear to be as follows:

(a) RAP, AJT and AP. These persons have (accidentally
and ? negligently) paid up dividends out of profits
which were not there except on the basis of certain
tax arrangements.

(b) TYB : he has been involved as partner in sundry
commodity dealing partnerships.

(c) RMG, DBP, WSC, TJN : These individuals have all been
directors of companies which entered transactions which
would have been impossible had the tax schemes not
worked.

(d) CK : He has taken on auditships at short notice and
in difficult situations.

It was decided that the company would contribute £50,000 to
any "disaster claim" but no more. The £50,000 could at the
individuals option be paid to him in the UK or be paid into
a trust fund abroad. At that individuals option, it could
be paid before that individuals bankruptcy (i.e. to help save
the bankruptcy) or after. If any individual thought that he
might have substantial claims against him, then it was up to
that individual to plan well in advance to reduce his UK estate
if he wished so that if there were claims against him of a
substantial sum, he would go bankrupt with a minimum of financial
loss.

The total provision for the above 9 individuals is 9 x £50,000
or £450,000 but it is thought that this could be discounted as
far as a present cash reserve were concerned to say- £300,000
(It is thought that interest should be rolled up on this

individual's bankruptcy (i.e. to help save the bankruptcy) or after. If any individual thought that he might have substantial claims against him, then it was up to that individual to plan well in advance to reduce his UK estate if he wished so that if there were claims against him of a substantial sum, he would go bankrupt with a minimum of financial loss.

Tucker did not overlook himself:

It was thought that RCT was in a different category from the rest as because of the unlimited liability in his business, he was much more likely to receive medium-size claims than the other individuals which he might reasonably want to pay. This might include excessive tax liabilities because of unfair disallowances in RT & Co. or might include negligence claims. It was thought that £50,000 should be paid to RCT (or his interests) up front on the basis that RCT took on all these risks personally.

Finally, those faithful, ever present, corporate servants, William Halliwell and Nigel Bruce-Watt, were not forgotten. They were left in the firing line on the hundreds of companies whose corporation tax liabilities had been spirited away under the Company Purchase Scheme but which now all faced tax assessments for money that had been paid on to the charities. Although, in the words of Tucker's report, 'the organisation did not have a disaster liability' to them, they were to be given a modicum of protection 'in appropriate circumstances' in the form of a £25,000 ex gratia payment each.

These preparations did little for Lewis-Grey's confidence in the efficacy of Rossminster's operations, but he did not have much time to dwell on such matters. The pace of the tax work had become even more hectic, and his private problems left little time for quiet contemplation. Tucker and Plummer were so concerned that Simon Raynaud was sent to Guernsey to evaluate the situation discreetly. He reported that all was well, but a week later Lewis-Grey informed MacMillan that he was leaving and returned to England the same day. Matters had come to a head in July when his wife left Guernsey with their two children and went to stay with her parents in Sussex. By then Lewis-Grey was, by his own admission, in a highly confused state, but after a few weeks he made up his mind to rejoin his family and to break from Rossminster. He resigned with effect from 12 October 1978.

In England Lewis-Grey was vulnerable to the Inland Revenue with its powers to compel the production of information. It was essential therefore to ensure his silence. Rossminster sought to achieve this by way of a draconian and intimidating severance agreement. Drafted by Desmond Miller, the agreement was made by Rossminster Trust not only with Lewis-Grey but also with his wife Miranda and, as her financial guarantor, her father, Dr Ronald Mowat. The agreement stated that Lewis-Grey had resigned because 'by reasons of ill-health' he had been incapacitated from performing his duties. In return for £95,000 paid for their house, bought with a £65,000 Rossminster mortgage which was written off, Lewis-Grey and his wife agreed to indemnify Rossminster against:

All losses, claims and damages which any of such [Rossminster] companies may suffer as a result of the loss, disclosure or publication whether by accident or otherwise of any . . . deeds, documents, correspondence or other papers or as a result of the disclosure by Mr Lewis-Grey or Mrs Lewis-Grey of any knowledge or information which is confidential to Rossminster or its subsidiary or associated companies or any client of any such companies.

Furthermore, they undertook that:

They will not and neither of them will make to any person any statement (whether by word of mouth or in writing) which has or might be considered likely to have an adverse or prejudicial effect on the standing, reputation or business of Rossminster or any company in the group of companies of which Rossminster forms part . . . or of any director or other officer or employee of any such company.

If they broke the agreement they would have to pay Rossminster £30,000 – a sum neither Lewis-Grey nor his wife could afford.

With the aid of the £95,000 carrot and this £30,000 stick Rossminster believed it had bought Lewis-Grey's silence. The list of companies and trusts he was to remain silent about ran to seventy-five Guernsey, Manx and Cayman Islands companies and twenty-four trusts which went to the heart of the personal finances of the Rossminster upper echelon. But the very nature of the agreement, with its built-in penalty for disclosing what he knew, only served to increase Lewis-Grey's doubts about what he had been doing in Guernsey.

Completion and signing of the severance agreement did not take place until four days before Christmas 1978. Living with his family in a rented house in Sussex, Lewis-Grey all at once had plenty of time to consider Rossminster and the role he had played:

From an extremely hectic life, I turned to doing nothing for a couple of months. It was in that period that I finally sorted out my thoughts on the true nature of the Guernsey operations. Rossminster to the outsider and indeed to the staff seemed an impressive organisation. Its chairman was a QC; four out of the five other shareholders were accountants. However, I reflected on the fact that I had never seen an opinion covering the operation of the offshore trusts and companies. The issue seemed to revolve around who controlled the trusts and companies. These trusts and companies were in truth puppets and not independent. In the cool light of day it seemed and still seems clear to me that the entire essence of the Guernsey operation was to obscure the control and ownership of the profits of the Rossminster group from the Inland Revenue. In January 1979 being troubled by these matters I contacted the Inland Revenue.

Lewis-Grey telephoned Somerset House and asked to speak to the only name he had – the inspector who had handled Bradman's tax schemes – but he was not available. When he explained the nature of his call, he was put through to Raymond Quinlan, one of Dermit's lieutenants in the Special Investigation Section. Quinlan and his superiors realised the significance of Lewis-Grey's offer to walk through their door. They were well aware of him from the tax-scheme documents which had started to flow into Melbourne House. This was the breakthrough the SIS had been seeking for almost a year.

Quinlan immediately suggested a meeting, the first of many Lewis-Grey was to have with the SIS team over the next three years. With no little trepidation about the repercussions of the course he had embarked upon, Lewis-Grey agreed to meet Quinlan at Melbourne House. He found the Revenue investigator low-key and friendly. At a second meeting, this time with Bill Dermit also present, Lewis-Grey outlined the way Rossminster, the offshore trusts and the associated companies worked.

The Revenue investigators now raised their intention to serve Lewis-Grey with a notice under Section 481 of the Income and Corporation Taxes Act – the means of seeking information relating to possible breaches of the law by transferring assets abroad or enjoying income from undeclared nonresident assets. Lewis-Grey indicated that he would be prepared to answer such a notice. At his next meeting, when presented with a list of some three hundred companies and individuals about which the Revenue wanted information, he whittled down the list by removing the names of companies linked to Rossminster clients. He decided he was only prepared to help the Revenue concerning Rossminster and its principals. The Revenue accepted his reduced list.

On 7 February 1979 Lewis-Grey was served with the Section 481 notice. This required him to furnish the Revenue by 30 March with all the information in his possession relating to events since he joined Roy

213

Tucker in November 1975. The notice was extremely detailed. The schedule of names attached to the notice was headed by the Keith, Leander, Ulysses and Trumpet trusts. It went on to list alphabetically Tucker, Plummer and twenty other executives and associates from John Arthur to Julian Walter. It concluded with a list of one hundred UK, Guernsey, Jersey, Manx and Gibraltar companies running from Abrale to Zeplan.

Lewis-Grey was now in a cleft stick of his own making. If he complied with the Revenue's request he would breach the severance agreement and might become liable for the £30,000 penalty. If he did not comply he could be the target of legal proceedings to ensure compliance. He consulted Steward Bates QC and was advised that unless he was physically or mentally unfit he had to supply the information demanded under the Section 481 notice.

On 28 February Lewis-Grey's lawyers wrote to Rossminster Trust asking for the views of his former employers to the receipt of the notice. The initial response was not unexpected – a call from Rossminster's lawyers making threatening noises about action under the agreement. But the next response was one which Lewis-Grey did not anticipate. Shortly before the 30 March deadline he was contacted by Richard Gardner.

Gardner had left Roy Tucker in 1978 and was self-employed, though still doing work for Rossminster and Tucker, with offices in Berkeley Square. Gardner attributes his decision to leave to a number of factors. One was the pressure of work related to his responsibilities for running the Gross Annuity Scheme. 'I was working eighteen hours a day for three months of the year, fifteen hours a day for three months and ten hours a day for the rest of the year,' he says. Another was his growing disenchantment with certain of the directions in which Tucker had taken Rossminster and his own practice. Gardner says that he was opposed to the increasing use of the Company Purchase Scheme. 'I didn't see why we had to take in other people's dirty laundry. We were making enough from selling tax schemes and taking a fee.' What concerned him were the repercussions if GAS did not work.

No provision had been made for paying tax because Robert Wright QC had said that the Rossminster-appointed directors of the company could rely on opinions from several other counsel to the effect that GAS and each other part of the scheme worked, so they could pay the company's funds out as donations to one of the charities. (Tom Benyon had also had doubts about the Company Purchase Scheme until he read all the legal opinions and checked with Robert Wright that he did mean what his opinion seemed to say could be done.)

But by paying away the cash in the Company Purchase Scheme companies, the taxpayer's traditional approach that if a tax scheme did not work the money was there to pay the tax was ignored. Now if the legal opinions on GAS were wrong and the Revenue succeeded with its challenge then there was no money with which to pay the tax due. Gardner was concerned at the Revenue's reaction to this step which it could construe as an attempt to deprive the Revenue of tax due, irrespective of the legal advice.

It is not certain whether all the relevant counsel read each other's opinions and so were able to see where, when laid end to end, the opinions led, nor that any counsel's opinion was ever sought on whether the nonprovision for tax that might become due was proper. As ever with the opinions elicited from the tax Bar, the key was in the instructions. What is certain is that Gardner's and Benyon's fears about the Revenue's reaction to the 'heads I win, tails you lose' nature of the Company Purchase Scheme were well founded. It is hard to see, whatever legal opinions were given on the intermediate stages, how the end result could be justified in the real world.

So Gardner decided to leave Tucker and sever his links to Rossminster. He says that he sold the shares held in his and his wife's name to the interests of Tucker and Plummer. 'I just let it go and ceased to have any interest,' he says of the shares in Rossminster held offshore in the Delta Trust, which he assumed went to the same purchasers.

The first Richard Gardner knew of the problem with Lewis-Grey was when he received a telephone call from Desmond Miller. 'I'm the sort that's often the oil poured on other people's troubled waters,' the bluff, bearded, burly accountant explains. He was asked if he would approach Lewis-Grey and try to persuade him to respond to the Section 481 notice 'sensibly' – without damaging his former employers.

Although surprised by the approach from Gardner, Lewis-Grey was not hostile, because of all the Rossminster principals he was on best terms with Gardner. Ostensibly Gardner wanted to discuss the purchase of Lewis-Grey's 25 per cent of Ocean Pegasus, a Guernsey company which had bought a 38-foot ketch and a Piper Aztec light aircraft at a combined cost of £90,000 in 1977. Both had since been sold and the company put into liquidation. Gardner suggested what was to be the first of a series of meetings in a variety of London pubs over the next few weeks. Lewis-Grey signed an agreement to sell Gardner his shares on 2 April but by then their discussions were concentrated on the more substantive topic of his intended response to the Revenue notice. Gardner sounded out Lewis-Grey about his likely course of action. According to Gardner, Lewis-Grey was very bitter, dismissive of Benyon and others, blaming Tucker and Plummer for not paying him enough, as a result of which he was now unable to buy back the house he had sold in order to move to Guernsey. He talked about 'the dossier' he was preparing and how harmful it would be to Rossminster. Despite these personal feelings Gardner detected that Lewis-Grey might be prepared to cooperate if a satisfactory financial settlement could be arranged and his fear of having to pay the £30,000 removed.

Lewis-Grey was still sufficiently unsure of his attitude towards the Revenue and conscious of his financial situation to agree to a meeting with Tucker and Plummer at their lawyers' office. Two such meetings took place. The atmosphere was, not surprisingly, very tense, especially when the outspoken Miranda Lewis-Grey was present. Lewis-Grey wanted the best financial deal; Tucker and Plummer wanted the most secure deal. To improve his bargaining position Lewis-Grey played on his former employers' fear of his unrestrained cooperation with the SIS. 'It's the one thing I did which I regret. I wish I'd never done it,' he says now.

Out of these discussions emerged a suggestion that Lewis-Grey, who had been effectively unemployed for most of the time since he left Guernsey, should work for Rossminster again. His job would be a very simple one, to resist complying with the Section 481 notice as long as possible and by every legal means. Lewis-Grey began to waver as the amount of money Rossminster were prepared to pay to buy his cooperation and silence rapidly climbed from an initial £30,000. The payment would enable the Lewis-Greys to enjoy the standard of living they had previously enjoyed in Guernsey, and to acquire the sort of house his wife wanted in order to keep horses.

To buy time from the Revenue while these negotiations continued, Lewis-Grey had written on 3 April saying that he would require longer to provide the information. He was given until 4 May. The negotiations were still in progress by the beginning of May so Lewis-Grey had to stall the

Revenue once more. He was given until 8 June to comply, but with the implied threat of legal proceedings for failure to do so.

Throughout this period Lewis-Grey was living what he described as a 'schizophrenic existence', for while waiting for the right offer from Rossminster and on paper stalling the Revenue over the Section 481 notice, he continued to meet SIS investigators and provide them voluntarily with information.

On 8 June Lewis-Grey had neither complied with the Revenue demand nor received a satisfactory offer from Rossminster. On 18 June the Revenue wrote advising him that consideration was now being given to prosecuting him for noncompliance and seeking the penalties laid down in the Taxes Management Act of a £50 fine plus £10 for every day of continued default.

Rossminster finally came through with a formal offer on Thursday 28 June. The proposal was a remarkable one: Lewis-Grey would become a consultant to Rossminster Holdings, the Manx master company, under an agreement with another Manx company, Horonet, set up for the purpose, which he would control. For a period of six years he would 'assist and advise' Rossminster regarding 'various taxation matters'.

Just what was entailed was left in no doubt:

It is expressly agreed that such services to be provided by Mr Lewis-Grey on behalf of Horonet shall include the provision of Mr Lewis-Grey's full cooperation in respect of all or any Appeals or proceedings whatsoever to defeat or nullify any Notice or Notices served on Mr Lewis-Grey by the Commissioners of Inland Revenue.

Rossminster would bear the full cost of the exercise, including any tax fines or interest penalties. Lewis-Grey in return was 'to pursue or make any such Appeals or proceedings or to raise any defences or counterclaims or abandon or vary the same in accordance with principles reasonably laid down by [Rossminster] Holdings or Rossminster [Trust]'.

Rossminster would select and instruct the legal counsel. If at the end of the legal road Lewis-Grey lost, then he was to discuss with Rossminster and its advisers the nature and details of any information which he supplied to the Inland Revenue. In return for keeping the SIS at bay Horonet was to receive, on signature of the contract, an immediate lump sum of £125,000 which Lewis-Grey could take taxfree.

The proposition was that I would have become some kind of nominal consultant to the group. Nobody expected me to perform any actual service other than the fact that I would devote myself to resisting all the Inland Revenue claims for information from me. I imagine what would have happened is that in two or three years hence when the Revenue had succeeded in proving that I was liable to give them certain information I would have forgotten large tracts of what I can now remember.[5]

'I was tempted,' Lewis-Grey admits. He was also advised by a company law counsel that it was all perfectly legal. Lewis-Grey was more concerned, however, with the morality of accepting what he saw as 'hush money'. Once again all his doubts about Rossminster and its activities resurfaced. The very consultancy deal itself, like the severance agreement, seemed to prove how justified those doubts were. He decided to take the weekend to decide.

That weekend Lewis-Grey invited a barrister friend to stay. 'He and I discussed the matter and resolved that I should not go any further. 'You don't want to spend the rest of your life looking over your shoulder,' he told me. First thing on Monday 2 July I indicated to the Revenue that I would cave in on the Section 481 notice. I'm glad I did because amazingly the Revenue knew all about the offer anyway.'

Events in Melbourne House now moved at a pace uncharacteristic of the Civil Service. Three days later, on Thursday 5 July, Lewis-Grey made a two-page statement. Attached to it was a photocopy of a crucial document. Headed 'RG & RT – 1977 Allocations' and signed by the six Rossminster principals, it referred to a distribution of £427,566 the year before to their interests and to three senior executives.

Because most of Rossminster's income was earned in the tax scheme season's peak months of February and March, bonuses were usually announced and paid to the staff by May, when it was clear what the profits would be for that year. For the year to April 1977 it was decided that the bonuses to certain senior staff would be paid to them offshore, using funds already available. In the case of the six principals this meant payments to the discretionary trusts in Guernsey. However, Tucker and Plummer instructed Lewis-Grey not to make the payments until they gave the word, much to the irritation of Gardner, Benyon and Trotman, who kept asking whether the money had been paid and when it was due. One reason for the delay was that it was decided that year to sort out various intergroup debts that existed between the various individuals and Rossminster. Tucker told Lewis-Grey that he was to be paid £113,000 from group funds. Finally, in February 1978, Rossminster's paymaster was given the go-ahead by Tucker and Plummer to make all the payments.

Because of the complexity and as a protection for himself against any future come-back from any of the individuals concerned, Lewis-Grey decided to prepare a list of the payments which they would all be asked to sign as his authority to pay the money. He drew up a schedule listing the payments to be made to the six principals plus Barry Pilkington and John Elmgreen. He listed the sums to be paid under a number of headings: bonus plus interest from June 1977; tax-scheme refunds plus interest; undrawn salary plus interest; car waiver (those who had not taken a company car); payments to Tucker; repayment of commissions earned on tax schemes; and interest due on deposits.

The completed document was sent by telecopier to John Trotman in London to be checked, and was returned on 10 March 1978. It was essentially the document Lewis-Grey had prepared but with certain amendments. The initials of Michael Coysh, the Rossminster banking manager, had been added beneath the original eight sets of initials. The car-waiver column was omitted and a new column covering interest to mid-March had been added. The document was signed by Tucker, Plummer, Miller, Gardner, Benyon and Trotman.

Tucker's interests were to be paid a total of £165,281 including £63,000 relating to St George's, £50,000 as a tax-scheme indemnity and £47,000 in interest foregone. There was also £7750 which related to a payment he had made to Plummer's Pandora Trust at the time in June 1977 that the Revenue had been pressing him for information about offshore interests. The money represented a loan made to him from an offshore trust, and could now be repaid.

Plummer's trusts were to receive a total of £39,424. There was a scheme refund of £7810, £13,280 in undrawn salary and £58,359 in interest foregone. Against these was £41,000 owed to Tucker and the group. Gardner's trust was to receive a total of £79,944, mostly from a £59,400 bonus. Miller was to receive £10,674 made up almost entirely from a tax-scheme refund. Trotman's trust was to receive £30,848. Benyon's interests were to be paid £57,050 made up of a £50,400 bonus and a refund on a tax scheme, but he had to repay £4500 of personal profits from his 1 per cent of the Commodity Carry Scheme partnerships (these could have made £450,000). Pilkington was to get £26,926, Elmgreen £13,195 and Coysh £4222.

Where the £433,802 to make these payments was to come from is made clear in another internal Rossminster document, headed 'Offshore Cash

TO: RAP/RCT

FROM: ABL-G

RE: OFFSHORE CASH RESOURCES - POSITION AS AT 19TH MAY 1978

1. The figures scheduled below show the position after 1977 bonus and adjustments payments totalling 433,802. In addition £20,000 to TJN/JA interests have been taken out of account.

2. The cash available should be reduced further for 'notional' interest due to RAP/RCT interests as from 1st Feb 1978 up 31 May 1978. £22,882 is owing to RAP interests for the period 1 Feb/30 April 1978 and £12,245 to RCT interests. It is estimated that by 31 May, RAP interests will be due £33,265 and RCT interest £19,175. Therefore, another £52,440 will need to be taken out of account.

		Now	Later	Total
(i)	BERMUDIAN GAS			
	(a) Sirius Group	125,000	220,000[1]	345,000
	(b) Jedvale	80,000	–	80,000
	(c) Illington/Illington Finance	35,000[2]	–	35,000
	(d) Victory Holdings Ltd	–	–	–
(ii)	GUERNSEY GAS	–	80,000[2]	80,000
(iii)	EXTERNAL GAS	5,000	–	5,000
(iv)	CCS/CPS	140,000	–	140,000
(v)	BAMBELLA	–	150,000	150,000
(vi)	DPCLS	40,000	–	40,000
(vii)	4TH AZURE[5]	45,000	20,000	45,000
(viii)	CIP/NAS	–	250,000[6]	250,000
				1,170,000

NOTES:

1. This figure is made up of £100,000 Sirius Share Capital plus 133 x £900 for U.K. S. Ltd's. It is arguable that the S Ltd 'Valuation' should be written down to nil as the Revenue are unlikely to give a tax clearance on liquidati

2. Dividends totalling approximately £100,000 will be payable by Illington Limit and Illington Finance Limited to Rossminster Trust Company as Trustee of 4th Azure Settlement. £65,000 of this amount will be put towards repaying over draft with RA(IOM) Ltd incurred in the purchase of Illington/Illington Finan from Victory Holdings Ltd.

3. Victory Holdings Limited has been taken out of account for the purposes of th Sched le (in fact has cash at bank of £107,000).

4. See ( ) above.

5. Cash surplus following payments due to RA, RT&Co. TJN & JA.

6. This figure is an estimate.

Resources – position as at 19 May 1978', which Lewis-Grey had sent to Tucker and Plummer marked 'Most Confidential – do not copy – please destroy ASAP'. This document disclosed that *after* the £433,802 had been paid to the six individuals or their trusts, there was still available offshore in a variety of accounts £1,170,000 which had not yet been distributed. The money to pay the 1977 allocations had come from Victory Holdings and the group of Manx companies which administered the Bermuda version of External GAS. Another £460,000 was still available in these companies. A further £80,000 was expected from the Guernsey-run version of GAS. The balance was made up of the anticipated profits amassed offshore from the Commodity Carry, Company Purchase, Deferred Purchase Capital Loss, Capital Income Protection and Net Annuity schemes plus Bambella. Tucker made various adjustments to Lewis-Grey's figures. There was also £57,000 to be paid to his and Plummer's trusts together with £20,000 to those of Nicholas and Arthur. He scribbled at the bottom of the document before returning it, 'Say £1 m.'

The payments of the 1977 allocations to the individuals' own trusts were made by Lewis-Grey on 23 May 1978. In his two-page statement accompanying the schedule of those payments Lewis-Grey told the Revenue:

At all material times I regarded the persons whose signatures appear on the document as being my employers and the owners of the group. In practice their ownership of the group was held through discretionary trusts of which Rossminster Trust was trustee. I was accustomed to act in accordance with the instructions of these signatories. I was also a protector or guardian of the discretionary trusts held for the benefit of the signatories and in addition a director of the subsidiary companies owned by these trusts.

The next day, Friday 6 July, Lewis-Grey produced the dossier he had mentioned to Gardner – a series of manuscript notes, running to more than 150 pages, detailing what he knew about the main Rossminster individuals, the Tucker and Plummer trusts and half the companies on which the Revenue had requested information together with a debunking of the Sark control myth and explanations of how the four smaller shareholders had taken up their 17 per cent of Rossminster offshore and the workings of internal GAS. (The remainder of the company information, another 47 pages of notes, was supplied a month later.) Lewis-Grey told Bill Dermit on 6 July, 'I'm keen to assist the Revenue in any way possible.'

The chairman of the board of Inland Revenue, Sir William Pile, referring to the document Lewis-Grey had produced, later admitted, 'Everything was changed by that one piece of paper which was on my desk the same day.'

To the Revenue that document appeared to indicate that a percentage of the fees Rossminster earned from Tucker's tax schemes had been diverted offshore for the benefit of the six individuals. No evidence of such funds existed in the individuals' previous tax returns. This suggested that Tucker and the others had the power to enjoy the funds paid into the offshore trusts, something they of course would deny. Tucker and Plummer maintain they had been advised that the Rossminster 'bonuses' were not declarable.

A lengthy report on the document and Lewis-Grey's allegations was prepared by Dermit and the Inland Revenue's solicitors. It was passed to Denis Moorcraft as the official responsible for the SIS who decided on prosecutions. The report suggested that there was prima facie evidence of tax fraud and that search warrants should be obtained to seek further proof necessary for any criminal prosecution. In normal circumstances Moorcraft, as an under secretary, would have made the decision on what action was to be taken, but the use of search warrants was a decision which could only be taken by the chairman – Pile had made that clear since the Finance Act 1976 had come into force. Because of the complexity of the case and the detailed nature of the report, Pile called for a meeting to give Moorcraft, Dermit and the Revenue solicitors the opportunity to support the case for using the search warrants.

Pile and the deputy chairman Alfred Dalton, a career Revenue man, were given a presentation by Dermit of the evidence against Rossminster. 'As a result of that document and the informer, we decided on the raids,' Pile says. 'It was a long meeting and a very carefully considered decision,' Dalton recalls. It was decided to apply for warrants under the powers granted by Section 20C of the Finance Act to search the homes and offices of the five Rossminster principals who still lived in England, on the basis that the Revenue had prima facie evidence to suspect a possible tax fraud.

Because of its role as a revenue collector, the Inland Revenue, like the Customs, is itself a prosecuting authority: its board alone decides on prosecutions. It does not need to consult either the Treasury, its political masters, or the Director of Public Prosecutions. Ministers only decide on policy; the execution of that policy, once it is law, is a matter for the

Revenue itself. Despite or maybe because of this, the Inland Revenue, unlike the Customs' VAT branch, was judicious in its use of its powers, especially the new power of search and seizure given against strong Conservative opposition in 1976.[6] There had only been eleven previous applications for search warrants.

Now that it had been decided to raid Rossminster, the political repercussions were in the forefront of everyone's mind. In the year since Lewis-Grey had made those payments, the Conservatives had come to power, Tom Benyon had become a Conservative MP, Peter Rees was the Treasury minister responsible for the Inland Revenue, the former Rossminster employee John Nott was trade minister, and Peter Walker, Rossminster's partner in the Talbex deal, was agriculture minister. Considerable political embarrassment could therefore be expected from the actions now planned. 'We all knew there would be a bit of an uproar,' says one of the senior Revenue officials involved. The position of Peter Rees made it especially sensitive; it was, as Dalton, the deputy chairman, says, 'a very carefully considered decision'. 'There was some concern over the raids because of the political involvement,' Sir William Pile admits. 'There was a bit of nail-biting but we still decided to do it.'

In preparation for his hoped-for political career Tom Benyon had quietly started to distance himself from Rossminster and had left the board in May 1978. He remained, however, an undisclosed shareholder through his offshore family trust. Explaining his decision, Benyon says, 'It was clear that Rossminster-style tax avoidance was over after retrospective legislation. I also felt a sense of *déjà vu* about tax. It was arid. I wanted to do something else. I also had a sense of concern about the past activities and was not keen to be involved in tax avoidance on that scale under a Conservative government which could be coming. So I decided to leave and await political events.' Plummer felt a similar party loyalty.

Although he had discreetly departed from Rossminster, Benyon continued to be involved in tax avoidance through a new company, NAS Financial Services, a Rossminster clone which operated from Tucker's old address in North Audley Street. He was managing director of NAS and also a director of Longfleet Leasing, a Rossminster-controlled company selling tax relief via leasing containers and canal boats. In early 1979 Benyon wrote to potential NAS clients offering the Tucker/Don Boyd film scheme, but Benyon's attentions were soon distracted from such matters as tax avoidance by the bomb blast at the House of Commons which killed

Airey Neave. Within weeks he had been elected Conservative MP for Abingdon. At thirty-six Tom Benyon could look forward to spending the next twenty to thirty years debating weighty issues instead of selling tax schemes. He resigned from NAS, which was later sold to Colin Emson.

There was no question but that the new MP's home would have to be raided. His signature was on the Lewis-Grey schedule and he had been identified as a Rossminster shareholder through his family trust.

Despite or maybe because of the political sensitivity, Sir William Pile decided that no advance warning should be given to ministers of the Revenue's intentions. No government is likely to welcome even a tyro backbench MP being involved in a tax scandal, especially one in which ministers' names could be mentioned. It might have been tempted to seek at least to delay matters for 'reconsideration', and there was the risk of a leak, even inadvertently, which could tip off Rossminster and lose the vital element of surprise.

On 12 July Raymond Quinlan took the five-minute journey from Melbourne House along Fleet Street to the Old Bailey to apply for a dozen search warrants.

During the 1976 debate the Labour government had agreed as a concession to the Conservatives that the Inland Revenue, unlike the Customs or even the police, would need to satisfy a circuit judge instead of a magistrate in order to obtain a search warrant. Quinlan went before the recently appointed Common Sergeant, Judge Leonard, a circuit judge with fifteen years' experience. In order to obtain a warrant under Section 20C of the Taxes Management Act the Revenue has to show that 'there is reasonable ground for suspecting that an offence involving any form of fraud in connection with or in relation to tax has been committed and that evidence of it is to be found on premises specified'. A Revenue official has to make a statement under oath specifying on what evidence the Revenue bases its suspicions. Quinlan relied heavily on the information provided by Lewis-Grey, in particular the schedule of 1978 payments. After examining Quinlan's evidence Judge Leonard granted the warrants: the raids were on. They were given the codename Operation Wimbledon, a reference to the annual tennis fortnight which had just ended.

The synchronised, military-style operation involved almost seventy Revenue officials backed up by twenty-eight police officers headed by members of Scotland Yard's Fraud Squad. The police always accompany the Revenue teams on raids in case there is any resistance, because the

Inland Revenue has no powers of arrest. The combined Revenue and Scotland Yard teams, each headed by a senior SIS inspector, set off soon after dawn to begin what Lord Denning, with some degree of hyperbole, later described as a seizure the like of which had not been seen in Britain for more than two hundred years.

At 7 am on Friday 13 July, senior Revenue investigators simultaneously knocked on the front doors of Roy Tucker's medieval manor Nettlestead Place in rural Kent, Ronald Plummer's town house in a quiet square just off Hyde Park, Tom Benyon's former rectory home near Oxford, and the Buckinghamshire and Sussex homes of John Trotman and Richard Gardner. In Mayfair other Revenue men were waiting outside the offices of Rossminster, AJR Financial Services and Gardner's company for the first employees to arrive. The element of surprise was complete.

Roy Tucker was not at home that morning, he was in Guernsey. His wife Annabel and their children watched as three Revenue officials swept the house clean of Tucker's papers, including even an old maths essay on infinite numbers written at St Paul's. They also took papers referring to his brother Keith.

Plummer was at home when the knock came at the door. He was woken up by three Revenue officers whom he describes as 'very nice chaps'. Here too the Revenue carried out a systematic search and collection of papers belonging not only to him but also to his wife and mother. The house in Radnor Place, the Plummers' cars, two garages and a safe-deposit box were searched.

Tom Benyon was in bed asleep when the Revenue arrived. He had returned home only a few hours before from a late-night sitting in the Commons. He described later how two Revenue officers raced upstairs, pushing past his wife, who had opened the door, in such a way that he thought he was being robbed. Once again the Revenue took away large quantities of documents. The Revenue also searched a flat Benyon shared in Westminster.

Richard Gardner had left his home in Sussex before the Revenue arrived. He found them waiting when he arrived at his Berkeley Square office just before 8 am. 'We were just about to break the door down,' he was told. Other Revenue officers were already searching his home. A further team were outside another office and flat he maintained in Cork Street.

John Trotman was at home in Gerrards Cross that morning. Like

Benyon and Gardner, he too had severed any public link with Ross-minster, resigning as finance director in March 1978. A thorough search of his house was carried out, and the Revenue officials displayed particular interest in a watch owned by Mrs Trotman which had been acquired from Asprey's by one of the offshore trusts at a cost of £850.

Although the Revenue teams had been briefed on what documents to look for, it was impossible to read every piece of paper, as required by the terms under which the search warrants are granted, before deciding that there is 'reasonable cause to believe' that it might be required as evidence. As a result the thorough searches of the Rossminster men's homes, which in some cases did not finish until the early afternoon, resulted in some unusual items finding their way into the black plastic rubbish bags brought by the Revenue: eleven-year-old Helen Plummer's school report, parking tickets, some letters to Roy Tucker from an old girlfriend. When Richard Gardner asked why a particular item was being removed he says he was told, 'Mr Gardner, we're taking everything.' At Trotman's home this bulldozer approach resulted in an embarrassing scene when certain personal letters written to Mrs Trotman were discovered, read and shown to Trotman – this was later cited as a factor in the breakup of his marriage.

While they were busy filling their plastic bags the Revenue officers refused to explain to Plummer, Benyon or the others just why they were there and what they were looking for. This and the seemingly indiscriminate and in some instances somewhat heavy-handed nature of the searches was to cost the Revenue dear.

Soon after 7.30 am the first employees arrived at Vogue House and round the corner at the AJR offices in St George's Street. The moment the Rossminster doors were opened the main task force of Revenue officers, led by Quinlan, poured through, police officers took over the switchboard and staff were politely but firmly taken to one side, questioned and then put in another room while the search went ahead. The Rossminster and AJR offices were emptied of files at the rate of one a minute over the next ten hours, as Plummer and his staff stood by helpless, and twelve vanloads were driven away containing some 2 million pieces of paper.

Richard Gardner had no knowledge of what was going on only five minutes' walk away in Hanover Square. The first clue came when he received a telephone call from Bill Cairns in Guernsey. Cairns asked him whether he was free to speak; he said no; Cairns said that this did not surprise him, from which Gardner assumed that the Rossminster offices were getting similar treatment.

Plummer had arrived at Vogue House soon after 9 am to find the search operation in full swing. He immediately consulted his lawyers to see if the raids could be stopped, and about 6.15 pm a High Court judge granted an injunction against the Revenue. This was the one piece of good luck Tucker and Plummer had that Friday the 13th. The injunction should not have been granted: it was in breach of the Crown Proceedings Act, which is supposed to prevent injunctions against officers of the crown.

Government ministers first learned of the raids through radio and television news reports that day. Sir Geoffrey Howe, then Chancellor, confirms, 'I knew nothing of the raids until I heard about them through the media. Neither myself nor any other Treasury minister was informed in advance. The news was out very quickly on the morning in question.'[7] As might be expected, the response of the Revenue's political masters was unenthusiastic. 'Why didn't you let us know sooner?' Howe is said to have commented at the time. But after listening to the Revenue's case there was a grudging acceptance that both the need for the raids and the security surrounding them had been justified.

The newspapers of Saturday 14 July carried reports of the raids. All focused on Benyon's involvement. 'Tax men search home of Tory MP' was the *Financial Times* headline. 'Tax squad visit MP's home,' said the more discreet *Daily Telegraph*. 'Taxmen in raid on Tory MP,' declared the blunter *Daily Mirror*. Had the press realised Rossminster's ministerial connections, the coverage would have been much greater.

The raid could not have come at a more inconvenient moment for Benyon. That night he had to face his local constituency association at its annual meeting. 'The effect was devastating on me,' Benyon recalls. He claims that as soon as he was adopted as the candidate for Abingdon he had asked Tucker and Plummer as well as the lawyer Roy Walkden, who handled all the dealings with the Inland Revenue on behalf of the clients, 'whether there was anything I should know' concerning either his own or the group's affairs. 'I asked Ron and Roy if there could be any problems as I knew we had made a lot of money.' He was assured there was nothing for him to worry about, everything had been done legally.

'My husband hasn't worked for Rossminster for over a year,' Jane Benyon declared.[8] Benyon himself made clear that he had never given tax advice. His solicitor John Clitheroe[9] emphasised that the MP 'had left

Rossminster eighteen months ago'. If he had been given notice of the investigation he would have 'given his fullest cooperation'. 'Mr Benyon has no dispute with the Inland Revenue,' said the lawyer.[10]

What was not said at the time was that Benyon's family interests had retained a 2½ per cent stake in Rossminster and that until he entered Parliament he had worked for the Rossminster-controlled Longfleet Leasing.

For their part, Rossminster and AJR denied any knowledge of tax offences. Roy Tucker said and continued to say, 'As far as we are concerned there is no fraud.'[11] Ronald Plummer echoed these sentiments: 'I categorically repeat that we have no knowledge of any tax fraud.'[12]

The stage was now set for a clash rivalling that between the Inland Revenue and the Vesteys, both in duration and in millions. This heavyweight contest would take place at Westminster and Whitehall, in Fleet Street newspapers and on television. It is still in progress today, seven years after those momentous events of Friday 13 July 1979.

THE SECRET WAR OF SQUIRREL NUTKIN

It did not take long for Tucker and Plummer to launch their legal counterattack against the Friday the 13th raids. Within four days Rossminster had obtained a High Court order for a judicial review to determine whether the Revenue officials had acted beyond the terms of the search warrants in the manner in which they had removed the 2 million pieces of paper. The Lord Chief Justice, Lord Widgery, decreed the review should be heard during the summer recess when Rossminster maintained that unless the seizure was declared illegal and the documents returned it could not continue in business as a bank.

The hearing, before three High Court judges, began on 30 July. Rossminster asked the court to quash the warrants and compel the Inland Revenue to disclose the basis for their suspicions and to specify which seized documents related to the allegations of fraud.

Lord Justice Eveleigh, sitting with Mr Justice Park and Mr Justice Woolf, ruled against Rossminster on 1 August. The raids had not been 'an abuse of power'. 'There have been occasions when a glance at a document will tell an investigation officer whether it is the kind of document he is entitled to take,' said the judge. 'No one would expect that they should stay on the premises to read the details of every document there.'

Once again Rossminster obtained an urgent hearing, this time before the Court of Appeal on 13 August in front of the Master of the Rolls, Lord Denning, well known for his support of the individual against the actions of the state. Three days later he delivered a typical Denning bombshell – the Inland Revenue raids, he held, were illegal. In his quiet, pronounced Hampshire accent Denning denounced the Revenue's actions. 'As far as my knowledge of history goes, there is no search like it and no seizure since

30 April 1763 when the Secretary of State issued a general warrant by which he authorised the King's Messenger to arrest John Wilkes and seize all his papers.'

Lord Denning showed that he, like many others, distrusted the powers given to the Revenue by the Finance Act 1976 to deal with tax evaders:

Those who defraud the Revenue in this way are parasites who suck out the lifeblood of society. . . The trouble is, the legislation is drawn so widely that in some hands it may be used as an instrument of oppression. Once great power is granted there is great danger in it being abused. It is the duty of the courts to construe the statute to see it encroaches as little as possible on the people of England.

Lord Denning was most definitely of the view that the Revenue officials conducting the search should have informed Tucker and Plummer of the nature of the allegations against them and could not be the sole arbiters of which documents could be seized. The Revenue case was that this could prejudice the investigation and reveal their informant. The Master of the Rolls was unimpressed. He concluded his judgment in typical style:

This case has given us much concern. No one would wish that any of those who defraud the Revenue should go free. They should be found out and brought to justice. But it is fundamental to our law that the means adopted to this end should be lawful. The means should not offend against the right of freedom and the elemental right of property.

It was a public humiliation for the Revenue and one that was keenly felt. 'All the Rossminster henchmen were there. It was the most despondent moment in my life,' recalls a senior Revenue official who was in court. Rossminster exploited its victory to the full. Denning had depicted the SIS just as Tucker and Plummer had done – as official bully boys out of control, ransacking honest accountant's homes without reason and removing any document that came to hand.

The tide of public opinion was running against the Inland Revenue, a fact clearly reflected in the reception given to the Denning judgment. 'Taxman tamed,' cried the *Daily Mail*, gleefully pointing to the seizure of Plummer's children's bank books, his wife and mother's private papers and Roy Tucker's passport. The Revenue inquiries into offshore discretionary family trusts and the use of tax-avoidance vehicles in foreign tax havens made such documents relevant but this was unrealised. As the Revenue remained silent about its suspicions, the newspapers were glad to accept the Rossminster version. 'I am no crusader but everybody should be pleased to see that the Inland Revenue's powers have got some limitation. It is a step back from 1984,' Plummer declared,[1] and announced that Rossminster would be pressing a claim for damages against the Revenue. It was claimed that the bank had already lost £2,500,000 in customers' deposits.

But that was the least of the Revenue's problems in the wake of the Denning judgment, for he also ruled that the SIS should hand back all that it had seized a month before together with all 'summaries, extracts and paraphrases'. Much of the contents from the twelve vanloads had not yet been fully analysed, and now they had to be returned. The whole Rossminster investigation was now jeopardised and there were serious implications for any future use of the search-warrant powers, making raids of the wide-ranging, Rossminster variety impractical. The Revenue appealed to the House of Lords.

The three-day hearing began on 29 October before five Law Lords – Wilberforce, Diplock, Salmon, Scarman and Viscount Dilhorne. They reserved judgment until 13 December when, not for the first or last time, the House of Lords firmly ruled against the Master of the Rolls. 'Appeals to eighteenth-century precedents of arbitrary action . . . did nothing to throw light on the issue,' declared Lord Wilberforce dismissively. By a vote of four to one the Law Lords held that the warrants were valid, the searches had been legally executed and the raids had not been an abuse of power.

Ironically, Tucker and Rossminster had run foul of the very factor they had consistently relied on for the eventual success of the tax schemes – the Lords' obeisance to the form of statutes rather than the substance of events. It was not part of the courts' duty or power 'to restrict or impede the working of legislation, even unpopular legislation, said Lord Wilberforce; 'to do so would be to weaken rather than advance the democratic process.' In his view the safeguards covering the issue of the search warrants were adequate. As to Tucker's and Plummer's right to know of what they were suspected, Lord Wilberforce declared, 'All that information was clearly protected by the public interest immunity that covered investigations into possible criminal offences . . . To require specification at the present investigatory stage would be impracticable given the complexity of 'tax frauds'."

After the euphoria that followed the Denning judgment, the House of Lords' decision was greeted with disappointed reserve by both Plummer and Fleet Street. Rossminster, Plummer said, 'had nothing to hide . . . We do not consider ourselves guilty of any tax fraud but the Revenue obviously now has a strong incentive to try and find something to justify themselves.' Rossminster would now press on with its civil action 'as a matter of principle'.[2]

Tucker and Plummer, having lost the legal war, intended to fight a publicity war against the Inland Revenue. They issued a seven-page statement attacking the Revenue's approach and exonerating themselves. This new high-profile policy had been foreshadowed on 9 October when the *Financial Times* published a lengthy article in which for the first time Tucker and Plummer discussed their activities and Tucker revealed that 'family trusts' set up by him and Plummer owned 83 per cent of Rossminster, which had earned '£5 million clear profit out of avoidance'. That figure omitted what had been made on the Ellerman, Bailey and Jacksons deals. The article declared that since March 1978 Rossminster had been out of the tax-avoidance business – 'Avoidance is very exhausting,' Tucker explained. Plummer confirmed this in an interview with the *Observer* a month later – 'It was such an exhausting business and we wanted to concentrate on other activities.'[3] Neither made any reference to the film scheme which was being sold only a few months before. The *Financial Times* article first put forward what was to become the authorised justification for Rossminster's and Tucker's activities. Tucker said, 'At the time it seemed a good thing to be doing. We thought it provided a safety valve. We really did stop people leaving the country and provided working capital for medium-sized companies'.[4] However, he rather undermined that argument in the *Observer*, admitting that, despite the slashing of the top tax rate from 83 per cent to 60 per cent by the new Conservative government, the demand for tax schemes was unabated. 'I think people may now have got into the habit and will find it difficult to change.'[5]

All these points were reiterated in the 13 December press statement. 'We accept that legal tax avoidance on a substantial commercial scale is a subject of legitimate concern.' However, the statement added, 'We have no moral qualms about the tax-avoidance schemes we have run as these were legal.' Legality rather than morality was always the issue.

Tax cases were being conducted by the Revenue as if taxpayers were defendants in a criminal trial. The SIS had been irritated, the statement claimed, by Tucker's use of a fighting fund for test cases enabling taxpayers to fight the Revenue on equal terms:

Many people in the SIS, if not the SIS as a whole, regard legal tax avoidance as being an equivalent evil to tax evasion and regard the matter of stamping out all tax avoidance as a crusade where the end justifies the use of any means . . . The SIS appear to be a law unto themselves within the Revenue . . . We believe that the SIS has become an elite which is too much responsible only to itself and is in danger of damaging the Revenue's relationship with the public.

Tucker and Plummer warned that all tax payers were now at the mercy of this new 'Gestapo'. As usual, the lengthy statement made no reference to the offshore arrangements for sheltering the up to £5 million Tucker and Plummer had each amassed through Rossminster. But they responded to the disclosures made in *Private Eye* and the *Sunday Times* about the use of charities in Rossminster's activities: the 'financial activities' entered into by St George's Elizabethan Theatre and Blessingwell 'made no use of charitable exemptions from tax whatsoever'. Apart from the use of HOVAS in the Plummer annuity scheme, the statement said, 'we have never been involved in the use of a charity for the purpose of obtaining a tax exemption due to its charitable status'.

This was not the full story. The Company Purchase Scheme relied on the fact that, following the implementation of the Gross Annuity Scheme, the profits could be paid on, free of any provision for Advance Corporation Tax, as uncovenanted donations. If the profits were paid as dividends to a parent company using group election, ACT would have to be deducted, but by making uncovenanted donations to a registered charity, that problem was bypassed. Also no mention was made of the short-lived Deprived Children's Aid Fund which, though not a registered charity, was a company with charitable purposes, and had been used in another annuity scheme.

The statement was accepted at face value by most of the press, like so much of what Tucker and Plummer said. Only *Private Eye* and the *Sunday Times* seemed in any way to question the Rossminster position.

The Charity Commissioners too were unconvinced. Once they discovered the real purpose of St George's and Blessingwell the Commissioners launched an investigation. They wrote to Halliwell and Plummer seeking an explanation regarding these and other charities. Halliwell replied at first, denying that the press reports were correct and offering to supply all the information to disprove them. 'Of course he never did,' recalls the secretary, David Forrest. Plummer replied, asking for the Commissioners' advice on how to deal with the Inland Revenue!

The Charity Commissioners concluded that they were unable to take any action as the Rossminster charities' activities in general were within the very wide investment powers granted by the deeds of trust. They queried one or two unsecured loans or assets acquired as being contrary to prudent practice but merely advised against any repetition. A memorandum prepared for the Commissioners by an official deputed to examine Blessingwell summed up their response. 'I have not been able to come up with any bright ideas for nailing Halliwell,' it began. Nor did the Charity Commissioners receive any help from the Inland Revenue, who never challenged the charities' status, preferring to rely instead on their own investigations. 'There was little really that we could do so we decided not to do anything,' admits Forrest.

Tucker's and Plummer's statements may have seemed to the lay journalist and reader to be clear and conclusive, but in fact were not. Defending the Company Purchase Scheme, Tucker told the *Observer*, 'No scheme or arrangement that I or Rossminster has had anything to do with has had as any part of its plan the creation of a tax liability in a company which that company wouldn't be able to pay. But I would not deny the elimination of such tax liability by the use of further schemes which counsel advised were lawful.'[6] The result was still the same: when the taxman got there the corporate cupboard was bare. But it did not quite sound that way.

The Rossminster Affair now disappeared from public view to be replaced by a secret war fought by Rossminster and its allies against the Inland Revenue and those who helped or supported it. Waged through the newspapers and in Parliament over the next three years, it was a campaign which relied on carefully engineered, discreet lobbying, press manipulation and 'dirty tricks'.

The first evidence of 'dirty tricks' came in August 1979, before the Court of Appeal hearing, when a typed, two-page anonymous letter arrived at *Private Eye*. The target of the letter was Lewis-Grey, whose role as its informant at that time was known only to the Revenue and Rossminster. After taking a few swings at the Revenue for failing to provide any information and at Sir William Pile for having been head of the prison service, the writer got down to business:

It might interest the Inland Revenue to know, since they do not conceivably already know, that their informer, Arthur Lewis-Grey, was dismissed from the Channel

Islands group company where he had been Managing Director for three or more years for a number of reasons.

These it proceeded to itemise under the headings of 'Incompetence', 'Dishonesty', 'Instability amounting to insanity', 'Scandal' and 'Debts'. The letter concluded:

Given the above it could be asked, was the spectacular and well publicised Gestapo-type morning raids on Rossminster . . . all part of a deliberate policy of harassment of Rossminster and other operators in the tax avoidance industry, really for the purpose of frightening away their customers, seizing all papers and records in order to effectively close down their business and generally to carry out a 'fishing' expedition?

Just who wrote the letter it is impossible to ascertain, but the sentiments were echoed in subsequent Rossminster statements. The allegations about Lewis-Grey – some of which contained an element of distorted truth, though he denies the dishonesty, debts and insanity – could only have been known to people connected with Rossminster. When *Private Eye* did not print any of this, the anonymous author did not attempt any further smears.

Rossminster's campaign against the Revenue really came to life after the Lords' ruling. It coincided with pressure within the Treasury against the investigation itself. The sıs investigators felt that Treasury officials were increasingly nervous about the wide scope of their inquiries because ministers were uneasy about the links now regularly made between Rossminster and Peter Rees and John Nott. Rees's position in particular, as the Treasury minister partly responsible for the Revenue, made the inquiry an ever present source of embarrassment. Suggestions were made that inquiries should be limited to the personal tax affairs of the Rossminster insiders, excluding such matters as the Commodity Carry Scheme, which would bring the investigation to the door of both Rees and Nott, or the Gross Annuity Scheme, on which Rees had also advised.

Revenue morale was not boosted by Rees's announcement in February 1980 that the government was to fulfil its election pledge and establish a committee to examine the tough new powers given to the Revenue only four years before. Some investigators found it difficult to separate the timing of this announcement with the outcry over the use of these powers against Rossminster. Coming from a former legal adviser to Roy Tucker, even one who as a minister had only recently publicly attacked tax-avoidance schemes, the announcement did little to reassure cynics inside and outside Melbourne House.

The political sensitivity of Peter Rees's position had already been highlighted on two occasions in the House of Commons by the Rossminster critic Jeff Rooker, Labour MP for Birmingham, Perry Barr. Rooker was angered by Rees's non-disclosure of his previous links to Tucker. His anger was further fuelled by a clumsy attempt by Tom Benyon to join in the 'dirty tricks' campaign. After Rooker had raised questions in the Commons about St George's Elizabethan Theatre in November 1979, Benyon approached the head of the Commons Secretaries Council about an alleged blacklist of MPs who treated their secretaries badly. Told there was no such list he asked 'Have you got anything on Jeff Rooker?' She had not and instead informed the Labour MP, who promptly raised the matter as a breach of Parliamentary privilege, an attempt to intimidate him and contempt of the House.

In the Christmas adjournment debate in December 1979 Rooker called for Peter Rees's resignation. 'The position of the minister of state as minister in charge of the Revenue is untenable,' he declared. 'I do not see how the Inland Revenue investigators can do their work properly and impartially if they know that their minister of state is someone whose papers they will be examining and whom they may wish to interview.' Rooker made a comparison with Reginald Maudling who in 1972, when Scotland Yard were called in to investigate his business associate John Poulson, had resigned as Home Secretary because of his nominal responsibility for the Metropolitan Police.

Rooker's point of view was not shared by the Leader of the House, Norman St John-Stevas. 'There is no inconsistency in having exercised a professional career in that area as a member of the Bar and his ministerial responsibilities,' said St John-Stevas, himself a barrister.

Undeterred, and spurred on by *Private Eye*'s disclosures of the concerns within the Revenue about a possible cover-up, Rooker returned to the attack in April 1980. Rees had suggested that the Revenue's powers might be curtailed. Rooker claimed this was clearly be taken as a warning to the Revenue from Rees to 'watch it'. St John-Stevas's answer was that the Revenue made its own decisions.

Some of the SIS investigators were not so sure, for that decision-making process did not take place in a political vacuum. Despite public assurances of independence, the Revenue team began to feel under pressure not only to limit the scope of their inquiries but to bring them to a speedy conclusion. However, the raids had produced an enormous amount of information on the tax affairs of Rossminster clients and former employees, all of which had to be followed up. The Rossminster case was living up to Bill Dermit's description of it as the most difficult investigation the Inland Revenue had ever undertaken.

The SIS chief admitted that there was 'some pressure' for a quick prosecution but said he was backed in his approach by 'one big man', believed to have been the Chancellor of the Exchequer, Sir Geoffrey Howe, no fan of tax avoidance or friend of its promoters. The Revenue also received some much-needed assistance in changing public opinion from an unlikely quarter – Lynette Binks, Roy Tucker's personal secretary.

After the twelve vanloads of documents once again made the journey from Vogue House to Melbourne House during December and January, it was discovered that Roy Tucker's desk diaries for the halcyon years of 1974 to 1977 and certain other documents were missing. On questioning Miss Binks, Revenue investigators eventually learned that they had been thrown away, despite an undertaking Tucker had given to the Court of Appeal.

The thirty-year-old Lynette Binks had taken over as Tucker's secretary on 1 December after working for Rossminster for two years. Her predecessor had explained to her that all Tucker's diaries had to be retained – six large red *Financial Times* desk diaries for the years 1974 to 1978, kept in two filing cabinets in the small two-room suite of offices Tucker now used at Vogue House. However, around the time of the House of Lords ruling on 13 December Lynette Binks, despite Tucker's instructions to throw nothing away, discarded all but the 1978 diary, all shorthand notebooks and possibly two files which had not been returned to the Revenue. An office cleaner recalled seeing the diaries and piles of other documents in the wastepaper bin – 'I said, Come and look at this, she's had a clear-out.'

On 7 February 1980 David Thomas and another SIS officer interviewed Lynette Binks. At first, according to the Revenue's evidence, she denied throwing the diaries away. 'I couldn't have thrown five diaries away without remembering,' she said. On 26 February she said she thought she had after all thrown the diaries away. By 3 March she was positive; she could almost visualise them on top of the wastepaper bin. Thomas said in his affidavit that he suspected that this had been 'put in her mind'.

The loss of the diaries was a blow to the Revenue. They had been used extensively by Tucker; 1976, a bumper year, required two volumes to record his meetings. They had already yielded a considerable amount of useful material about Tucker's offshore interests and given clues to possible cracks in the tax schemes' defences. In its evidence later to the Court of Appeal, the Revenue pointed to certain apparent significant inconsistencies. For example, a diary entry for 30 May 1974 recorded a visit to two lawyers in Vaduz and one in Zurich. In June 1975 a Liechtenstein *Anstalt*, Donmark Establishment, had been set up in Vaduz. The *Anstalt* is a virtually impenetrable vehicle for controlling assets whose real owners are securely hidden by the rigid secrecy laws of Liechtenstein. Donmark held certain Malaysian tin-mining shares. Keith Tucker, as a nonresident, had personally claimed the repayment of UK tax deducted from dividends which equalled the dividend paid to Donmark on these shares. However, in a 1977 document seized by the Revenue, Donmark had been included in a statement of Roy Tucker's 'Personal Financial Affairs' among his 'trust interests': 'Donmark . . . is owned by my brother, Keith, but . . . I also have signing powers.' Donmark had its main bank account in Luxembourg. 'I get statements sent to me in relation to this bank account regularly,' Tucker wrote.

Two other diary entries, for 12 May and 21 May 1974, recorded meetings of the Rocquaine Trust, a Guernsey company, in Tucker's office. This caused the Revenue to wonder whether it was within UK tax jurisdiction.

The Revenue also claimed in their affidavit evidence to have discovered a pattern of significant inconsistencies between the diaries and the board minutes of certain tax-scheme companies where Tucker was a director and where he had agreed transactions as part of an orchestrated scheme sequence. On 14 April 1972 he was apparently attending a meeting of Masterdene Finance, a key company in the Reverse Annuity Scheme, while also visiting Copenhagen and Stockholm. He was recorded as present at a 15 November 1978 board meeting in London of Spinfare, a Thornwright-controlled company, yet his diary showed him to be in Venezuela that day. On 29–30 June 1978 he was minuted as attending board meetings of Butleycourt, Interbridge (both Thornwright-controlled companies), Spinfare and Goldcog (although he was not made a director of that company until September) companies active in the Commodity Carry Scheme; but according to his diary he was in Ireland on both days.

The investigators clearly believed that the missing diaries could have produced even more crucial evidence of what seemed to be an amazing ability by Tucker to be in two places at once.

These apparent inconsistencies encouraged Revenue suspicions that approval of transactions in a tax scheme and signing of the relevant documents might not always have happened on the dates indicated, because of the pressure of work, and were later backdated. If this could be proved it would be crucial to challenging the schemes in the courts. A Tucker tax scheme had to be synchronised: if one of the interlinked transactions was not carried out as stated it was invalid, and then the whole sequence of events could be null and void. But while there were clues to follow in this connection for 1972 and 1973 and also 1978, the loss of the diaries effectively blocked the Revenue from examining the years in between – Tucker's most active.

The Inland Revenue decided in April 1980 to bring proceedings against Roy Tucker, asking for his imprisonment for contempt of court. The hearing took place before Lord Denning on 22 May. The SIS officers David Thomas and Eric Wrigglesworth, in their evidence by affidavit, stressed the significance of the material that had disappeared. Tucker had told the Revenue that Forwood was a Channel Islands company owned by a trust that he looked after but in which he had no interest; Thomas pointed out that Forwood was in fact a Manx company and other evidence showed it to hold Tucker's commodity portfolio of tin and silver contracts as well as a large amount of cash.

In his affidavit, Wrigglesworth said Tucker could have committed perjury in relation to his answers about the Ridge Trust. Tucker was entitled to 25 per cent of £50,000 set aside to fight a test case on the Exempt Debt Scheme. Despite this, 'there was no mention of the Ridge Trust in the list of Tucker's interests'. Nor had Tucker mentioned the Magnum Trust, which had received a £6559 loan from Ridge, or the Iota Trust, known as a 'black hole trust', having no known beneficiary. According to Thomas, Iota's main assets were shares and loans to Forwood. The Revenue produced a schedule estimating Tucker's assets both on and offshore – in total some £5,500,000.

In her affidavit for Tucker's lawyers, Lynette Binks denied the Revenue's version of events. She had never categorically denied throwing the diaries away. She had simply forgotten her boss's instructions. Nobody had put any ideas in her head to explain what had happened. And most certainly Roy Tucker had not told her to throw the diaries away. Lord Denning and the two other judges, Lord Justice Brightman and Sir Patrick Browne, listened to these explanations with expressions of increasing displeasure. The Revenue counsel, Brian Davenport, described Tucker's secretary's effort to absolve him from blame as 'incredible'. Their displeasure grew when Davenport revealed that Tucker had refused to make an affidavit or give evidence to explain what steps he had taken to ensure all his documents were kept securely. 'He would have been expected to make such an affidavit,' the Master of the Rolls remarked disapprovingly. 'Something went very wrong for the diaries to have been destroyed. I am not sure how far the court should accept all that Miss Binks says.' As Davenport stressed, she could not have been properly instructed by Tucker and it was up to him to ensure that the diaries were kept safe. Tucker had not said that he believed his secretary; in fact he had said nothing. There was, said the Revenue counsel, insufficient explanation.

An increasingly grim-looking Tucker, smartly dressed and with his normally long hair neatly trimmed, remained silent at the front of the court. His counsel, Roger Titheridge, ineffectually stood up to convey Tucker's regrets and apologies to the court. This clearly irritated Lord Denning, who no doubt felt he had been made to look foolish. His ringing defence of Tucker's rights, equating the tax-scheme promoter with John Wilkes and the Revenue with the forces of oppression, had not only been proved wrong in law by the House of Lords but had enabled the destruction of vital evidence that, the Revenue suggested, showed Tucker to be one of Lord Denning's 'parasites who suck out the blood of our society'.

The faltering Titheridge attempted to explain that 'there is a difficulty'. The issue of the missing diaries 'touched on allegations that may well be the subject of prosecutions', in particular, Forwood and the overseas trusts. It would, said the QC, be improper for the court to allow cross-examination on these broad matters. 'The allegations will be answered at the proper time. There is an answer,' he assured the court. As for the contradictions between Tucker's diary and the minutes of companies where he was a director, 'there is an answer and it will be given.' He was seeking to reassure the judges.[7]

They were far from reassured. 'Tucker is the person responsible for the undertaking,' Lord Denning declared pointedly. Lord Justice Brightman said it was 'astonishing that Tucker had not put in any words of his own to

say that he was not to blame.' Tucker looked as unhappy as his counsel
sounded, and gave the impression of a man seeing the prison gates swing
open before him as Lord Denning began his summing up. In his characteristic, slow delivery the Master of the Rolls indicated from the start how
seriously he viewed the disappearance of the diaries – 'very important
matters, desk diaries'. Almost as serious was Tucker's failure to come
before the court and explain.

Let me say at once and perhaps most important of all, I should have thought that Mr
Tucker himself should have given his own explanation to the Court. He should have
made an affidavit making his apologies . . . saying what steps he had taken to see that
these diaries were stored and kept in a proper place. His secretaries should have
received proper instructions . . . There was no such affidavit by Mr Tucker. No
explanation by him . . . one cannot help wondering whether the reason why Mr Tucker
has not made an affidavit to explain his action is because of the fact that he may be
cross-examined . . . To my mind the explanation given by Mr Tucker is not in the least
satisfactory. It seems to me that this was a serious breach of an undertaking given to the
Court . . . Explanations seem to fall far short of the truth, particularly in the absence of
any affidavit by Mr Tucker himself.

Tucker now looked very worried indeed. Then Lord Denning pronounced sentence – £1000 fine plus costs – and for the first time that day
Roy Tucker smiled. That was petty cash to a man who controlled assets
worth more than £5 million.

The Revenue investigators were angry at the leniency of the sentence.
As they gathered in the coffee shop across the Strand from the court, the
consensus was that the punishment had far from fitted the crime. A
relieved Roy Tucker meanwhile left the court with his smiling secretary,
who told waiting journalists that he was 'a super boss' and how it was 'really
all my fault'. Was there any danger of her being fired? 'Oh, good God, no,'
she replied.[8] Her only fear, she joked, was that the fine might be deducted
from her salary.

Roy Tucker too could afford to laugh. The vital desk diaries were no
longer available to the Revenue and an explanation had been given
described by Lord Denning as falling 'far short of the truth', and he had
given no explanation at all, yet the cost was a derisory fine.

The revelation of the disappearing diaries and Tucker's refusal to give
evidence gave the Revenue a compensatory publicity bonus: for the first
time Tucker and Rossminster did not appear to be pristine white Robin
Hoods victimised by a Gestapo like Inland Revenue. To repair their image

Tucker and Plummer launched a new public-relations offensive, enlisting the support of a highly unorthodox public-relations man.

Unknown to Tucker and Plummer, Bill Taylor of W. A. Taylor and Associates had always had a problem in telling fact from fiction, usually an asset for a PR man. In 1973 Taylor left Britain for Rhodesia. On arrival he gave his full name as Paul William Alfred Taylor, born at Felpham in Sussex on 21 June 1944. The registrar of births for that district could find no trace of a Paul William Alfred Taylor born on that day, but Scotland Yard's Criminal Records Office had a record of a Paul William Taylor, beginning in 1959. In 1969 Taylor had been convicted on thirteen charges of making false income-tax statements. In January 1970 he had been convicted of falsely claiming unemployment benefit. In November 1971 he had been jailed for two years on charges of deception.

Taylor's career as a journalist was just as colourful. In 1964 he was censured for the first time by the Press Council for supplying a false story to the *Daily Sketch*. Two years later he was being described by the *People* as 'the most congenital liar and original inventor of news who has come to our knowledge'. Taylor had earned these plaudits by journalistic 'scoops' such as the germ-warfare establishment that turned out to be a fuel storage depot, the shock report on airline pilots' morals from a nonexistent league for moral reform, the invisible cat who swallowed a £3200 ring and the nondiscovery of Cromwell's helmet being used as a flower pot.

The first PR stunt Taylor orchestrated for Tucker and Plummer involved commemorating the anniversary of the raids. On Sunday 13 July 1980 Roy Tucker solemnly walked into his local police station in West Malling, Kent, and asked fatuously, 'Am I on your wanted list?' He was told by a surprised police officer that he was not. About the same time Ron Plummer telephoned Paddington Green police station with the same inane query and, not surprisingly, was given a similar dusty answer. Word of this stage-managed nonevent was immediately circulated to Fleet Street via the Press Association news agency, and fulsomely reported on the front page of the *Daily Telegraph*. The whole exercise was nothing more than an opportunity for Tucker and Plummer to go once more into their Gestapo routine. Plummer told the *Daily Telegraph*, 'We have reason to believe that some members of the SIS of the Revenue are politically motivated and have decided to draw their own moral lines about perfectly legal tax avoidance.'[9]

On 16 July the government announced the setting up of the Committee on Enforcement Powers of the Revenue Departments under the Law

Lord and tax expert Lord Keith. No one could miss the relevance to Rossminster since the raids had been brought back to prominence by the Taylor-inspired publicity stunt.

When he was elected Conservative MP for Brigg and Scunthorpe in 1979, Michael Brown became, at twenty-eight, the youngest member of the House. On 18 July Brown tabled a question in the Commons to the Chancellor, Sir Geoffrey Howe, asking whether payments were made out of a 'slush fund' to Inland Revenue informers in tax-evasion cases. Explaining the background to his unusual enquiry, Brown declared, 'I have uncovered the tip of what could be a very big iceberg.'[10] He went on to allege that the Rossminster raids had been made after information was supplied by an informant who had been 'intimidated by the Special Investigation Section of the Inland Revenue and misled into believing his life could be ruined by Revenue harassment'.[11] Brown claimed to have two witnesses who would swear affidavits confirming this. 'He believed his only escape from this predicament – imaginary or otherwise – was to cooperate with the investigators by supplying information.'[12]

The only problem was that Lewis-Grey did not confirm this version of events. Instead he told the *Daily Telegraph*, 'As far as I am concerned Mr Brown's allegations are completely wrong and perhaps you should ask him who he is acting for. I have absolutely no criticism to make of the Inland Revenue.'[13] Undeterred, the MP explained that he considered the serving of a Section 481 notice 'a form of harassment'. Brown similarly was not put off by the reply from Peter Rees to his question, pointing out that since 1890 payments could be made for information about offences. Rees denied that a 10 per cent bounty could be rewarded, as Brown claimed; only £1445 had been paid out since January 1974. Michael Brown said he would still be pursuing the matter as he had 'no reason to doubt' the information given to him.[14] Explaining this curious episode Brown says that after he had raised a question in the House about overzealous taxmen, 'An intermediary, not in the House of Commons, contacted me. He may well have been in touch with Rossminster's public-relations man.' The choice of Michael Brown may not have been entirely coincidental. One of his constituents was a regular introducer of clients to Tucker. The MP would not identify who contacted him but admits that he was unknowingly used to help Rossminster by being given incorrect information with which to embarrass the Inland Revenue.

Bill Taylor's most audacious effort on Rossminster's behalf was nothing less than an attempt to compromise the head of the SIS, Bill Dermit. In early July – just before the anniversary stunt – Dermit was contacted by a man calling himself David Aitken, from the Black Star Press Agency, who said that he was acting for a Fleet Street newspaper. A 'mole' in Guernsey had supplied him with Rossminster documents which were very compromising, and he wanted to check their authenticity in return for sharing the information in them with the Revenue. Dermit agreed to meet 'Aitken', who gave a telephone number for the Black Star Press Agency. A check with Post Office records disclosed that the number was listed to an empty office in a particularly run-down part of Caledonian Road, in north London.

At the meeting in Melbourne House, 'Aitken' was accompanied by two other men, one of whom identified himself as an accountant. Bill Dermit, already suspecting an attempt to 'set him up', had brought as witnesses Detective Sergeant Eric Lilley – a personal friend and the collator of information for Scotland Yard's Fraud Squad – and another police officer. Both men were unintroduced and remained silent throughout what turned out to be a very brief meeting.

'Aitken' began by talking about the documents relating to Rossminster and a man in Sussex who had committed a tax fraud. Dermit listened, then asked 'Aitken' to identify the Fleet Street newspaper for which he was acting. 'Aitken' refused. Dermit asked why the telephone number he had been given was in an empty office. 'Aitken', now becoming nervous, attempted to explain this away by talking about an office move. Then the SIS chief delivered the *coup de grâce*: he asked why the Inland Revenue could not trace any tax returns for 'Aitken', Black Star or the other two men at the meeting. This was a bluff but it worked. The three men looked at each other, spluttered about not expecting to be treated in this fashion and then, as one of those who remained put it, 'ran from the room'.

Bill Dermit was convinced that the meeting had been a clumsy attempt to compromise him by getting him either to handle stolen documents or breach the Official Secrets Act by discussing Rossminster's affairs with the Press. This evidence could then be used to discredit him and the investigation, causing the government to put pressure on the Revenue and maybe even halt the SIS inquiries. Shortly after this meeting Dermit described 'Aitken' to a journalist who knew Bill Taylor, and it became clear that they were one and the same man. A subsequent check of the Caledonian Road address showed that the Rossminster PR man had an office there as W. A. Taylor Assurance. There is no evidence that he discussed the attempt to 'set up' the head of the SIS with his clients. Taylor was still working for Rossminster some months after the 'Aitken' incident.

Throughout 1980 *Private Eye* had been almost alone in continuing to report new aspects of the Rossminster story, so it was not altogether surprising that an attempt should be made to influence if not silence that source of anti-Rossminster comment. In August a Mrs C. M. O'Collins sat down at her home in Kent and wrote a long letter to Richard Ingrams, the editor of *Private Eye*, which she tucked inside a copy of a famous children's book:

On the strength of your TV charisma – almost impossible to reconcile with those nasty little articles you publish in *Private Eye* – I am sending you the tale of Squirrel Nutkin . . . It has occurred to me that in many ways Nutkin's adventures resemble Roy Tucker's of Rossminster.

Mrs O'Collins then disclosed that she was Tucker's mother-in-law. Explaining the similarities between the master of tax schemes and the intrepid squirrel, she wrote:

Nutkin, unlike Roy, was impertinent and lazy. However, both managed to avoid giving 'nice' official presents and both exercised their own special talents, unchecked and to a maddening degree, until in Nutkin's case, Mr Brown (the Inland Revenue?) goaded beyond all endurance suddenly pounced and grabbed him, prior to skinning him alive. An excessive punishment would you not think? Fortunately Nutkin escaped, albeit with half his tail. Roy has now been metaphorically skinned alive for just over a year.

She went on to give a mother-in-law's-eye view of the great tax expert:

Roy, who is really rather clever, would, even if criminally inclined [not] do anything so abysmally stupid [as fraud] . . . I admit that if Roy was proposing to rob a train he would be unlikely to confide in his mother-in-law nevertheless and notwithstanding . . . I do sincerely believe Roy to be a person of absolute integrity, i.e. more so than is normal. (His wife says his honesty is positively irritating) . . . I am not saying he is a saint, understandably his legal but artificial tax avoidance schemes were experienced by the Government as damaging and doubtless they had to be stopped. But surely this could have been done much sooner without cost . . . if somebody had condescended to talk to him. They never have and to this day he remains unenlightened as to what he is accused of. In short it appears he is being unjustly victimised.

After a year of fairly relentless pressure from the SIS, Tucker and Plummer seemed to be feeling the strain of the war of attrition, despite their publicity gestures and brave pronouncements. The Inland Revenue, with blanket opposition to all Tucker's tax schemes, had taken action against all companies involved, and raised assessments claiming tax of at least £100 million. Pressure was also being exercised in other ways. Rossminster companies had always been slow to file accounts with the Registrar of Companies – a fact which usually caused problems only for those seeking information about their activities – but in August 1980 Halliwell and Bruce-Watt were fined £400 and £525 respectively after admitting eleven charges brought by the Department of Trade and Industry of failing to supply accounts and annual returns during 1976 to 1979 for five internal Rossminster companies.

By the summer of 1980 there were some ninety tax cases pending on Tucker schemes between the Special Commissioners and the House of Lords. The great majority were at the first stage, awaiting a Special Commissioners hearing, and threatened to clog up the courts for at least ten to fifteen years. Tucker estimated that if all his clients asked for a hearing before the Special Commissioners it would take some of them 120 years to get there.

Where the tax scheme had succeeded before the courts, the Revenue now refused to accept test cases and allow relief to all those clients who had done similar schemes; each client was asked to prove his own scheme as if the court ruling had not happened. The Revenue also refused to deal with Tucker or Rossminster directly; instead, their clients faced demands for all the documentation on every transaction in the tax scheme. The clients and their advisers needed to produce innumerable original documents, board minutes, old bank statements and cheques – most of which they had handed over to Rossminster. Tucker was threatened with a tidal wave of demands for advice, assistance and documents, which quickly proved impossible to handle. He had assigned the task of dealing with the Revenue on the clients' schemes to Roy Walkden, who was soon inundated with clients' and advisers' files and requests to advise – and that was only for the earlier schemes.

Faced with the costs involved, Tucker gave up the struggle and withdrew his promise of the test case, the fighting fund and the after-sales services. Early in August 1980 Tucker's former clients received the bad news that they were on their own. A letter from Tucker to clients who had bought the Advance Interest Scheme explained why. Naturally the Inland Revenue were to blame:

This decision . . . is caused by the Inland Revenue whose attitude is having the effect of escalating costs to a level not previously imagined . . . If this firm were to advise on each and every case exactly what documents should be provided to the Revenue, it would in effect become involved in conducting the skilled preliminary work of each appeal in detail. We regret that this work would go far beyond this firm's strict obligations and also beyond its resources . . . It is likely that the Reserve Fund set aside for fighting this case to the House of Lords – £35,000 – will be considerably exceeded merely in fighting the case through the Special Commissioners.

Tucker's former clients were informed that neither he nor Walkden would provide more than 'reasonable assistance of a general nature', that is, explaining the principles of the tax schemes and how they related to the reliefs claimed. As neither Roy Tucker & Co. nor Rossminster ever acted as professional advisers to the clients they did not owe them any continuing care beyond what was spelled out in the small print of the agreements. The clients were now recommended to make 'political representations' against the 'oppressive' Revenue and its use of public funds.

To many clients the guarantee to fight the test case, the fighting fund and the free after-sales service had influenced their decision to go ahead more than the small print of the legal opinions. Now the small print revealed that security to be a delusion. They had a choice between putting up the substantial cost of fighting the Revenue legally and dropping the claim for relief they had paid Tucker and Rossminster to produce. The umbrella had been taken away just as the storm broke.

News of Tucker's decision reached Lorana Sullivan at the *Sunday Times* from two anxious former clients of the Advanced Interest Scheme. On 24 August she published the details of Tucker's letter in a prominent article. This was another blow to the keenly fostered image of honest businessmen who had merely tried to do their best for overtaxed clients and who were making a principled stand against the despotic Inland Revenue, and Tucker responded quickly. That Sunday afternoon he issued a statement pledging to spend 'whatever it costs' to fight the Revenue challenges to his tax schemes – 'unlikely to be less than £1 million', more than twice the 1978 estimate. Tucker emphatically denied that he had 'abandoned' clients: all commitments were being fulfilled, and twelve test cases were being fought all the way to the House of Lords. 'It could be ten years before all the cases are settled. We remain confident, however, that all schemes will be vindicated as legal and that our clients will, at the end of the day, have made the planned tax savings.' Plummer's response was very different. Rossminster promptly sued for libel.

Tucker and Rossminster continued to receive a sympathetic press in some quarters, particularly but perhaps not surprisingly *Accountancy Age*. On 10 October the weekly magazine chronicled the Revenue's latest 'excess': using documents seized in the raids to challenge before the Special Commissioners Plummer's £150,000 claim for relief against capital gains tax from using the Deferred Purchase Capital Loss Scheme. With, by his own estimates, £15 million in clients' tax at stake, Plummer was upset when, without warning, the Revenue cross-examined him on the seized documents. Plummer protested but the Commissioners ruled they were admissible. Plummer complained to *Accountancy Age*:

We are victims of a serious abuse of justice. We believed all along that there was a cynical attempt to discredit – and thereby frighten off – all those engaged in perfectly legal tax avoidance activities. But we never dreamed that the Revenue would have the cheek to produce the seized tax papers in a civil case. We have always maintained that the raids might have had an ulterior motive.

Plummer also complained to the Lord Chancellor.

Plummer's umbrage was understandable. The seized documents had exposed gaping flaws in the scheme's documentation and execution, and as a result the Special Commissioners had seemed unconvinced by the traditional semantic arguments voiced by Andrew Park QC. But Plummer did not pass on that part of the story to the Press. Plummer's shouts of 'foul' were eagerly picked up by Fleet Street's regular Rossminster apologists in the *Daily Telegraph* and the *Observer*.

A week later, on 19 October, the pro-Rossminster lobby reached its widest audience with the help of BBC television's *Money Programme*. Tucker and Plummer made their usual protestations of innocence and ignorance of what was suspected. Explaining the raids, Tucker declared, 'I think the Inland Revenue were worried about the growth of the tax-avoidance industry . . . They wanted to terrify our competitors and our clients or our potential clients to stop them doing tax-avoidance schemes for the future, quite certain about that. Terror is one of their motives.' The programme showed the Inland Revenue in general and the SIS in particular in the overbearing role Tucker and Plummer had chosen for them. The raid on Nettlestead Place was re-enacted with a frightened-looking Tucker (he appeared to have forgotten that he was not there but in Guernsey that day) peering anxiously with his wife from an upstairs window as the BBC jackboots crunched up the gravel path to their front door. Sir William Pile was subjected to a series of leading questions without any evidence to justify the innuendo behind them – had not the raids been a fishing expedition, had the SIS engaged in telephone tapping, did the Inland Revenue have enough control over this special squad? The former chairman's denials were bound to seem unconvincing.

Roy Tucker showed considerable less enthusiasm for a *World in Action* documentary about Rossminster on which I had been working since the summer. After three invitations for an interview had been declined it became clear that Tucker had no wish to take part in a programme which he foresaw was unlikely to be favourable.

Shortly before the programme was to be broadcast Rossminster announced, on 21 November, that it was closing down in Britain. 'This move signals the end of the road for Rossminster,' Plummer told the *Financial Times.*[15] He blamed the raids for causing a loss of confidence, particularly in the bank, where deposits had halved to £3 million. Banking profits had declined from £371,000 in 1979 to £133,000. Group profits of £872,000 and £1,061,000 for 1978 and 1979 had largely been earned by E. Bailey's commodity dealings. In the year to July 1980, with no Bailey contribution, they were just £82,000.

The decision to close the bank had largely been forced on Rossminster by the growing realisation that it was most unlikely to be licensed by the Bank of England – which had now replaced the Department of Trade and Industry as the approving authority under the 1979 Banking Act – while the Inland Revenue investigation continued. (First London Securities and Rossminster Acceptances had been recognised as banks by the DTI but not by the Revenue.) The bank would have to close if it was not approved by 31 March, 1981. Plummer accepted the inevitable and closed voluntarily.[16]

1980 was also the end of the road for Plummer as a British resident. His London home was up for sale at £275,000.

The Rossminster name would only be retained in order to take legal action against the Revenue for damages, as Plummer had threatened to do if the Revenue did not bring charges within a year of the House of Lords judgment – by mid-December 1980. This seemed unlikely. The Revenue were only just starting to take witness statements from Lewis-Grey and certain former clients. They had caused perturbation inside Rossminster, however, by approaching some twenty former employees of the firm and Roy Tucker & Co. with an invitation to answer questions about their personal tax affairs. Many of the former employees had used tax schemes to avoid tax on their annual bonuses or had received special taxfree payments when moving from one part of the group to another. Tucker swiftly sent a circular to all present and past staff members:

Certain individuals have recently been approached by the SIS for a meeting allegedly concerning their own taxation affairs. We are advised that no one is under any compulsion to agree to attend such a meeting or even to discuss their affairs over the telephone . . .

Please note that you are not authorised to discuss the affairs of your employer or former employer or any associate of your employer with the Inland Revenue or with anyone else. We mention this in case you find that the real purpose of the Inland Revenue is to broaden the discussion beyond your personal affairs.

The *World in Action* documentary was broadcast on 1 December. Tucker's response was that it 'was very biased, just as I expected it to be'.[17] Labour MPs were particularly incensed at revelations regarding the role of Peter Rees. Robert Hughes caused an uproar in the Commons when he asked whether Rees's position as a Treasury minister was a case of 'set a thief to catch a thief'.[18] Two days later, Rees was stoutly defended in the Commons by the prime minister, also a barrister.

On 11 December some 200 accountants and lawyers, gathered at the Café Royal in London to discuss and decide on the tactics with which to meet the Revenue's challenge to all Tucker's tax schemes. Tucker had been pressed to summon the meeting by former clients and their advisers alarmed at the Revenue's hard line attitude of picking off scheme users one by one. Philip Hardman, senior tax partner of Thornton Baker, was appointed chairman of a working party to try and negotiate a deal with the Revenue.

Tucker had concluded his appearance on the *Money Programme* by repeating the assurances both he and Plummer had given since the raids: 'I'm confident that at the end of the day, in most if not in all of our schemes, our clients will win because the schemes were good, soundly conceived and well implemented.' This confidence was about to be proved totally mistaken.

THE REAL WORLD INTERVENES

By the end of the seventies the tax-avoidance boom, which had begun some ten years before, was making its impact felt in the courts with a lengthening queue of cases. At the beginning of 1979 two Tucker schemes – Plummer with the HOVAS Reverse Annuity Scheme and Ramsay with the Exempt Debt Scheme – had either reached the Court of Appeal or were awaiting an appearance there. Plummer had succeeded in both the High Court and the Court of Appeal; Ramsay had succeeded in the High Court. Two Bradman schemes were also heading for the Court of Appeal – one had been vindicated in the High Court, the other had not – and a third was due to be heard by the High Court. Each was different but they were all artificial schemes, relying largely on the use of tax reliefs created for genuine commercial transactions.

The courts were still applying the Tomlin doctrine even if it came tottering forward from another age. Form was still all; substance was irrelevant. As recently as 1971 an attempt to revive the substance argument had been firmly quashed by Lord Wilberforce – 'In a matter of taxation it is necessary to consider and respect the legal form.'[1] Wilberforce was now the senior Law Lord in tax cases. In a 1974 Lords judgment on what he admitted were 'two blatant tax-avoidance schemes', Lord Simon recognised the problem but saw no solution:

It may seem hard that a cunningly advised taxpayer should be able to avoid what appears to be his equitable share of the general financial burden and cast it on the shoulders of his fellow citizens . . . Disagreeable as it may seem that some taxpayers should escape what might appear to be their fair share of the general burden of national expenditure it would be far more disagreeable to substitute the rule of caprice for that of law.[2]

In the five years that followed, the Law Lords had considered five artificial avoidance schemes, ruling for the taxpayer only twice. But from the way in which judges in the lower courts approached the more sophisticated and complex schemes that Bradman and Tucker had devised, there was little reason to believe that Lord Clyde's shovel was about to be placed back in the taxman's hands. There was, however, one voice in the courts which did speak out consistently against the growing menace presented by artificial tax avoidance both to the Treasury and the interests of other taxpayers. That was Sir Sydney – now Lord – Templeman.

In 1975, three years after becoming Mr Justice Templeman, he had delivered a withering critique of the tax scheme used by the film actress Julie Christie. Using terms like 'trick' and 'fake', he spoke dismissively of the complex arrangements created by the scheme promoters, and he made a point which went to the heart of the 'form' versus 'substance' argument. Quoting Lord Wilberforce, Templeman said, 'It is legitimate to consider the "scheme as a whole" where there is evidence . . . that each separate step is dependent on others being carried out.' Yet persistently, as the more modern and more artificial schemes emerged from the Bradman and Tucker stables, the judges were pressed to ignore that view and to take instead the blinkered, step-by-step approach, never raising their eyes above the pile of documentation to see the escaping taxpayer. In a series of judgments during his six years as a Chancery Division judge, Templeman showed that those who used the services of 'an inventor and purveyor of tax-avoidance schemes' could expect no mercy. Fortunately for Bradman, Tucker and their rivals, Templeman's approach was not reflected among his fellow High Court judges. When he gave judgment for the Revenue in a case involving N. M. Rothschild's clients the Chinn family, founders of Lex Garages, this decision was overruled by the Court of Appeal. Despite this difference in attitude Templeman was highly regarded by his legal peers and in 1978, when fifty-eight years old, was appointed to the Court of Appeal.

At the beginning of 1979 Roy Tucker held an unbeaten record in his legal contests with the Inland Revenue, helped by the narrow, legalistic Tomlin view. Mr Justice Walton in his July 1977 judgment for Plummer had declared, 'it is quite impossible to leave the contractual or other arrangements out of account.'[3] (Shortly afterwards the same judge found for the Vesteys in their battle with the Revenue.) In March 1978 Mr Justice Goulding overruled the Special Commissioners and allowed the claim for relief against corporation tax made by W. T. Ramsay, following use of the Exempt Debt Scheme. When the Inland Revenue appealed the Plummer decision to the Court of Appeal, its argument that the HOVAS annuity was entered into with the sole object of tax avoidance met with little sympathy from Lord Justice Buckley. 'It is in my opinion quite fallacious to regard the fiscal advantages as constituting any part of the consideration for the bargain' was his remarkable conclusion.[4]

Tucker and Plummer were therefore fairly confident as the Revenue's appeal in the Ramsay case came up for hearing in May 1979 – despite the presence of Lord Justice Templeman among the three Court of Appeal judges. However, there had been a worrying development: a similar capital gains tax scheme marketed by the tax lawyer John Memery had lost in the High Court in July 1978.[5] Mr Justice Slade had ruled against the scheme on the narrow point that a £10,000 payment made by the taxpayer, with money borrowed from the promoters, was the price for the promoters' completing the remaining stages of the scheme and so was not 'wholly and exclusively' for the purpose claimed. Slade's decision in the *Eilbeck* v. *Rawling* case indicated a potential crack in the Tomlin doctrine. That crack turned into a gaping fissure in May 1979 when the Court of Appeal gave its decision in the Ramsay case.

The key judgment was given by Lord Justice Templeman – a choice that signalled which way the verdict had gone. The Exempt Debt Scheme was, said Templeman:

Yet another circular game in which the taxpayer and a few hired performers act out a play; nothing happens save that the Houdini taxpayer appears to escape from the manacles of tax . . . The taxpayer and the consultants revolved and exchanged money through companies controlled by them or their directors and thereby at neglible cost to the taxpayer, and without earning a gain or suffering a loss, created for the taxpayer a claim for a non-taxable gain and for a tax-deductible loss thus achieving no result save a manufactured claim to entitlement to tax relief.[6]

Despite his open dislike for this type of scheme, Templeman decided the case on a very narrow point – if the crucial second loan the taxpayer sold to the scheme promoters at a profit was a security, the profit was taxable. The Tucker argument was that the loan was not a security but a debt to a creditor. Lord Scarman said, 'In simple English (not of course appropriate to the complications of a taxing statute) the distinction is between a loan and an investment.' He and Lord Justice Ormrod agreed with Templeman that it was an investment and so the gain was taxable, which meant the

Exempt Debt Scheme did not work. If Ramsay had to pay tax on selling the second loan, the proceeds would not cancel out the loss on the sale of the first loan, which had been created to claim tax relief against the real capital gain made from the farm sale.

The Ramsay decision was the first clear signal that the mood of the courts was turning against artificial tax avoidance. It came only two weeks after the Conservatives' victory in the general election under the banner of lower taxes. A little under two months later the Rossminster raids took tax avoidance out of the law reports and onto the front pages. Further evidence of the rapidly changing public perception of tax avoidance came from the *Financial Times*'s legal columnist 'Justinian'. Commenting on the Ramsay judgment, he concluded, 'Surely it cannot be past the wit of Parliamentary draftsmen to distinguish legitimate 'tax planning' from indulgence in schemes which amount, in truth, to raids on the nation's purse?'[7]

On 1 November 1979 the Law Lords gave their decision in the Plummer case. House of Lords judgments are no longer read out in full in open court. Instead, on the day, counsel, lawyers and clients attend in the peers' lobby around 1.30 pm, collect the judges' opinions which are printed together like a pamphlet on distinctive green paper, flip to the end of each one and see who has won. Then at two o'clock they all troop into the Lords' chamber for the brief formality of hearing each of the five judges solemnly declare their decision for or against the appeal for the reasons either given in their own printed judgment or that of a fellow Law Lord. The whole process takes only a few minutes.

The first judgment from Lord Wilberforce, while rejecting the Revenue's appeal against Plummer, displayed unease about the Reverse Annuity Scheme. It was, he said, 'an extreme case' entitled to 'a fair, if not a particularly benevolent, analysis'. The court should look at the scheme as a whole but must not 'disregard the legal form and nature of the transactions carried out'. 'If it were possible to disregard the legal form of the documents and to look behind them for an underlying substance,' said Wilberforce pointedly, 'there would be attractions beyond those of ingenuity in this argument.' But on the basis of the legal documents he held that the Plummer annuity to HOVAS was not simply a repayment of the capital sum paid to him by the charity. The manner in which he chose to make the payments was 'completely irrelevant'. Nor did it matter that the payments were part of a sequence designed solely to avoid tax, and not a bona fide commercial transaction. Lord Wilberforce concluded his judgment by saying:

The familiar argument was used that Parliament can never have intended to exempt from the taxing provisions an arrangement solely designed to obtain fiscal advantages. But this is not the question . . . The question is whether a certain series of transactions in a certain legal form do or do not fall within the taxing words. If they do not and if Parliament dislikes the consequence, it can change the law.[8]

This traditionalist view was not acceptable to Viscount Dilhorne, who, from the start of the second judgment, made it clear that he had little liking or sympathy for 'an ingenious, complicated and well thought-out scheme'. In his view it was 'a scheme to avoid the payment of tax by those who participated and to raid the Treasury using the technicalities of Revenue law as the necessary weapon'.

Dilhorne was said to have been influenced partly by the involvement of Slater, Walker in financing the scheme. In April 1978 he had ruled in favour of the extradition of the Slater, Walker director Richard Tarling to Singapore to face Companies Act charges arising out of a management incentive scheme for Jim Slater and fellow executives. In a dissenting opinion – the Law Lords ruled three to two against the Singapore government – Dilhorne said there was prima facie evidence of dishonesty. He was also angered by the lower courts' decision not to extradite Slater, who had been charged with Tarling. 'Slater, Walker was like a red rag,' says a fellow judge.

Dilhorne made much of the fact that HOVAS had been unable to obtain charitable status from the Revenue and had not appealed that decision. But mainly he attacked the view that it was not for the courts to seek to interpret what Parliament intended. Dilhorne declared, 'It is open to the courts when considering particular transactions and whether they come within the definition, to conclude that Parliament cannot have intended that they should be treated as doing so; and to decide, if that conclusion is reached, that they do not.'

The key issue was whether the payments Plummer made to HOVAS were part of his income arising out of a settlement. If Plummer was the settlor of such an arrangement then he was caught by Section 457 of the Income and Corporation Taxes Act. The Wilberforce line was that Parliament could not have intended such a wide meaning of either 'settlor' or 'settlement' that all transactions would be caught. Nor was it open to the courts to read into the wording an exemption excluding any transaction which was not bona fide.

Dilhorne disagreed: 'The question to be decided is whether Parliament can have intended that the arrangement of which *the* main object was the obtaining of tax advantages should be outside the operation of Section 457. In my opinion the answer is in the negative.' He therefore found for the Revenue.

So did the next judge, Lord Diplock. 'Whatever kind of transaction Parliament may have intended to exclude it cannot have been this one,' he declared. He found this despite 'the blinkers that the court by *Inland Revenue Commissioners* v. *Duke of Westminster* and cases that have followed it is enjoined to wear in Revenue cases'.

It seemed that over forty years of legal precedent was about to be overturned by the first of the off-the-peg tax schemes to be considered by the Law Lords. But with the vote two to one against, the traditionalist cavalry came over the hill to rescue Lord Wilberforce and Ronald Plummer. Lords Fraser and Keith both accepted that the money in the scheme was in fact provided by Plummer from his income and not by HOVAS from a settlement he had made. The narrow interpretation of Section 457 therefore could apply and he was entitled to claim the tax relief. HOVAS had relieved Plummer's suffering if no one else's. Plummer had won and £15 million in tax had been avoided for Tucker's clients – or so it seemed. But even Lord Wilberforce says now that the Reverse Annuity Scheme 'was very near to the edge'. For the new-style tax avoiders it was to be their first and last hurrah.

Three weeks later the Law Lords also ruled in favour of the Vestey family over the Revenue's attempt to tax income of £2,600,000 emanating from the family's offshore trusts and in a highly unusual decision overturned a 1948 ruling designed to enforce the provisions against the transfer of assets abroad.

To tax experts the Lords' decision was seen as nothing short of astounding. It opened up 'a yawning gap' in Section 478 of the ICTA which supposedly caught those UK residents with 'the power to enjoy' assets held abroad. For the Lords ruled that the Revenue could not – as the statute appeared to say – decide which of the beneficiaries of a trust should be taxed and how much. So, while the transferor of assets abroad could be taxed, his family could not, 'even though they participated in the tax avoidance'. Speaking of that decision now, Lord Wilberforce, who had appeared for the Revenue against the Vesteys when at the Bar, says,

You don't know how much it hurt me to decide in favour of the Vesteys. I sometimes wake up at night and ask myself, was it right that I should have decided the case in a way that the Vesteys did not pay millions in tax? It would have been easy to do. We could have relied on the earlier decision. The problem was that the Revenue couldn't produce any real evidence for their contention about their discretion to decide who should be taxed and how much. In the end that principle was more important.

Eleven months later, in October 1980, the *Sunday Times* highlighted the Vesteys' long and successful battle to preserve their £1000 million fortune from the taxman, suggesting that the courts had a greater concern for the injustices of the tax laws on the Vesteys than for the injustice of such practices on less well-advised and less wealthy taxpayers. The result was a storm of protest both inside and outside Parliament. Sir Geoffrey Howe immediately promised legislation to close up the Vestey loophole – a year after Viscount Dilhorne had remarked on the 'urgent need' for action – and said, 'Anyone living here and enjoying the benefits ought to pay our taxes.'[9] The Vestey loophole was slammed shut in the Finance Act 1981.

The Revenue raids and subsequent disclosures had begun to change the public perception of Tucker and Plummer, and with the top tax rate slashed to 60 per cent, some tax-avoidance practitioners closed up shop. Increasingly, judges and others began to see the Bradmans and Tuckers as, in Lord Justice Templeman's words, scripting pantomimes 'of a kind which would render the payment of tax a voluntary exercise by the ignorant, the conscientious, the idle and the generality of taxpayers'.[10]

Plummer felt the full force of this change in attitude in February 1981 when the Special Commissioners gave their verdict on his £150,000 claim for tax relief through the Deferred Purchase Capital Loss Scheme. His appeal was rejected, the Commissioners terming the transactions and the documentation 'shams and nullities . . . by no stretch of the imagination . . . a real transaction of commerce'. Such harsh language had never been used before to strike down a Tucker scheme. For the first time the belief of the SIS investigators that the schemes could be defeated – if *all* the facts were before the court – had been vindicated, thanks to the documents discovered in the raids.

At Westgate Farm near Gainsborough, the Vestey and Rossminster developments were being followed closely by farmer Robert Ramsay, for he was due shortly to follow in Ronald Plummer's and Lord Vestey's footsteps to the House of Lords in a bid to overturn the Court of Appeal's decision on the Exempt Debt Scheme. Unlike Plummer, his family company had paid the £177,000 corporation tax claimed on the sale and lease-back of the farm and was seeking repayment of the tax on the basis of the capital loss he had bought through the scheme.

W. T. Ramsay was one of twenty-seven Pilbrow clients who had done the scheme. Three were selected by the Inland Revenue as candidates for a test case. When the first choice, an elderly man, died, Ramsay replaced him. 'My only regret is that we were selected as the guinea pig,' says Robert Ramsay. 'Others had the money for about ten years, earning interest, while we had paid the tax and then had to spend all that time trying to get it back.' Ramsay was quite confident in the scheme even though he could not follow all its intricacies or the sophisticated legal arguments. 'I thought we would win,' he says.

Pilbrow gave odds of at worst 60:40 that the Law Lords would rule in their favour and overturn the decision of Lord Justice Templeman – now nicknamed 'Sid Vicious' after the punk pop star, because of his hostile views. Robert Ramsay travelled from Lincolnshire to London, for the House of Lords hearing which began on 26 January 1981. 'I didn't understand a word.' However, he did at least meet the scheme's architect, Roy Tucker. 'We all felt reasonably confident when it ended,' he recalls. Tucker, Pilbrow and their counsel Charles Potter QC also felt that the hearing had gone well and that Lord Wilberforce and his four colleagues, who this time did not include the Plummer critics Dilhorne and Diplock, were sympathetic. They had, they thought, the best five judges to hear the case.

After a distinguished career at the tax Bar, Richard Wilberforce, a direct descendant of the Great Emancipator, had been appointed a Law Lord in 1964. A small, neat, ascetic-looking figure, he was considered one of the great legal intellects and had for more than fifty years been a Fellow of All Souls, Oxford. 'I was brought in to give the Lords tax expertise' is how he explains his appointment after only three years as a Chancery Division judge. 'A cool head, a theoretical judge, not a liberal judge' is how he describes himself. While practising at the Bar, Wilberforce would give advice on tax affairs but not on tax schemes. 'I would say, I'm not prepared to do that. I was only prepared to advise on whether something was within the law.' He has little time for those at the tax Bar who became opinion fodder for the tax-scheme promoters. 'As a judge you'd say, "Oh, not him again,"' he said of a well-known QC much used by Tucker and Bradman. 'You listen to those who are fair, not those who retail opinions.'

After seventeen years in the House of Lords, Wilberforce was seen both as the keeper of the Duke of Westminster blinkers and the protector of the faith in form over substance. Wilberforce denies that he was anti-Revenue. 'I'm in favour of people paying their share of tax. I don't see it as a moral issue but in terms of what the law says. I would look at a tax scheme critically to see if it failed. I liked to challenge counsel's opinions.' Nevertheless, in only one major tax-avoidance case to come before the House of Lords while he had been the senior judge had he supported the Revenue.

The Scottish judge Lord Fraser was seen as a 'theoretical' judge similar to Wilberforce. Lord Russell, the son of a Law Lord, was described by one of his colleagues as 'a Tomlin man'. Lords Roskill and Bridge were both 'new boys', having been appointed Law Lords only the previous year, 1980. Roskill had been a leading commercial lawyer while Bridge was a former Treasury counsel. 'Morality judges who would look at what was right' was how they were described by another Law Lord. Both were likely to follow the lead given by the three senior judges.

It had been decided that the House of Lords would hear, at the same time as Ramsay, the appeal in the Eilbeck case, which had lost in the Court of Appeal in February 1980. All three judges had ruled against the taxpayer, Rawling, but Templeman's judgment, typically, was the most scathing. Referring to the Memery scheme, which was 'characteristic of many tax-avoidance schemes which have lost the country millions of pounds in revenue', he declared, 'So far as the taxpayer is concerned, he began with nothing, by contract he gained nothing and lost nothing and he ended with nothing. The effect of the contract was that he paid £9985 for an argument which proves to be worth nothing.'[11]

The Memery and Tucker schemes had the common feature of seeking to create a loss allowable against capital gains tax together with a matching but not taxable capital gain – a device basic to the art of artificial tax avoidance as it had developed since Bradman. It was clear that the Law Lords' decision in the Ramsay and Eilbeck cases would be crucial for the future of every fill-in-the-numbers artificial tax scheme. This significance was certainly felt by the two senior judges, Wilberforce and Fraser. Wilberforce recalls:

One was aware that there was a changing tide of opinion, a lot of criticism of schemes. You met professors, counsel, other judges, read knowledgeable articles by financial journalists. You would be asked, 'When is the House of Lords going to do something about these schemes, when is it going to catch up with the real world?' I felt it was time to set out the position as far as the House of Lords was concerned on tax avoidance.

'We're really like a jury,' Wilberforce says, describing how the highest court goes about making its decisions. The judges discuss the case during the hearing and over lunch. Then there is a formal meeting at which views are exchanged and the likely decision emerges, and it is decided which judge will write the main judgment. Wilberforce was in favour of multiple judgments. The draft judgments are then circulated and suggestions made. Once these have gone the rounds and been emended they are printed and a date is set for the decision to be given.

The Law Lords gave their decision on the Ramsay and Eilbeck cases on 12 March 1981. Robert Ramsay arrived at the House of Lords that day feeling full of confidence. 'The Revenue thought we'd won. I've never seen so many miserable faces.' During the hearing the Revenue counsel, Peter Millett QC, had launched a broad attack on both schemes on the basis that they should be disregarded as artificial and a fiscal nullity because they produced neither gain nor loss. Charles Potter QC had termed such an approach 'revolutionary'.

At seventy-four, Lord Wilberforce seemed an unlikely convert. 'Counsel for the Revenue probably didn't expect his view to be accepted by us,' he said, smiling. Wilberforce began by addressing 'the fundamental issue' which was 'of great importance both in principle and in scope'. He noted certain essential features of the schemes: once started they would proceed to the end, and at the end the taxpayer's position was identical to that at the beginning except for the payment of the promoter's fee. 'In some cases one may doubt whether in any real sense any money existed at all.' The 'whole and only purpose' was the avoidance of tax: 'The taxpayer merely had to state the figure involved – the amount of the gain he desired to counteract – and the necessary particulars were inserted in the scheme.'

Lord Wilberforce then veered off on a historic tack from which he did not depart until his judgment was concluded. The Tomlin doctrine should not be 'overstated or overextended'; it did not compel the court to look at documents or transactions 'in blinkers'. The judges were not 'bound to consider individually each separate step in a composite transaction intended to be carried through as a whole', nor did Wilberforce accept that a drastic anti-avoidance approach was a matter for Parliament rather than the courts:

While the techniques of tax avoidance progressed and were technically improved, the courts were not obliged to stand still . . . To force the courts to adopt . . . a step-by-step, dissecting approach . . . would be a denial of the true judicial process . . . The capital gains tax was created to operate in the real world, not that of make-believe. It was a tax on gains not on arithmetical differences . . . It would be an excess of judicial abstinence to withdraw from the field now before the House.

Because the scheme was not designed to produce any result but the payment of fees, it would, said Lord Wilberforce:

be quite wrong, and a faulty analysis, to pick out and stop at the one step in the combination which produced the loss . . . The true view, regarding the scheme as a whole, was to find that there was neither gain nor loss.[12]

The descendant of the Great Emancipator was not to free the tax avoiders this time. He ruled against the Exempt Debt Scheme, and so did all the other judges. Robert Ramsay and those on the Tucker side were stunned – it was as if the earth had suddenly been proved to be flat – and the Revenue side were equally surprised. 'The Revenue almost threw their briefcases in the air,' Ramsay recalls. It was a famous landmark victory, the 'death knell for artificial avoidance schemes', as the *Times Law Report* described it. The Ramsay judgment meant that any tax-avoidance scheme which lacked commercial justification – and that meant most, if not all schemes – was now likely to fail.

For the Ramsay family it meant that, after seven years, they would not after all get back the tax they had paid; indeed, they had to pay another £1200. Today Robert Ramsay is philosophical about his losing battle with the Inland Revenue. 'I don't regret doing the scheme or having lost. I don't think they could have given us the decision. A lot of money was riding on it.' He feels the Vestey case had affected public opinion and the Law Lords' view of tax avoidance. 'Perhaps it was a good thing as it worked out,' he says wryly. But the decision has had other repercussions for him apart from putting the Ramsay name into the legal textbooks. 'We still get a lot of trouble from the Inland Revenue. Our accounts are under the microscope. We can't get away with anything,' he jokes.

Once the shock had worn off, the reaction on the Tucker side was to suspect that the judges had been in some way pressed by the Conservative government to put tax avoidance out of business. Some even went so far as to suggest intervention by the prime minister or Lord Hailsham, the Lord Chancellor. But just how much of a legal upset was it?

Since the Plummer and Vestey victories, the House of Lords had on two occasions under Lord Wilberforce (the first being the Chinn case) ruled against tax-avoidance arrangements involving the transfer of assets to overseas trustees in order to avoid capital gains tax. The *Financial Times* columnist 'Justinian' wrote a short time before that 'a loud alarm bell is ringing that the courts are determined to act against tax-avoidance schemes'.[13] Even in his Plummer judgment Lord Wilberforce had indicated that he was far from enthusiastic about finding against the Revenue. And when dropping the Vestey bombshell he had shown that he was prepared to interpret what Parliament meant or did not mean if that prevented injustice.

Lord Wilberforce's explanation of why the Law Lords reached their historic decision in Ramsay is simplicity itself, if somewhat unflattering to Roy Tucker. 'The scheme did not succeed technically. We realised that very quickly. It was self-cancelling, as there was no gain and no loss.' Once that had been agreed, both Wilberforce and Fraser felt the need to use the decision to generalise about the tax-avoidance issue. 'The Law Lords were under pressure to do something,' says Fraser. 'There was a lot of criticism about loopholes just being closed and then new ones opening.' 'I felt it was wrong that these schemes should be sold widely,' says Wilberforce, 'that people out there should make a lot of money out of selling tax avoidance; people had to pay their fair share of tax.'

As a judge in tax cases Wilberforce says he did not think his role was to shape society or respond to it:

I don't see myself as involved in social engineering, that's for others. I believe that the law should be clear and fair. It will reflect changes in public opinion but some way behind . . . My main aim in the judgment was to set out guidelines for the future, to say Tomlin still stands but it must be redefined. We knew Ramsay was going to mark a change. The House of Lords had to make its position clear.

Fraser is even more candid: 'Tax avoidance had got out of hand. Something had to be done.'

It was nevertheless a remarkable legal volte-face. For the tax-avoidance industry it was the biggest nail yet in the coffin of artificial, off-the-peg schemes, following those hammered home by retrospective legislation and the cut in tax rates. Certainly Roy Tucker was quick to inform the 2000 clients who had used the fifty schemes he had produced that they now had little choice but to wave the white flag and pay the tax – if they could. 'I need to look at each of the schemes but I do think it is likely that we will come to the conclusion that many of the schemes are ineffective,' he told the *Sunday Times* two days after the judgment.[14] 'It will have a severe effect on a lot of people caught up in the middle. We are now likely to see a number of bankruptcies.' Tucker realised that the Ramsay judgment also meant difficulties not only for clients but also for those former employees of his and of Rossminster who had used schemes to shelter their bonuses.

Repercussions were soon felt within Rossminster itself as one by one the remaining group companies were wound up because of tax liabilities which, after Ramsay, could no longer be denied or after the Company Purchase Scheme, paid. First London Securities went into liquidation on 13 July 1981 owing unsecured creditors, essentially the Inland Revenue, £3 million against assets of just £2000. As at July 1978, the Rossminster bank faced potential tax liabilities of up to £9,450,000. FLS was followed into liquidation by other key companies like Rossminster Acceptances (renamed Southgrange Acceptances), which owed £1,470,000; Firstwatch, the original Rossminster Group (£141,000); Kemforth (£890,000); Thornwright (£912,000); Spinfare (£1,719,000) and HOVAS (£2,244,000). Their total assets amounted to little more than £60,000 with which to pay these debts, thanks to the Company Purchase Scheme, the St George's and Blessingwell charities and the legal opinions which had made the whole disappearing trick possible.

On 3 December 1981 Lord Diplock, in another case involving what Lord Fraser called the 'magic result of creating a tax loss that was not a real loss', gave a warning to the tax-avoidance promoters in case they had failed fully to recognise the watershed marked by the Ramsay decision because of the subsequent Law Lords ruling in favour of a Bradman scheme in the Garvin case. Overturning a lower court's decision in favour of the taxpayer, Lord Diplock declared:

It would be disingenuous to suggest, and dangerous on the part of those who advise on elaborate tax-avoidance schemes to assume, that Ramsay's case did not mark a significant change in the approach adopted by this House in its judicial role to a preordained series of transactions (whether or not they include the achievement of a legitimate commercial end) into which there are inserted steps that have no commercial purpose apart from the avoidance of a liability to tax which in the absence of those particular steps would have been payable.[15]

The courts were now more concerned with distinguishing between 'straightforward' transactions and those which had no other purpose but the avoidance of tax. Lord Scarman emphasised, 'It is now crucial when considering any such scheme to take the analysis far enough to determine where the profit, gain or loss is really to be found.'[16]

Two weeks later, Tucker's former employee Bill Cairns' appeal over the Advance Interest Scheme he had used on his 1974 bonus failed in the High Court, on technical grounds rather than because of the new anti-avoidance mood in the courts. The Special Commissioners had ruled against the scheme in August 1979 influenced by Plummer's evidence that it relied on circular money and Tucker's failure to give evidence about his creation although present at the hearing. Mr Justice Nourse held that the 'advance interest' was not interest at all but a payment to discharge a purely artificial liability and even if it was interest it was not 'annual' interest as required by law. Cairns took his case a year later to the Court of Appeal, where the Advance Interest Scheme was defeated for a third and final time. Even without the 'icy blast of the Ramsay case', the Master of the Rolls, Sir John Donaldson, saw little merit in the scheme. The transactions 'had a character so artificial and so devoid of any purpose, other than a fiscal purpose, as to disqualify them from consideration in the context of taxation'. As Cairns had paid no fee, it 'lacked all reality'.[17] Another of Roy Tucker's creations had failed to withstand close legal scrutiny.

The culmination of this attack on artificial tax avoidance came in February 1984. *Furniss* v. *Dawson* involved a bid to defer rather than avoid capital gains tax on the sale of shares in a textile company. The Revenue had lost all the way to the House of Lords, but there, Lords Fraser, Roskill and Bridge took the opportunity to restate, for the benefit of Roy Tucker's imitators and their fellow judges, the highest court's hostility towards the type of tax avoidance represented by the Ramsay case. Lord Roskill declared:

The ghost of the Westminster case has haunted the administration of this branch of the law for too long ... I had hoped that that ghost might have found quietude with the decisions in Ramsay and Burmah. Unhappily it has not. Perhaps the decision of this House in these appeals will now suffice as exorcism.[18]

The House of Lords, said Lord Bridge, was now taking an 'increasingly critical approach to the manipulation of financial transactions to the advantage of the taxpayer'. Lord Brightman said judges had been determined to resist 'a deplorable inroad into the sacred principles of the Westminster case'. To make sure there would be no future misunderstandings he set out the tests by which any tax scheme or avoidance arrangement must be judged:

There must be a preordained series of transactions or ... one single composite transaction. This composite transaction may or may not include the achievement of a legitimate commercial end ... There must be steps inserted which have no commercial purpose apart from the avoidance of a liability to tax ... If those two ingredients exist, the inserted steps are to be disregarded for fiscal purposes. The court must then look at the end result.

These criteria would now determine what Lord Scarman termed 'the limit beyond which the safe channel of acceptable tax avoidance shelves into the dangerous shallows of unacceptable tax evasion'. Nine years after his first attack, in the Julie Christie case, Lord Templeman's judicial peers had come to share his view that 'a tax avoidance industry of the scale that developed in the 1970s had to be destroyed'.[19]

Artificial tax avoidance was finally dead. Roy Tucker had killed it, by the way he had tried to use the courts to abuse the legal loopholes he could spot by a few minutes' study of the tax laws. The Law Lords were merely the undertakers; they had taken Lord Clyde's famous shovel and used it to bury the body.

But in their zeal of the convert to abolish tax avoidance, Tucker-style, they also put under threat any fiscal arrangement which had as its primary object the avoidance of tax. Two months after the Law Lords' decision in *Furniss* v. *Dawson*, it was Peter Rees, now the Chief Secretary to the Treasury, who had to reassure Conservative MPs inside Parliament and Conservative voters and their advisers outside that the Inland Revenue would not seek to apply the strictest letter of the judgment against transactions already cleared or against popular tax-avoidance devices like covenants or pension plans. Such comments from their former adviser were unlikely to reassure Tucker and Plummer, by now seeking to defend the offshore fortunes Rossminster and tax avoidance had created against the onslaught of an Inland Revenue armed not only with the *Furniss* v. *Dawson* blunderbuss but also with the post-Vestey anti-avoidance provisions against offshore trusts. But, at least, by 1984 the threat from the civil courts was all that remained.

NO INSPECTOR CALLS

After the hiccups caused by the Revenue's defeat in the Court of Appeal, Bill Dermit (who had been awarded a CBE in the 1980 New Year's honours, once the House of Lords had vindicated the Special Investigation Section) and his team had set to work in earnest. A dozen senior inspectors of taxes were engaged full time on the inquiry: each Rossminster founder had one or more assigned to their tax affairs, while others pursued the smaller fry, past and present Rossminster and Tucker staff. 'Anybody who is a target will be shot at' was their motto as the Revenue investigation went forward from early 1980 on the broadest of fronts. They wanted to establish whether there had been a conspiracy to defraud the Revenue not only of income tax on the profits from selling the schemes, but also of corporation tax, which should have been paid on the profits that disappeared into the Company Purchase Scheme. No provision had been made for the tax to be paid, on the assumption that the Gross Annuity Scheme escape route was effective, but the Ramsay judgment had made clear that it was not. Those profits were now offshore since the Rossminster banks, which had received them as interest, fees and loan repayments, had been sold through the same Company Purchase Scheme to Blessingwell.

One line of approach taken by the Revenue was to construe the group of individuals who had devised and promoted each scheme in the pre-Rossminster period as a partnership: Tucker, Plummer, Pilbrow and Moser with the Exempt Debt Scheme; Tucker, Plummer and Cardale with the Reverse Annuity Scheme. Rossminster itself could be seen as a partnership of the six founders. If it could be proved that there was a de facto partnership, the profits of each partnership should have been distributed to the partners, who would then have had to pay tax on them.

The offshore family trusts, with their ownership of everything from Rossminster itself to Tucker's and Plummer's homes and certain of their contents, were a prime target. The Revenue wanted to prove that Tucker and Plummer not only controlled these trusts but had the 'power to enjoy' their assets or income and so could be taxed on both, regardless of whether the money stayed offshore or was distributed to them or their families in the UK.

Lewis-Grey was crucial to the Revenue case and its inquiries. He was able to chart a course for the investigators through the paper maze erected from the 1200 companies on and offshore and the dozens of trusts. With the experience of more than two years at the heart of Rossminster's offshore operations, and with photographic recall, he could identify the key companies and explain transactions which might otherwise have baffled the Revenue. Month after month through 1980 and 1981 Lewis-Grey regularly travelled up from Sussex to Melbourne House to meet one or more investigators. Time and time again he went over the minutest detail of transactions involving not just Tucker, Plummer and Benyon but many of the lesser lights. Between February 1980 and September 1981 Lewis-Grey made nearly twenty statements on a wide range of subjects and personalities. But when two years had passed since his first statement, which had led to the raids, he began to feel some disquiet. He had no sense that the investigation had yet obtained a sharp focus.

Throughout that period the Revenue had tried to discover a London equivalent of Lewis-Grey in Vogue House or North Audley Street, but without success. There were former employees who were no longer close to Tucker and Plummer and who, after the Ramsay judgment, felt they had been left to face the consequences of doing the schemes. Some were not in principle opposed to assisting the Revenue and would have liked to negotiate a sympathetic approach towards their own pressing tax problems. However, any inclination they had to cooperate dissolved in the face of the Revenue's tactics at interviews. The individual would usually be confronted by two investigators who would produce three types of documents – those that could be copied, those from which notes could be taken and those that could only be read. But the conversation would not last long before the ex-employee would be formally cautioned of his possible arrest on criminal charges – at which point he would leave. The Revenue's response to criticism of their actions is that the judges' rules covering interviews made it essential to administer the caution if the individual was considered a possible prosecution target. The Revenue was not prepared, unlike the police, to do deals in order to obtain witnesses or to grant immunity from prosecution. But the effect of its tactics was firmly to close mouths that, if opened, could have been very helpful.

Mrs Thatcher's first ministerial reshuffle, in September 1981, transferred Peter Rees from the Treasury to become Minister of Trade. This switch, nine months after it had been demanded by Labour MPs because of his Rossminster links, was seen by those close to the Revenue investigation as clearing the political path for any prosecution and reducing government embarrassment if charges were brought against anyone at Rossminster. But the end of 1981 came and went without any news.

As the third anniversary of the raids neared in 1982 there was a distinct and growing impression outside the Revenue that the investigation had become lost in detail. Scotland Yard detectives in contact with Melbourne House commented, 'No fraud, however complex, takes three years to investigate.' How, they asked, would a jury understand and convict on something so complicated that it took three years to produce a case? Inside the Revenue, the SIS were pursuing several clear lines of inquiry but the investigation was far more complex than they had realised, and it was noticeable as 1982 progressed that there were no longer bold predictions about prosecution emanating from Melbourne House. The investigation seemed to be flagging, going back over old ground as if stuck in a groove. The demands on Lewis-Grey to make himself available gradually petered out.

A major obstacle to some Revenue inquiries, despite the help of Lewis-Grey, was that they had no power to compel witnesses or documents from the offshore trusts and their satellite companies in Guernsey and the Isle of Man. This became clear when, as a result of studying the documents they had seized and listening to Lewis-Grey, the Revenue pressed for information about not just the 1977 bonus paid to the principals but its predecessors and the assets which, it seemed, had been transferred offshore, like the shares in Rossminster itself. Benyon replied to their queries in February 1981, claiming that the Alpha and Pythagoras trusts had not been set up by him, he did not control them and was not a beneficiary, although he understood that the trusts' assets could 'enure' for the benefit of his family or himself. He had not given any instructions about the trusts' transactions – these were handled by the administrators, among them Lewis-Grey. He had not asked for the 1977 bonus to be paid to his trust or received any of the £57,000: this money had been paid without legal obligation and he had not been given the opportunity to receive it himself. The £27,000 he had received in cash were loans: interest had been paid and the loans were being repaid. He therefore had no 'power to enjoy' these assets or any income from them.

Lewis-Grey contradicted much of what Benyon told the Revenue. In particular, he denied that he rather than the MP controlled the trusts, and he quoted the sale of the Hillcoll shares to Matula and the Manx company's purchase of control of NAS Financial Services. He also denied that he had ever prepared any documents providing for interest to be paid on the £27,000 or for the money itself to be repaid. Further, he said he had produced a statement showing that the trusts' assets totalled £250,000, which had surprised and pleased Benyon. But how to *prove* what lay behind the offshore defensive wall of silent and inaccessible trustees and nominee directors?

The bonus document, which showed a total of £433,000 paid to nine people in May 1978, had triggered the raids because it suggested that the recipients might have failed to declare similar bonuses in earlier years. But they had not completed their tax returns for 1978 when the raids took place in 1979, so no prosecution could be based on the bonus document alone. Asked whether he would have declared the £57,000 he was shown as receiving, Tom Benyon smiled and said, 'I would have had to take advice.' Plummer denied that anything needed reporting.

Furthermore, so much of what Tucker and Plummer had done was based on a bedrock of opinions from the best and brightest tax and company law experts, and it is an accepted principle that taking legal advice almost precludes 'mens rea' or intent to break the law. This was another stumbling block for the Revenue. After three and a half years without the threatened prosecution, even those with little sympathy for Tucker and Plummer felt that the Revenue should either bring charges or drop the investigation.

Lewis-Grey, who after several months of unemployment had embarked on a new career, taking over the management of an ailing lead-pellet business, was disillusioned by the delay. Almost four years after he had first contacted the Revenue it appeared that his public-spirited action and the personal anxiety this had provoked had been for nothing. 'I can't remember all this for ever', he said on one occasion in frustration when enquiring, without success, about the likelihood of a prosecution. Lewis-Grey began to detect a noticeable cooling in his relationship with the Revenue. As reticence turned to silence, he became convinced that no prosecution was likely and decided to put both Rossminster and the Inland Revenue behind him and concentrate on running his business. 'It became something I didn't want to think about,' he says. 'A closed chapter in my life.'

His forebodings seemed to be confirmed just before Christmas 1982 when the *Mail on Sunday* published a Rossminster-inspired leak. Under the headline 'Ron and Roy off the hook', the City editor, Maurice Barnfather, wrote that 'the Inland Revenue, I understand, has been told by counsel that it would be "unwise to proceed" . . . In effect the Revenue has been told on present evidence there is no case to answer.'[1]

If it had been as simple as that, it would not have taken so long to reach this conclusion. The Revenue had been considering a number of cases based on different sets of possible charges, and the leaked opinion was given in response to only one of these. However, Robin Auld QC, the senior counsel brought in to advise the Revenue together with two juniors who were tax specialists, had considerable and understandable doubts about the chances of bringing a successful fraud prosecution. He was worried less by the time elapsed since many of the events and the lack of supporting witnesses than by the mindbending complexity of the case. It would have to be presented to an Old Bailey jury probably lacking accountants or other financial sophisticates, and this made it very difficult to be confident of a conviction, whatever the evidence. But at the time of the *Mail on Sunday* article the SIS were still discussing a possible prosecution over Rossminster with counsel and no final decision to abandon the case had been taken.

Confirmation that the criminal investigation was still alive came in February, when the Keith Committee published its report on the Revenue's enforcement powers and pointed out that the 'investigation is not yet concluded'. This was also confirmed by the Treasury minister Nicholas Ridley on 7 February in reply to a question from Jeff Rooker.

Much to the surprise of the Revenue's critics and those in the Conservative Party whose pressure had led to the committee being set up, Lord Keith vindicated the use of the Revenue's 'search and seize' powers. Fifteen searches had produced twelve prosecutions and eight convictions out of nine cases brought to trial. Although Lord Keith felt, in the light of the Ramsay and Burmah judgments, that 'there was now no market for marketed tax-avoidance schemes', he recommended that, far from being reduced, the Revenue's powers should be extended to deal with the more determined tax avoider. Taxpayers should be forced to indicate on their tax return if they had taken advantage of a possible legal loophole. (After almost four years, none of Lord Keith's recommendations have been acted on by the Conservative government which appointed his committee.)

But, without any charges being brought, the Inland Revenue investigation had already claimed one victim – Tom Benyon MP. At the beginning of February 1983, *World in Action* returned to the subject of tax with a documentary contrasting the treatment of Social Security 'scroungers' with that of tax evaders. Lewis-Grey featured again, this time talking in uncompromising terms about the tax arrangements entered into by the MP for Abingdon. Convinced now that no Revenue prosecution was likely and no longer intimidated by the threatened £30,000 penalty – he had been advised the agreement was unenforceable in England – the former Rossminster managing director felt it was time to make public certain matters which he had told only to the Revenue investigators.

'The sole purpose of my being in Guernsey was to organise Benyon's affairs so that he did not pay a penny piece in tax,' he declared on television. The purpose of the trusts, he said, was 'to obscure the ownership of these funds from the Inland Revenue.' By 1978 these funds had totalled £250,000 and were controlled by Benyon. The Tory MP had paid no tax 'because he had managed to disclaim ownership of these assets by putting them supposedly in the hands of other people'. Asked whether these arrangements amounted to tax evasion, Lewis-Grey was in no doubt: 'Yes, because they relied on the Inland Revenue not finding out who organised these trusts, who owned them in truth.'[2]

Benyon declined on legal advice, because of the still pending investigation, to appear in the programme to answer Lewis-Grey's charges. He now says this was 'a bad mistake' as he could have answered them. 'The programme was very damaging to me. I did not realise how damaging.' The timing of Lewis-Grey's allegations was highly unlucky for Benyon. The Abingdon constituency was to be merged into a new constituency, Wantage, before the general election expected later in 1983. As the sitting MP, Benyon confidently expected to be selected unopposed for the new seat. The local Conservative association had asked him, in preparation for this, if he expected to be prosecuted by the Revenue, and he had fruitlessly tried to get clearance from the Inland Revenue, the Director of Public Prosecutions and the government Whips. 'I replied that I did not know but it was possible. That was fatal.'

In April 1983 Benyon was put forward as the sole nominee for Conservative candidate in Wantage. At the selection meeting, which was unusually well attended, the only question put to him about Rossminster and the Revenue was why he had not sued over Lewis-Grey's allegations on *World in Action*. Benyon left the meeting feeling confident that the nomination was a formality, but when he returned home that evening from a dinner in Oxford he discovered that the meeting had divided 135 for, 135 against, and the chairman had declined to use his casting vote in his favour. Benyon had alienated certain elements in the local party and his opponents had made great use of the TV progamme, to the extent of circulating a transcript of Lewis-Grey's allegations, to gather support against his nomination. (Ironically, the only other significant matter on the agenda at that meeting was a move to avoid having to pay capital gains tax on the Abingdon Conservatives' building which was to be transferred to the Wantage association. The property was to be left in the name of the old association and leased by the new. This was in line with the advice from Conservative Central Office, naturally after consulting tax counsel.)

Faced with such a deep rift within the constituency party, another selection meeting was set for 16 May with Benyon as just one of several candidates. Shortly before it was due to start a very bitter Tom Benyon, suspecting that he was unlikely to get the nomination, stood down and announced his retirement from politics. He blamed the Rossminster taint stemming from the still unresolved Revenue investigation. 'It has been difficult to know how to rebut the inevitable cloud which developed over everyone involved,' he said.[3]

Had he been able to wait only a few more weeks that cloud would have been dispersed. But with the general election less than a month away Wantage had to have a Conservative candidate to take over as MP.

Peter Rees's return to the Treasury as chief secretary following the Conservatives' landslide victory on 9 June was a clear hint that the decision on Rossminster had been made. Just as his departure to the Department of Trade two years before had indicated the removal of any political obstacle to a prosecution, so it seemed inconceivable to those who had followed the politics of the Rossminster investigation that the former Tucker adviser would be returning to the Treasury if his one-time client was to be prosecuted. And on 30 June the Attorney-General, Sir Michael Havers, disclosed in a written parliamentary answer that the Inland Revenue indeed had decided against criminal prosecution of Rossminster or any of its principals. This decision had been taken by the Board of Inland Revenue on the advice of leading counsel and – significantly, given that the board alone could decide – after consultation with the Attorney-General. Instead the Revenue would 'now be taking steps to deal with the liabilities for tax and, where appropriate, for interest and penalties that have come to light in the course of the investigation'.

The Special Investigation Section had been confident that the Inland Revenue's biggest and most complex investigation would end in a prosecution for the tax-fraud offences that they suspected when they obtained the search warrants. Why had their confidence proved misplaced? Was the Attorney-General's announcement tantamount to clearing Tucker and Plummer of any offence, proving that there was no case to answer, as they and their apologists have sought to show?

The Revenue could probably have brought a prosecution on the basis of the documentary evidence and Lewis-Grey's testimony. Discussions with Auld and his juniors had continued until a short time before the Attorney-General's announcement. One of the senior SIS investigators emphasised that 'the Attorney-General's reference to penalties was evidence that he accepted there could have been evasion either involving wilful default or fraud, as penalties are not required for negligence'. (The 'penalty' for negligence is merely paying the tax underpaid plus £50 for each year. But if either fraud or wilful default – defined as 'careful breach of duty' – is proved then the Revenue can ask for twice the amount underpaid.)

But whether the prosecution would have been successful was another matter. The Revenue's legal advisers were heavily influenced by the immense problems of complexity and comprehensibility, by the evidential problems related to the offshore trusts and by the difficulties of proving intent, given the piles of legal opinions. And the Revenue's dilemma over whether to risk an unsuccessful prosecution came at a time when there was growing concern in government and legal circles about the length and cost of prosecuting complex fraud cases, in the wake of some highly publicised failures.[4]

The Inland Revenue was particularly conscious of the need for any prosecution in the Rossminster case to result in a conviction; that had been the message from the Treasury ever since 1979, because of the political dimension and the publicity surrounding the raids. The adverse publicity from a failed prosecution could be worse than from no prosecution at all. The Revenue was sensitive to such possible bad publicity since the decision of an Old Bailey judge in 1981 to halt the William Press trial and acquit all the defendants. Before Rossminster, the raids on William Press had been the most publicised use of the search and seizure powers and the collapse of the Press prosecution had been seen as a humiliation for the Revenue. (Few knew that the following year Press had reached a civil settlement with the Revenue whereby it paid £250,000 in tax.) If at the end of four years of investigation and a hugely expensive and inordinately lengthy trial there had been no convictions, Somerset House would once again have been covered in egg.

The option of civil action was less risky. The burden of proof for nonpayment of tax was less onerous. If the tax assessments were challenged there would be no jury problem and after Ramsay the courts were likely to be sympathetic. As none other than John Nott, when a junior Treasury minister, had explained in Parliament nine years before: 'Cases involving tax very often are complicated and of a kind not easy to deploy before a jury. If the Inland Revenue was required to take some cases before the courts in criminal prosecution there is no doubt there would be far less penalties paid for tax evasion than there are now.'[5]

Those of the original Rossminster team at the s i s endeavoured to make the best of the decision, but there is little doubt that they realised they had failed. Extracting penalties and interest, even on large amounts of tax, was little consolation. Two weeks after Sir Michael Havers announced the decision, William Dermit C B E, head of the Special Investigation Section, retired from the Inland Revenue. He chose to leave on the fourth anniversary of the Rossminster raids.

However, not everybody who had been involved in that original decision saw the result as a defeat for the Inland Revenue. 'What it did do was to ensure all of this activity came to an end,' says one senior official. 'My only regret is that we didn't do it earlier.'

AN UNFUNNY VALENTINE

For months after the Havers announcement all was quiet on the Rossminster front. But behind the scenes both sides were preparing for the next phase of their private war.

At Melbourne House the Inland Revenue set to work on the tax assessments to be served on Tucker, Plummer and the others. These would cover the entire period from 1972 to the closure of Rossminster in 1980.

Meanwhile, at new offices in Curzon Street, Mayfair, Tucker and Plummer, who now commuted weekly from his Guernsey home, spent much of their time planning the reactivation of the legal action against the Revenue, held in abeyance since the raids. They had decided to start new legal proceedings on a much more ambitious scale, claiming that the SIS had not only acted improperly in the method of the searches but had been wrong in the way it obtained the warrants and in relying on Lewis-Grey, who they claimed had provided false information for vindictive reasons. The eminent and highly expensive QC Robert Alexander was brought in to advise on the lengthy statement of claim to accompany the proposed writ.

The main protagonists continued to shadowbox in anticipation of the coming rounds in their heavyweight battle; others were affected more immediately by the legal fallout from the raids.

Michael Preston, the former head of Rossminster Corporate Services, had made profits of just over £24,000 from the sale of a 35 per cent interest in a dealing company, Gymboon, in January 1977, before he left Rossminster. But he maintained that no capital gains tax was payable because, he claimed, he had tax losses totalling £40,000 to offset against that profit. The SIS queried why the value of the Gymboon shares had risen so much since he sold a 15 per cent interest at cost in 1975, and Preston was asked to provide 'full details' of the purchase and sales of his Gymboon shares. The Revenue did not appear to realise, from the information Preston supplied, that the profit was the result of Gymboon being sold to St George's Elizabethan Theatre through the Company Purchase Scheme, so it offered to drop any further inquiries if Preston would drop his claim for tax relief. Preston decided this would be politic and agreed to do so in July 1978.

When the Revenue obtained the Gymboon accounts in the raids, it realised that the sale by Preston had been part of a tax scheme. In July 1982, when he could no longer claim the tax reliefs he had forgone, Preston was asked for more information. He reminded the Revenue of the 1978 agreement and was informed it had been cancelled, on the grounds that he had not provided full disclosure of all the facts as requested. He was also reassessed for capital gains tax on the share sale. Preston disputed this version of events, claimed that the 1978 agreement was binding and accused the Revenue of acting unfairly, as he could no longer claim the tax reliefs given up by that agreement.

Preston won a High Court ruling in his favour in February 1983, but this was overturned by the Court of Appeal in a decision confirmed by the House of Lords in April 1985, and he was left with a tax bill exceeding £10,000 and very substantial legal costs.

Much more serious, however, were the consequences of the discoveries made in the raids about Michael Buckley and Jerrold Moser.

Buckley, a former Jim Slater protégé, had been an early Rossminster client thanks to the Slater, Walker link. In 1978 the Revenue had begun an investigation into his tax affairs but this had been closed when the trail ran out in Gibraltar among the companies and trusts formed there by Rossminster's lawyer Louis Triay. Information obtained from the raids caused the investigation to be reopened. Buckley was served with a Section 481 notice in July 1982 demanding information about his tax affairs, and in January 1983 he was charged with making a false statement concerning a Gibraltar trust which had received £270,000. He was acquitted at the Old Bailey in November 1983.[1]

Moser also received a Section 481 notice after the raids. He replied to it in May 1981 and two years later, just two weeks after the attorney-general's 'no prosecutions' announcement, was charged with making a false statement. This related to the funds in the Marx Trust, which had received a share of the Exempt Debt Scheme proceeds plus certain introductory commissions from Tucker. In February 1986 Moser pleaded guilty to making a false statement to the Inland Revenue concerning the affairs of a client and was fined £10,000.[2] The Section 481 notice charge relating to the Marx Trust was dropped, but the Revenue is still pursuing Moser for tax it claims is due.

Early in 1984, in preparation for launching their legal action, Tucker and Plummer's lawyers asked the Inland Revenue to return all the documents seized in the raids and explain why the raids had been carried out. The reply they received was not the one they expected.

On St Valentine's Day 1984 the Inland Revenue issued a barrage of tax assessments including the largest it has ever issued against one individual. Tucker and Plummer received estimated assessments which in total added up to a minimum £16 million each. Richard Gardner and Desmond Miller both received assessments totalling between £1,500,000 and £2 million; Tom Benyon and John Trotman, assessments exceeding £1 million. Each individual received a number of assessments covering several years calculated a number of varying ways. Much smaller assessments were sent to about a dozen former Tucker and Rossminster employees and associates.

The recipients, especially Gardner and Benyon, were staggered. Miller, resident in Guernsey, was angry – 'The Revenue's figures bear no relation to reality' – but he was anyway beyond its jurisdiction. Tucker and Plummer adopted a calmer approach, at least in public. 'I'm extremely relaxed about it,' said Plummer, who now enjoyed dual tax residence, having moved to Guernsey.

The use of assessments is designed to ensure that any possible liability is not underestimated and to encourage the recipient to respond as soon as possible with either the tax or evidence of why it is not owed in order to avoid interest payments. Certainly, in the case of the four smaller shareholders, it would be difficult to prove a tax liability of more than £1 million even including interest. This was as much as they had made, and in the case of Benyon and Trotman probably considerably more. After all, Lewis-Grey had only estimated the worth of the Benyon trusts in 1978 at £250,000. Gardner admits to having made £1 million out of Rossminster.

All six lodged appeals against the assessments, since when there has been little movement apart from the Revenue informing certain of the individuals at the end of 1984 that it intended to seek penalties for wilful neglect or default. This enables the Revenue to claim penalties for the underpayment of tax going back more than six years. As the Havers statement had hinted, to the Revenue the evidence rules out simple negligence or neglect.

It was more than a year before Tucker and Plummer responded with their own legal move on 16 May 1985, suing the Inland Revenue, Dermit, Quinlan and the Metropolitan Police for £7 million in damages. The action's sixty-page statement of claim, endorsed on the writ contrary to normal practice, made the expected allegations that the Revenue had acted 'unfairly and without reasonable skill or care' as well as having 'negligently and unfairly failed to properly or at all consider, alternatively to appreciate, what constituted an offence involving fraud'. The writ also alleged that the raids were intended 'to disrupt the business and affairs of the plaintiffs and to damage their reputations'.

As evidence of the Inland Revenue's determination to destroy Rossminster, the writ alleged that in March 1979 Bill Dermit had told Lewis-Grey that 'we will have Roy Tucker's balls' and that the Revenue 'had been waiting for a long time for an opportunity to go in with the pantechnicon and clear out the offices of Tucker and Rossminster'. For some months Tucker and Plummer's lawyers had, without saying why, been seeking to persuade Lewis-Grey to provide a statement. He had declined, but would anyway have been of little help. When questioned by the Inland Revenue, he denied that Dermit had ever made the statements claimed.

Rossminster itself claimed a total of £5,491,000; AJR Financial Services £277,000. Tucker and Plummer both claimed for loss of earnings of £927,000 and £252,000 respectively, and they also claimed exemplary damages and interest. They were joined as plaintiffs by their wives, Benyon and his wife, Gardner and Trotman. In its details of the events of 13 July 1979, the writ is a work of legal art. It received wide Press coverage, as it was clearly designed to do by including the sixty pages of detail.

Tucker and Plummer laid the public relations groundwork for their legal offensive against the Revenue in a novel way – by collaborating in the publication of a book setting out their version of the Rossminster story. (They already knew that this book was in preparation and realised it was unlikely to be helpful in that regard.) The author of the pro-Rossminster book was an accountant turned journalist, Nigel Tutt, another Arthur Andersen alumnus, whose comments in *Accountancy Age* had been consistently sympathetic. The publishers were Financial Training Publications, part of the Park Place Investments group, headed by the accountant Mervyn Frankel, whose Channel Island subsidiary acted for Tucker's old Vogue House neighbour and rival Michael Hepker.[3] Publication of the book was timed to coincide as closely as possible with the writ against the Revenue.

The Tax Raiders is unsubtle in its support for Tucker and Plummer. The second paragraph of the introduction describes how the book 'reveals how the taxman used every dirty trick in his book to bring tax avoidance in the UK to a grinding halt'.[4] The Revenue is treated in emotive terms, being described as going 'over the top to beat tax avoiders'[5] and 'wanting blood'.[6] Words like 'tough', 'ruthless' and 'smear' are frequently used to describe the Revenue's response to Tutt's heroes, who for their part had been responsible for 'no deception of the Revenue'.[7] Lorana Sullivan, who had written critically of Rossminster, was depicted as little more than a pawn of the Revenue's 'dirty tricks department', as was *Private Eye*.

Tutt's book was published at the end of May, barely two weeks after the Tucker/Plummer writ. The book's cover, usually printed some weeks ahead of publication, contained a reference to the legal claim being filed in May: Tutt and the publishers had been kept well informed. Those invited to a cocktail party to launch *The Tax Raiders* were to meet not only the author but also 'former members of the Rossminster Group'.

By their unprecedented legal action Tucker and Plummer intend to force the Revenue to explain not only the reason for the raids but also the failure to prosecute given the prima facie evidence of fraud required to obtain the search warrants. The Revenue is defending the action which has yet to come to court. It is expected to plead Crown privilege to prevent disclosure of its internal documents concerning the raids and the subsequent investigation. All of this suggests a long legal tussle.

Today few signs remain in Britain of Rossminster and its clusters of companies. Although in liquidation, Rossminster and AJR Financial Services have been kept in existence as pegs on which to hang the legal action against the Revenue. Offshore too there has been a major corporate clear-out. Most of the Guernsey companies have been wound up, as have the bulk of the Manx companies, including those linked to the offshore trusts of the six founders. Trust and Mercantile Management in Jersey is no longer active. Among the handful of companies that still function is Dreadnought, through which the trusts used to exercise their control of

Rossminster. What is left is now run by Bill Cairns and a handful of loyalists in Guernsey.

Rossminster Holdings itself, the Manx parent company, was wound up in 1982, but not before the shareholders had been repaid £5,465,000 from the debentures plus £401,500 for the £2650 they had invested in preference shares. Rossminster Acceptances (IOM) has been replaced by the Douglas Bank with the same bank manager.

Deal Investments and Nadine were wound up in 1980.[8] Within a year Nadine had distributed £4,660,000 to its owners, the Plummer trusts. The Tucker-linked Hartopp, Forwood, Darmas and Peroneus had all been wound up by 1983. Peroneus was by then owned by Kazan Corporation in Panama, the new and safer haven Tucker and Plummer now favour.

The Central American funk hole is a favourite among those with something to hide because company and banking information is almost totally hidden from tax inspectors and anyone else, including governments. In 1980, once the House of Lords had shown that Rossminster was not to be saved from the Inland Revenue, the home-grown tax havens with their susceptibility to British government pressure were no longer secure repositories for the Tucker and Plummer family fortunes. Soon an increasing number of Panamanian companies began to appear. Tucker and Plummer already knew the local lawyer Ricardo Durling who formed most of the companies.

The first public sign of Tucker's and Plummer's Panamanian preference came in November 1981 with the transfer of Rossminster Holdings' 60 per cent stake in Jacksons Bourne End to Laurel Company SA. Laurel acquired the Rossminster subsidiary Avonwalk, which held half the shares, and then acquired another Panamanian company, Megastar Investment, which had bought the balance of the former Rossminster holding.[9]

In normal circumstances the purchase of a 60 per cent stake in a public company triggers a takeover bid for the remainder of the shares under the rules of the Stock Exchange and the City Takeover Panel. But exemption from this requirement was given by the Panel because it was told that the ultimate ownership of the Jacksons shares had not changed, and that link was confirmed in 1983 when Plummer was reappointed a Jacksons director.

After two further share reshuffles, 78 per cent of the Jacksons shares are held by five companies. Metox Investments, a Manx company, received half the ex-Rossminster stake, by then switched entirely to Megastar, in January 1985. Terrell SA[10] held 7 per cent, acquired during 1984, until June 1986 when it disposed of these shares to Millfield, a Manx company controlled by Douglas Financial Services (Panama), which also controls Metox. DFS' directors include Keith Tucker and Roy Tucker's old associate, Simon Cardale. A further 5 per cent is held by Wenlock Investment S.A. The other half of the Megastar holding went to a Manx company, Grampton which raised its stake to 31 per cent before disposing of the holding to a Panamanian company, Casaya, in June 1986.[11] It is not clear in all cases which companies represent Tucker or Plummer interests, but the equal distribution of the Megastar holding shows that the Tucker and Plummer interests were still operating jointly in January 1985, just as they had done twelve years before when Rossminster was founded.

Today the Tucker and Plummer interests seem to control shares in Jacksons worth at least £4,000,000 most of which cost £450,000 to £475,000. They control property and cash assets worth close to £7 million, the remaining seven and a half Bourne End acres having been sold for £3,700,000. The dividend income of £90,000 a year plus any capital profits from a future sale of this highly successful investment go offshore taxfree. 'It was the best deal we ever did,' says Tom Benyon, adding ruefully, 'But I never had any shares.'

Roy Tucker has also based several of his less successful post-Rossminster ventures in Panama. Tucker became involved with the record and video producer Simon Lait in 1978 when he became a director of Radialchoice, in which Forwood took a 49 per cent interest. (A year later Rossminster was involved in a tax scheme for the furniture importers Philip Lait.) After three years as a director Tucker was replaced by his brother Keith on a new company, Radialchoice Group, in which Vazon Nominees – a Guernsey company which along with Rocquaine Nominees was regularly used to shield Tucker or Plummer interests – took a 49 per cent stake. Further financial support to Radialchoice came from Blessingwell and another Panamanian company, Pimila SA.[12] Despite producing one of 1982's most successful records Radialchoice went into receivership in December 1983 after losses exceeding £600,000.

Through Avonwalk, which it acquired in 1981, Laurel SA also came to own Calpernium, a Tucker/Plummer company run from Curzon Street in which were collected several venture capital projects associated with Plummer, who was a director, through the Rossminster bank. These included Flexibrick, Lottery Developments, Jackpot Promotions and the hotel owners Boblean as well as an interest in the rump of the Waterlooville site owned by Bryan Forbes and friends. Douglas Bank pumped £685,000 into Calpernium but in the three years to 1982 it lost over £145,000. Most of the underlying investments went into receivership or liquidation and Calpernium itself was wound up in 1984. So too was Video Village, a video-cassette retailer of which Tucker became a director, after only six months in business. Romanwalk, a company in which the Tucker interests held 50 per cent, lost £70,000 in Video Village.

For the majority of their clients Roy Tucker and Ronald Plummer have become just expensive memories. After the Ramsay judgment most realised that further resistance was hopeless and paid the tax they thought had been avoided – if they could. It is estimated that at least 85 per cent of the 350 clients (200 individuals and 150 companies) have paid up. For many of the 100 or more clients of the Company Purchase Scheme there is still the threat of apportionment of the £100 million plus corporation tax due on the profits of the companies ultimately sold to St George's and Blessingwell. The Price Waterhouse chartered accountant, Colin Bird, is liquidator on behalf of the creditors, essentially the Inland Revenue, in 180 companies. He has only agreed about half their tax liabilities. Any shortfall in assets with which to pay the tax agreed – and there will be a shortfall in most cases – will have to be met by the original shareholders who sold to Rossminster.

Not even the forty or so purchasers of the original Reverse Annuity Scheme escaped. The Revenue refused to accept Plummer's victory in the House of Lords as a test case, and proceeded to challenge every other individual who had done the scheme to prove that it was effective. Subtle differences from the Plummer version in each case made this possible. Few could afford to take on the Revenue and after Ramsay it was pointless, so most settled. Armed with what it had discovered through the raids plus the Ramsay decision, the Revenue relitigated the HOVAS linked scheme. In April 1984 the Special Commissioners ruled in the Revenue's favour over a client who had bought the Reverse Annuity Scheme in 1971, holding that it was a 'fiscal nullity'. Two months later the Special Commissioners ruled against the Deprived Children's Aid Fund version for the same reason, saying, 'The transaction had no place in the real world.' As for Plummer, the Revenue only accepted that the Law Lords had cleared his claim for relief on the first of his five payments under the scheme and challenged his claims for relief on the subsequent payments. And once again, after Ramsay, it had to win.

Almost everyone who did business with Tucker and Rossminster had only found an expensive way of deferring payment of a tax bill. Once fees and interest were added it would have been cheaper for most, if not all, to have paid the tax.

Most clients accepted this setback philosophically. One who hit back, with good reason, was Michael Harris who, with George Miller, had bought the Advance Interest Scheme in 1974. Since March 1975 Rossminster had been demanding repayment with interest of the £60,000 'loan' claimed to represent half the fee due on the tax scheme which had been made redundant by William Stern's bankruptcy. Despite threats of legal action it was not until August 1978 that Rossminster seriously attempted to obtain payment of what had now grown with interest to £104,000. Plummer claimed that the original loan had not after all been part of the fee but was a separate loan made through Rossminster's account at the National Westminster Bank to enable Miller and Harris to pay the advance interest.

The case did not reach court until 1980. Unable to pay the £60,000 into court in order to defend the action, both men had judgment entered against them. By now, however, the alleged debt had embarked on a journey around the Rossminster corporate empire: it had been assigned from Rossminster Acceptances to Thornwright and from there to a new company, Sparebound, from where it moved again, to Giantlands[13]. This Tucker/Plummer company chose only to proceed against Harris, the financially weaker partner. It obtained judgment for £30,000 in January 1980.

In August 1982 Giantlands obtained a bankruptcy order against Harris, but these proceedings were set aside a year later when it was disclosed that at the time of the assignment from Sparebound, Giantlands had been in liquidation. Avonwalk then attempted to reinstate the order and claimed to have been assigned the debt and judgment by Giantlands.[14] This move was rejected by the courts. Although he has not been made bankrupt, Michael Harris still has the judgment outstanding against him. Ironically, it is a debt he need never have had: he could have claimed that his half share of the Little Benton profit was a gift from Miller and untaxable. Harris has now issued his own proceedings against Tucker and Plummer in a bid to have the receiving order rescinded. He is claiming £104,000 compensation for the money paid to Tucker and Rossminster.

George Miller, never less than irrepressible, extricated himself from the consequences of dealing with Rossminster and Stern, albeit at the cost of the initial £60,000 fee plus £70,000 paid to settle an action brought by the First National Bank of Chicago. He also had to contend with the Inland Revenue, which tried to tax him as if he had received the £1 million for Little Benton. He was eventually able to convince the General Commissioners that all he had ever received was £200,000 – half the payment made by Stern – and so had made a loss; but that took until 1984 and cost a further £20,000. However, early in 1986 Miller was made bankrupt as a result of a claim arising from an unrelated 1974 US property deal. Rossminster, through its corporate alter egos, has filed a claim for its £30,000 six years after it obtained the court judgement.

Many former Tucker and Rossminster employees have fared no better than the clients. Several now face large tax assessments relating to bonuses received in the boom years which they had tried to shelter from tax through one or other of Tucker's schemes provided at a discount. Without the protection of substantial private funds or offshore trusts, several of these bit players in the Rossminster story have suffered considerable financial hardship in addition to carrying the handicap of their past Rossminster associations.

The leading characters are now mostly pursuing different careers; some have gone back to what they did before meeting Tucker and Plummer.

Richard Gardner and John Trotman are back in practice as accountants in Brighton and London. Tom Benyon is involved with an electronics company and Lloyd's as well as taking a leaf out of that other former Tory MP Jeffery Archer's book and writing a novel. 'I have had my own experiences in financial chicanery', he says.[15] Bill Cairns is running his own trust company in Guernsey. Nicholas Pilbrow is back from the United States – the Inland Revenue have served him with a Section 481 notice – and with Tim Nicholas and John Arthur at London Investment Trust. Colin Emson runs bankers Robert Fraser. Godfrey Bradman now concentrates on his property company Rosehaugh and is part of the circle of businessmen close to Mrs Thatcher. Don Boyd is back producing films. The Joyners, the Dawes and Patricia Falle are still in the rent-a-director business on Sark. Lewis-Grey has discovered a new career reviving ailing companies. Sir William Pile, Denis Moorcraft and Bill Dermit have all retired. So too has Lord Wilberforce. Peter Rees is on the backbenches after being sacked by Mrs Thatcher as chief secretary of the Treasury in September 1985. He will also retire from politics after the next election. John Nott is knighted, has left politics and is chairman of Lazards, a leading City merchant bank with close ties to the Conservative Party. Desmond Miller and Rose Plummer have both died.

St George's Elizabethan Trust and Blessingwell, on which Tucker and Plummer expended so much attention but rather less money, are dormant. St George's Theatre itself, however, is still in the Shakespeare business. Of the other charities, the Rossminster Foundation has filed no accounts since 1979 so it is impossible to detect any signs of charitable life.

This illustrates once again the continued impotence of the Charity Commissioners. Despite the abuses revealed by Rossminster's activities in St. George's and Blessingwell under the guise of charity no changes in the law have been proposed or are even contemplated.

'Reforms are needed to ensure that no tax clearance is given for a charity without it presenting accounts so that we can see what is being done,' says Charity Commissioners' secretary David Forrest. To be effective, he says, the Commissioners also need more specialist staff and greater co-operation and information from the Inland Revenue. At present there is little or no exchange of information where a supposed charity is claiming tax relief. This is withheld by the Revenue because of its obsession with confidentiality even where tax evasion may be suspected. Without this co-operation the Charity Commissioners, understaffed and under-motivated, can do little to check if a charity is acting correctly within the terms of its deed or articles and if necessary remove its charitable taxfree status. So the abuses and the tax evasion continue.

Ronald Plummer has become active in venture capital projects, Jacksons Bourne End and Florida real estate, as well as the Euthanasia Society. The Ronald Plummer Charitable Settlement meanwhile supports school chamber-music competitions. He can consider the continuing battle with the Revenue with the detached, relaxed attitude of a punctilious, cautious man for whom events have largely gone as anticipated and who has planned accordingly.

The same cannot be said of the more intuitive but equally forward-looking Roy Tucker. A remarkable sequence of unrelated and unpredictable events currently threatens to unravel the truth about the ownership and operations of the Tucker trusts. The root of Tucker's present problems lies in his decision to join up with a former schoolteacher,

Willem 'Wimpie' Ackermann, in buying South Africa's only emerald mine. Tucker first met Ackermann, then twenty-six years old, in 1980. Neither he nor Plummer saw any moral problem in investing in South Africa at a time when other British companies were disinvesting because of the increasing opposition to apartheid.

One of the Tucker trusts took a 50 per cent stake in Ackermann's gem-dealing company, Marquis Diamonds International, in February 1982. Marquis had been formed in Panama but operated from Johannesburg. Keith Tucker became a director of both this company and its British subsidiary, which shared the Curzon Street office. According to Roy Tucker, his brother 'controls' the trusts that made this investment, although he admits, 'my children and those of my brother are beneficially interested'.[16] This would seem to indicate the Keith Number Two and Keith Number Three trusts, although Plummer was also to be a beneficiary of the latter.

The Gravelotte emerald mine was owned by local South African Asian interests through Promogem, a Swiss company. On 12 November 1982 Promogem sold the mine to the Manx company Altina Holdings for £1,775,000 cash. Altina had remained dormant since being formed in 1980 by Commercial Trust and Management, who had had a long business connection with Rossminster. Ten days before the sale of the mine, Ackermann and Cairns were appointed directors of Altina, the Douglas Bank became secretaries and, six days later, Cairns's company Weighbridge Trust was issued with 38 of the 40 Altina shares. On 1 December Altina sold the Gravelotte mine to Envox, another Manx company owned by the Tucker trusts. Envox promptly negotiated to sell the mine to a new Canadian company, Cobra Emerald Mines, in a deal which resulted in Altina receiving £2,420,000 – a £645,000 profit in less than three months. Envox received Cobra shares worth £615,000 plus shares worth £131,000 in another Canadian mining company which had taken over the Gravelotte debts. Envox also invested another £630,000 in more Cobra shares. Altina was wound up in November 1983, by which time its assets were just £1000. It is not known what had happened to the £645,000 made on the mining deal or why Altina was interposed in the deal between Promogem and Envox, except simply to take out a cash profit before the mine was sold to Cobra. The beneficial ownership of Altina is also unknown despite the presence on the board of Ackermann and Tucker's former employee Cairns.

Gravelotte was not the end of Roy Tucker's South African mining ambitions. In April 1984 the Tucker trusts invested £1,250,000 in the Helam diamond mine through another Panamanian vehicle, White Channel. Ackermann became chairman of Channel Mining, to which Helam was transferred. Roy Tucker, now describing himself as a 'financial consultant', was also a director.[17] Further, towards the end of 1984, Jacksons Bourne End purchased 50 per cent of the Ingogo coal mine for £500,000.[18]

By the middle of 1984, the glitter had gone off Gravelotte. Marquis Diamonds International was the marketing agent for its emeralds but these were of low quality and the only real market was in India. The prices realised turned out to be much lower than Cobra had anticipated and so it terminated the marketing agreement. A bitter row developed, resolved in August 1984 by an agreement under which Marquis retained a stock of emeralds, took over Cobra's overdraft at the Douglas Bank and agreed to pay $400,000. In addition Envox handed back its remaining 350,000 Cobra shares.[19]

Cobra insisted, however, on a guarantee of the $400,000 payment by Roy Tucker. Its lawyers would not accept a guarantee from Marquis or Envox – an indication of where they felt the real power and money lay, although Tucker had merely been a consultant on the original deal. Tucker initially refused but when Cobra insisted he agreed to give the guarantee in return for a $50,000 fee and assurances from Ackermann that it would not be called upon. Cobra was to be paid the $400,000 in two stages in November 1984 and January 1985 from the proceeds of Marquis's sale of its stock of emeralds, but it proved impossible to sell the emeralds at worthwhile prices and so the first $200,000 was not paid.

In December 1984 Cobra began High Court proceedings in London to enforce Tucker's guarantee. Two months later, when Tucker continued to refuse to pay, it obtained a judgment for $202,794 including interest, and a month later it obtained judgment for nonpayment of the second $200,000, bringing the total due to $414,900 – equivalent to £328,952. When Tucker still refused to pay, Cobra began bankruptcy proceedings. On 10 August 1985 Roy Tucker was declared bankrupt.

Why Tucker allowed himself to be made bankrupt mystified those who had followed Rossminster and knew the man. There is little doubt that, despite the series of business failures, the Tucker trusts could have raised £329,000. The Inland Revenue's initial suspicion was that it was a

Machiavellian ploy by the ever resourceful and inventive Tucker either to provide a convincing argument against claims that he controlled the assets in the trusts and had the 'power to enjoy' them or to show in the civil case how much he had been damaged by the raids. But the bankruptcy had unattractive consequences for Tucker: all nonessential possessions seized, all bank accounts frozen, no credit, loss of his professional status, a ban on any involvement in managing a business, and social stigma. It also had repercussions for the civil case launched only two months before the receiving order was made against him. As a bankrupt Tucker would be in no position personally to finance the case and so might be unable to continue as a plaintiff. Already Rossminster and AJR were in the unusual position of suing while in liquidation, but this had been possible because the Tucker and Plummer trusts had made the funds available.[20]

On balance, therefore, it appeared that Tucker's was an enforced rather than an arranged bankruptcy. Certainly there was little love lost between Cobra's lawyers in South Africa and Tucker. But two events subsequent to the bankruptcy decision kept alive suspicions about the genuine nature of this unexpected development.

Following the bankruptcy there was a formal meeting of Tucker's creditors on 3 September. Only three turned up: the representatives of Cobra, the Inland Revenue and the lawyer Louis Glatt, a long-time Tucker and Plummer associate who worked from their offices in Curzon Street. Glatt represented Tucker's landlord at Nettlestead Place, the Manx company Cambury, and disclosed that Tucker owed a year's rent, £2000. Asked if he had taken legal action to recover the money or evict Tucker, the lawyer admitted he had done neither. Normally a committee of creditors is formed at the meeting to liaise with the Official Receiver on the bankruptcy. Glatt enquired if such a committee was being formed, and was quickly informed by the Cobra and Revenue representatives that as there were so few creditors, and the minimum for a committee was three, they did not feel it was necessary. In fact, both suspected the real purpose of Glatt's presence.

All bankrupts have to go through a public examination at which they are questioned about the causes of their bankruptcy and what they had done with their money, in order to see that no assets have been hidden from creditors. Tucker's public examination was set for 6 December. A few days beforehand, Cobra received an offer from a Panamanian company associated with Ronald Plummer to buy its claim against Tucker. As

Tucker had disclosed assets of only £24,000, Cobra saw the offer as its best chance of at least obtaining most of the £329,000 it was owed, and sold the debt to the Plummer company at an undisclosed discount. Plummer's action removed a large claim against the Tucker estate, since it was most unlikely that he would enforce the claim. The bankruptcy proceedings could not be halted or reversed but now Tucker would face hostile questioning from only one major creditor – his old enemy, the Inland Revenue. The man who had been appointed Tucker's trustee in bankruptcy and deputed to discover what had happened to the millions Tucker had made out of tax avoidance was the insolvency expert Colin Bird, already the liquidator of 180 Rossminster companies.

The bankruptcy court section of the Law Courts in the Strand lacks the grandeur or sense of occasion found in the courtrooms where the celebrated civil cases are heard. Room 38A, the small, bare courtroom set aside for the initial public examination of debtors, seemed an ill-fitting venue for a man facing the biggest ever claim by the Inland Revenue. On the morning of 6 December Roy Clifford Tucker was not even first on the list of that day's cases before Mr Registrar Dewhurst. He had to sit at the back of the room on a row of wooden chairs alongside the SIS' Bernard Quigley, three Revenue officials, and Michael Harris (who has a finely developed sense of *Schadenfreude*) while the court dealt with a Bengali tradesman whose debts came to a few thousand pounds. His examination completed, Tucker's then began. 'Is the debtor present?' asked the clerk of the court, giving Tucker, who not long before had threatened to cost the country at least £200 million in lost revenue, the same lowly status as any other bankrupt. It was a changed Roy Tucker who stepped forward to begin answering questions from the Official Receiver's counsel about his professional life since leaving Arthur Andersen all those years before. No longer was he the confident, assertive encyclopedia of the taxes acts but a nervous, hesitant defendant. This was the first occasion since the diary case in 1981 that Roy Tucker had faced questioning under oath and this time there was no alternative but to answer.

Tucker's own statement of affairs disclosed debts of £350,895 and assets of £362,663, producing a surplus of £11,768 – but, in typical piece of Tucker-style accounting, he had included as an asset the sum of £338,500 representing what he expected to receive from the action against the Inland Revenue (50 per cent – 'to allow for uncertainties') less his own admitted tax liability of £250,000. It was, he admitted, 'a figure taken from the air'. Without that piece of creative accounting there was a deficit of £326,732, and that ignored the Revenue's assessments, which had grown to £18,500,000. Tucker estimated that between 1972 and April 1978, when he stopped marketing tax schemes, he had earned £2 million in fees, producing a profit of 'several hundred thousand pounds'. 'Surely you earned much more than £2 million?' said the Official Receiver's counsel. Tucker replied, not for the last time that day, that he did not have the answer. In his one-hour cross-examination Tucker displayed a remarkable lack of knowledge about his own affairs and those of the family trusts. One reason was that he had produced no accounts for the years 1972 to 1976, although required to do so. The accounts for the period 1976 to 1980 showed fees of £1,700,000 and profits of £212,000. In the years from 1980 to March 1985, when he ceased to practice, the fees declined from £239,000 to £58,000. But these figures ignored his arrangements with Rossminster for receiving a share of the fees paid by its tax clients. More significantly, there was no accounting for the profits made by Rossminster itself. Profits which Plummer had admitted to a newspaper shortly after the Havers announcement had made Tucker and himself 'a lot of money'.[21] These, said Tucker, had gone to the shareholders and were 'not income in the hands of any UK resident', i.e. they were not his and not taxable. Tucker admitted that the Keith Number One trust, of which he was a 'discretionary beneficiary', had held shares in Rossminster, but he was merely 'an adviser' to the company; he had had 'considerable say' – 'but I did not have any control in an administrative sense.' Who then controlled Rossminster? 'I would say Mr Plummer controlled Rossminster,' he replied – an answer that would have surprised those who had seen how Plummer regularly deferred to Tucker.

The picture Tucker gave the court was that he had been junior not only to Plummer but also to his own brother, now a farmer in Belgium. (Keith Tucker declined an interview for legal reasons.) Tucker said that he was employed as a consultant at £1000 a month by Douglas Investment Services, a subsidiary of Douglas Financial Services and an associate of the Douglas Bank which was now controlled by a Plummer trust. Like Avonwalk, Plummer and Louis Glatt, Douglas Investment Services can be found at 42 Curzon Street. The Keith Number One trust had been but was no longer a half-shareholder in the bank. This was just one of several recent changes that Tucker disclosed in the affairs of the trusts. The ownership of Cambury and with it Nettlestead Place had changed. So too had the trustees of the Keith trusts, who were now in Panama although the trusts were still run from Guernsey. 'I'm no longer always sure of what it does,' its 'discretionary beneficiary' declared concerning Keith Number One. It seemed that steps had been taken to ensure that the creditors would come up empty-handed if they were able to make any claims on that trust.

Tucker was also unable to provide any information about the fate of the proceeds from the sale of the Douglas Bank shares or the farm land at Nettlestead sold to Cambury for £130,000 in 1980 or the Westbourne Park house Cambury had acquired from him for £80,000 in 1984 or the loan repaid to Cambury from the 1985 sale of a Bayswater flat for £44,000.

The disastrous South African venture, he explained, had come about as a result of acting for Golcondra Enterprises in the purchase of the Gravelotte mine by Envox.[22] Who owned Envox? 'I believe it's my brother through a trust, but not a trust I have any interest in.' The same arrangement applied to Marquis Diamonds International. Tucker did not mention that his children were beneficiaries of that particular trust. 'I was through Golcondra asked to perform various services for it from time to time.' He also advised his brother 'from time to time'. Keith Tucker had assured him that 'he would not let me be called on the [Cobra] guarantee, he would put further funds into Marquis,' Tucker explained. There was, however, no explanation of why both his brother and 'Wimpie' Ackermann had let him down and so made him bankrupt. Why, therefore, had he signed the $400,000 guarantee when he did not by his own admission have the means to pay? enquired the Official Receiver's counsel. 'I've often asked that question of myself,' Tucker replied ruefully.

After brief adjourned hearings in April and October 1986 the full public examination of Roy Tucker is expected to resume in February 1987 following the completion by the trustee of his inquiries. These have included seeking a court order for documents from the trusts in Guernsey and taking the unusual step of seeking to examine in private witnesses who could have knowledge of Tucker's affairs. Most significant among these is Keith Tucker. His decision to resist legally the court order obtained by the trustee to compel his evidence is one reason for the continued delay in resuming Tucker's examination. Before the private examinations this promised to be the longest in British bankruptcy history. It was estimated to last twenty days in court, a measure of just how complex is the task of unravelling where are the millions earned by Roy Tucker from tax avoidance.

While Roy Tucker continues to struggle with the consequences of his involvement with Rossminster, tax avoidance in Britain is far from dead. Despite the ruling in *Furniss* v. *Dawson*, which now allows the Inland Revenue to ignore any step in a composite transaction inserted purely for the purpose of avoiding tax, avoidance is thriving, but in different and mostly less sophisticated versions than the highly complex and artificial forms devised by Tucker and Bradman. The fashion now for those seeking to avoid income tax is to take advantage of capital allowances or the ingenious and worthwhile tax reliefs offered by investment in forestry (costing the Revenue perhaps £25 million a year[23]) or the shares of new companies set up under the Business Expansion Scheme (up to £150 million invested). The charity loophole is still being exploited but more by the use of private charities for the benefit of the donor or their relatives. A Victorian relic, the friendly society, has become a vehicle for selling tax-exempt bonds.

Needless to say, there have been excesses which the government has been forced to prevent. There has been legislation to remove capital allowances on leasing and film financing and limit the types of business eligible for the Business Expansion Scheme to those which create employment, as the scheme originally intended. The massive use of sophisticated 'dividend stripping' on government stocks, turning income into capital, has had to be banned. So too has a scheme for avoiding stamp duty on major company takeovers which is estimated to have cost £35 million in 1983 alone. Some of the wilder excesses of the investment funds which attracted hundreds of millions of pounds into Jersey and Guernsey seeking to avoid capital gains tax have also been banned. The Revenue has recently been given powers to curb the abuse of friendly societies' taxfree status.

Despite such anti-avoidance moves, the tax which has been most successfully avoided is the Labour government's proud, modern version of estate duty, the Capital Transfer Tax. This has had little or no impact on the redistribution of wealth in Britain, and in 1986 was replaced by the more flexible Inheritance Tax. Means of avoiding capital transfer tax were so numerous that only those who were ignorant of the loopholes or wanted to pay did so. One loophole alone, the Discounted Gift Scheme, which used a life-assurance policy maturing only if the policyholder reached the age of 105, is believed to have removed £1000 million from the grasp of

CTT in three years. After this loophole was blocked a successor, the Inheritance Trust Scheme, is estimated to have attracted nearly £2000 million in five years.

Britain is certainly no more honest or socially responsible about its taxpaying today, after seven years of Conservative government and lower tax rates, than it was when the Labour Party was in power. As Roy Tucker suggested, tax avoidance tends to be habit-forming. The complex, sophisticated tax scheme which was the hallmark of Tucker and Bradman has not been revived because of the legal vetoes they forced the courts to impose. But current unease in legal circles about the *Furniss* v. *Dawson* blunderbuss placed in the Inland Revenue's not always sensitive hands by the Law Lords suggests that it may not be long before the House of Lords turns the decision on its head. Since May 1985, three tax schemes have already successfully defeated in the High Court Revenue challenges relying on *Furniss* v. *Dawson*.[24] In each case the judge accepted that the transactions concerned were separate or had a purpose apart from tax avoidance and were not preordained or prearranged as in Ramsay. If these decisions are not reversed and others follow, further eroding *Furniss* v. *Dawson*, the floodgates against artificial avoidance schemes will start to creak once again. And they will burst wide open if a future Labour government carries out anything like the shadow chancellor Roy Hattersley's initially proclaimed intention of a return to 'penal' tax rates – although below 98 per cent – an investment income surcharge and extra capital taxes, all designed to raise the effective rates paid by 'the rich'.[25] Since making that declaration in 1985 Labour policy has sought to move away from a pledge of high marginal tax rates towards slashing the allowances enjoyed by the top 5 per cent of taxpayers – the 250,000 to 500,000 who earn more than £27,000 a year. They, Hattersley warns, 'will lose out substantially'.[26] It all sounds depressingly familiar.

To put the clock back to 1974 would prove that the Labour Party has learned nothing from its taxation failure of the seventies. It would also be the kiss of life for which the next generation of Tuckers and Plummers are waiting.

NOTES

CHAPTER I

1 – The Committee on Enforcement Powers of the Revenue Departments had been set up in July 1980 as the Conservative government's reaction to the backlash from its supporters against the often needless excesses of the Customs and Excise in collecting VAT and the increasingly aggressive Inland Revenue which, over Conservative objections, had been given tough new powers by the previous Labour government.

2 – *Ayrshire Pullman Motor Services and David M. Ritchie v. Commissioners of Inland Revenue* (Annotated Tax Cases, p. 531).

3 – (As note 2.)

4 – *CIR v. the Duke of Westminster* (1936 *Appeal Cases* 1).

5 – *Lord Vestey's Executors and Vestey v. CIR* (vol. 31 *Tax Cases* 80).

6 – *Sothern-Smith v. Clancy (Inspector of Taxes)* (1941 *Kings Bench* 276).

7 – *Latilla v. CIR* (1942 1 *All England Law Reports* 287).

8 – *Daily Mail*, 6 October 1980.

9 – *Sunday Telegraph*, 14 March 1976.

10 – The invulnerability of discretionary trusts was ended by the introduction of Capital Transfer Tax in 1975. This assessed such trusts every ten years. As a result discretionary trusts were replaced by accumulation and maintenance settlements. These allow lower-taxed income to be converted into taxfree capital to be paid out many years later, for instance to a child on reaching the age of twenty-five. The tax payable is at most 45 per cent.

11 – *Black Nominees Ltd v. Nicol (IoT)* (1975 *Simon's Tax Cases* 372).

12 – *Inland Revenue Commissioners v. Goodwin* (1975 *Weekly Law Reports* 640).

13 – *Financial Times*, 8 March 1980.

14 – *Financial Times*, 31 January 1986.

15 – Godfrey Bradman declined to be interviewed. He said his tax-avoidance activities were a long time ago and he did not wish to discuss them. He now runs a £300-million-plus property group, Rosehaugh, which has developed several major City and West End sites. Bradman family trusts have shares in Rosehaugh worth £30 million at the time of writing.

CHAPTER 2

1 – Rossminster brochure published in 1977.

2 – A similarly flattering version of events is provided by Nigel Tutt in *The Tax Raiders* (Financial Training Publications, 1985). Tutt records that Tucker left St Paul's because he 'was impatient to experience the world'. However, a London *Evening News* profile (29 October 1979) confirms that

he had intended to read mathematics at Oxford but 'was unsuccessful in the scholarship examinations'.

3 – *Financial Times*, 9 October 1979.

4 – The Inland Revenue challenged the trust's tax-exempt status on the grounds that it was merely enabling income to be added to capital taxfree in the foundation. This argument was finally rejected by the Court of Appeal in 1980 on the grounds that, as the Slater Foundation was a charity and its funds were not being misapplied, the trust's donations could be taxfree.

5 – (As note 3.)

CHAPTER 3

1 – *CIR* v. *Plummer* (1979 *STC* 793).

2 – HOVAS appealed against the Inland Revenue's refusal to pay the tax rebate but lost at a hearing before the Special Commissioners of Tax. By April 1976 the company was virtually insolvent. As a consequence of the Special Commissioners' decision it faced a corporation tax liability of £904,000 as a result of the now not allowable income tax which the taxpayers had had deducted at source. HOVAS did not even have the money to finance an appeal to the High Court.

3 – *Financial Times*, 9 October 1979.

4 – (As note 3.)

5 – The Deprived Children's Aid Fund continued in existence until 1981, paying a further £390 to charity.

6 – DCAF did not seek to challenge the Revenue's decision in the courts. Instead it used another Tucker scheme, involving the purchase and sale of the rights to receive annuity payments, in a bid to remove its tax liability.

7 – The battle over DCAF was to take even longer. It was not until June 1984 that a ruling, in favour of the Inland Revenue, was made by the Special Commissioners. The appeal was brought by Richard Sotnick, the 'pessimistic solicitor' and a former Lord Mayor of Portsmouth, who in 1972 had agreed to pay £45,000 to DCAF (on which he claimed tax relief) which agreed to repay him £37,700, the difference including the fee. One major reason for the delay in this case was that it was not until 1979 that the Revenue obtained documents confirming that DCAF was not a qualifying charitable company and therefore the annuities were not tax effective. A further factor in the delay was that Sotnick had been charged in 1981 with the theft of £1600 relating to a property transaction. He was convicted of deception in 1983 but that conviction was quashed in December 1984.

CHAPTER 4

1 – In 1978 a contingent interest in the trust's assets was appointed to Moser and he sold that to a Jersey company for £56,000. The trust had grown as a result of a subsidiary, Sacrone Investments, receiving commissions paid by Tucker for clients Moser introduced. Some five or six payments totalling about £100,000 were made.

2 – *W. T. Ramsay Ltd* v. *CIR* (1979 1 *WLR* 974).

3 – *Financial Times*, 9 October 1979.

CHAPTER 5

1 – *Financial Times*, 9 October 1979, and *Sunday Times*, 6 June 1976.

2 – Plummer to Glauser, 14 October 1974.

3 – Letter, Miller to Perrot, 2 October 1975.

4 – Letter, Plummer to Lewis-Grey, 7 February 1977.

5 – This growth has continued unabated despite a Conservative government and lower taxes on the wealthy and high income earners. By 1984 there were 6400 corporation tax companies in

Jersey, over 8000 companies in Guernsey and 16,500 in the Isle of Man. The receipts from the tax on these companies was more than £1,700,000 in Jersey, £900,000 in Guernsey and £1 million in the Isle of Man. Bank deposits, not entirely from UK residents, have reached almost £30 billion Jersey, £6,500 million in Guernsey and more than £2000 million in the Isle of Man. In all three islands the financial sector is either the largest or second largest contributor to the economy.

CHAPTER 6

1 – This involved twelve steps, beginning with the purchase of a UK company owned by the client by another UK company controlled by a nonresident trust set up by him in Guernsey. Slater, Walker (Guernsey) provided the finance. The UK company was taken over for one share in the acquiring company at a price equal to 1/100th of the underlying assets. This was then sold at that same value to establish the loss required. The trust was then sold on to a nonresident at the full value of the underlying assets, establishing a matching 'profit' for the client to cancel the earlier 'loss'.

2 – Tutt, p. 21.

3 – *World in Action*, 1 December 1980.

4 – Letter, Gardner to Miller and Harris, 31 October 1973.

5 – Letter, Gardner to Miller and Harris, 14 March 1974.

6 – (As note 5.)

7 – *World in Action*, 1 December 1980.

8 – (As note 7.)

9 – (As note 7.)

10 – *Financial Times*, 9 October 1979.

11 – Minute of meeting on 29 October 1974.

CHAPTER 7

1 – *Sunday Times*, 6 June 1976.

2 – *Guardian*, 5 June 1976.

3 – (As note 2.)

4 – (As note 2.)

5 – Section 38 of the Finance Act 1976 denied tax relief on any interest paid after 8 June 1976 when a tax scheme had been entered with the sole or main purpose of avoiding tax.

6 – This was introduced after bank interest on loans for nonbusiness purposes ceased to be tax deductible in Healey's first budget of March 1974. It was replaced in 1976 by the Non-Deposit Scheme Mark 3 using share dealing. Peter Rees provided one of the legal opinions for this scheme.

7 – The loan was repaid in March 1977 and replaced by one from Hallpark Financiers. This was repaid in 1979 with loans from Mandeville, Robinhill and Ogbourne which were still outstanding when Middlelane was wound up in 1981 owing creditors, mainly the Inland Revenue, £4,240,000.

CHAPTER 8

1 – *World in Action*, 1 December 1980.

2 – *Daily Telegraph*, 12 February 1977.

3 – (As note 1.)

4 – The Bermuda version was run by Bill Cairns, the former clerk in Tucker's office. He was joined by partners from the local lawyers Cox & Williamson and two Americans, Gordon and Maureen Copley, who ran a supermarket. This was the supposed Bermudan 'control'. In fact they all took instructions directly from London, as did their opposite numbers in Guernsey and Sark. After little more than a year Tucker closed the Bermuda operation as too costly and inaccessible.

5 – The onshore 'S' companies differed with every deal but the vital offshore companies remained largely unchanged. These were Illington, Illington Finance, Lambgill, Highbarrow, Kemploy and Jedvale in the Bermuda version and Alrate, Adverton, Blackwood, Brindleton and Copwell in the Sark version.

6 – A year or so later Morgan sold Plummer a seventeenth-century Jonathan Speed atlas for £9500.

7 – (As note 1.)

8 – In 1980 and 1981 the original St George's Elizabethan Theatre company gave £7000 to its successor. The original company was put into voluntary liquidation in September 1982 with its liabilities, including unspecified tax claims, far exceeding its assets.

9 – No further accounts have been published by Blessingwell, in contravention of both the Companies and Charities acts. But during 1982 it was involved in a £2,500,000 London property deal partly financed by Douglas Bank, the successor to Rossminster Acceptances (IOM).

CHAPTER 9

1 – Subsequently the arrangement with Cambury was modified so that Tucker paid a very modest rental of £2000 a year while enjoying the protection of a statutory tenant. Tucker claimed to have invested £120,000 in the 400 acres he farmed at Nettlestead. Following losses Tucker put at £54,000, the farming business was sold to the Cambury-controlled Farming Acre, of which Tucker was a director, for £130,000 in 1980.

2 – *Evening News*, 29 October 1979.

3 – Starkeep, formed in 1979 and controlled first by Darmas and then by another Manx company, Forwood, was believed to own certain of the *objets d'art* at Nettlestead as part of its declared business as art dealers. In 1981 the company held £11,000 in works of art and cameras worth £222. Tucker's friend Jelko Yuresha was his codirector and held a 25 per cent interest.

4 – The majority of the group's 82 subsidiaries, including most of the 'mechanical' scheme companies, were taken over by Thornwright, a parallel company owned by the same six interests, and then put into liquidation. Thornwright had been formed in September 1976 and capitalised with £2,500,000 in debentures from the shareholders. In its first year Thornwright paid £273,000 in interest to the offshore debenture holders. In the ten months to July 1978 it made a profit of £3,855,000. The debentures were paid off in April 1978 and the company sold to Blessingwell through the Company Purchase Scheme.

5 – The biggest slice of these profits came from the banks. In the year to July 1976 Rossminster Acceptances made £851,000 and paid a £519,000 dividend. This was largely possible because of a tax charge of only £107,000. Without the use of Tucker tax schemes the tax charge would have been £698,000 higher. Rossminster Acceptances had made advances during the year of £51,600,000 although deposits were only £4,100,000. In the same year First London Securities produced a £281,000 profit and a £165,000 dividend. A £1,260,000 provision for tax would have been required without the use of tax schemes. FLS had deposits of only £7,900,000, yet it advanced no less than £542 million to customers of the Advanced Interest Scheme. Ashleymore, a major player in that tax scheme, was also a substantial contributor, producing profits of £1,736,000 in the year to March 1977 despite a tax liability of £2,750,000. A year later it passed on £1,335,000 to Blessingwell although the tax liability remained unresolved. For the year to July 1977 Rossminster Acceptances made £491,000 – though advancing only £366,000 to customers. However, it had a potential tax liability of £1 million. FLS' profits soared to £1,698,000 from the £13 million it lent to customers. Its potential tax liability was at least £2,400,000 and possibly up to £4,250,000 if the tax schemes did not work. This was a result of the Inland Revenue withdrawing FLS' recognition as a bank, a status Rossminster Acceptances had never obtained.

CHAPTER 10

1 – The Guernsey authorities later had to compensate depositors as it was proved that they had failed to monitor the bank's activities correctly and so prevent it attracting deposits when it was already in difficulties.

2 – *World in Action*, 7 February 1983.

CHAPTER 11

1 – It was later revealed that Minet chairman John Wallrock and two key executives, Peter Cameron-Webb and Peter Dixon, had also been involved in secret offshore reinsurance companies into which £39 million had disappeared, of which £13 million is still missing.

2 – A Bradman-linked client was his former personal assistant Michael Goddard who bought the Advanced Interest Scheme in 1976 for his property company Woodpath Securities. Goddard later became the expert on tax avoidance through leasing.

3 – WLE, renamed Farmost, received an assessment for £18,200,000 corporation tax. It was put into liquidation in April 1979 with the tax assessment still unresolved, as it remains in 1986, and with assets of only £10,000.

4 – Group Houses made a £814,000 donation to St George's plus a further £803,000 when its share capital was reduced on its becoming an unlimited company. This was the normal practice once companies were inside the charity and bound for liquidation. Going unlimited and repaying the share capital reduced even further the amount left in the company from which any tax assessment could be met. The Inland Revenue issued a corporation tax assessment on Group Houses for the tax due on its £810,000 profit and also a protective assessment – protecting its right to claim tax that might be due – on the interest paid of £842,000. The tax position was still unresolved when Group Houses went into liquidation in September 1981 owing £456,000 but having assets of less than £5000.

5 – One of these was an annuity scheme to avoid £208,000 in corporation tax. But the following year the company provided for the payment of this tax not expecting the scheme to succeed in the courts. In the three years 1976 to 1979 Brown & Jackson managed to pay only £16,000 in tax on profits that totalled £6 million. As a result its shares (50 per cent owned by a company in Guernsey's smaller neighbour, Alderney) rose by 500 per cent. The offshore owners, believed to be linked to family trusts associated with Bailey and Duffy, in 1980 sold shares worth £8 million taxfree. Soon afterwards the bubble burst and the profits collapsed as did the shares.

6 – The three MFC deals gave Rossminster a taste for tax avoidance at sea and the opportunities ships presented as sources of tax losses. Courtwise Shipping was formed in 1978 and through Savannah Shipping acquired two small cargo ships at a cost of $6,700,000. Lord Young's accountant brother Stewart, later chairman of the BBC, was a partner in the City firm of Hacker Rubens Young who were auditors to some of the MFC companies.

7 – One company, Blackenden Investment, was wound up in 1981 owing £809,000, mainly to the Inland Revenue, from assets of £502. Merlbrook Investment was also wound up, leaving £1290 to pay debts of £1,149,000.

8 – The flotation of Speyhawk on the stock market in 1981 gave Osborne shares worth more than £6 million.

CHAPTER 12

1 – *Newsweek*, 12 March 1984.

2 – Emson & Dudley sold interests in seven limited partnerships called either Monday or Tuesday Films to finance the making of four films including *Sunburn* starring Farrah Fawcett, *The Passage* starring Anthony Quinn and *Cattle Annie and Little Britches* with Burt Lancaster. Among those who invested were Lord Forte and his son Rocco, who put in more than £100,000; George

Harrison; Cliff Richard backed up by two of his Shadows, Hank Marvin and Bruce Welch; and Pam Ayres.

3 – Posgate was at the centre of one of the biggest Lloyd's scandals when in 1982 it was revealed that $55 million of insurance premiums from Howden syndicates had been misapplied into offshore companies connected with the Howden chairman and three of his fellow directors. Posgate was sacked by the new management at Howden and suspended by Lloyd's. He denied any knowledge of the offshore companies' ownership but admitted receiving certain benefits from them. He was expelled by Lloyd's in 1985 but this was then reduced to a suspension. However, Lloyd's later refused to let him re-enter the insurance market on the grounds that he was not 'a fit and proper person' to be an active underwriter.

4 – However, the Inland Revenue has subsequently re-litigated the scheme before the Special Commissioners who held in 1986 that it was ineffective on the grounds that the full facts proved that the partnerships were not carrying on a trade and so could not claim the tax losses. The loophole enabling members of limited partnerships to claim tax relief equal to four times their investment was finally closed by the Finance Act 1985 which restricted relief to the actual amount invested.

CHAPTER 13

1 – Letter, Walker to author, 21 November 1980.

2 – (As note 1.)

3 – Ellerman Lines and the breweries were sold for almost £50 million in 1983.

4 – Alanvale Property Trust, Alanvale Securities and Hillcoll all went into liquidation between October 1980 and August 1981. Alanvale Securities had assets of precisely £5.14, Hillcoll was better placed with £880. Both had and still have unresolved tax assessments against them regarding their profits on the Ellerman transaction. Alanvale Property Trust had to be put into liquidation because of its liabilities, which included tax assessments on profits of £1,100,000. Its assets were just £900.

CHAPTER 14

1 – The Conservative Party chairman was a policyholder in European Life and Pensions, a Manx company. ELAP policies had been marketed from 1972 until 1978 as a means of avoiding Capital Gains Tax. The key legal opinions on the effectiveness of the insurance policies and the tax scheme had been provided by Desmond Miller before he joined Rossminster. The essence of the scheme was ELAP's claimed ability to make taxfree dealing profits in government stocks. After ten years ELAP policyholders were promised up to a 150 per cent taxfree profit. However, in 1979 the Inland Revenue successfully proved that the offshore insurance company through which ELAP made much of its taxfree dealing profits was liable for tax as far as UK policyholders were concerned. Then, in May 1981, the Special Commissioners ruled that an ELAP policy was not an insurance policy at all but an investment and furthermore was not a bona fide transaction but one entered into purely for the avoidance of tax and thereby ineffective. ELAP was put into receivership in 1984, leaving Lord Thorneycroft and the other policyholders facing possible claims for Capital Gains Tax after all.

2 – There was no mention of Slater, Walker in the Rossminster publicity material on Benyon's background, according to which he spent the years from 1969 to 1973 as a 'director of an insurance broking group'. A similar non-reference appeared later in his parliamentary profile once he became an MP. This is perhaps not so curious, given Slater, Walker's near collapse in 1975 and Slater's subsequent prosecution on Companies Act offences.

3 – Conservative Central Office, in a press release issued at the time of Benyon's first appearance

as a candidate, said he left the army in 1967, but Rossminster in its publicity had him serving Queen and Sultan for another two years.

4 – Yeo eventually became MP for Suffolk South in 1983 after three years as a director of the Spastics Society.

5 – Tutt, p. 17 and p. 77.

6 – Letter, Walker to author, 13 December 1985.

7 – *Daily Telegraph*, 11 February 1975.

8 – *Daily Telegraph*, 21 November 1975.

9 – *Sunday Times*, 6 January 1980.

10 – (As note 9.)

11 – *Hansard*, 12 May 1977.

12 – One of those interviewed on the programme was Tucker's rival Michael Hepker, whose Marchmont Taxation Group was based on the floor below in Vogue House.

CHAPTER 15

1 – A 1981 United States Treasury estimate put the yearly loss in tax at $1300 million.

2 – *Financial Times*, 25 June 1980.

3 – Bambella Trading had been dealing in cocoa and sugar since 1968. Among its director shareholders was the Duke of Marlborough. The dealing was handled by another director, Jake Morley of the commodity brokers M. L. Doxford. Doxford crashed later, owing investors £4 million.

4 – Interview recorded for 1980 *World in Action* programme.

5 – *Hansard*, 11 April 1978.

6 – *Hansard*, 12 April 1978.

7 – *Hansard*, 27 April 1978.

8 – *Hansard*, 12 July 1978.

9 – (As note 8.)

10 – *Hansard*, 27 April 1978.

11 – (As note 10.)

12 – *Hansard*, 12 July 1978.

13 – (As note 12.)

14 – (As note 12.)

15 – In the May 1974 House of Commons free vote on the establishment of a compulsory public register of MPs' interests Rees voted against the proposal and in favour of a Conservative motion proposing that disclosure should be left to the individual MP's judgement. This was rejected by the majority of MPs, who voted for the compulsory register. Nott also voted against the register. Peter Walker, however, voted in favour.

16 – *Hansard*, 28 April 1977.

17 – *Hansard*, 11 March 1969.

18 – *Erskine May's Parliamentary Practice*, 19th edn, p. 412.

19 – Interview recorded for 1980 *World in Action* programme.

20 – *Hansard*, 12 July 1978.

21 – Coltpearl had a near £4,500,000 tax liability which it sought to dispose of by way of an extremely large GAS transaction involving the receipt of £104 million and the payment of £67 million. Algrave Investments was listed as the parent company but during the year Coltpearl and/or Algrave had become owned by a 'UK registered charity'.

22 – Pectineus and Tanror had been formed on the same day in October 1977; Valen was formed in January and Darmas in March 1978; Kallow was a 'shelf' company formed back in 1971.

23 – Both Darmas and Valen soon took advantage of the rise in the LIT share price to sell. Darmas, which initially held 1,489,300 shares, had sold completely by January 1981. Valen switched its similar-sized holding to another Manx company, Valen Securities, and had sold out by February 1983. Kallow sold its 317,500 shares by June 1982. Miller sold his 215,000 shares during 1980. Pectineus sold two thirds of its 305,000 in May 1980 and the balance by 1982. Tanror continued to hold its 90,000 shares.

CHAPTER 16

1 – Interview recorded for 1980 *World in Action* programme.
2 – (As note 1.)
3 – Tutt, p. 114.
4 – (As note 1.)
5 – (As note 1.)
6 – Peter Rees had been among the most critical of the 'odious provisions'.
7 – Letter, Sir Geoffrey Howe to author, 23 January 1986.
8 – *Daily Mail*, 14 July 1979.
9 – Clitheroe's firm Kingsley, Napley were also acting for the civil engineers William Press in the criminal case brought by the Inland Revenue as a result of information provided by one of Benyon's Abingdon constituents. This had resulted in a highly publicised raid on the Press offices in March 1978.
10 – *Daily Telegraph*, 17 July 1979.
11 – *Observer*, 5 August 1979.
12 – *Daily Mail*, 17 August 1979.

CHAPTER 17

1 – *Daily Express*, 17 August 1979.
2 – *Daily Mail* and *Financial Times*, 14 December 1979.
3 – *Observer*, 4 November 1979.
4 – *Financial Times*, 9 October 1979.
5 – (As note 3.)
6 – (As note 3.)
7 – That answer was given years later to the ever sympathetic Tutt. Referring to the Ridge Trust, Tucker said, he considered himself as having an influence over some of the monies but that did not mean he was a beneficiary. The trustees however would have taken account of his wishes. On Iota, he admitted, it was a clerical error on a small amount of money. He knew he had an interest in some trusts but did not declare those he did not have an interest in. As to those board meetings, the answer was that they were 'held in an informal way . . . some were held on the phone'. (Tutt, pp. 245 and 250.)
8 – *Daily Mirror*, 4 June 1980.
9 – *Daily Telegraph*, 14 July 1980.
10 – *Daily Telegraph*, 26 July 1980.
11 – *News of the World*, 20 July 1980.
12 – *Observer*, 20 July 1980.
13 – (As note 10.)
14 – (As note 10.)
15 – *Financial Times*, 22 November 1980. In fact Rossminster group companies had been going into voluntary liquidation since July. Among them was the former Rossminster parent company, now called Maplecrown. This was helped on its way by a corporation tax assessment on profits of £1,500,000 for 1978.
16 – A new bank, Mallinhall, owned by a trust for the benefit of former Rossminster employees,

was set up with Rossminster's assistance to replace it. Mallinhall did obtain a banking licence. It ceased business in 1984.
17 – *Daily Mail*, 3 December 1980.
18 – *The Times*, 3 December 1980.

CHAPTER 18
1 – *Inland Revenue Commissioner* v. *Europa Oil (NZ) Ltd* (1971 *A C* 760).
2 – *Ransom* v. *Higgs* (1974 *S T C* 559).
3 – *Inland Revenue Commissioners* v. *Plummer* (1977 *WLR* 1227).
4 – *IRC* v. *Plummer* (1978 *WLR* 459).
5 – The scheme involved the creation of an allowable capital loss by buying and selling an interest in a Gibraltar settlement (a 'loss' offset by the 'profit' from buying and selling an interest in a Jersey settlement).
6 – *W. T. Ramsay Ltd* v. *IRC* (1979 *STC* 582).
7 – *Financial Times*, 20 September 1979.
8 – *IRC* v. *Plummer* (1979 *STC* 793).
9 – *Financial Times*, 9 October 1980.
10 – *IRC* v. *Garvin* (*Times Law Report*, 29 February 1980). Templeman made this comment in giving a dissenting judgment against a Bradman capital gains tax scheme in the Court of Appeal. This was the only Bradman scheme to succeed in the House of Lords, the Inland Revenue losing an appeal there in May 1981, largely because there would otherwise have been double taxation on the same capital gain. As Lord Scarman commented, 'Those who used the services of an inventor and purveyor of tax avoidance schemes could expect no mercy; but they were entitled to justice.' (*TLR*, 15 May 1981.)
11 – *Eilbeck (IoT)* v. *Rawling* (1980 *STC* 192).
12 – *W. T. Ramsay* v. *IRC* (1981 *STC* 174).
13 – *Financial Times*, 9 February 1981.
14 – *Sunday Times*, 15 March 1981.
15 – *IRC* v. *Burmah Oil* (1982 *STC* 30).
16 – (As note 15.)
17 – *Cairns* v. *MacDiarmid (IoT)* (1983 *STC* 178).
18 – *Furniss (IoT)* v. *Dawson* (1984 *STC* 153).
19 – *Financial Times*, 19 October 1985.

CHAPTER 19
1 – *Mail on Sunday*, 19 December 1982.
2 – *World in Action*, 7 February 1983.
3 – *The Times*, 17 May 1983.
4 – In November 1983 the government had set up a committee of inquiry under Lord Roskill, a Law Lord, to consider changes in the law and procedure governing the investigation and prosecution of fraud. The committee reported in January 1986, making 112 recommendations including, most controversially, the replacement of trial by jury with trial by a judge, assisted by two lay assessors, in highly complex cases. Lord Roskill declared, 'We are satisfied that the Fraud Trials Tribunal would considerably reduce the length and cost of trials while at the same time increasing the prospects of a sound verdict being reached. The savings of judges and court time and the greatly improved comprehension of the matters under enquiry would allow more, if not all, complex fraud cases to be brought to trial.' This proposal was supported by the Attorney-General and the Director of Public Prosecutions. It was, however, rejected by the Conservative

government in October 1986. But many of the other Roskill recommendations for improving the investigation and prosecution of fraud were accepted.

5 – *Hansard*, 18 January 1974.

CHAPTER 20

1 – Buckley had told the Inland Revenue, 'I am not aware of any settlement created on my behalf in Gibraltar.' At the trial he maintained that he thought 'on your behalf' meant 'for your own benefit' and so had not answered deliberately falsely.

2 – Moser's client was the millionaire George Jackson, who had been engaged in massive, long-standing tax evasion. Jackson was also arrested but did a private settlement with the Inland Revenue involving the payment of £6,800,000. Jackson was not prosecuted, on the grounds of ill health. However, his two accountants and Moser were committed for trial, although charges against the accountants were later dropped.

3 – By 1985 Hepker was himself the target of an investigation by the Inland Revenue concerning the profits made by his Marchmont group. He had also become a central figure in the controversy surrounding the near collapse of Johnson Matthey Bankers, from whom offshore companies that he advised and his family interests controlled had borrowed and not repaid £1 million.

4 – Tutt, p. vii.

5 – Tutt, p. viii.

6 – Tutt, p. 231.

7 – Tutt, p. 177.

8 – Benyon's and Trotman's Manx companies were also wound up in 1980.

9 – Laurel had been incorporated in December 1980 and Megastar in September 1981. Laurel's first directors were the trusted Sark duo of Douglas and Pamela Dawe plus Rossminster's man in Guernsey, Ian McMillan. They were later replaced by the local lawyer Ricardo Durling and McMillan's successor David Dickens, both directors of Megastar. Its registered office is in Guernsey.

10 – This company, like Kazan Corporation, was registered in 1981 with McMillan and the Dawes as directors.

11 – Douglas Financial Services, formed in November 1981, is a key company in the Tucker interests' Panamanian operations. Although incorporated in Panama its registered office is at the Douglas Bank in the Isle of Man. The Dawes have authority over Casaya.

12 – This company was registered in October 1980 with Keith Tucker's wife Angela and the Dawes as directors.

13 – Giantlands, formed in February 1980, was a subsidiary of Conifer and both Tucker and Plummer were directors. It was initially much involved with financing deals relating to the former MFC ships. The company was voluntarily wound up in July 1982.

14 – Avonwalk was registered in February 1981 as a Rossminster Holdings subsidiary but in November that year was transferred to Laurel as part of the Jacksons Bourne End ownership reshuffle to Panama. During 1982 Douglas Financial Services became its other shareholder. Apart from the Jacksons shares and Calpernium, Avonwalk's other interests, as at March 1982, included £891,000 of book debts and a Cornish holiday camp. It had been assigned assets valued at £330,000 by Giantlands in July 1982, just before that company was wound up. These included some land in Sussex, a bank deposit and the Harris debt, valued at just £200. Avonwalk was financed with the aid of a £1,200,000 bank loan and £500,000 from Laurel.

15 – *London Standard*, 19 August 1986.

16 – Tucker affidavit in Cobra legal action, 22 January 1985.

17 – In October 1984 White Channel (directors Keith Tucker and Cairns) made a £1 million offer of shares in Channel Mining Investments on the Johannesburg Stock Exchange. White

Channel and Ackermann owned 70 per cent of the company. A third of the proceeds went to repay loans from White Channel. Profits were predicted to exceed £1 million by 1987, but by the end of 1985 White Channel's stake was worth only £600,000.

18 – This company went into liquidation in February 1986 owing Jacksons £500,000. The money was repaid by Metox and Grampton, the Manx companies associated with Tucker and Plummer interests.

19 – Envox had held 1,976,000 Cobra shares at the time dealings began on the London Stock Exchange in June 1983, worth 63p each. By August 1984 the shares were more than double that price, enabling Envox to sell the majority of its holding very profitably.

20 – Tucker's trustee in bankruptcy has reached an agreement whereby no funds are provided for the litigation from Tucker's assets but Tucker can continue as a plaintiff in his personal capacity rather than the trustee doing so on his behalf. In return the trustee, on behalf of Tucker's creditors, mainly the Inland Revenue, will receive a share of any award received by Tucker from the Inland Revenue!

21 – *Guernsey Evening Press*, 2 July 1983.

22 – Golcondra had been registered in 1981. Keith Tucker was a director of its Panamanian parent, Goliath Trading, as was the old Rossminster hand Nigel Bruce-Watt.

23 – Report by the British Association of Nature Conservationists, *Guardian*, 13 February 1984.

24 – *Craven (IoT)* v. *White* (*TLR*, 6 June 1985); *IRC* v. *Bowater Property Developments* (*TLR*, 23 October 1985); *Bayliss (IoT)* v. *Gregory* (*TLR*, 2 December 1985).

25 – Speech at Ilford, *Daily Telegraph*, 26 September 1985.

26 – BBC Radio interview, 18 September 1986.

INDEX

Porter, Eric 90, 97
Posgate, Ian 155, n299
Posgate & Denby 155
Poster, Harold 139
Potter QC, Charles 61, 176–7, 258–60
Poulson, John 195, 236
Preston, Michael 158–66, 175, 205,
 275–6
Price QC, Leolin 177
Price, Tim 159–61
Price Waterhouse 17, 158, 282
Private Eye viii, ix, 159, 233–6, 245, 279
Promogem 286
Prudential Assurance 132–3
Pythagoras Trust 112, 268

Quigley, Bernard 289
Quinlan, Raymond 213, 224, 226
Quinn, Anthony n298

Radialchoice 281
Radialchoice Group 281
Ralli Brothers 27
Ralli International 62
Ramsay, Robert 39–41, 251, 253, 258–61
Ramsay, William 39
W. T. Ramsay 39–40, 253, 258–61
Ransom v Higgs n302
Rasklith 109
Raynaud, Simon 115, 208, 211
Rees, QC MP, Peter: personal background
 62, 177; political career 62, 176–7; and
 Tucker 176–8; and tax schemes 177–8;
 and tax 178; and Non-Deposit Scheme
 61–2, 67, 73–4, n296; and Gross
 Annuity Scheme 95; and Commodity
 Carry Scheme 183–9; appears on *London
 Programme* 178–9; non-disclosure of
 Tucker link 194–7; parliamentary
 speeches 193–4, n301; declarations of
 interest 196, n300; becomes Trade minister
 268; becomes Chief Secretary of
 Treasury 265, 272; and Keith Committee
 235; attacked in Parliament 236; and
 World in Action programme 250; present
 situation 284–5
Reverse Annuity Scheme 23–32, 37, 251,
 253–6, 282–3
Register of MP's interests 195, n300
Regstane 112
Remnant, Lord 97
Restmor 139
Richard III 97
Richard, Cliff n299

Richstock 79
Ridge 35, 49
Ridge Trust 35, 40, 239, n301
Ridley MP, Nicholas 270
Ritchie, David 3–4
Riverflow 161
R. M. Enterprises 148–50
Robinhill n296
Rocquaine Nominees 281
Rocquaine Trust 35, 49–50, 59, 84, 113,
 119–20, 124, 238
Romanwalk 282
Romeo and Juliet 97–8, 151
Roney, Patrick 44, 72, 115
Roney Vincent 183–7, 194
Rooker MP, Jeff 178–9, 236, 270
Rosehaugh 284, n294
Roskill, Lord 259, 264, n302
Roskill Committee (Fraud Trials
 Committee) n302–3
Rossminster: formation 42; shareholdings
 46; relationship with Roy Tucker & Co
 46–8; and Conservative Party 75, 88,
 168, 170; cash extraction exercise 105–7;
 takeover by Blessingwell 110–13; and
 films 151–7; and E. Bailey 173–4;
 Revenue raid 226–7; Court of Appeal
 case 229–30; House of Lords case 231;
 closes down 249; sues Revenue 231–2;
 and commissions 68; and clients 282–3;
 Staff Disaster Fund 209
Rossminster Acceptances 59–74, 87–8,
 100, 166, 249, 263, 283, n297
Rossminster Acceptances (IoM) 94–5, 109,
 121, 148–9, 280, n297
Rossminster Corporate Services 158–66,
 173, 175
Rossminster Finance 57, 59, 84, 92–3
Rossminster Financial Services 56, 59, 87
Rossminster Foundation 76, 285
Rossminster Group 48, 74, 84, 88, 100–1,
 105, 110, 263
Rossminster Group Holdings 105, 110
Rossminster Holdings 109–15, 125,
 148–9, 217, 280, n303
Rossminster Holdings (C.I.) 56
Rossminster Limited 109, 153–6, 231, 249,
 278–9, 288
Rossminster Trust 109, 124, 209, 212, 214
Rothschild, N. M. 252
Rountree, Diana 55, 88, 119, 123
Rountree, Frank 55, 88, 119, 123
Rowland, R. W. 'Tiny' 139
Royal Bank of Canada 110, 124, 126
Russell, Lord 12, 259